Nonkilling Societies

Edited by
Joám Evans Pim

Center *for* Global **Nonkilling**

© The Authors, 2010
© Center for Global Nonkilling, 2010 (this edition)

  First Edition: September 2010

  ISBN-13 978-0-9822983-4-3
  ISBN-10 0-9822983-4-X

  Cataloging in Publication Data (CIP)

  Nonkilling Societies / Edited by Joám Evans Pim
      ISBN   978-0-9822983-4-3
      1. Nonkilling 2. Peace. 3. Pacifism – Nonviolence.
      I. Title. II. Evans Pim, Joám, ed. lit.

  CDU - 172.4 : 327.36

  A catalogue record is also available from the Library of Congress.

Center *for* Global **Nonkilling**

Post Office Box 12232
Honolulu, Hawai'i 96828
United States of America
Email: info@nonkilling.org
http://www.nonkilling.org

"Anything that exists is possible."

Kenneth Boulding

"A nonkilling global society is possible."

Glenn D. Paige

Contents

Foreword

Joám Evans Pim
Center for Global Nonkilling

This volume arises from a crucial question formulated by Professor Glenn D. Paige, a political scientist, in his seminal work *Nonkilling Global Political Science* (2009 [2002]): "Is a Nonkilling Society Possible?" Paige defines this form of society as "a human community, smallest to largest, local to global, characterized by no killing of humans and no threats to kill; no weapons designed to kill humans and no justifications for using them; and no conditions of society dependent upon threat or use of killing force for maintenance or change." (2009 [2002]: 21; See also Paige, 1993, 1996, 2002, 2005, 2006; Abueva, Ed., 2004; Bhaneja, 2006, 2008; Paige and Evans Pim, Eds., 2008; Evans Pim, Ed., 2009; Evans Pim, 2010.)

The term "nonkilling" may sound odd to some readers, but it is certainly not foreign to anthropological literature. For example, in his essay *Our Kind*, Marvin Harris (1990) actually uses it in the title of three of the chapters ("The Nonkilling Religions," "The Origin of Nonkilling Religions," and "How the Nonkilling Religions Spread"). Following a cultural materialist approach, Harris explains how nonkilling religions emerged, in a confluence of brutal and costly wars, environmental depletion, population growth and rise of cities, food shortages, widespread poverty and rigidified social distinctions (1990: 444). A scenario that certainly resembles our own.

Even before that, Houar used the expression in his 1984 article "Nonviolent societies and non-killing warfare," describing a form of battle present in various North American Indian societies who practiced the "counting coup," where "[t]o touch an enemy, to enter battle unarmed and take an opponent's weapon or horse was the highest feat of bravery one could accomplish" (Houar, 1984: 50). Not to mention much earlier works that without using the term explicitly tackle the problems associated to it. (See Sponsel's "Introduction" for a revision of the literature of the field.)

Even if the term itself is not new, Paige provided "a way to think about the issue in a systematic way," through the simple but far reaching question set above (Urbain, 2009: 90). Paige's approach, characterized by the measurability of its goals (killing and nonkilling can be quantified and related to specific causes) and the open-ended generative systems nature of its realization (appealing to infinite human creativity and variability), trespasses the limits of an ideology for social change entailing a new scientific model based on the refutation of killing-accepting science and the societal premises rooted in the widespread acceptance of lethality (in all of its forms) and lethal intent. As Collyer reminds us, the "familiar word, nonviolence, is almost comforting in its generality" while nonkilling "confronts and startles us with its specificity" (2003: 371), urging us to take concrete action.

Even if written from the stand point of political science, an explicit request is directed to other fields to bring about a "disciplinary shift to nonkilling creativity," through a four-part logic of analysis focused on the causes of killing; the causes of nonkilling; the causes of transition between killing and nonkilling; and the characteristics of killing-free societies (2009 [2002]: 73). The fourth item in this framework implies the need to understand existing killing-free societies, setting an appeal to anthropologists, sociologists and others. Recalling Kenneth Boulding's so-called "First Law" ("Anything that exists is possible"), Paige (and much of the evidence brought forward in this book) reminds us that nonkilling societies do exist in spite of having passed largely unnoticed to most in the scientific community.

To counter the "historic and current systemic bias of the disproportionate amount of attention given to violence and war" (Sponsel, 1996: 113-114) peace, nonviolence and nonkilling need not only be held as legitimate subjects of research but must be considered seriously, systematically and intensively. As Sponsel points out: "you cannot understand or achieve something by ignoring it" (1996: 14). Readers have probably realized that what is being said here is not in any way a revelation. Most authors who are contributing to this volume have been repeating the same crucial fact for decades: nonkilling societies, as those imagined by Paige in his book, are not a utopian dream; they are a genuine, real actuality that is currently in existence and has been so for millenia. It can probably be said louder but not more clearly. This volume provides firm evidence that the only feasible answer to Paige's question ("Is a Nonkilling Society Possible?") is undoubtedly affirmative.

In the following pages the reader will find examples of such nonkilling societies as the Semai (Dentan), the Paliyans (Gardner), or contemporary "autonomous zones" (Niman, Dentan), described with some detail. Many other societies are mentioned and an extensive bibliography featured in the various reference sections. Certainly not all chapters deal with societies where killing is absent. Gomes and Preston examine the cases of societies with peaceful values (Menraq and Cree) where conflict has erupted as a consequence of disruptive external influence. Niman's account on the Rainbow Family gatherings presents a similar dynamic. McClusky brings the vision of a society seeking to reduce normalized (domestic) violence, the Maya of southern Belize, and Sponsel challenges the long-held assumptions of the Yanomano as the canonical example of fierce Hobbesian savages. As expressed in the Introduction, a nonkilling anthropology must not focus exclusively in societies that can be considered "peaceful" or "killing-free" but must scrutinize the still prevailing Hobbesian view of humans as inherently violent beings and provide a firm basis for the realization of nonkilling societies through revised socio-cultural heuristic models.

Besides the above-mentioned studies which deal with particular societies, the first five chapters of this volume are aimed at questioning killing-accepting assumptions providing examples from diverse cultures and new insights on contemporary anthropological problems. In his Introduction, Sponsel sets out to reply to the questions "Are nonkilling societies possible?" and "What are the possibilities for a nonkilling anthropology?" A wide range of aspects are covered including the involvement of anthropologists with the military establishment and some proposals for a revised curriculum.

Sussman and Hart criticize the "Man the Hunter" theories on innate human violence, linking them to a set of Western ethnocentric values conceived in the frame of Judeo-Christian cultures. The authors establish that the dominant social tool among most primate societies and individuals is cooperation and not aggression. Giorgi further expands this argument stating that killing among humans is a cultural aberration that came into being during the last 7,000 to 8,000 years. Neurobiological evidence is provided indicating how violent social behaviors are defined after birth and are not subject to congenital biological factors but specific cultural models.

Fry, Schober and Björkqvist prove through evolutionary theory that nonkilling is the "the normal state of affairs" not only among humans but also in many other animal species. Through a comparison of physical aggression and aggression avoidance strategies across species, the authors come to the conclusion that selection pressures rarely favor killing rather than other mechanisms such as display and tournament contests.

Dentan presents egalitarian mutual-aid groups as the primordial societal formation and argues that humans tend toward these particular social arrangements as they favor the inhibition of killing and other aggressive behaviors. The author analyzes diverse forms of egalitarian acephalous groups, ranging from foragers such as the Semai to contemporary experiences of "autonomous zones" as the Rainbow Family (also discussed in depth by Niman). Dentan prefigures future nonkilling egalitarian anarchic societies even if the transitional prospects are presented in dimmer terms.

The two last chapters in the book bring a sociological perspective. On the one hand Clammer explores the relationship between nonkilling and the sociology of the body through the lens of "deep sociology," seeking to go beneath the surface levels of social relations and forms of organization to tackle deeper existential aspects. On the other hand Lee discusses the role of religion in the formation of killing or nonkilling attitudes and behaviors through an examination of particular cases of what Paige called collective or individual transitions or oscillations from killing to nonkilling and vice versa (2009 [2002]: 74).

In fact, this volume draws from contributions of the members of both the Nonkilling Anthropology and the Nonkilling Sociology Research Committees. Beyond practical reasons, the convergence of anthropology— namely social anthropology—with sociology in many aspects increasingly justifies joint efforts aimed at understanding nonkilling societies and specific practices and attitudes of our own. Even if only the two last chapters come from our Nonkilling Sociology Committee, gradually more and more scholars from this field are focusing on these problems, following historical examples of sociologists such as Jane Addams, W. E. B. Du Bois or Pitirim Sorokin. (See "Nonkilling Sociology" by Feltey, 2009, and Finley, 2010.)

Other research activities relevant to the issues tackled in this volume recently developed by the Center for Global Nonkilling are projects such as the "Exploratory Colloquium on Neuroscience and Nonkilling," held in Philadelphia in July 2009, which gathered seven brain researchers with the expressed purpose of identifying the state of knowledge related to killing and nonkilling. Moving beyond biological imperatives, one of the main recommendations focused on the need to promote early childhood care as a means of preventing violence and killing (Center for Global Nonkilling, 2009; on this aspect, also see Prescott, 2002). Significantly, the first issue of the new series *Global Nonkilling Working Papers* was devoted to the problem "Are Humans Inherently Killers?" featuring a critique by Robert W. Sussman and Joshua L. Marshack (2010) and a response by Richard Wrangham (2010).

Finally, some acknowledgments need to made. Les Sponsel has been extremely supportive in setting a firm anthropological basis for the Center's research component. His essay "Reflections on the Possibilities of a Nonkilling Society and a Nonkilling Anthropology" headed the collective volume *Toward a Nonkilling Paradigm* (Evans Pim, Ed., 2009) pointing at new research needs, some of which are now developed in this volume (his essay serves as an introduction). Les' use of this approach and materials in his "ANTH/PACE 345 Aggression, War and Peace" course at the University of Hawaiʻiᶦ has also been a great encouragement to continue to prepare new publications and research initiatives that will hopefully make it through to graduate and undergraduate programs. As he will be retiring this year, and in anticipation of well-deserved *festschrift*, the Center for Global Nonkilling would like to dedicate this volume to him as a small tribute honoring his life-long dedication to nonviolence and nonkilling. The final form of this publication must also be credited to former CGNV Secretary Glenda H. Paige, whose invaluable dedication and talent are gratefully appreciated.

References

Abueva, Jose V., Ed. (2004). *Towards a Nonkilling Filipino Society: Developing an Agenda for Research, Policy and Action.* Marikina City: Kalayaan College.

Bhaneja, Balwant (2006). "A Nonkilling Paradigm for Political Problem Solving," *Asteriskos. Journal of International and Peace Studies*, 1: 273-277.

Bhaneja, Balwant (2008). "Nonkilling Political Science," in Kurtz, Leslie, Ed. *Encyclopedia of Violence, Peace and Conflict.* San Diego: Elsevier.

Center for Global Nonkilling (2009). *Exploratory Colloquium on Neuroscience and Nonkilling, July 2009* [Report]. Honolulu: Center for Global Nonkilling. Available at: <http://www.nonkilling.org/pdf/2009neurosciencereport.pdf>.

Collyer, Charles E. (2003). "A Nonkilling Paradigm for Political Scientists, Psychologists, and Others," *Peace and Conflict*, 9(4):371-372.

Evans Pim, Joám (2010). "Nonkilling, A New Paradigm," in Young, Nigel J., Ed., *The Oxford International Encyclopedia of Peace*, Vol. 3. New York: Oxford University Press, pp. 161-164.

Evans Pim, Joám, Ed. (2009). *Toward a Nonkilling Paradigm.* Honolulu: Center for Global Nonkilling. Available at: <http://www.nonkilling.org>.

Feltey, Kathryn (2009). "Nonkilling Sociology," in Evans Pim, Joám, Ed., *Toward a Nonkilling Paradigm.* Honolulu: Center for Global Nonkilling, pp. 371-378.

Finley, Laura L. (2010). "Examining Domestic Violence as a State Crime: Nonkilling Implications," *Global Nonkilling Working Papers*, 2: 7-45.

Harris, Marvin (1990). *Our Kind: Who We Are, Where We Came From, Where We Are Going.* San Francisco: Harper Perennial.

Houar, Michael A. (1984). "Nonviolent societies and non-killing warfare: The case of American Indian Tribal Groups," *Social Alternatives*, 4(1): 49-54.

Paige, Glenn D. (1993). *To Nonviolent Political Science: From Seasons of Violence.* Honolulu: Center for Global Nonviolence.

ᶦ Course syllabus available at: <http://nonkilling.org/pdf/3451 0syllabus.pdf>.

Paige, Glenn D. (1996). "'To Leap Beyond yet Nearer Bring.' From War to Peace to Nonviolence to Nonkilling," *Peace Research*, 28(4).

Paige, Glenn D. (2002). "A Nonkilling Korea: From Cold-War Confrontation to Peaceful Coexistence," *Social Alternatives*, Vol. 21, Issue 2.

Paige, Glenn D. (2005). "Nonkilling Global Society," Aharoni, Ada, ed., *Encylopedia of Life Support Systems (Peace Building)*. Oxford: EOLSS Publishers.

Paige, Glenn D. (2006). "Korean Leadership for Nonkilling East Asian Common Security," *Korea Observer*, 37(3):547-563.

Paige, Glenn D. (2009 [2002]). *Nonkilling Global Political Science*. Honolulu: Center for Global Nonkilling. Available at: <http://www.nonkilling.org>.

Paige, Glenn; Evans Pim, Joám, Eds. (2008). *Global Nonkilling Leadership First Forum Proceedings*. Honolulu: Center for Global Nonviolence; Spark Matsunaga Institute for Peace, University of Hawai'i.

Prescott, James W. (2002). *The Origins of Love and Violence. Sensory Deprivation and the Developing Brain Research and Prevention* [DVD]. Solvang: Touch the Future.

Sponsel, Leslie E. (2009). "Reflections on the Possibilities of a Nonkilling Society and a Nonkilling Anthropology," in Evans Pim, Joám, Ed., *Toward a Nonkilling Paradigm*. Honolulu: Center for Global Nonkilling, pp. 35-70.

Sussman, Robert W.; Marshack, Joshua L. (2010). "Are Humans Inherently Killers?" *Global Nonkilling Working Papers*, 1: 7-28.

Urbain, Olivier (2009). "Nonkilling Arts," in Evans Pim, Joám, Ed., *Toward a Nonkilling Paradigm*. Honolulu: Center for Global Nonkilling, pp. 73-91.

Wrangham, Richard (2010). "Chimpanzee Violence is a Serious Topic: A response to Sussman and Marshack's critique of Demonic Males: Apes and the Origins of Human Violence," *Global Nonkilling Working Papers*, 1: 29-47.

Introduction

Reflections on the Possibilities of a Nonkilling Society and a Nonkilling Anthropology

Leslie E. Sponsel
University of Hawai'i

> That since wars begin in the minds of men, it is in the minds of men that the defenses of peace must be constructed (UNESCO Constitution, November 16, 1945).

> Everyone has the right to life, liberty and security of person. (UN, Universal Declaration of Human Rights, December 10, 1948, Art. 3)

> The time has come to set forth human killing as a problem to be solved rather than to accept enslavement by it as a condition to be endured forever (Paige, 2002: 145).

Is a nonkilling society possible? What are the possibilities of a nonkilling political science? These are the two elemental, central, and pivotal questions that Glenn D. Paige (2002) raises and explores in his ground breaking book which is generating a quiet but accelerating and far-reaching revolution in theory and praxis throughout the world (Bhaneja, 2008). The present essay addresses these two questions and related matters from one anthropologist's perspective and cites some of the extensive literature for documentation and as sources for further information, although no attempt has been made at a thorough literature review, especially for periodicals.

The particular approach to anthropology used here needs to be clearly specified at the outset. American anthropology may be defined as the holistic scientific and scholarly study of human unity and diversity in all of its aspects throughout time and space. It encompasses the five subfields of archaeology, biological (or physical) anthropology, cultural anthropology, linguistic anthropology, and applied anthropology. In varying ways and degrees, American anthropologists share a concern for human evolution, human diversity (biological, cultural, and linguistic), culture and cultures, fieldwork, and comparison (especially cross-cultural). Anthropology is also unique in its scope which ranges from in-depth studies of local communities to surveys of the human species as a whole (Birx, 2006; Perry, 2003; Salzman and Rice, 2004).

Nonkilling Society

Is a nonkilling society possible? Without any hesitation, my answer is affirmative. As a political scientist, Paige pursues the framework of nation states or countries noting that today there are 195 such entities. In contrast, an anthropologist would more likely pursue the framework of cultures. Estimates of the number of extant cultures in the world today are around 7,000 (Summer Institute of Linguistics, 2008). Furthermore, whereas countries typically range in age from a few decades to a few centuries, cultures are centuries to millennia old. Accordingly, examples of nonkilling and peaceful cultures can also be important evidence in answering Paige's first question in the affirmative. Such socio-cultural systems generally accord with Paige's (2002: 1) definition of a nonkilling society as "... characterized by no killing of humans and no threats to kill; no weapons designed to kill humans and no justification for using them; and no conditions of society dependent upon threat or use of killing for maintenance or change."

At the same time, the logic that Paige pursues regarding the frequency of killing by humans is affirmed as well by anthropology. He argues that women seldom kill other humans, and that only a minority of men kill other humans (cf. Levinson, 1994; WHO, 2002). To phrase it another way, the overwhelming majority of humans have not been involved directly in any kind of killing. The Yanomami are an anthropological case in point. They were stereotyped and stigmatized in a derogatory way as "the fierce people" by Napoleon Chagnon (1968, 1992). However, if one actually scrutinizes his own ethnography (description of a culture), then it is apparent that most individuals within Yanomami society do not kill others. There is no mention of a woman killing a man or another woman. Raids and other forms of intergroup aggression are not ubiquitous in space and time by any means. Not all men from a village participate in a raid on another village. Also, Chagnon mentions that often many members of a raiding party find excuses to retreat rather than participate in the entire process (Sponsel, 1998).

Other anthropologists who have conducted research with the Yanomami, some living with them for many more years than Chagnon, such as Bruce Albert, Gale Goodwin Gomez, Kenneth Good, Jacques Lizot, and Alcida Ramos, have all called into serious question Chagnon's characterization of the Yanomami as the "fierce people." Apparently as a result of such authoritative criticism, Chagnon dropped that subtitle from later editions of his book, yet his characterization in the text persists anyway (Sponsel, 1998). The ethnography by Chagnon together with the wealth of dozens of other books on the Yanomami could be examined to identify a multitude of examples of nonkilling and peaceful behaviors that prevail in the daily life of most individuals and communities (see especially Dawson, 2006; Ferguson, 1992, 1995; Good, 1991; Lizot, 1985; Peters, 1998; Ramos, 1987, 1995; Smole, 1976; Sponsel, 1998, 2006c).

A nonkilling society is not only just a possibility as Paige theorizes, rather in reality many such societies actually exist today. The most famous one is the Semai of the Malaysian forest. They fit Paige's criteria for a nonkilling society and were first described through field research by Robert Knox Dentan (1968). Years later Clayton Robarcheck (1979, 1992, 1996, 1998a, b) independently confirmed Dentan's characterization of the Semai. Much later Clayton and Carole Robarcheck worked among the Waorani who were supposedly one of the most violent societies known, as will be discussed here later. In an ingenious comparison between the Semai and Waorani, the Robarchecks (1992, 1998a) concluded that the worldview of each of these two cultures was the single most important influence on whether they were peaceful or warlike. Otherwise, they were very similar in many respects such as their subsistence economy.

Beyond the Semai, dozens of other nonkilling societies have been extensively documented in the anthropological record. David Fabbro (1978) published the earliest modern cross-cultural study identifying the basic attributes of existing peaceful societies which accord with Paige's criteria. The most systematic and extensive documentation of such societies is by Bruce D. Bonta (1993, 1996, 1997). He compiled an annotated bibliography of 47 cultures that are generally nonviolent and peaceful (Bonta, 1993). A wealth of information on these and other aspects of this subject are archived on his encyclopedic website called "Peaceful Societies" (http://www.peacefulsocieties.org). By now there are several other surveys and inventories of nonviolent and peaceful societies including those by Baszarkiewicz and Fry (2008), Bonta and Fry (2006), Melko (1973, 1984), and van der Dennen (1995). Three edited books of ethnographic case studies of nonviolent and peaceful cultures also have been published (Howell and Willis, 1989; Montagu, 1978; Sponsel and Gregor, 1994). Most recently, Fry (2006, 2007) has systematically and vigorously argued with ample evidence for the human potential and actuality of nonviolence and peace.

Given this extensive documentation of nonkilling and peaceful sociocultural systems, the only way that any author, scholar, or scientist can possibly assert that human nature is inherently murderous and warlike is by ignoring the ample evidence to the contrary from a multitude of diverse sources. Nevertheless, that fact has not prevented many from doing so as apologists for warfare (Barber, 1996; Cannel and Macklin, 1974; Ehrenreich, 1998; Feibleman, 1987; Ghiglieri, 1987, 1999; Guilaine and Zammit, 2001; Kaplan, 1994, 2000; Keeley, 1996; LeBlanc and Register, 2003; Otterbein, 1993, 1999, 2004; Smith, 2007; Wrangham and Peterson, 1996). Either they have not adequately covered the documentation that is readily available in the published literature, or they just purposefully ignore other arguments and evidence that do not fit their own ideology, theory, arguments, advocacy, and so on. In either of these two instances, their science, scholarship, and writing is seriously deficient and suspect, to say the very least (Frankfurt, 2005, 2006). Yet the unproven assumption that human nature is inherently murderous and warlike still dominates publications by a vocal minority of anthropologists and others to the nearly total exclusion of any serious and systematic attention to nonkilling and peace. For a most recent example, see Holmes (2008).

Most simple hunter-gatherer bands epitomize Paige's attributes of a nonkilling society (Kelly, 2000). They are grounded in an ethos of routine cooperation, reciprocity, and nonviolent conflict resolution as documented for the San and Mbuti of Africa, Semai of Malaysia, and many others (Bonta, 1993, 1996, 2008; Dentan, 1968; Fry, 2006, 2007; Kelly, 2000). Furthermore, for 99% of human existence, from more than two million to roughly 10,000 years ago, humans lived almost exclusively as simple hunter-gatherers (Hart; Sussman, 2009; Kelly, 2000; Lee and DeVore, 1968; Shepard, 1973). Accordingly, although captivating, William Golding's (1999) novel *Lord of the Flies* which was originally published in 1954, and the ensuing two movies are not by any means accurate anthropologically as a reflection on human nature. A more recent variant on the Hobbesian theme is the film called *Apocalypto* which appears to have been made to insult the Mayan people.

With regard to nonlethal weapons and weapon-free societies (Paige, 2002: 109, 113), it is important to note that weapons specifically designed for warfare do not appear archaeologically until very late in human prehistory, although tools employed in hunting such as a spear or a bow and arrow could easily be used to kill or injure another human being. The archaeological record does not evidence any regular warfare until relatively late in human prehistory (Ferguson, 2002, 2006; Fry, 2006, 2007; Grossman, 2008; Guilaine and Zammit, 2001; Keegan, 1993; Keeley, 1996; Kelly, 2000; LeBlanc and Register, 2003).

Paige (2002: 101) refers to the 20th century as "the era of lethality." Anthropology, with its unique combination of temporal depth and spatial breadth offers great hope in this regard, because such widespread lethality is an extremely recent aberration in human nature, judging by evidence from evolution and prehistory accumulated by archaeologists and evidence from the record of some 7,000 cultures in the world (ethnographies) and from cross-cultural comparisons (ethnology). Torture, terrorism, genocide, weapons of mass destruction, and the like are all relatively rare in the vast range of human experience (cf. Levinson, 1994). The "era of lethality" endures for decades or so, not millennia or millions of years. However, structural violence in various forms and degrees is coincident with the origin of inequality (social stratification) which emerges most of all with civilization at the state level of sociopolitical organization and complexity (Bodley, 2008a).

Actually warfare and the institution of the military are relatively recent inventions, as noted long ago by Margaret Mead (1940). There is relatively little evidence of warfare until the Neolithic some 10,000 years ago, depending on the region. The military as a social institution is mostly coincident with the evolution of the state around 5,000 years ago, depending on the region (Bodley, 2008a; Fry, 2006, 2007; Keegan, 1993; Kelly, 2000). Moreover, anyone who is a genuine evolutionist realizes that change is inevitable; thus, there is no reason to think that warfare and the institution of the military, not to mention other lethal aspects of humankind or a culture, are inevitable and eternal. Humanity as a whole cannot return to a hunter-gatherer lifestyle, at least at the current level of world population and given economic dependence and preference (Shepard, 1973). However, hunter-gatherers can provide heuristic models of the socio-cultural possibilities of a nonkilling society (Fry, 2006, 2007; Kelly, 2000).

Resource scarcity and the resulting competition may well lead to conflict, violence, and even warfare as many have asserted (Hastings, 2000; Homer-Dixon et al., 1993; Kaplan, 1994, 2000; Klare, 2001, 2002; Lanier-Graham, 1993; Myers, 1996; Renner, 1996). But as Fredrik Barth (1956) demonstrated for three different ethnic groups in the Swat Valley of Pakistan, niche differentiation may be an alternative. They effectively reduced most direct competition by developing different foci for land and resource use as well as complementary trading relationships. However, this interethnic system was probably seriously disrupted by refugees from the successive Soviet and American invasions of Afghanistan.

The above are indisputable scientific facts, this in spite of the biased approaches, pseudoscience, and disinformation campaigns of a few anthropologists and others who have gained notoriety. Without meaning to denigrate the substantial contribution of anthropologists who have focused on studying warfare and other forms of aggression, such as Eller (1999, 2006), Ferguson (1995, 2007) and Nordstrom (1997, 1998), clearly a vocal minority are in effect apologists for war (cf. Paige, 2002: 136). (For additional case studies, see compilations such as those by Fried et al., 1968; Ferguson and Farragher, 1988; Ferguson and Whitehead, 1992; Ferguson, 2003; Nordstrom and Robben, 1995.) Since at least the 1960s the apologists for war pursue and even champion the pivotal assumption that humans are innately, instinctively, genetically, or biologically programmed to be aggressive, and, therefore, that war is an inevitable manifestation of human nature (Ardrey, 1961; 1966, 1976; Chagnon, 1992; Ghiglieri, 1987, 1999; Keeley, 1996; Lorenz, 1966; Morris, 1967, 1969; Otterbein, 1993, 1999, 2004, 2008; Wrangham and Peterson, 1996). Their absolutist, universalist, and essentialist posture conveniently ignores the contrary examples within our own species of *Homo sapiens* and, as will be discussed later, from our closest relatives in the animal kingdom, the chimpanzees (see Bonta, 1993, 1996; Dennen, 1995; Fry, 2006, 2007; Howell and Willis, 1989; Melko, 1973, 1984; Montagu, 1978; Sponsel, 1996a; Sponsel and Gregor, 1994).

Some of these apologists for warfare claim to have discovered extraordinarily violent and warlike societies, such as the Yanomami in the Brazilian and Venezuelan Amazon. However, the Yanomami, although not free from low levels and frequencies of some types of aggression do not pursue warfare by any meaningful definition of the term and are relatively nonviolent in their daily lives (Barash and Webel, 2002; Gelvin, 1994; Keegan, 1993; Jeong, 2000; Sanders, 2008; Sponsel, 1998; Stoessinger, 2008). Chagnon (1968, 1992) stereotyped and stigmatized the Yanomami as the "fierce people," and even after he dropped that designation as the subtitle of his famous (now infamous) book, his fixation on aggression still exaggerated it to the point of being misleading (Good, 1991; Sponsel, 1998, 2006c). Chagnon exemplifies some anthropologists who have been so focused on the violent aspects of a society, often to the point of obsession, that they have provided a grossly distorted and problematic perspective, neglecting the far greater frequency of nonviolence and peace in the daily life of most people in the society.

It should also be noted that, even within relatively violent societies, most people are nonkilling in their own behavior (cf. Nordstrom, 1997, 1998). Furthermore, there are individuals, groups, and subcultures that explicitly pursue nonkilling and pacifism such as the Amish. In addition, even in the midst of wars, such as the recent ones in Afghanistan and Iraq, there are medical doctors and other persons who are saving lives and reducing suffering instead of the opposite. Nevertheless, the prevalence of many forms of violence in American society and culture to the point of obsession in the media and elsewhere should be obvious, especially with inventories like that by Paige (2002). Transcending this phenomenon is as much a problem for science as for society as Paige discusses.

History provides examples of nation states such as Germany and Japan that have been transformed from a society frequently engaged in war to one pursuing peace. Costa Rica is an instructive example as well. This country abolished the military and instead invested its resources in life-enhancing activities. Cases like Costa Rica merit much greater recognition, documentation, and analysis by anthropologists and others (Biesanz et al., 1982).

Among ethnographic cases, perhaps the most remarkable example of a rapid transformation from a killing to a nonkilling society is the Waorani of the Ecuadorian Amazon, as amply documented by the Robarcheks (1992, 1996, 1998a,b). Traditionally the Waorani were frequently involved in intergroup feuding. Through contact with American missionaries the Waorani imagined the possibilities of a nonkilling and peaceful society; they considered this to be far more attractive, and within a few decades the majority of the Waorani communities voluntarily changed. The Waorani demonstrate the plasticity and adaptability of human nature. Accordingly, they hold the promise for the possibility of other societies undergoing such a transformation, another case of an affirmative answer to Paige's first question. Also it is noteworthy that many societies in Oceania and elsewhere which had traditionally engaged in some kind of warfare to some degree were rapidly pacified by Western colonial forces, albeit often through violent means (Bodley, 2008b; Ferguson and Whitehead, 1992; Rodman and Cooper, 1979).

There are also societies which have courageously persisted in their pacifist commitment in the face of terrible violence. The Amish are pacifists, like the Hutterites, Mennonites, and Quakers. Americans and many in the rest of the world were shocked when a psychotic gunman shot to death five girls and wounded five others in an Amish one-room school in Lancaster County, Pennsylvania, on October 2, 2006. Many people were impressed as well when representatives from the same Amish community attended the funeral of the gunman whom police had killed in order to forgive and comfort his widow and children. The Amish did not respond to this horrific crime by initiating a cycle of blood revenge (Kraybill, 2008; Kraybill, et al., 2006). This should have been a lesson to the larger world, and especially American society in general and its government. It has direct relevance to the aftermath of the terrible unjust tragedy of the 9-11 attacks. What if a similar Christian response had been pursued then? What if the federal government of the USA had responded to 9-11, not by military attack on Afghanistan, but instead capitalized on world sympathy and advocated concerted action by its leaders through the United Nations, Interpol (International Criminal Police Organization), and other nonkilling means? Whether or not this would have brought to justice the surviving perpetrators of the 9-11 attacks is uncertain. However, it is certain that U.S. militarism has not achieved that goal in the many years since 2001. Moreover, it is certain that in the interim hundreds of thousands of innocent civilians, including women, children, and elderly, have been killed and injured, so-called collateral damage. Millions have been displaced as refugees internally and beyond their homeland in Afghanistan and Iraq. Billions of dollars have been sacrificed from constructive life-enhancing initiatives to promote nutrition, health, education, economy, and other things in the USA and elsewhere. As Mahatma Gandhi observed, an eye for an eye leads to blindness. All of the vast resources— personnel, financial, institutional, technological, and so on—of the Pentagon, State Department, C.I.A., and other U.S. federal government agencies failed to prevent 9-11. The time is long overdue to open the minds of government leaders and the populace regarding the nonkilling alternatives available for dispute resolution and conflict prevention (Barnes, 2007; Bonta, 1996; Fry and Bjorkqvist, 1997; Kemp and Fry, 2004; Ury, 1999, 2002).

Tibet also provides a particular case to illustrate several crucial points previously identified. During its long history, in spite of some episodes of violence, Tibet was transformed into a mostly nonviolent society. The spread of Buddhism was the seminal influence in this transformation. Today the power and wealth of Tibetans are not military, political, and/or economic, but religious and cultural. That Tibetans have suffered terribly since the 1950 invasion and occupation by the Chinese with more than a million killed and thousands imprisoned and tortured to this day, and that more than 100,000 Tibetans have risked their lives in the Himalayan winter to flee to exile as political refugees in adjacent countries and beyond, does not diminish this power. Although initially there was militant resistance to the Chinese invasion by some Tibetans, subsequently under the leadership of His Holiness the XIVth Dalai Lama of Tibet, Tibetans appear to present the most outstanding case of a nonviolent response to violent invasion, occupation, and suppression. While this nonkilling approach has not liberated Tibet from Chinese imperialism, it has avoided far worse conflict and suffering by the Tibetans who are greatly outnumbered and outgunned by the Chinese. It may be only a matter of time before the situation improves significantly, although it could be decades or more before the central government of the People's Republic of China promotes a more democratic society and moral civilization in the entire country. However, there is reason for optimism, given the religiosity, courage, and resilience of Tibetans. There is also some hope, given historical precedents such as the expulsion of the British colonial empire from India, the dissolution of the apartheid system in South Africa, and the overthrow of the Ferdinand Marcos regime in the Philippines, all generated by the nonviolent actions of courageous and persistent leaders and commoners in the face of overwhelming lethal force. (For more on Tibet see Blondeau; Buffetrille, 2008; Dalai Lama, 1987; Kapstein, 2006; Shakya, 1999; Sperling, 2004; Thurman, 2008, and the official website of the Tibetan Government in Exile at <http://www.tibet.com>.)

To go even deeper, into human nature, that is, while many biologists and psychologists might favor nature over nurture as the primary determinant and shaper of aggression, some have revealed strong evidence to the contrary. Of all of the species in the animal kingdom, the closest to humans are the common and pygmy chimpanzees, *Pan troglodytes* and *P. paniscus*, respectively. Only after many years of observations on a few social groups of the common chimpanzee at Gombe Stream Reserve in Tanzania did Jane Goodall and her research associates discover what they described as the rudiments of war (Goodall, 1986; Wrangham and Peterson, 1996; Ghiglieri, 1987, 1999). However, Margaret Power (1991) and others have argued that this aggression may be influenced by external factors, at least in part, and especially by the primatologists provisioning the chimpanzees with bananas in order to bring them closer for more detailed observation.

In sharp contrast to some groups of the common chimpanzees, independent studies of the pygmy chimpanzees, also called bonobos, have not revealed comparable aggression either in the wild or in captive colonies. In fact, they are just the opposite. They seem to pursue behavior according to the motto make love and not war! Bonobos use a wide variety of sexual behaviors to avoid or reduce tensions within the group on a daily basis (Kano, 1990, 1992; Waal, 1989, 1996, 2006; Waal and Lating, 1997). However, the "scientists" who favor the Hobbesian view of human nature, apparently have ideological blinders that channel them to emphasize violence to the near exclusion of nonviolence, stressing the common chimpanzees at Gombe and largely ignoring other common chimpanzee groups elsewhere where such behavior has not been observed. They also downplay the evidence of the peaceful bonobos. (See Aureli and de Waal; 2000; Harcourt and de Waal, 1992; Kohn, 1990.)

As a heuristic exercise, Leslie E. Sponsel (1996a) marshaled the arguments and evidence for the natural history of peace, pursuing just the opposite position from that of the apologists for war. The fields of biology, primate ethology, human ethology, human palaeontology, prehistoric archaeology, ethnography, and ethnology were surveyed. The basic conclusions were that: (1) although conflict is inevitable and common, violence is not;

(2) human nature has the psychobiological potential to be either nonvio-lent/peaceful or violent/warlike; (3) nonviolence and peace appear to have prevailed in many prehistoric and pre-state societies; (4) war is not a cul-tural universal; and (5) the potential for the development of a more nonvio-lent and peaceful world is latent in human nature as revealed by the natural history of peace (Sponsel, 1996a :114-115).

Douglas P. Fry (2006, 2007) elaborated this approach further in much greater detail. He observes that the "Man the Warrior" model asserts that war is ubiquitous in time and space, natural, normal, and inevitable. Fry as-serts that this reflects a Western cultural bias that selectively focuses on certain kinds of evidence to the exclusion of contrary evidence. He ob-serves that this Hobbesian model also stems from muddled thinking that confuses almost any kind of aggression such as homicide or blood feuding with warfare. Fry concludes that the "Man the Warrior" model is fantasy in-stead of fact. Moreover, he warns that this model is dangerous because it may contribute to policies of belligerent militarism as well as to inaction by peace advocates, if war is considered to be an inevitable manifestation of human nature. Fry argues that evolutionary pressures would select for re-straint and for the ritualization of aggression to reduce harm, as well as for alternatives in nonviolent conflict resolution because the costs of aggression can far exceed any possible benefits. He affirms that war can be eliminated in the 21st century by transcending the narrow, unrealistic, and culturally bi-ased mentality of "Man the Warrior" and the associated belligerent milita-rism, and replacing it with an emphasis on extending nonviolent conflict management alternatives practiced within democratic nation states to an in-ternational system of world and regional cooperative governance and jus-tice such as in the United Nations and the European Union.

Such studies are an independent and objective confirmation of the asser-tions in the UNESCO "Seville Statement on Violence" of May 16, 1986, cited by Paige (2002: 39-40). (See Adams, 1989.) They affirm as well the statement in the charter of UNESCO; namely, that just as war begins in the minds of men, then so can peace (Barnaby, 1988). They sustain Mead's (1940) conten-tion that war is only an invention, and that, as such, it can be transcended.

What is needed more than ever is a collaborative project to research nonviolence and peace in both theory and practice with a commitment, ex-pert personnel, and adequate resources on a scale equivalent to the Man-hattan Project of WWII. If that war effort was so important to the world, then why isn't a peace effort even far more so? Modern warfare is simply much too expensive in terms of human deaths, injuries, and suffering as well as money, resources, and the environment (Andreas, 2004; Cranna and Bhinda, 1995; Hastings, 2000; Lanier-Graham, 1993; U.S. Army, 2008). Indeed, war is rapidly becoming an unaffordable anachronism in the 21st century (cf. Younger, 2007). Just consider the fact that a significant percentage of the American troops returning from Afghanistan and Iraq are bringing the war home in the form of not only physical injuries, but also post-traumatic stress syndrome, substance abuse, domestic violence, homelessness, and even suicide. The expense of all of this—medical, psychological, and social as well as economic—will be long-term and immense (Grossman, 1995; Hedges and Al-Arian, 2007; McNair, 2002). (Also see "Iraq Body Count" at <http://www.iraqbodycount.org>.) Incidentally, the facts that soldiers have to be trained to injure and kill other human beings, and that many of those who do so often suffer serious emotional problems that may endure over many years, are yet another line of evidence invalidating the Hobbesian myth of dismal human nature. (Also see <http://www.refusingtokill.net>.)

As in political science (Paige, 2002: 74), likewise in anthropology, authors who have dared to consider the possibilities of nonviolence and peace have been variously accused, stigmatized, and dismissed as unrealistic, idealistic, romantic, or utopian dreamers (Otterbein, 1999; Sponsel, 1990, 1992, 2000b, 2005). But such feeble attempts at a counter-argument are not sustainable in the face of the wealth of scientific evidence that has been rapidly accumulating since the 1970s.

In summary, although anthropology certainly has its limitations, it offers a far broader temporal and spatial perspective than that of political science which tends to be constrained by its focus on the governments and politics of historic and contemporary nation states (Barash and Webel, 2002; Jeong, 2000). Anthropology offers not only an affirmative answer to Paige's first question, but also amplification and substantiation based on numerous and diverse well-documented cases in the real world. Paige discusses how individuals in different contexts from different professions or disciplines and countries answer his elemental question. No doubt he would also find a variety of responses to this question if he were to ask individuals in societies such as the Amish, Semai, Tibetans, Waorani, and Yanomami. Hopefully, future anthropological researchers may do just that.

Nonkilling Anthropology

What are the possibilities for a nonkilling anthropology? At first glance, probably most anthropologists would be puzzled to consider the idea of either a killing anthropology or a nonkilling anthropology. However, consider this logic: either you are part of the solution or a part of the problem; there is no space for neutrality. For example, if you witness a person who is apparently being beaten to death and do nothing to intervene, such as call for anyone nearby to help and telephone the police, then are you not complicit in murder to some degree? Similarly, if you are an anthropologist in a killing society and do nothing to intervene in any way, then are you not complicit in the killing to some degree? Moreover, even from an egocentric perspective, it might be argued that ignoring the human suffering caused directly and indirectly by a killing society diminishes one's own humanity and increases one's own suffering, because we are all interconnected and interdependent (cf. Dalai Lama, 1999). Such considerations may stimulate some to contemplate the possibilities of a killing anthropology and a nonkilling anthropology.

Answering Paige's second question is much more difficult than answering the first one because it requires thinking more "outside of the box," since much of anthropology supports, indirectly if not directly, and inadvertently if not intentionally, the military-industrial-media-academic complex. To be blunt, the modern war-making machine's main effect, if not primary purpose, is usually to generate death, destruction, and suffering, as for example in the March 2003 U.S. "shock and awe" bombing campaign over the city of Baghdad. At the same time, it should be mentioned that I respect those in the military who serve honorably and even place themselves in harm's way; however, I respect even more highly someone like the courageous First Lieutenant Ehren Watada who refuses to serve in an unjust Iraq War in spite of tremendous institutional, social, and legal pressures to conform (<http://www.thankyoult.org>). Another difficulty with the nonkilling aspects of anthropology is that they are so diffuse that a special effort is required to identify and explicate them. Furthermore, much of what would help generate a nonkilling anthropology is at the early stage of critical analysis and focused on the military as an institution, its origin, evolution, structure, functions, beliefs, values, symbols, rituals, customs, and practices, rather than on positive alternatives, such as the interrelated human rights and peace movements and organizations throughout the world.

In recent decades, an increasing number of publications have critically analyzed in historical perspective the relationships between anthropology and war since colonial times to the current wars in Afghanistan and Iraq. This endeavor is not to be confused with the anthropological study of war as such. (See Ben-Ari, 2004; de Wolf, 1992; Frese and Harrell, 2003; Goldschmidt, 1979; Gordon, 1988; Gough, 1968; Gusterson, 1996, 2003, 2007; Hickey, 2003; Hymes, 1999; Jell-Bahlsen, 1985; Mabee, 1987; Neel, 1994; Patterson, 2001;

Penny and Bunzl, 2003; Price, 2008; Schaft, 2004; Simons, 1997, 1999; Starn, 1986; Stauder, 1999; Suzuki, 1986; Wakin, 1992; Williams, 1986.) Among other influences, pursuit of this subject reflects the correlated development since the 1960s of a code of professional ethics for anthropologists emphasizing the primary ethical principle of "do no harm." That code was largely stimulated by the reaction to covert counter-insurgency research by anthropologists in Thailand during the American war in Vietnam and adjacent countries, although its roots are deeper in time and broader in experience (Fluehr-Lobban, 2002, 2003; Hymes, 1999; Whiteford and Trotter, 2008; Wakin, 1992).

At the same time, some anthropologists have been pacifists, such as Edward B. Tylor and Franz Boas, although rarely does this surface in their research and publications. It was not until the 1960s, and in connection with the Vietnam War in particular, that a variant of what might be called nonkilling anthropology began to develop. Perhaps more than any other single anthropologist before or since, Ashley Montagu as a prominent public scientist pioneered the groundwork for a nonkilling anthropology through many of his publications addressing nonviolence and peace as well as violence, including even structural violence (racism, sexism, ageism) (Lieberman et al., 1995; Montagu, 1968, 1972, 1989, 1998; Sponsel, 2006b; cf. Paige 2002: 97). He rigorously challenged the idea that there is any biological basis for racial superiority, distinguishing between biological and social ideas about race (Montagu, 1998). Montagu (1972) was one of the leaders in the development of the UNESCO Statement on Race. Likewise, he critically analyzed and dismissed the Hobbesian view of human nature (Montagu, 1976). He edited the first anthology documenting nonviolent and peaceful societies (Montagu, 1978). Montagu and Matson (1983) scrutinized dehumanization as a tactic facilitating violence toward "the other" (Hinton, 2001; Staub 1989). More recently, several other pioneers laying the groundwork for a nonkilling anthropology stand out in various ways, including Baszarkiewicz and Fry (2008), Bodley (2008a,b), Bonta (1993, 1996, 1997), Dentan (1968), Ferguson (1995, 2002, 2003, 2006, 2007, 2008), Fry (2006, 2007), Gonzalez (2004), Graebner (2004), Gusterson (1996, 2003, 2007), Hymes (1999), Kyron and Rubenstein (2008), Lutz (2001, 2002), Nordstrom (1997, 1998), Nordstrom and Robben (1995), Price (2004, 2008), Sanders (2008), Sluka (2000), Sponsel (1994a,b,c, 1996a,b,c, 1997a,b, 2000b, 2006b), Sponsel and Good (2000), and Strathern and Stewart (2008).

Recently, the U.S. military initiated the special program called the Human Terrain System (HTS) that embeds anthropologists and other social scientists with troops on the ground in conflict zones in Afghanistan, Iraq, and probably elsewhere as well. The main purpose appears to be to enhance the cultural information and understanding of the soldiers in order to help make their operations more effective (Kipp et al., 2007; McFate, 2005 a, b; Renzi, 2006; Sewall et al., 2007). It is claimed that HTS reduces conflict, saves lives, and may shorten the wars; however, so far these assertions have not been proven. One HTS anthropologist, Marcus Griffin, even maintains a website from Iraq (<http://marcusgriffin.com>).

The American Anthropological Association is the major professional organization of anthropologists in the USA, with a membership of well over 10,000. Its executive officers charged a special commission with investigating the role of anthropologists in the HTS (AAA ad hoc Committee on the Engagement of Anthropology with US Security and Intelligence Communities, or CEAUSSIC). The results of their inquiry were summarized in an Executive Board Statement on October 31, 2007. Their 62-page Final Report was posted on November 4, 2007. The main conclusion is that anthropologists involved in HTS may compromise or violate the principles in the 1998 AAA Code of Ethics in various ways. They may not be able to openly disclose their purpose or obtain voluntary consent from informants, and their information may be used by the military in ways that harm their informants and/or others in their community. Another concern was that anthropologists working anywhere in the world might be mistakenly identified as associated with the U.S. military and/or HTS and thereby their personal safety might be placed at risk (<http://www.aaanet.org>). In addition, a number of prominent anthropologists have been very critical of HTS, among them Roberto J. Gonzalez (2007, 2008), Hugh Gusterson (2003, 2007), and David H. Price (2000, 2007). An organization also was formed among such critics called the Network of Concerned Anthropologists (<http://concerned.anthropologists.googlepages.com>). (Ferguson, 1988; Fluehr-Lobban, 2002, 2003; Glazer, 1996; Whitehead and Trotter, 2008.)

There is no doubt that anthropology can be relevant in facilitating cross-cultural understanding and communication as, for example, in the pioneering research by Edward T. Hall (1990) on proxemics (spatial relationships). The main problem is the ends to which anthropology is a means—causing harm or promoting welfare, violence or nonviolence, war or peace, militarism or pacifism, and so on. As part of the creative challenge of a nonkilling anthropology it is imperative to imagine the practical possibilities of a nonkilling alternative to HTS. For example, some anthropologists might have less concern if the field anthropologists were engaged with the U.S. Department of State instead of the Department of Defense, but that would also depend on current government policies. For instance, by now it is widely recognized in the USA and worldwide that many of the policies of President George W. Bush's admini-stration have been disastrous, to say the least (Carter, 2005; Chomsky, 2001; Gore, 2007; Govier, 2002; Singer, 2004; Wright and Dixon, 2008).

In thinking through Paige's chapter 3, one of the challenges is that an-thropologists usually focus on culture and community, whereas political sci-entists tend to focus on power and polity, especially in the context of the nation state. However, anthropology also deals with many subjects basic to political science such as human nature, the origin of the state as civilization, and the emergence and maintenance of social inequality. In any case, think-ing through the relevance of this chapter for anthropology has the potential to transform the discipline, if not even to revolutionize it. In the first para-graph of chapter 3, Paige poses several questions about political science that can be pursued through anthropology as well as other disciplines. For example, his third question asks what values would inspire and guide the work? His sixth question asks what uses of knowledge would we facilitate? These two questions were previously answered in another context by the present author who pointed to the various United Nations declarations and conventions on human rights as a framework for developing anthropological thinking and actions (Sponsel, 1994a; 1995: 277-278; 1996b, c; 1997a, b; 2001). Before and since then, many other anthropologists have conducted re-search on human rights theory and practice (Bell et al., 2001; Downing and Kushner, 1988; Messer, 1993; Nagengast and Turner, 1997; Nagengast and Vélez-Ibáñez, 2004). Anthropologists have also addressed the important issue of universal human rights versus cultural relativism mentioned by Paige (2002: 117). (See Bell et al., 2001; Herskovits, 1972; Nagengast and Turner, 1997.) Three tasks for applied science that Paige (2002: 104) identifies are preven-tion, intervention, and post-traumatic nonkilling transformations, and each of these can be pursued through various forms of applied anthropology (e.g., Rubenstein, 2008). Articulating teaching, research, and service with human rights, even just in a general way as a conceptual framework, can generate more social meaning and significance in the anthropological endeavor.

For the professional training of nonkilling anthropologists, the curriculum and the pedagogy would need to be substantially changed, if not revolution-ized (cf. Paige 2002: 127-129). The curriculum would need to be reoriented from a structure around standard courses on subfields, topics, areas, and methods to one more explicitly focused on the important problems and is-sues of contemporary society and the world. It would have to emphasize as-pects of nonviolence and peace, although not to the exclusion of also consid-ering violence and war. These are among some possibilities for a curriculum:

- Unity and Diversity of Humankind
- Professional Values and Ethics in Anthropology
- History of Anthropology from War to Peace
- History of Colonial and Development Anthropology
- Anthropology of Colonialism and Neocolonialism
- Cultural Evolution, Change, and Revolution
- Anthropology of Violence and War
- Anthropology of Nonviolence and Peace
- Science, Technology, and Economics as if People Mattered
- Quality of Life: Environment, Water, Food, and Health
- Anthropology of Environmentalism, Environment, and Gaia
- Comparative Religion: Worldviews, Values, and Spiritual Ecology
- Alternative Political and Legal Systems
- Culture in Conflict Management and Resolution
- Problems and Solutions in Applied Anthropology
- Human Rights and Advocacy Anthropology
- Collaborative Ethnographic Methods

Each of these courses would address as feasible Paige's (2002: 72-74) four principles of logical analysis (see below). (Also see McKenna, 2008; Smith, 1999.) Although some of these courses mirror traditional ones, the focus would be significantly changed. For example, the orientation of a course on Alternative Political and Legal Systems, formerly political and legal anthropology, would shift to themes such as the mechanisms of nonviolent dispute resolution traditionally practiced by hunter-gatherer cultures (Avruch, 1998; Bonta, 1996; Bonta and Fry, 2006; Fry and Bjorkqvist, 1997; Greenhouse, 1985; Kemp and Fry, 2004; Rubinstein, 2008; Wolfe and Yang, 1996).

The faculty would be dedicated as much to teaching and service as to research, genuinely recognizing and rewarding the significance of all three. They would be engaged in cooperative rather than competitive activities aimed at applying their science to understanding and helping to resolve practical problems and issues, rather than advancing egocentric career trajectories by pursuing the latest academic fashions and theoretical fantasies. Accordingly, overall there would be a shift in emphasis, albeit not exclusively, from basic to applied aspects of anthropology (Barker, 2004; Fry and Bjorkqvist, 1997; Gwynne, 2003; Johnston, 2007; Johnston and Barker, 2008; Kemp and Fry, 2004; Paine, 1985; Sponsel, 2001; and Ury, 1999, 2004).

At the same time, there are economic obstacles to be overcome. For example, at the University of Hawai'i, in spite of near unanimous opposition from faculty and students, some top administrators and a few researchers in the physical sciences recently embraced a 5-year contract for $50,000,000 from the U.S. Navy for the development of a University Applied Research Center. At the same time, it is simply inconceivable that even a fraction of that amount would ever be invested in the annual budget of the Spark M. Matsunaga Institute for Peace at the University of Hawai'i. Such are the priorities in a killing society and in the most militarized state in the union (Blanco, 2009; Kajihiro, 2007). Killing remains more profitable than nonkilling. As General Dwight Eisenhower also warned in his farewell presidential speech to the nation on January 17, 1961: "The prospect of domination of the nation's scholars by Federal employment, project allocations, and the power of money is ever present—and is gravely to be regarded." (See Feldman, 1989; Giroux, 2007; Simpson, 1998.)

Likewise, within the professional organization of the American Anthropological Association and others, the structures and priorities would have to radically change. For example, within the AAA the Committee on Ethics and the Committee for Human Rights would have to be given top priority with corresponding financial and other resources. The themes of the annual conventions would have to place far greater emphasis on the more applied aspects of anthropology. Current priorities are crystal clear. For instance, the topical index of key words from sessions at the 2008 annual convention of the AAA lists ten sessions on violence and eight on war, but only one on peace and none on nonviolence. On the other hand, it lists nine sessions on human rights and a dozen on ethics which is more positive, a much larger number than prior to the 1990s (AAA, 2008). Incidentally, the AAA is not atypical in this respect. As another example, the second edition of the multidisciplinary *Encyclopedia of Violence, Peace, and Conflict* (Kurtz, 2008) contains 289 entries, but only ten (3.5%) with nonviolence and 29 (10%) with peace in their titles, although these topics may receive some attention in articles without these words in their titles.

Many of the phenomena that Paige (2002: 133) worries about were not problems until the evolution of the state, and especially modern nations, so they are very recent (Nagengast, 1994). Contemporary issues include abortion, capital punishment, conscription, war, armed revolution, terrorism, genocide, criminality, social violence, disarmament, and economic demilitarization (Paige, 2002: 133; cf. Levinson, 1994). According to Paige (2002: 111-112), five problems that are globally salient are: continued killing and the need for disarmament, poverty and the need for economic equality, violations of human rights and the need for greater respect for human dignity and human rights, destruction of nature, and other-denying divisiveness that impedes problem-solving cooperation. (See Donnelly, 2003; Mahoney, 2007.) In one way or another, anthropologists have been addressing these and related matters to varying degrees. Indeed, there are many books on each of these subjects, but if any one might be singled out, including as a possible textbook, then it would be *Anthropology and Contemporary Human Problems* by John H. Bodley (2008a).

Paige concludes chapter 3 by inviting "... thought about what political science would be like if it took seriously the possibility of realizing nonkilling societies in a nonkilling world." He goes on to write that "Acceptance of such a possibility implies active political science engagement in nonviolent global problem-solving" (Paige, 2002: 97). This is certainly a provocative question for anthropology as well. Applied, advocacy, action, public, and engaged are various qualifiers associated with anthropology that deals with practical problem solving in promoting human survival, welfare, justice, dignity, and rights in various ways and degrees (Barker, 2004; Besteman and Gusterson, 2005; Eriksen, 2006; González, 2004; Gwynne, 2003; Hinton, 2001; Johnston, 1994, 1997, 2007; Johnston and Barker 2008). Already many anthropologists are contributing to the development of a nonkilling society and nonkilling world, although not exactly with those terms in mind. There is still enormous potential for further work in this regard. However, a major obstacle is that often such practical work is not considered to be as prestigious or valuable as basic research, as for example, in the assessment for tenure and promotion of academic faculty at universities and colleges, and especially among those who are still under the illusion that science is apolitical and amoral (cf. Giroux 2007).

The framework and questions for research and praxis that Paige develops so boldly and profoundly in his book and other work opens up an entire new world of exciting and promising possibilities for anthropological research, teaching, and service with potentially far reaching practical consequences. His pursuit of a medical model for the sciences, humanities, and other professions pivoting around a central concern for saving lives, reducing suffering, and promoting well being calls for a paradigm shift, if not even a revolution. While he emphasizes nonkilling, ultimately this transcends stopping the negative—lethality, to also advance the positive—protection and enhancement of the quality of life. In the present author's opinion, the subject of human rights provides the conceptual and practical framework for such a noble endeavor.

Discussion

Paige challenges the prevailing assumption that (1) killing is an inescapable or inevitable part of human nature or of the human condition, and the corollary that (2) it must be accepted in political theory and practice as well as elsewhere. He implies that this assumption stems from the long history of American warfare and militarism by citing numerous examples (Paige, 2002: 7-8). Even more revealing and disturbing are the more detailed historical inventories of these aggressive activities in sources such as Andreas (2004) and Churchill (2003). Thus, a systemic bias toward violence including war appears to be a product of Western and especially American history and culture (Duclos, 1997; Hofstadter and Wallace, 1971; Keegan, 1993; Lewis, 2006; Palmer, 1972; Sponsel, 1994a, 1996a). The USA is grounded in the invasion and conquest of the continent by European colonial displacement or compulsory relocation, forced assimilation and acculturation, and downright ethnocide and genocide of a multitude of indigenous societies (Bodley, 2008b; Churchill, 1997; Diamond, 1999; Ferguson and Whitehead, 1992; Jaimes, 1992; Kroeber, 1961; Patterson, 2001; Starkey, 1998; Steele, 1994). Another factor is the militarism and warfare that permeates U.S. history (Andreas, 2004; Churchill, 2003; Hedges, 2002; Hillman, 2004; Ury, 2002). Since at least WWII, the Hobbesian view of human nature has been increasingly reinforced by the development of the industrial-military complex that President Dwight Eisenhower warned about in his farewell speech to the nation.

Moreover, subsequent developments have resulted in an industrial-military-media-academic complex that infiltrates American society like a cancer, with the most rapid and penetrating growth during the presidential administration of George W. Bush as part of the post-911 paranoia it helped to create and maintain. Thus, for instance, for several years Americans were kept terrified with a system of periodic color coded alerts and other tactics that helped generate the lucrative profits of the weapons, military, and security industries since 9-11. The interconnected weapons and oil industries are not only the most profitable ones in the world along with illegal drugs, but also the most powerful politically as well as economically (Andreas, 2004). Accordingly, it is most sad to say that peace is likely to emerge and prevail globally only when it becomes more profitable than war.

American anthropologists who stress a Hobbesian view of human nature may be culturally as well as ideologically biased (Clark, 2002; Curti, 1980). On the one hand not all American anthropologists share the ideology that encompasses the Hobbesian view (Kegley and Raymond, 1999: 20-21, 245;

Patterson, 2001). On the other hand, to some degree all American anthropologists share the same generic culture. In anthropology, the common assumption about dismal human nature and the inevitability of war and other forms of aggression still appears to prevail, even though most reject simplistic and reductionistic biological determinism. For instance, this is reflected in the fact that there are many more books on violence and war than on nonviolence and peace, whether general surveys or particular case studies. Those on nonviolence and peace number about a dozen, whereas there are many times more that number on violence and war (Ferguson and Farragher, 1988; Sponsel, 1994a, b, 1996a, c; Wiberg, 1981). Members of the American Anthropological Association may list their specializations in a special online directory. The specializations available for listing in the AAA form include conflict, conflict resolution, ethnic conflict, violence, and warfare, but revealingly, neither nonviolence nor peace are listed.

The idea of human nature also needs to be problematized (Cannel and Macklin, 1974; Curti, 1980; Sponsel, 2007; Stevenson and Haberman, 1998). Logically, human nature may or may not exist, it may be uniform or multifarious, it may good or bad, and so on. For example, some anthropologists would argue that there is no single, uniform human nature; instead, there are numerous human natures as expressed in the diversity of some 7,000 different cultures extant in the world today. From such a perspective, human nature is manifest in cultural diversity and is generated by nurture (social environment) instead of nature (genetics). Human nature is tremendously plastic and adaptable as well as diverse, the latter the expression of the former two attributes (Sponsel, 2007). Thus, many anthropologists would see cultural relativism as their primary disciplinary value, while some extreme cultural relativists would even dispute the existence of any meaningful cross-cultural universals common to all of humanity (Brown, 1991; Herskovits, 1972). Furthermore, within science and academia, there are many different theories of human nature (Cannel and Macklin, 1974; Curti, 1980; Feibleman, 1987; Stevenson and Haberman, 1998). Likewise, each of the world's religions has a somewhat different concept of human nature distinctive to their own worldview (Matthews, 2004). This diversity itself undermines the assumptions of a single, uniform human nature, and of the inevitably of violence and war in spite of the reductionistic and simplistic speculations of the apologists for war.

As a political scientist concerned with international relations, Paige tends to focus on the modern nation state. Anthropology also problematizes this focus because the state is actually a relatively recent invention and could well be a transitory stage of political organization in cultural evolution (cf.

Ferguson, 2003; Nagengast, 1994). As conceived by anthropologists, the state is basically coincident with civilization and only about 5,000 years old, depending on the region. Actually 99% of human existence from origins dating back to at least two million years ago was dominated exclusively by hunting-gathering lifestyles. If there is anything universal in human culture and/or such a thing as human nature, it then most likely is a result of this hunter-gatherer legacy (Lee and DeVore, 1968; Shepard, 1973). Moreover, the overwhelming majority of hunter-gatherer societies are mostly egalitarian, cooperative, nonkilling, and peaceful, as demonstrated by evidence from archaeology, ethnohistory, ethnography, and ethnology, this notwithstanding the contrary opinions of the apologists for warfare (Kelly, 2000).

As a political scientist, Paige considers power to be pivotal in society and in his discipline, and power is political with economics, religion, and other factors secondary. The parallel focus in anthropology is culture. Culture is pivotal in society and in the discipline. However, both of these are only partial considerations, albeit very important ones. Particular circumstances can be decisive. For instance, in the case of Tibet as previously discussed, Buddhism as a religion is pivotal, and the power of the Dalai Lama as a spiritual leader is primary even in exile. Given the relationship of Tibetans with China and other countries, these factors also become political, but that is secondary, even though it is often difficult to consider the religious and political as separate in this case, especially given Tibet's history since the Chinese invasion and occupation. Similarly, in the case of the Middle East, religion is a tremendous influence; it is not simply a matter of secular politics. Indeed, in Islam politics is subordinated to religion. It is impossible to understand the Middle East purely in secular terms (Eickelman, 2002; Eickelman and Piscatori, 1996; Esposito and Mogahed, 2007; Khan, 2006).

Paige is challenging not only the inevitability of killing, but also its efficacy and legitimacy. A nonkilling anthropology would reject these tenets as well. However, legitimacy invokes normative considerations, and some might reject this by claiming that science must be amoral as well as apolitical to maintain neutrality for the sake of objectivity. But that is an illusion. To take an extreme case, the Manhattan project was grounded in hard science. Yet Paige (2002: 81) notes that 19 out of 150 scientists on the Manhattan Project voted against any military use of the atomic bombs. Personally, the present author does not see any difference in incinerating Jews in the Nazi concentration camps and in incinerating Japanese in the cities of Hiroshima and Nagasaki. Both are absolutely immoral. Furthermore, the scientists who made these atrocities possible cannot be considered amoral and apolitical. Indeed, they can be considered complicit in such crimes against humanity (cf. Christopher, 1999).

Postmodernists have called into question the assertion that science is neutral, objective, apolitical, amoral, and the like. As an example, in the controversy over the scandalous behavior of some researchers working with the Yanomami generated by the publication of the book *Darkness in El Dorado* by investigative journalist Patrick Tierney (2000), some of those who portrayed themselves as scientists clearly exhibited behavior that was just the opposite of scientific, lacking in objectivity, rife in political ideology, and downright unethical and immoral (Borofsky, 2005; Fluehr-Lobban, 2003; Gregor and Gross, 2004; Gross, 2004; Robin, 2004; Sponsel, 2006a; Sponsel and Turner, 2002; Tierney, 2000). The larger hidden agenda of many of the negative responses to Tierney was to try to invalidate a penetrating critic of one example of Cold War anthropological research (also see Neel, 1994; Price, 2008; Wax, 2008).

The above are some of my reservations, qualifications, and elaborations regarding Paige's book and thesis. At the same time, what he has to say is obviously extremely important, and increasingly so given the so-called global war on terrorism, the dire problems of globalization, the developing consequences of global warming with all of its widespread and profound impacts on society and the environment, and the increasing militarization of the planet including its infiltration of scientific and academic institutions (Giroux, 2007). These are all interrelated and acting in synergy to the point of being not only alarming, but potentially catastrophic, to say the least.

Consequently, the time is not only most propitious, but also most urgent to consider the possibilities of a nonkilling society at every level—family, community, national, international, and global. Paige's four-component logical analysis is most valid and useful; namely, to consider the conditions, processes, and consequences of (1) a killing society, (2) a nonkilling society, (3) the transition from a nonkilling to a killing society, and (4) the transition from a killing to a nonkilling society. Tibet could be a very revealing case study for illuminating these four components. In various ways anthropology offers evidence and insights that are very relevant to all four of these components, ranging from the earlier work of Franz Boas, Margaret Mead, Ruth Benedict, and Ashley Montagu, and others to the most recent work of pioneers previously mentioned.

Finally, Paige (2002: 143) asserts that: "Every political scientist and each person can be *a center* for global nonviolence to facilitate transition to a nonkilling world." More anthropologists need to become such a center. In 1993, I was privileged to participate in a small multidisciplinary conference titled "What We Know About Peace" in Charleston, South Carolina, sponsored by the Harry Frank Guggenheim Foundation (Gregor, 1996). However, I quickly became very disappointed and even disillusioned when it became clear that almost all of the participants were actually talking about war instead of peace. One participant even went to the extreme of asserting that peace is the presence of war (Tuzin, 1996: 3). Thank you, Glenn Paige, for opening some minds to the social and scientific possibilities of nonkilling and peace.

Conclusions

Glenn Paige (2002) has dared to ask the very profound and provocative primary question: Is a nonkilling society possible? From my perspective as an anthropologist who has paid some attention to anthropological aspects of peace and nonviolence, and not only war and violence unlike most colleagues, I find the answer to this question quite simple. A nonkilling society is not only possible to conceive of theoretically, such societies exist in reality as revealed by the overwhelming evidence from archaeology, ethnohistory, history, ethnography, and ethnology. Thus, nonkilling is an actuality, not merely a possibility. Nonkilling and peace are scientific facts; the evidence is overwhelming and undeniable, as alluded to in this essay and sustained by the accumulating documentation, such as Bonta's website. The time is long overdue to systematically make this explicit and pursue it in every constructive way possible to create a nonviolent and life-enhancing society for the realization of the human potential for freedom, justice, peace, harmony, and creativity. Anthropology has an important role to play in such a noble and vital endeavor, if only more anthropologists can open their minds to the revolutionary possibilities of a nonkilling society and a nonkilling anthropology.

References

Adams, David (1989). "The Seville Statement on Violence: A Progress Report," *Journal of Peace Research*, 26(2):113-121.

American Anthropological Association (2008). *Program American Anthropological Association 107th Annual Meeting, November 19-23, 2008, San Francisco, California*. Arlington: American Anthropological Association.

Andreas, Joel (2004). *Addicted to War: Why Can't the U.S. Kick Militarism*. Oakland: AK Press. Also see: <http://www.addictedtowar.com>.

Ardrey, Robert (1961). *African Genesis: A Personal Investigation into the Animal Origins and Nature of Man*. New York: Atheneum.

Ardrey, Robert (1966). *The Territorial Imperative: A Personal Inquiry into the Animal Origins of Property and Nations*. New York: Atheneum.

Ardrey, Robert (1976). *The Hunting Hypothesis: A Personal Conclusion Concerning the Evolutionary Nature of Man*. New York: Atheneum.

Aureli, Filippo; Waal, Frans B.M. de, eds. (2000). *Natural Conflict Resolution.* Berkeley: University of California Press.

Avruch, Kevin (1998). *Culture and Conflict Resolution,* Washington: United States Institute of Peace Press.

Barash, David P.; Webel, Charles P. (2002). *Peace and Conflict Studies.* Thousand Oaks: Sage Publications.

Barber, Benjamin R. (1996). *Jihad vs. McWorld: How Globalism and Tribalism Are Reshaping the World.* New York: Ballantine Books.

Barker, Holly M. (2004). *Bravo for the Marshallese: Regaining Control in a Post-Nuclear, Post-Colonial World.* Belmont: Wadsworth/Thomson Learning.

Barnaby, Frank, ed. (1988). *The Gaia Peace Atlas.* New York: Doubleday.

Barnes, Bruce E. (2007). *Culture, Conflict, and Mediation in the Asian Pacific.* Lanham: University Press of America.

Barth, Fredrik (1956). "Ecological Relationships of Ethnic Groups in Swat, North Pakistan," *American Anthropologist,* 58:1079-1089.

Baszarkiewicz, Karolina; Fry, Douglas P. (2008). "Peaceful Societies," in Kurtz, Lester, ed., *Encyclopedia of Violence, Peace, & Conflict,* San Diego: Elsevier 2:1557-1570.

Bell, Lynda S.; Nathan, Andrew J.; Peleg, Ilan, eds. (2001). *Negotiating Culture and Human Rights.* New York: Columbia University Press.

Ben-Ari, Eyal (2004). "The Military and Militarization in the United States," *American Ethnologist,* 31(3):340-348.

Besteman, Catherine; Gusterson, Hugh, eds. (2005). *Why America's Top Pundits are Wrong: Anthropologists Talk Back.* Berkeley: University of California Press.

Bestman, Catherine, et al. (2009). *Network of Concerned Anthropologists: The Counter-Counterinsurgency Manual or, Notes on Demilitarizing American Society.* Chicago: Prickly Paradigm Press.

Bhaneja, Balwant (2008). "Nonkilling Political Science," in Kurtz, Lester, ed., *Encyclopedia of Violence, Peace, & Conflict,* San Diego: Elsevier 2:1356-1363.

Biesanz, Richard; Biesanz, Karen Zubris; Biesanz, Mavis Hitunen (1982). *The Costa Ricans.* Prospect Heights: Waveland Press, Inc.

Birx, H. James, ed. (2006). *Encyclopedia of Anthropology.* Thousand Oaks: Sage.

Blanco, Sebastian (2009). *U.S. Militarism in Hawai'i: A People's History.* Kihei: Koa.

Blondeau, Anne-Marie; Buffetrille, Katia, eds. (2008). *Authenticating Tibet: Answers to China's 100 Questions.* Berkeley: University of California Press.

Bodley, John H. (2008a). *Anthropology and Contemporary Human Problems.* Lanham: AltaMira Press.

Bodley, John H. (2008b). *Victims of Progress.* Lanham: AltaMira Press.

Bonta, Bruce D. (1993). *Peaceful Peoples: An Annotated Bibliography.* Metuchen: Scarecrow Press.

Bonta, Bruce D. (1996). "Conflict Resolution among Peaceful Societies: The Culture of Peacefulness," *Journal of Peace Research,* 33:403-420.

Bonta, Bruce D. (1997). "Cooperation and Competition in Peaceful Societies," *Psychological Bulletin,* 121:299-320.

Bonta, Bruce D. (2008). "Peaceful Societies: Alternatives to Violence and War," Available at: <http://www.peacefulsocieties.org>.

Bonta, Bruce D.; Fry, Douglas P. (2006). "Lessons for the Rest of Us: Learning from Peaceful Societies," in Fitzduff, M.; Stout, C. E., eds., *The Psychology of Resolving Global Conflicts: From War to Peace*. Westport: Praeger 1:175-210.

Borofsky, Robert, ed. (2005). *Yanomami: The Fierce Controversy and What We Can Learn from It*. Berkeley: University of California Press.

Brown, Donald E. (1991). *Human Universals*. New York: McGraw-Hill, Inc.

Cannel, Ward; Macklin, June (1974). *The Human Nature Industry: How Human Nature is Manufactured, Distributed, and Consumed in the United States and Parts of Canada*. Garden City: Anchor Press/Doubleday.

Carter, Jimmy (2005). *Our Endangered Values: America's Moral Crisis*. New York: Simon and Schuster.

Chagnon, Napoleon A. (1968). *Yanomamo: The Fierce People*. New York: Holt, Rinehart and Winston.

Chagnon, Napoleon A. (1992). *Yanomamo*. Fort Worth: Harcourt Brace Jovanovich.

Chomsky, Noam (2001). *9-11*. New York: Seven Stories Press.

Christopher, Paul (1999). *The Ethics of War and Peace: An Introduction to Moral and Legal Issues*. Upper Saddle River: Prentice Hall.

Churchill, Ward (1997). *A Little Matter of Genocide: Holocaust and Denial in the Americas 1492 to the Present*. San Francisco: City Lights Books.

Churchill, Ward (2003). *On the Justice of Roosting Chickens: Reflections on the Consequences of U.S. Imperial Arrogance and Criminality*. Oakland: AK Press.

Clark, Mary E. (2002). *In Search of Human Nature*. New York: Routledge.

Cranna, Michael; Bhinda, Nils (1995). *The True Cost of Conflict: Seven Recent Wars and Their Effects on Society*. New York: New Press.

Curti, Merle (1980). *Human Nature in American Thought: A History*. Madison: University of Wisconsin Press.

Dalai Lama, His Holiness the XIVth (1987). *The Buddhism of Tibet*. Ithaca: Snow Lion Publications.

Dalai Lama, His Holiness the XIVth (1999). *Ethics for the New Millennium*. New York: Riverhead Books.

Dawson, Michael (2006). *Growing Up Yanomamo*. Enumclaw: WinePress.

Dennen, J.M.G. van der (1995). *The Origin of War*. Groningen: Origin Press.

Dentan, Robert K. (1968). *The Semai: A Nonviolent People of Malaya*. New York: Holt, Rinehart and Winston.

Diamond, Jared (1999). *Guns, Germs, and Steel: The Fates of Human Societies*. New York: W.W. Norton & Company.

Donnelly, Jack (2003). *Universal Human Rights in Theory and Practice*. Ithaca: Cornell University Press.

Downing, Theodore E.; Kushner, Gilbert, eds. (1988). *Human Rights and Anthropology*. Cambridge: Cultural Survival.

Duclos, Dennis (1997). *The Werewolf Complex: America's Fascination with Violence*. New York: Berg.

Ehlers, Tracy Bachrach (1980). "Central America in the 1980's: Political Crisis and the Social Responsibility of Anthropologists," *Latin American Research Review* XXV(3):141-155.

Ehrenreich, Barbara (1998). *Blood Rites: Origins and History of the Passions for War*. New York: Holt.

Eickelman, Dale F. (2002). *The Middle East and Central Asia: An Anthropological Approach*. Upper Saddle River: Prentice Hall.

Eickelman, Dale F.; Piscatori, James (1996). *Muslim Politics*. Princeton: Princeton University Press.

Eller, Jack David (1999). *From Culture to Ethnicity to Conflict: An Anthropological Perspective on International Ethnic Conflict*. Ann Arbor: University of Michigan Press.

Eller, Jack David (2006). *Violence and Culture: A Cross-Cultural and Interdisciplinary Approach*. Belmont: Thomson Higher Education.

Eriksen, Thomas Hylland (2006). *Engaging Anthropology: The Case for a Public Presence*. New York: Berg.

Esposito, John L.; Mogahed, Dalia (2007). *Who Speaks for Islam?: What A Billion Muslims Really Think*. New York: Gallup Press.

Fabbro, David (1978). "Peaceful Societies: An Introduction," *Journal of Peace Research*, XV(1):67-83.

Feibleman, James Kern (1987). *The Destroyers: The Underside of Human Nature*. New York: Peter Lang.

Feldman, Jonathan (1989). *Universities in the Business of Repression: The Academic-Military-Industrial Complex and Central America*. Boston: South End Press.

Ferguson, R. Brian (1988). "Anthropology and War: Theory, Politics, Ethics," in Turner, Paul R.; Pitt, David, eds., *The Anthropology of War and Peace: Perspectives on the Nuclear Age*. Cambridge: Bergin and Garvey Publishers, pp. 141-159.

Ferguson, R. Brian (1992). "Tribal Warfare," *Scientific American*, 266(1):108-113.

Ferguson, R. Brian (1995). *Yanomami Warfare: A Political History*. Santa Fe: School of American Research Press.

Ferguson, R. Brian (2002). "The 'Violent' Human: Archaeological and Historical Evidence," in Ury, William, ed., *Must We Fight? From the Battlefield to the Schoolyard: A New Perspective on Violent Conflict and Its Preservation*. San Francisco: Jossey-Bass, pp. 26-38.

Ferguson, R. Brian, ed. (2003). *The State Under Siege: Political Disintegration in the Post-Cold War World*. London: Routledge.

Ferguson, R. Brian (2006). "Archaeology, Cultural Anthropology, and the Origins and Intensification of War," in Arkush, Elizabeth N.; Allen, Mark W., eds., *The Archaeology of Warfare: Prehistories of Raiding and Conquest*. Gainesville: University Press of Florida.

Ferguson, R. Brian (2007). "Eight Points on War," *Anthropology News*, 48(2):5-6.

Ferguson, R. Brian (2008). "Ten Points on War," *Social Analysis*, 52(2):32-49.

Ferguson, R. Brian; Farragher, Leslie E. (1988). *The Anthropology of War: A Bibliography*. New York: Harry Frank Guggenheim Foundation Occasional Paper 1.
Ferguson, R. Brian; Whitehead, Neil L., eds. (1992). *War in the Tribal Zone: Expanding States and Indigenous Warfare*. Santa Fe: School of American Research.
Fluehr-Lobban, Carolyn (2002). "A Century of Ethics and Professional Anthropology," *Anthropology News*, 43(3):20.
Fluehr-Lobban, Carolyn, ed. (2003). *Ethics and the Profession of Anthropology: Dialogue for Ethically Conscious Practice*. Walnut Creek: AltaMira Press.
Frankfurt, Harry G. (2005). *On Bullshit*. Princeton: Princeton University Press.
Fluehr-Lobban, Carolyn (2006). *On Truth*. New York: Alfred A. Knopf.
Frese, Pamela R.; Harrell, Margaret C., eds. (2003). *Anthropology and the United States Military: Coming of Age in the Twenty-first Century*. New York: Palgrave Macmillan.
Fried, Morton; Harris, Marvin; Murphy, Robert, eds. (1968). *The Anthropology of Armed Conflict and Aggression*. Garden City: Doubleday & Company, Inc.
Fry, Douglas P. (2006). *The Human Potential for Peace: An Anthropological Challenge to Assumptions about War and Violence*. New York: Oxford University Press.
Fry, Douglas P. (2007). *Beyond War: The Human Potential for Peace*. New York: Oxford University Press.
Fry, Douglas P.; Bjorkqvist, Kaj, eds. (1997). *Cultural Variation in Conflict Resolution: Alternatives to Violence*. Mahwah: Lawrence Erlbaum Associates, Publishers.
Gelvin, Michael (1994). *War and Existence: A Philosophical Inquiry*. University Park: Pennsylvania State University Press.
Ghiglieri, Michael P. (1987). "War among the Chimps," *Discover*, 8(11):67-76.
Ghiglieri, Michael P. (1999). *The Dark Side of Man: Tracing the Origins of Male Violence*. Reading: Perseus Books.
Giroux, Henry A. (2007). *The University in Chains: Confronting the Military-Industrial-Academic Complex*. Boulder: Paradigm Publishers.
Glazer, Myron Peretz (1996). "Ethics," in Levinson, David; Ember, Melvin, eds., *Encyclopedia of Cultural Anthropology*, vol. 2. New York: Henry Holt, pp. 389-393.
Golding, William (1999 [1954]). *Lord of the Flies*. New York: Penguin Books.
Goldschmidt, Walter, ed. (1979). *The Uses of Anthropology*. Washington: American Anthropological Association Special Publication 11.
Good, Kenneth; Charnoff, David (1991). *Into the Heart: One Man's Pursuit of Love and Knowledge among the Yanomami*. New York: Simon and Schuster.
González, Roberto J., ed. (2004). *Anthropologists in the Public Sphere: Speaking Out on War, Peace, and American Power*. Austin: University of Texas Press.
González, Roberto J. (2007). "Towards Mercenary Anthropology?," *Anthropology Today*, 23(3):14-19.
González, Roberto J. (2008). "Imperial Tactics: Bribing the 'Tribes,'" *Z Magazine*, 21(2):37-40.
González, Roberto J. (2009). *American Counterinsurgency: Human Science and the Human Terrain*. Chicago: Prickly Paradigm Press.

Goodall, Jane (1986). *The Chimpanzees of Gombe: Patterns of Behavior*. Cambridge: Cambridge University Press.

Gordon, Robert (1988). "Apartheid's Anthropologists: The Genealogy of Afrikaner Anthropology," *American Ethnologist*, 15(3):535-553.

Gore, Al (2007). *The Assault on Reason*. New York: Penguin Books.

Gough, Kathleen (1968). "Anthropology and Imperialism," *Monthly Review*, 19(11):12-24.

Govier, Trudy (2002). *A Delicate Balance: What Philosophy Can Tell Us About Terrorism*. Boulder: Westview Press.

Graeber, David (2004). *Fragments of an Anarchist Anthropology*. Chicago: Prickly Paradigm Press.

Greenhouse, Carol (1985). "Mediation: A Comparative Approach," *Man*, 20(1):90-114.

Gregor, Thomas A., ed. (1996). *The Natural History of Peace*. Nashville: Vanderbilt University Press.

Gregor, Thomas A.; Gross, Daniel R. (2004). "Guilt By Association: The Culture of Accusation and the AAA's Investigation of *Darkness in El Dorado*," *American Anthropologist*, 106(4):687-698.

Griffin, Marcus. *Human Terrain System Anthropologist* <http://www.marcusgriffin.com>.

Gross, Paul R. (2004). "Politics and Science," in Salzano, Francisco M.; Hurtado, A. Magdalena, eds., *Lost Paradises and the Ethics of Research and Publication*. New York: Oxford University Press, pp. 59-69.

Grossman, Dave (1995). *On Killing: The Psychological Costs of Learning to Kill in War and Society*. New York: Little, Brown.

Grossman, Dave (2008). "Evolution of Weaponry," in Kurtz, Lester, ed., *Encyclopedia of Violence, Peace, & Conflict*, San Diego: Elsevier 3:2442-2455.

Guilaine, Jean; Zammit, Jean (2001). *Origins of War: Violence in Prehistory*. Malden: Blackwell Publishing.

Gusterson, Hugh (1996). *Nuclear Rites: A Weapons Laboratory at the End of the Cold War*. Berkeley: University of California Press.

Gusterson, Hugh (2003). "Anthropology and the Military: 1968, 2003, and Beyond?" *Anthropology Today*, 19(3):25-26.

Gusterson, Hugh (2007). "Anthropology and Militarism," *Annual Review of Anthropology*, 36:155-175.

Gwynne, Margaret A. (2003). *Applied Anthropology: A Career-Oriented Approach*. Boston: Allyn and Bacon.

Hall, Edward T. (1990). *The Hidden Dimension*. New York: Anchor Books.

Harcourt, A.H.; Waal, Frans B. M. de (1992). *Coalitions and Alliances in Humans and Other Animals*. New York: Oxford University Press.

Hart, Donna; Sussman, Robert W. (2009). *Man the Hunted: Primates, Predators, and Human Evolution*. Boulder: Westview Press.

Hastings, Tom H. (2000). *Ecology of War & Peace: Counting Costs of Conflict*. Lanham: University Press of America.

Hedges, Chris (2002). *War Is a Force that Gives Us Meaning*. New York: Public Affairs.

Hedges, Chris; Al-Arian, Laila (2007), "The Other War," *The Nation*, 285(4):11-31.

Herskovits, Melville J. (1972). *Cultural Relativism: Perspectives in Cultural Pluralism*. New York: Random House.

Hickey, Gerald C. (2002). *Window on a War: An Anthropologist in the Vietnam Conflict*. Lubbock: Texas Tech University Press.

Hillman, James (2004). *A Terrible Love of War*. New York: Penguin.

Hofstadter, Richard; Wallace, Michael, eds. (1971). *American Violence: A Documentary History*. New York: Random House.

Holmes, Bob (2008). "How Warfare Shaped Human Evolution," *New Scientist*, 2682.

Homer-Dixon, Thomas F.; Boutwell, Jeffrey H.; Rathjens, George W. (1993). "Environmental Change and Violent Conflict," *Scientific American*, 268(2):38-45.

Howell, Signe; Willis, Roy, eds. (1989). *Societies at Peace: Anthropological Perspectives*. New York: Routledge.

Hymes, Dell, ed. (1999). *Reinventing Anthropology*. Ann Arbor: University of Michigan Press.

Jaimes, M. Annette, ed. (1992). *The State of Native America: Genocide, Colonization, and Resistance*. Boston: South End Press.

Jell-Bahlsen, S. (1985). "Ethnology and Fascism in Germany," *Dialectical Anthropology*, 9:337-347.

Jeong, Ho-Won (2000). *Peace and Conflict Studies: An Introduction*. Aldershot: Ashgate.

Johnston, Barbara Rose, ed. (1994). *Who Pays the Price? Examining the Sociocultural Context of the Environmental Crisis*. Washington: Island Press.

Johnston, Barbara Rose, ed. (1997). *Life and Death Matters: Human Rights and the Environment at the End of the Millennium*. Thousand Oaks: AltaMira Press.

Johnston, Barbara Rose, ed. (2007). *Half-Lives & Half-Truths: Confronting the Radioactive Legacies of the Cold War*. Santa Fe: School for Advanced Research Press.

Johnston, Barbara Rose; Barker, Holly M. (2008). *The Rongelap Report: Consequential Damages of Nuclear War*. Walnut Creek: Left Coast Press, Inc.

Kajihiro, Kyle (2007). "A Brief Overview of Militarization and Resistance in Hawai'i," Honolulu: DMZ-Hawai'i/Aloha 'Aina, pp. 1-12 (<http://www.dmzhawaii.org>).

Kano, Takayoshi (1990). "The Bonobo's Peaceful Kingdom," *Natural History*, 11:62-71.

Kano, Takayoshi (1992). *The Last Ape: Pygmy Chimpanzee Behavior and Ecology*. Stanford: Stanford University Press.

Kaplan, Robert D. (1994). "The Coming Anarchy," *Atlantic Monthly*, 273(2):44-76.

Kaplan, Robert D. (2000). *The Coming Anarchy: Shattering the Dreams of the Post Cold War*. New York: Random House/Vintage.

Kapstein, Matthew T. (2006). *The Tibetans*. Malden: Blackwell Publishing.

Keegan, John (1993). *A History of Warfare*. New York: Random House/Vintage.

Keeley, Lawrence H. (1996). *War Before Civilization: The Myth of the Peaceful Savage*. New York: Oxford University Press.

Kegley, Jr., Charles W.; Raymond, Gregory A., eds. (1999). *How Nations Make Peace*. New York: St. Martin's Press.

Kelly, Raymond C. (2000). *Warless Societies and the Origin of War*. Ann Arbor: University of Michigan Press.

Kemp, Graham; Fry, Douglas P., eds. (2004). *Keeping the Peace: Conflict Resolution and Peaceful Societies Around the World*. New York: Routledge.

Khan, Arshad (2006). *Islam 101: Principles and Practice*. San Jose: Khan.

Kipp, J.; Grau, L.; Prinslow, K.; Smith, D. (2006). "The Human Terrain System: ACORDS for the 21ˢᵗ Century," *U.S. Army Professional Writing Collection*, 4:1-9.

Klare, Michael T. (2001). "The New Geography of Conflict," *Foreign Affairs*, 80(3):22-49.

Klare, Michael T. (2002). *Resource Wars: The New Landscape of Global Conflict*. New York: Harry Holt.

Kohn, Alfie (1990). *The Brighter Side of Human Nature: Altruism and Empathy in Everyday Life*. New York: Basic Books.

Kraybill, Donald B. (2008). *The Amish of Lancaster County*. Mechanicsburg: Stackpole.

Kraybill, Donald B.; Nolt, Steven M.; Weaver-Zercher, David L. (2006). *Amish Grace: How Forgiveness Transcended Tragedy*. New York: Jossey-Bass.

Kroeber, Theodora (1961). *Ishi in Two Worlds: A Biography of the Last Wild Indian in North America*. Berkeley: University of California Press.

Krug, E. et al., eds. (2002). *World Report on Violence and Health*. Geneva: World Health Organization.

Kurtz, Lester, ed. (2008). *Encyclopedia of Violence, Peace, & Conflict*. San Diego: Elsevier.

Kyrou, Christos N.; Rubenstein, Robert A. (2008). "Cultural Anthropology Studies of Conflict," in Kurtz, Lester, ed., *Encyclopedia of Violence, Peace, & Conflict*. San Diego: Elsevier 1:515-521.

Lanier-Graham, Susan D. (1993). *The Ecology of War: Environmental Impacts of Weaponry and Warfare*. New York: Waker and Company.

Lassiter, Luke Eric (2005). *The Chicago Guide to Collaborative Ethnography*. Chicago: University of Chicago Press.

LeBlanc, Steven A.; Register, Katherine E. (2003). *Constant Battles: The Myth of the Peaceful, Noble Savage*. New York: St. Martin's Press.

Lee, Richard B.; DeVore, Irven, eds. (1968). *Man the Hunter*. Chicago: Aldine.

Levinson, David (1994). *Aggression and Conflict: A Cross-Cultural Encyclopedia*. Santa Barbara: ABC-CLIO.

Lewis, Andrian R. (2006). *The American Culture of War: The History of U.S. Military Force from World War II to Operation Iraqi Freedom*. New York: Routledge.

Lieberman, Leonard; Lyons, Andrew; Lyons, Harriet (1995). "An Interview with Ashley Montagu," *Current Anthropology*, 36(5):835-844.

Lizot, Jacques (1985). *Tales of the Yanomami: Daily Life in the Venezuelan Forest*. New York: Cambridge University Press.

Lorenz, Konrad (1966). *On Aggression*. New York: Harcourt, Brace and World.

Lutz, Catherine (2001). *Homefront: A Military City and the American 20th Century*. Boston: Beacon Press.

Lutz, Catherine (2002). "Making War at Home in the United States: Militarization and the Current Crisis," *American Anthropologist*, 104(3):723-735.

Mabee, Carleton (1987). "Margaret Mead and Behavioral Scientists in World War II: Problems in Responsibility, Truth, and Effectiveness," *Journal of the History of the Behavioral Sciences*, 23:3-13.

MacNair, Rachel M. (2002). *Perpetration-Induced Traumatic Stress: The Psychological Consequences of Killing*. Westport: Praeger Publications.

Mahoney, Jack (2007). *The Challenge of Human Rights: Origin, Development, and Significance*. Malden: Blackwell Publishing.

Matthews, Warren (2004). *World Religions*. Belmont: Wadsworth/Thomson Learning.

McFate, Montgomery (2005a). "Anthropology and Counterinsurgency: The Strange Story of Their Curious Relationship," *Military Review*, 24-38.

McFate, Montgomery (2005b). "The Military Utility of Understanding Adversary Culture," *Joint Force Quarterly*, 38:42-48.

McKenna, Brian (2008). "A Good Military Education is Hard to Find," *Society for Applied Anthropology Newsletter*, 19(2):13-18.

Mead, Margaret (1940). "Warfare: It's Only an Invention—not a Biological Necessity," *Asia*, 15:402-405.

Melko, Matthew (1973). *52 Peaceful Societies*. Oakville, Ontario: Canadian Peace Research Institute.

Melko, Matthew (1984). "Peaceful Societies," in Laszlo, Ervin; Youl Yoo, Jong, eds., *World Encyclopedia of Peace*. New York: Pergamon Press, 2:268-270.

Messer, Ellen (1993). "Anthropology and Human Rights," *Annual Review of Anthropology*, 22:221-249.

Montagu, Ashley (1968). *The Natural Superiority of Women*. New York: Macmillan.

Montagu, Ashley (1972). *Statement on Race: An Annotated Elaboration and Exposition of the Four Statements on Race Issued by the United Nations Educational, Scientific, and Cultural Organization*. New York: Oxford University Press.

Montagu, Ashley, ed. (1976). *The Nature of Human Aggression*. New York: Oxford University Press.

Montagu, Ashley (1978). *Learning Non-Aggression: The Experience of Non-Literate Societies*. New York: Oxford University Press.

Montagu, Ashley (1989). *Growing Young*. Granby: Bergin & Garvey Publishers.

Montagu, Ashley (1998). *Man's Most Dangerous Myth: The Fallacy of Race*. Walnut Creek: AltaMira Press.

Montagu, Ashley; Matson, Floyd (1983). *The Dehumanization of Man*. New York: McGraw-Hill.

Morris, Desmond (1967). *The Naked Ape: A Zoologist's Study of the Human Animal*. London: Cape.

Morris, Desmond (1969). *The Human Zoo*. New York: McGraw-Hill.

Myers, Norman (1996). *Ultimate Security: The Environmental Basis of Political Instability*. Washington: Island Press.

Nagengast, Carole (1994). "Violence, Terror, and the Crisis of the State," *Annual Review of Anthropology*, 23:109-136.

Nagengast, Carole; Turner, Terence, eds. (1997). "Universal Human Rights versus Cultural Relativity," *Journal of Anthropological Research*, 53(3):267-381.
Nagengast, Carole, Vélez-Ibáñez, Carlos G., eds. (2004). *Human Rights: The Scholar as Activist.* Oklahoma City: Society for Applied Anthropology.
Neel, James V. (1994). *Physician to the Gene Pool: Genetic Lessons and Other Stories.* New York: John Wiley.
Nordstrom, Carolyn (1997). *A Different Kind of War Story.* Philadelphia: University of Pennsylvania Press.
Nordstrom, Carolyn (1998). "Deadly Myths of Aggression," *Aggressive Behavior*, 24(2):147-159.
Nordstrom, Carolyn; Robben, Antonious, eds. (1995). *Fieldwork Under Fire: Contemporary Studies of Violence and Survival.* Berkeley: University of California Press.
Otterbein, Keith F. (1993). *Feuding and Warfare: Selected Works of Keith F. Otterbein.* New York: Gordon and Breach.
Otterbein, Keith F. (1999). "A History of Research on Warfare in Anthropology," *American Anthropologist*, 101(4):794-805.
Otterbein, Keith (2004). *How War Began.* College Station: Texas A&M University Press.
Otterbein, Keith F. (2008). "Clan and Tribal Conflict," in Kurtz, Lester, ed., *Encyclopedia of Violence, Peace, & Conflict.* San Diego: Elsevier, 1:268-275.
Paige, Glenn D. (2009 [2002]). *Nonkilling Global Political Science.* Honolulu: Center for Global Nonkilling. Available at: <http://www.nonkilling.org>.
Paine, Robert, ed. (1985). *Advocacy and Anthropology.* St. John's: Memorial University of Newfoundland Institute of Social and Economic Research.
Palmer, Stuart (1972). *The Violent Society.* New Haven: College and University Press Publishers.
Patterson, Thomas C. (2001). *A Social History of Anthropology in the United States.* New York: Berg.
Penny, H. Glenn; Bunzl, Matti, eds. (2003). *Worldly Provincialism: German Anthropology in the Age of Empire.* Ann Arbor: University of Michigan Press.
Perry, Richard J. (2003). *Five Key Concepts in Anthropological Thinking.* Upper Saddle River: Pearson Education, Inc./Prentice Hall.
Peters, John F. (1998). *Life Among the Yanomami: The Story of Change among the Xilixana on the Mucajai River in Brazil.* Orchard Park: Broadview Press.
Power, Margaret (1991). *The Egalitarians—Human and Chimpanzee: An Anthropological View of Social Organization.* New York: Cambridge University Press.
Price, David H. (2000). "Anthropologists as Spies," *The Nation*, 271(16):24-27.
Price, David H. (2004). *Threatening Anthropology: McCarthyism and the FBI's Surveillance of Activist Anthropologists.* Durham: Duke University Press.
Price, David H. (2007). "Counterinsurgency Anthropologist Montgomery McFate's," *Counterpunch*, October 30. Available at: <http://www.counterpunch.org/price10302007.html>.
Price, David H. (2008). *Anthropological Intelligence: The Development and Neglect of American Anthropology in the Second World War.* Durham: Duke University Press.

Price, David H. (2008). David H. Price Faculty Homepage. Available at: <http://www.homepages.stmartin.edu/fac_staff/dprice>.

Ramos, Alcida Rita (1987). "Reflecting on the Yanomami: Ethnographic Images and the Pursuit of the Exotic," *Cultural Anthropology*, 2(3):284-304.

Ramos, Alcida Rita (1995). *Sanuma Memories: Yanomami Ethnography in Times of Crisis*. Madison: University of Wisconsin Press.

Renner, Michael (1996). *Fighting for Survival: Environmental Decline, Social Conflict, and the New Age of Insecurity*. New York: W.W. Norton & Company.

Renzi, Fred (2006). "Networks: Terra Incognita and the Case for Ethnographic Intelligence," *Military Review*, 16-22.

Robarcheck, Clayton A.; Robarcheck, Carole J. (1992). "Cultures of War and Peace: A Comparative Study of the Waorani and Semai," in Silverberg, James; Gray, J. Patrick, eds., *Aggression and Peacefulness in Humans and Other Primates*. New York: Oxford University Press, pp. 189-213.

Robarcheck, Clayton A.; Robarcheck, Carole J. (1996). "Waging Peace: The Psychological and Sociocultural Dynamics of Positive Peace," in Wolfe, A. W.; Yang, H., eds. *Anthropological Contributions to Conflict Resolution*. Athens: University of Georgia Press, pp. 64-80.

Robarcheck, Clayton A.; Robarcheck, Carole J. (1998a). "Reciprocities and Realities: World Views, Peacefulness, and Violence among Semai and Waorani," *Aggressive Behavior*, 24:123-133.

Robarcheck, Clayton A.; Robarcheck, Carole J. (1998b). *Waorani: The Contexts of Violence and War*. Fort Worth: Harcourt Brace College Publishers.

Robin, Ron (2004). *Scandals & Scoundrels: Seven Cases that Shook the Academy*. Berkeley: University of California Press.

Rodman, Margaret; Cooper, Matthew, eds. (1979). *The Pacification of Melanesia*. Ann Arbor: University of Michigan Press.

Rubenstein, Robert A. (2008). *Peacekeeping Under Fire: Culture and Intervention*. Boulder: Paradigm Publishers.

Salzman, Philip Carl; Rice, Patricia C., eds. (2004). *Thinking Anthropologically. A Practical Guide for Students*. Upper Saddle River: Pearson Education/Prentice Hall.

Sanders, Andrew (2008). "Anthropology of Warriors," in Kurtz, Lester, ed., *Encyclopedia of Violence, Peace, & Conflict*. San Diego: Elsevier, 3:2432-2442.

Schafft, Gretchen E. (2004). *From Racism to Genocide: Anthropology in the Third Reich*. Urbana: University of Illinois Press.

Sewall, Sarah et al. (2007). *The U.S. Army/Marine Corps Counterinsurgency Field Manual*. Chicago: University of Chicago Press.

Shakya, Tsering (1999). *The Dragon in the Land of Snows: A History of Modern Tibet Since 1947*. New York: Penguin Group (USA) Inc.

Shepard, Paul (1973). *The Tender Carnivore and the Sacred Game*. New York: Scribner.

Simmons, Anna (1997). *The Company They Keep: Life Inside the U.S. Army Special Forces*. New York: Free Press.

Simmons, Anna (1999). "War: Back to the Future," *Annual Review of Anthropology*, 28:73-108.

Simpson, Christopher, ed. (1998). *Universities and Empires: Money and Politics in the Social Science during the Cold War*. New York: New Press.

Singer, Peter (2004). *The President of Good and Evil: Questioning the Ethics of George W. Bush*. New York: Penguin Group.

Sluka, Jeffrey A., ed. (2000). *Death Squad: The Anthropological State of Terror*. Philadelphia: University of Pennsylvania Press.

Smith, David Livingstone (2007). *The Most Dangerous Animal: Human Nature and the Origins of War*. New York: St. Martin's Press.

Smith, Linda Tuhiwai (1999). *Decolonizing Methodologies: Research and Indigenous Peoples*. New York: Zed Books Ltd.

Smole, William J. (1976). *The Yanomama Indians: A Cultural Geography*. Austin: University of Texas Press.

Sperling, Elliot (2004). *The Tibet-China Conflict: History and Polemics*. Washington: East-West Center Washington.

Sponsel, Leslie E. (1990). "Ultraprimitive Pacifists: The Tasaday as a Symbol of Peace," *Anthropology Today*, 6(1):3-5.

Sponsel, Leslie E. (1992). "Our Fascination with the Tasaday: Anthropological Images and Images of Anthropology," in Headland, Thomas N., ed., *The Tasaday Controversy: Assessing the Evidence*. Washington: American Anthropological Association Special Publication No. 28, ch. 18, pp. 200-212.

Sponsel, Leslie E. (1994a). "The Mutual Relevance of Anthropology and Peace Studies," in Sponsel, Leslie E.; Gregor, Thomas A., eds., *The Anthropology of Peace and Nonviolence*. Boulder: Lynne Rienner Publishers, ch. 1, pp. 1-36.

Sponsel, Leslie E. (1994b). "Toward a Pedagogy of the Anthropology of Peace," in Sponsel, Leslie E.; Gregor, Thomas A., eds., *The Anthropology of Peace and Nonviolence*. Boulder: Lynne Rienner Publishers, ch. 11, pp. 259-269.

Sponsel, Leslie E. (1994c). "Book Review: *Societies at Peace: Anthropological Perspectives* co-edited by S. Howell and R. Willis," *American Ethnologist*, 20(2):396-397.

Sponsel, Leslie E. (1995). "Relationships among the World System, Indigenous Peoples, and Ecological Anthropology," in Sponsel, Leslie E., ed., *Indigenous Peoples and the Future of Amazonia: An Ecological Anthropology of an Endangered World*. Tucson: University of Arizona Press, ch. 13, pp. 263-293.

Sponsel, Leslie E. (1996a). "The Natural History of Peace: A Positive View of Human Nature and Its Potential," in Gregor, Thomas A., ed., *The Natural History of Peace*. Nashville: Vanderbilt University Press, ch. 4, pp. 95-125.

Sponsel, Leslie E. (1996b). "Human Rights and Advocacy Anthropology," in Levinson, David; Ember, Melvin, eds. *The Encyclopedia of Cultural Anthropology*. New York: Henry Holt and Co., 2:602-607

Sponsel, Leslie E. (1996c). "Peace and Nonviolence," in Levinson, David; Ember, Melvin, eds., *The Encyclopedia of Cultural Anthropology*. New York: Henry Holt, 3:908-912.

Sponsel, Leslie E. (1997a). "Human Rights," *The Dictionary of Anthropology*,

Barfield, Thomas, ed. Oxford: Blackwell Publishers, pp. 248-250.

Sponsel, Leslie E., (1997b). "Peace and Nonviolence," *The Dictionary of Anthropology*, Barfield, Thomas, ed. Oxford: Blackwell Publishers, pp. 350-352.

Sponsel, Leslie E. (1998). "Yanomami: An Arena of Conflict and Aggression in the Amazon," *Aggressive Behavior*, 24(2):97-122.

Sponsel, Leslie E. (2000b). "Response to Otterbein," *American Anthropologist*, 102(4):837-840.

Sponsel, Leslie E. (2001). "Advocacy in Anthropology," in Smelser, N.J.; Baltes, Paul B., eds., *International Encyclopedia of the Social and Behavioral Sciences*. Oxford: Pergamon Press, pp. 204-206.

Sponsel, Leslie E. (2005). "Noble Savage and Ecologically Noble Savage," in Taylor, Bron, ed., *Encyclopedia of Religion and Nature*. New York: Continuum, 2:1210-1212.

Sponsel, Leslie E. (2006a). "Darkness in El Dorado Controversy," in Birx, H. James, ed., *Encyclopedia of Anthropology*. Thousand Oaks: Sage Publications, 2:667-673.

Sponsel, Leslie E. (2006b). "Ashley Montagu," in Birx, H. James, ed., *Encyclopedia of Anthropology*. Thousand Oaks: Sage Publications, 4:1620-1622.

Sponsel, Leslie E. (2006c). "Yanomamo," in Birx, H. James, ed., *Encyclopedia of Anthropology*. Thousand Oaks: Sage Publications, 5:2347-2351.

Sponsel, Leslie E. (2007). "Human Nature," in Robbins, Paul, ed. *Encyclopedia of Environment and Society*. Thousand Oaks: Sage Publications, 3:886-889.

Sponsel, Leslie E.; Good, Kenneth R. (2000). "Anthropologists Debate Future of War," *Anthropology News*, 41(2):19-20.

Sponsel, Leslie E.; Gregor, Thomas A., eds. (1994). *The Anthropology of Peace and Nonviolence*. Boulder: Lynne Rienner Publishers.

Sponsel, Leslie E.; Turner, Terence (2002). "Counterpoint: Charges of Wrongdoing by Anthropologists," *The Chronicle of Higher Education*, 2 (Reviews), B13.

Starkey, Armstrong (1998). *European and Native American Warfare, 1675-1815*. Norman: University of Oklahoma Press.

Starn, Orin (1986). "Engineering Internment: Anthropologists and War Relocation Authority," *American Ethnologist*, 13:700-720.

Staub, Ervin (1989). *The Roots of Evil: The Origins of Genocide and Other Group Violence*. New York: Cambridge University Press.

Stauder, J. (1974). "The 'Relevance'" of Anthropology to Colonialism and Imperialism," *Radical Science Journal*, 1:38-61.

Steele, Frank (1994). *Warpaths: Invasions of North America*. New York: Oxford University Press.

Stevenson, Leslie; Haberman, David L. (1998). *Ten Theories of Human Nature*. New York: Oxford University Press.

Stoessinger, John G. (2008). *Why Nations Go to War*. Belmont: Thomson.

Strathern, Andrew J.; Stewart, Pamela J. (2008). "Anthropology of Violence and Conflict, Overview," in Kurtz, Lester, ed., *Encyclopedia of Violence, Peace, & Conflict*. San Diego: Elsevier, 1:75-86.

Summer Institute of Linguistics (2008). *Ethnologue*. <http://www.ethnologue.com>.

Suzuki, Peter T. (1981). "Anthropologists in the Wartime Camps for Japanese Americans: A Documentary Study," *Dialectical Anthropology*, 6:23-60.

Thurman, Robert (2008). *Why the Dalai Lama Matters: His Act of Truth as the Solution for China, Tibet, and the World*. New York: Simon & Schuster/Atria Books.

Tierney, Patrick (2000). *Darkness in El Dorado: How Scientists and Journalists Devastated the Amazon*. New York: W.W. Norton & Company.

Tuzin, Donald (1996). "The Spectre of Peace in Unlikely Places: Concept and Paradox in the Anthropology of Peace," in Gregor, Thomas, ed., *A Natural History of Peace*. Nashville: Vanderbilt University Press, pp. 3-33.

Ury, William L. (1999). *The Third Side: Why We Fight and How We Can Stop*. New York: Penguin Putnam, Inc.

Ury, William L., ed. (2002). *Must We Fight? From the Battlefield to the Schoolyard—A New Perspective on Violent Conflict and Its Preservation*. San Francisco: Jossey-Bass.

U.S. Army (2008). *War Surgery in Afghanistan and Iraq: A Series of Cases, 2003-2007*. Washington: U.S. Department of Defense.

Waal, Frans de (1989). *Peacemaking Among Primates*. Cambridge: Harvard University Press.

Waal, Frans de (1996). *Good Natured: The Origins of Right and Wrong in Humans and Other Animals*. Cambridge: Harvard University Press.

Waal, Frans de (2006). *Primates and Philosophers: How Morality Evolved*. Princeton: Princeton University Press.

Waal, Frans de; Lating, Frans (1997). *Bonobo: The Forgotten Ape*. Berkeley: University of California Press.

Wakin, Eric (1992). *Anthropology Goes to War: Professional Ethics and Counterinsurgency in Thailand*. Madison: University of Wisconsin Center for Southeast Asian Studies, Monograph No. 7.

Wax, Dustin M., ed. (2008). *Anthropology at the Dawn of the Cold War*. Ann Arbor: Pluto Press.

Whitehead, Linda M.; Trotter II, Robert T. (2008). *Ethics for Anthropological Research and Practice*. Long Grove: Waveland Press, Inc.

Wiberg, Hakan (1981). "JPR 1964-1980—What Have We Learned About Peace?," *Journal of Peace Research*, XVIII(2):111-148.

Williams, Emilio (1986). *A Way of Life and Death: Three Centuries of Prussian-German Militarism: An Anthropological Approach*. Nashville: Vanderbilt University Press.

De Wolf, Jan J. (1992). "Ethnology in the Third Reich," *Current Anthropology*, 33(4):473-475.

Wolfe, A.W.; Yang, H., eds. (1996). *Anthropological Contributions to Conflict Resolution*. Athens: University of Georgia Press.

Wrangham, Richard; Peterson, Dale (1996). *Demonic Males: Apes and the Origins of Human Violence*. Boston: Houghton Mifflin Company.

Wright, Ann; Dixon, Susan (2008). *Dissent: Voices of Conscience*. Kihei: Koa Books.

Younger, Stephen M. (2007). *Endangered Species: How We Can Avoid Mass Destruction and Build a Lasting Peace*. New York: HarperCollins Publishers.

Chapter One

Gentle Savage or Bloodthirsty Brute?

R. W. Sussman
Washington University, St. Louis

Donna Hart
University of Missouri - St. Louis

Many anthropologists and biologists have theorized about the behavior of the earliest hominins and how this conduct might be related to the biological basis of modern human behavior. There seem to be only extreme depictions of Mr. or Ms. Average Hominin. Radical positions have been taken on this issue with few centrist opinions. On one side of this theoretical chasm, our human ancestors are painted as gentle ape-like versions of Jean-Jacques Rousseau's noble savage. On the other side, our ancestors are portrayed as bloodlusting demons, i.e., killer apes.

It appears that the killer ape theory easily toppled the gentle vegetarian ape theory in the mid years of the twentieth century. One of the fathers of modern physical anthropology and American field primatology, Sherwood Washburn, synthesized this dichotomy in statements he made at Princeton University in 1956:

> The world view of the early human carnivore must have been very different from his vegetarian cousins. The desire for meat leads animals to know a wider range and to learn the habits of many animals. Human territorial habits and psychology are fundamentally different from those of apes and monkeys (quoted in Ardrey, 1976: 10-11).

But was Washburn correct in his assumptions? In the inaugural decades of the twentieth century, it was thought the first humans must have had large brains and primitive, ape-like bodies. Easy acceptance in 1912 of the Piltdown Man, with its human skull and ape-like jaw as the "missing link" between humans and apes was facilitated by a preconceived bias about our large brains (Sussman, 2000). Just such a preconception concerning characteristics of early humans also fostered resistance to accepting *Australopithecus africanus*, uncovered in Africa in 1924 by Raymond Dart, as our earliest ancestor. However, in the early 1950s with the discovery that Piltdown

Man was a fraud—and with many more australopithecine fossils recovered —scientists realized that our earliest ancestors were more like nonhuman primates than like modern humans. That realization, in turn, led to a number of attempts to reconstruct the behavior of our earliest hominin ancestors, often using primate models.

It seems that each decade since the acceptance of australopithecines in our evolutionary past, a recurrent theme has emerged and reemerged; it focuses on the importance of hunting and its relationship to an innate propensity for human violence. Many scenarios concerning the evolution of violence and its biological basis in modern humans have been constructed based upon Man the Hunter.

In the 1960s Washburn was among the first to develop a hunting-man theme for human evolution and behavior (Washburn and Lancaster, 1968). In the 1970s E.O. Wilson, one of the major founders of the subfield of sociobiology, explained much of current human behavior as an outcome of our hunting past (Wilson, 1975). In the 1980s with the discovery of earlier hominin fossils in Ethiopia, anatomist Owen Lovejoy and Donald Johanson (the paleontologist who discovered Lucy) explained many of the features of hominin evolution with a modified version of male hunting and provisioning (Johanson and Edey, 1981). A more recent version of this recurrent theme is authored by Wrangham and Peterson (1996) and Wrangham (1999). Describing his theory, Wrangham links human hunting to an inherent propensity for violence shared alike by humans and common chimpanzees. Stanford (1999) and Ghiglieri (1999) also have emphasized comparable ideas.

Where did these different theories of hunting and innate violence originate? Are they coincidence? Valid scientific theory? Ethnocentrism? Our view is that the recurrent theme of Man the Hunter has more to do with the myths of Judeo-Christian culture than with objective science.

Let's go back again to Raymond Dart and how Man the Hunter became the paradigm for human origins in Western society. Dart's view of human evolution was infused with obvious moral judgments. In fact with their innovative new subsistence pattern (i.e., hunting), Dart believed that the earliest hominins also created a new moral code devoid of altruism. Dart waxed poetic with his claims of australopithecine primal urges: "confirmed killers ... carnivorous creatures that seized living quarries by violence, battered them to death, tore apart their broken bodies, [and] dismembered them limb from limb, greedily devouring livid writhing flesh." He had arrived at a point where he could explain "[t]he loathsome cruelty of mankind to man is explicable only in terms of man's carnivorous and cannibalistic origin" (1953: 209). Our ancestors were branded with the mark of Cain and were more allied with bloodthirsty carnivores than their primate relatives.

Dart's vision of early human morality, however, is not new in Western myth, religion, or philosophy. The hunting hypothesis, as it is often referred to, was deconstructed by Cartmill (1993, 1997) who studied the history of human hunting. He calls the hunting hypothesis a "bleak, pessimistic view of human beings and their ancestors as instinctively bloodthirsty and aggressive" (Cartmill, 1997: 511). Cartmill shows that it is reminiscent of the earlier Greek and Christian views of human morality. Dart himself began his seminal Man the Hunter paper with a quote from a seventeenth century Calvinist divine, Richard Baxter: "Of all the beasts the man-beast is the worst, / to others and himself the cruellest foe" (Dart, 1953: 201). In 1772 James Burnet reaffirmed the Man the Hunter theme, arguing that "when necessity forced man to hunt, the wild beast part of him became predominant, war succeeding hunting, and he became fiercer than any other animal —when not subdued by laws and manners" (quoted in Bock, 1980: 202). As Cartmill notes, the early Christian philosophers believed that free will gave human beings the choice to be good or bad; therefore, humans can be corrupted, a distinctively Christian philosophy that extrapolates to nature itself having gone rotten. This view of the depravity of human nature is related to the idea of man's fall from grace and of the Christian notion of original sin. As we shall see, these medieval myths still pervade many modern, so-called "scientific" interpretations concerning the evolution of human behavior, human nature, and human morality.

What about Cannibalism among Hominins?

"Where did we come from?" and "What were the first humans like?" are questions that have been asked since Darwin first proposed his theory of evolution. The commonly accepted Man the Hunter answer tells us that our early ancestors were killers of other species and of their own kind, prone to violence, natural born killers. But the label of human as cannibals also is common in the popular and scientific literature. As quoted earlier, Dart (1953) had exclaimed "[t]he loathsome cruelty of mankind to man is explicable only in terms of man's carnivorous and cannibalistic origin." There are few more disparaging or ignominious descriptions of our fossil relatives than "Man the Cannibal." In fact, it is surprising how frequently the label is attached as an explanation for the condition of human fossil remains. For example, BBC News (2006) reported: "Starvation and cannibalism were part of everyday life for a population of Neanderthals living in northern Spain 43,000 years ago, a study by Dr. Antonio Rosas of the National Museum of Natural Sciences in Madrid says ..."

In tackling Man the Cannibal allegations, we find that almost all of the alleged cannibalistic sites have been lacking in evidence to support this claim; recent, perhaps less sensational analyses listed below have not found substantiation of cannibalism but instead find evidence of natural disasters, including predation on hominids:

Paranthropus: Raymond Dart thought that robust australopithecines in South African caves were killing and eating each other. However, the individuals killing and eating fossil hominins were hyenas and big cats (Brain, 1981).

Homo erectus: Decades of anthropology students were instructed that the Zhoukoudian Cave in China was the scene of hominin cannibalism. However, it seems that giant *Pachycrocuta* hyenas were using the cave and most likely feeding on hominins (Boaz et al., 2000).

Homo antecessor: Atapuerca, containing the "Pit of Bones," is a famous fossil site in Spain dated at approximately 800,000 years before the present. The very name "Pit of Bones" conjures up a ghoulish specter of the alleged cannibalism thought to be the cause of bone deposits. But, new analyses find that the hominin bone accumulations were the result of a natural catastrophic event not cannibalism (Monge and Mann, 2007).

Homo neanderthalensis: Neanderthals have been tarnished with the accusation of cannibalism almost since their fossil remains were first discovered. "As for Neanderthals, scholars in the early part of this [the 20th] century assumed almost routinely that they practiced cannibalism, an idea that fitted the prevailing view of Neanderthals as shambling, uncultured brutes ..." (Bahn, 1992: 330). Trinkhaus, however, estimates there is only one confirmed instance of violence in the Neanderthal fossil record. He noted, "The identification of traumatic injury in human fossil remains has plagued paleontologists for years. There has been a tendency to consider any form of damage to a fossil as conclusive evidence of prehistoric violence between humans ..." (2000:133).

A single Neanderthal skull found at Monte Circeo, Italy in a "ring of stones" had been assumed to be ritual cannibalism. But a careful analysis suggested instead that the "ring" was the result of a landslide, and Monte Circeo was a hyena den at the time the hominin bones were deposited there. The damage to the single skull is consistent with the method used by hyenas to crush skulls and extract brains (Bahn, 1992: 330).

There is a century of history behind accusations of cannibalism at Krapina in former Yugoslavia. Neanderthal bones were discovered between

1899-1905 when crude methods were used to excavate and preserve hominid remains. Cannibalism was the fallback explanation for the bone deposits, but wolf, bear, and hyena remains at the site might point to predators being responsible for the hominin cache (Klein and Edgar, 2002). Although media reports continue to identify Neanderthal remains at Krapina as a confirmed "cannibal feast," we invoke Bahn's review of cannibalism: "This gruesome image does not stand up to scrutiny. The bones display no evidence of the impact fractures characteristic of marrow extraction by humans. Instead, the extensive fragmentation can be explained by roof-falls, crushing by sediments, and the use of dynamite during excavation" (Bahn, 1992: 330).

Homo sapiens: Fontbrégoua is a cave in southeastern France that was inhabited by anatomically modern humans after the domestication of animals about 4,000-6,000 years ago (Klein, 1999; Bahn, 1992). The bones of a dozen people in proximity to pits containing animal bones stirred allegations of cannibalism at this site. Alternative explanations exist, including the practice of flesh removal from bones (defleshing) and secondary burial, mortuary preparations often found in traditional cultures such as Australian Aborigines (Bahn, 1992).

Some words of caution about allegations of cannibalism are in order. Accusations of cannibalism stretch back to Greek myths and seem to titillate the human mind. However, cannibalism among humans appears to be extremely rare, and is an atypical, extraordinary exception to normal human behavior that is prompted only by the most singular circumstances, such as the famous instance that occurred when survivors of a plane crash in the Andes consumed their dead fellow passengers. After careful study, Bahn (1992) finds there are no reliable witnesses to ritual or habitual cannibalism and that reports of it are based on hearsay. Bahn (1992: 330) states: "Where prehistory is concerned, cannibalism has long been a favourite and dramatic theory ... All these interpretations depend on indirect clues and on assumptions, as nobody has yet found definite evidence of the practice, such as human remains inside preserved human coprolites ..."

The Hunting Myth and Sociobiology

Although more spectacular than the claims of contemporaneous scientists, Robert Ardrey, the writer who popularized Dart's theory, held views of human nature that did not differ greatly from the scientists, nor from the ancient Christian beliefs of a fall from grace and original sin. To Ardrey, however, sin is good; it is a strength that "Cain's children" possess by virtue of their enlarged brain and their carnivorous lifestyle: "Man is a predator whose natural instinct is to kill with a weapon" (1961: 316). Ardrey argues that humans are not the product of special creation; they have naturally, rightfully, and nobly inherited genes that carry the "scars of the ages" (1961: 326). For Ardrey it is war and the instinct for territorial acquisition that led to the great accomplishments of Western man.

Ardrey's statements might be considered the beginning of what has been called evolutionary ethics (Ruse, 1993), a genre introduced in the mid-1970s by E. O. Wilson and other proponents of sociobiology which became the next major scientific statement on the importance of hunting in the formulation of human nature. Wilson (1975) describes a number of behavioral traits that he claims are found in humans generally and are genetically-based human universals. These include: (1) territoriality, (2) aggressive dominance hierarchies, (3) male dominance over females, (4) permanent male-female bonds, (5) matrilineality (female offspring stay with the troop they are born into while males leave to find a new social group when they reach sexual maturity), and (6) extended maternal care.

The argument Wilson uses to support his idea that these traits are biologically fixed and genetically-based characteristics rests on their relative constancy among our primate relatives and their persistence throughout human evolution and in human societies. But, other than the last—extended maternal care—these behavioral characteristics are neither general primate traits nor human universals. Permanent male-female bonds and matrilineality are found in some cultures but not consistent throughout primate or human societies. Let's look at the remaining traits that deal with subjects more related to a discussion of aggression.

Is Territoriality a Human Universal?

The concept of "territory" was first developed in studies on birds. The essence of the concept is that an animal or group of animals "defends" all or part of its range. Thus there are two major components—the space itself and the active defense of that space. However, many animals maintain exclusive areas simply by vocalizing, displaying, or in some way signaling to possible intruders, and very rarely if ever, actually fighting at borders (Waser and Wiley, 1980). The concept of territoriality is highly complex, and there are real difficulties in relating various spacing methods used by different species to one single, strict concept. For primate groups, spacing mechanisms are extremely variable. Groups of gibbons and the South American titi monkey could be considered territorial in that they actually have ritualized battles at borders of their almost-exclusive ranges. A number of other primates have specialized loud calls that presumably help them maintain exclusive areas. However, most species of primates have overlapping group ranges and often share resources. Thus, in primates territoriality in the strict sense of the word is rare (Fedigan, 1992; Sussman, 2003a, b).

In humans the concept of territory, as used to define the way birds defend an area, is not at all useful. Most hunters and gatherers do not have exclusive, defended ranges, and agricultural peoples have a multitude of ways of dealing with land use. Lumping these into a simple concept of territory is nonsensical. Modern warfare, particularly, has little to do with directly defending borders. How is a political decision to send troops to Somalia, Bosnia, or Iraq similar to a bird or a gibbon displaying at the border of its range?

Are Aggressive Dominance Hierarchies Human Universals?

Again, we are dealing with a very complex concept. Dominance hierarchies in animals are defined by a number of criteria, including priority of access to food, space, or mates. In addition dominance involves such delicate social situations as who grooms and who gets groomed ... who is the leader of group progression ... or who will be the winner in aggressive encounters. These often are not positively correlated—that is, the animal who wins fights does not always lead the group (Bernstein, 1981). In fact defining the group hierarchy by any one of the above criteria usually does not help us to understand the complexities of primate group organization or structure. Furthermore, there are many primate species in which dominance hierarchies are unclear, ambiguous, or absent altogether. Dominance hierarchies have not been demonstrated in most prosimians, nor in many New and Old World arboreal monkeys, nor in terrestrial patas monkeys, nor in gibbons. However, they do seem to be present in baboons, macaques, and chimpanzees. But even among the latter primate species, hierarchies are often unstable, and the genetic influence and consequences of hierarchies are unknown. For one example, in a baboon troop rank changes may occur on an average of every two weeks among males; in many studies of baboons and macaques in which paternity is known, little correlation between rank and reproductive success has been found. Generally, the relationship between rank and reproductive success has remained obscure (Walters and Seyfarth, 1987; Bercovitch, 1991; Ellis, 1995; Hausfater, 1995; Takahata et al., 1999; Silk et al., 2003).

When we consider humans, the presence of dominance hierarchies based on aggression becomes even more problematic. An aggressive dominance hierarchy is determined by winners and losers of head-to-head aggressive encounters and is normally defined within a closed social group. You might ask yourself the following: Is your status in society based on your fighting ability or aggressiveness? As you walk down the street or the halls of your school or work place, do you "display" aggressively to the people who you pass? Or, in the same situations, are you forced to give way to others and allow them to pass? How many face-to-face fights have you had in your lifetime? What is your status (based on aggressive encounters) in your social group? And, by the way, what are the limits of your own closed social group? We think these situations are rarely relevant in human societies.

Is Male Dominance over Females a Human Universal?

Male dominance over females is not by any means one of the traits that permeates the primate order. Smuts (1987), who studied the male-female relationships in baboons, has identified five major types of adult male-adult female dominance relationships in nonhuman primates. In three of the five, males are not dominant to females. These include species in which sexual differentiation in body size is slight and in which females are clearly dominant to males; species in which body size differences are slight and the sexes are codominant; and species in which males are larger than females but females sometimes dominate often through female-female coalitions. In fact the only species in which females rarely dominate males are those in which the males are much larger than females. Size difference (sexual dimorphism) in humans is slight, and female coalitions are quite common. If this *is* a human universal, we would need to believe that male dominance over females is ubiquitous, in other words "women prove everywhere to be second-class citizens in the public-political domain" (Brown, 1991: 91). (Tell this to Margaret Thatcher, Hilary Rodham Clinton, Oprah Winfrey, or former and current Prime Ministers of Germany, Norway, Pakistan, Sri Lanka, India, Israel, and Indonesia.) Many traditional societies have a truly egalitarian distribution of power. For example, tropical hunters and gatherers, such as the !Kung San of the Kalahari Desert and Mbuti Pygmies of Central Africa, are known for a fairly equal distribution of domestic and public power between males and females.

Let us pause to state clearly that we're not proposing a complete absence of a biological basis to human behavior. But, as Franz Boas—a sane voice in the decades of Social Darwinist theory—stated over 70 years ago, "unless the contrary can be proved, we must assume that all complex activities are socially determined, not hereditary" (quoted in Degler, 1991: 148).

Chimpanzee and Human Males as Demonic Killers

One of the new claims to the importance of killing and the biological basis of morality is proposed by Wrangham and Peterson (1996). Twenty to twenty-five years ago scientists thought human aggression was unique because research on the great apes had revealed that those species were basically unaggressive, gentle creatures. Although early theorists proposed that hunting, killing, and extreme aggressive behavior were biological traits inherited from our earliest hunting hominin ancestors, many anthropologists still believed that patterns of aggression were environmentally and culturally determined, learned behaviors. Our sins were thought to be acquired and not inherited characteristics, no more genetic than all the other acquired and culturally transmitted traits manifested by the human species. Wrangham and Peterson's argument proposes that killer instincts are not unique to humans because we share this characteristic with our nearest relative, the common chimpanzee. In fact it is this inherited propensity for killing that allows hominins and chimps to be such good hunters.

Here's the demonic male theory in a nutshell: The split between humans and common chimpanzees happened at least eight million years ago. Furthermore, humans may have split from the chimpanzee-bonobo (pygmy chimp) line after gorillas, with bonobos separating from chimps only 2.5 million years ago. Because a chimp-like being may be the common ancestor of all these forms, and because the earliest australopithecine was quite chimpanzee-like, Wrangham speculates that: "The most reasonable view for the moment is that chimpanzees are ... an amazingly good model for the ancestor of hominins ... [and if] we know what our ancestor looked like, naturally we get clues about how it behaved ...that is, like modern-day chimpanzees" (1995: 5). Finally, if modern chimpanzees and modern humans share certain behavioral traits, these traits have "long evolutionary roots" and are likely to be fixed, biologically-inherited components of our nature and not culturally determined.

Further to the demonic male theory, there are a number of cultural traits shared by early hominins and chimpanzees. However, it is not these cultural traits that are of the most interest, rather it is presumed shared patterns of aggression between chimps and humans. The proponents claim that only two animal species—chimpanzees and humans—live in patrilineal, male-bonded communities that exhibit intense territorial aggression, including lethal raids seeking vulnerable enemies to kill. Wrangham asks:

> Does this mean chimpanzees are naturally violent? Ten years ago it wasn't clear ... In this cultural species it may turn out that one of the least vari-

able of all chimpanzee behaviors is the intense competition between males, the violent aggression they use against strangers, and their willingness to maim and kill those that frustrate their goals ... As the picture of chimpanzee society settles into focus, it now includes infanticide, rape, and regular battering of females by males (1995: 7).

Since chimpanzees and humans share these violent urges, the demonic male paradigm emphasizes that chimpanzees and humans also share an inborn morality. Those long evolutionary roots of bloodlust, those aggressive urges rise out of a eight-million year old curse we share with our closest genetic kin.

Let's look at a few details before we proceed any further with demon chimps and devil humans. Certainly humans hunt, and chimpanzees are also hunters who have specific predatory strategies in specific geographic populations. But, neither humans nor chimpanzees are the only primates that hunt for food. Some prosimians are highly insectivorous, and many catch and eat small snakes, lizards, and amphibians. Neither are humans and chimpanzees the only primate hunters of mammals. The baboons of Africa and the capuchin monkeys of South America are hunters of small mammals. And chimpanzees and humans are not the only "higher" apes who hunt. Chimpanzees are the most carnivorous of our close relatives, but orangutans have been observed out on successful hunting forays as have bonobos and gibbons (Hart, 2000).

Humans and chimpanzees are not even the only primates that hunt and eat other primates. Orangutans prey on lorises and gibbons; baboons eat bushbabies and vervet monkeys; blue monkeys prey on bushbabies; capuchin monkeys prey on titi monkeys and owl monkeys; red ruffed lemurs prey on infant ringtailed lemurs; and dwarf lemurs have been observed hunting and eating smaller mouse lemurs (Hart, 2000).

But, only a few instances of primates preying on other primates are relatively well-studied, and the emphasis has been on chimpanzee predation. At Gombe National Park in Tanzania, chimpanzee predation on red colobus is extensive, alleged to result in the death of a minimum of one-sixth to a maximum of one-third of the red colobus monkey population every year since the study began (Fourrier et al., 2008). There are other locations where chimpanzees also prey on red colobus monkeys (chimpanzees, for the record, have been seen preying on twenty different primate species), but not at the heavy rate observed in Gombe. Boesch (1994) believes that human presence has had a much stronger impact on chimpanzee hunting of red colobus in Gombe than in the Tai Forest where he studies chimpanzees. Indeed, if the high killing rates at Gombe went on for long, the red colobus monkeys at Gombe would quickly disappear (Bernstein, 1997, Fourrier et al., 2008).

So, there seems to be no doubt that many primate species will hunt and eat meat. Where we differ from Wrangham and Peterson (and Dart, Washburn, and Wilson before them) is in the theory that *killing and violence* are inherited from our ancient relatives. We further disagree with the Wrangham and Peterson argument that killing and violence are traits shared by hominins and chimpanzees and that it is this violent nature and natural blood lust which makes both humans and chimpanzees such good hunters.

The bonobo (the "gentle" pygmy chimpanzee) helps the Demonic Male adherents to their conclusions. They claim that bonobos have lost the desire to kill, as well as losing the desire to hunt; that they have suppressed both personal and predatory aggression; that even though bonobos evolved from a chimpanzee-like ancestor who was both a hunter of monkeys and a hunter of its own kind, during the evolution of bonobos the males *lost* the desire to kill each other and the desire to kill prey; and finally, that bonobos and chimps tell us murder and hunting are very similar. Wrangham and Peterson (1996) believe that blood lust ties killing and hunting tightly together, but in his scenario it is the desire to kill that drives the ability to hunt.

Thus, the book *Demonic Males* states that humans and chimpanzees might share biologically-fixed behaviors based on two assumptions: First, humans and chimps are more closely related to each other than chimps are to gorillas; secondly, chimps are a good model for our earliest ancestor and retain so-called "conservative" traits shared by both.

In fact, chimpanzees have been evolving for as long as humans and gorillas, and there is no reason to believe that ancestral chimps were highly similar to present-day chimps. The fossil evidence is extremely sparse for the great apes. It is likely that many forms of apes have become extinct during millions of years—just as many forms of hominins have become extinct. Furthermore, even if chimpanzees are a good model for the ancestor to chimpanzees and humans and a "conservative" representative of this particular branch of the evolutionary bush, it would not follow that humans would necessarily share specific behavioral traits. As the authors of *Demonic Males* emphasize, chimps, gorillas, and bonobos are all very different from one another in their behavior and in their willingness to kill others of their species. It is exactly because of these differences, in fact, that the authors agree that conservative retention of traits alone cannot explain the drastic behavioral similarities and differences.

Let's examine the "proof" of Wrangham and Peterson's theory which, we must reiterate, doesn't rest on theoretical grounds but depends solely on the circumstantial evidence that violence and killing in chimpanzees and humans are behaviors that are similar in pattern, have ancient shared evolutionary roots, and are inherited. *Humans and chimpanzees kill members of neighboring groups of their own species*—we can't argue that this happens, particularly with humans. *This is a startling exception to the norm for animals*—actually, there are many exceptions, such as lions, wolves, spotted hyenas, and a number of other predators. *Fighting adults of almost all species normally stop at winning: They don't go on to kill*—the fact is that most species do not have the weapons to kill one another as adults. Aggressive, unfriendly behavior between adults of many species is common in various circumstances (Small, 1997), but certainly it would take two adult squirrels, rabbits, or aardvarks much more energy than it is worth to kill their opponent rather than to drive it away. They just don't have the tools. Chimpanzees and humans do, although the tools they use are radically different.

Chimpanzee Aggression

Just how common is it for chimpanzees to kill other chimpanzees? This is where the real controversy may lie. During the first fourteen years of study at Gombe Reserve in Tanzania (1960-1974), chimpanzees were described as a peaceful, unaggressive species. In fact, during a year of concentrated study, Jane Goodall (1968) observed 284 agonistic (i.e., aggressive) encounters. Of these 66% were due to competition for introduced (that is, human-provisioned) bananas, and only 34% could be classified as "attacks occurring in 'normal' aggressive contexts" (1968: 278). Furthermore, as Goodall recorded:

> Only 10 percent of the 284 attacks were classified as "violent," and even attacks that appeared punishing to me often resulted in no discernable injury ... Other attacks consisted merely of brief pounding-hitting after which the aggressor often touched or embraced the other immediately (1968: 277).

Chimpanzee aggression before 1974 was considered no different from patterns of aggression seen in many primate species. Goodall explained that she used data mainly from after 1975 because the earlier years presented a behavioral contrast of the Gombe chimps as being "far more peaceable than humans" (1968: 3). Other early naturalists' descriptions of chimpanzee behavior were consistent with those of Goodall prior to 1975 and confirmed her first fourteen years of observation. Even different communities were observed to come together with peaceful, ritualized displays of greeting (Goodall, 1965; Reynolds and Reynolds, 1965; Sugiyama, 1972; Ghiglieri, 1984). Nevertheless, between 1974 and 1977, five adult males from one subgroup at Gombe were attacked and disappeared from the area, presumably dead. Why after fourteen years did the patterns of aggression change?

Was it because the stronger group saw the weakness of the other and decided to improve its genetic fitness (the sociobiological explanation)? Surely there were stronger and weaker animals and subgroups before this particular time. We can look to Goodall's own observations for an answer. In 1965 Goodall began to provide "restrictive human-controlled feeding." A few years later she realized that:

> [T]he constant feeding was having a marked effect on the behavior of the chimps. They were beginning to move about in large groups more often than they had ever done in the old days. They were sleeping near camp and arriving in noisy hordes early in the morning. Worst of all, the adult males were becoming increasingly aggressive. When we first offered the chimps bananas, the males seldom fought over the food; ... [now] not only was there a great deal more fighting than ever before, but many of the chimps were hanging around camp for hours and hours every day (1971: 143).

By this time the social behavior and ranging patterns of the animals were already disrupted, and the increasing aggression eventually created so many problems that observation was almost ended at Gombe (Wrangham, 1974).

The possibility that human interference was a main cause of the unusual behavior of the Gombe chimps was the subject of a book by Power (1991). She believes that much of the behavior of the Gombe chimpanzees reflected stress related to years of human interference and provisioning. Wrangham and Peterson state that, yes, the aggression by males at Gombe might have been unnatural behavior if it weren't for new evidence of similar behavior occurring since 1977 "elsewhere in Africa." What is this evidence? We summarize three examples below.

1) Between 1979 and 1982 the Gombe group extended its range to the south and conflict with a southern group (named "Kalande" by researchers) was suspected. One day in 1982 a so-called raiding party of males reached Goodall's camp and "some of these raids may have been lethal" (Wrangham and Peterson, 1996: 19). However, Goodall described the only reported raid as follows: One female "was chased by a Kalande male and mildly attacked. Her four year old son ... encountered a second male—but was only sniffed" (Goodall, 1986: 516). Although Wrangham and Peterson imply that these encounters were similar to previous lethal attacks at Gombe, in this single observed raid, no violence was ever witnessed

2)   From 1970 to 1982 six adult males from one community disappeared at a Japanese study site in the Mahale Mountains of Tanzania, west of Gombe. The six disappeared one by one over this twelve-year period. None of these animals was ever observed being attacked or killed, and one was sighted later roaming as a solitary male. Nishida and his colleagues who study the chimps at Mahale puzzled over the gradual, successive disappearance of the adult males. They went on to speculate that at least some of these males may have been killed by chimpanzees from another group (Nishida et al., 1985). The rationale for Nishida's research group to pinpoint other chimpanzees as the perpetrators was the Gombe intergroup conflict resulting in five male deaths between 1974 and 1977. We now know that provisioning caused migration and disturbance of the chimpanzees in Gombe and that predation on chimps by large cats can be a significant factor in mortality (Hart and Sussman 2009). Lions often pass through Mahale and regularly eat chimpanzees (Tsukahara, 1993). An alternate explanation for the missing chimps—i.e., that any unaccounted-for males were eaten by lions— seems highly probable (see Hart and Sussman, 2009; Ferguson, 2009).

3)   In the Tai Forest, Cote d'Ivoire, West Africa, Wrangham and Peterson (1996: 20) report that researchers Christophe and Hedwige Boesch believe that "violent aggression among the chimpanzees is as important as it is in Gombe." Referring to the original paper by Boesch and Boesch (1989: 567), however, the authors simply state that encounters by neighboring chimpanzee communities are more common in their site than in Gombe and that this may lead to larger, more cohesive group structure and a "higher involvement of the males in social life." There is no mention of any violence or killing during these encounters.

By 2006, the claim of chimp male-to-male violence was updated to 19 "certain killings" (although only 14 of these were observed) and another 16 suspected cases of killing among male chimpanzees in four out of nine long-term research sites (Wrangham et al., 2006). (Two further "certain" female killings also were reported, although these are events that do not fit the demonic male theory.) However, interestingly, only two of the four long-term research sites involved "certain" intercommunity killings; the other two (Mahale and Budongo) accounted for three "certain" intra-community kills. Using the above authors' own calculations, this adds up to 19-35 cases in 1,970 "male chimpanzee years" of combined observation at five long-term sites (including Tai Forest but not including the other long-term research sites where, to that time, no male killings had been reported), or one male-male killing every 56-103 chimpanzee male observation years. Of course, we acknowledge that killings do occur and a few more cases have been reported since the above article was published (see Boesch et al., 2008). However, the context of these attacks is rarely described and the fact that each of the study sites suffers intense interference from habitat encroachment and loss, introduced diseases, hunting and poaching pressure, food provisioning, tourism and/or constant surveillance by primatologists is not addressed (Sanz, 2004; Ferguson, 2009; Hart; Sussman, 2009). In fact, there typically has been a nearly complete separation in the scientific literature between the "natural" behavior of primates (and theories thereof) and the literature reporting influence of human threats and the conservation status of these primates.

More evident in follow-ups to *Demonic Males* is a development of the theoretical argument purporting to explain chimp and human violence in several ways. First is the belief that warfare in humans and violent, deathly attacks in chimpanzees are examples of a phenomenon Wrangham (1999) labels "coalitionary killing." According to his explanation, adult male chimps and humans collaborate to kill or brutally wound other adults: "The ancient origin of warfare is supported by ... evidence that...chimpanzees and humans share a common ancestor around 5-6 mya" (Wrangham, 1999: 3).

Next, Wrangham believes the principle adaptive explanation linking coalitionary killing in chimpanzees and humans is the "imbalance-of-power" hypothesis. Accordingly, chimpanzee males will attack other groups if they outnumber them and have a low risk of injury to themselves. Because of the complexity of modern warfare, these types of lethal raids can be seen more readily in humans in "primitive" warfare among "pre-state" societies.

Finally, the long-term evolutionary explanation of coalitionary killing is a "dominance drive" that favors *unprovoked* aggression through an opportunity to attack at low personal risk. The dominance drive is related to increased genetic fitness, allowing the killers to leave more of their dominant-killer genes to the next generation.

Wrangham assumes certain behaviors resulting in conspecific killing among ants, wolves, chimpanzees, and humans (especially those in "primitive, pre-state" societies) are similar phenomena. Presumably they have the same biological bases and motivations, and are driven by the same underlying natural causes. He gives these behaviors a label "coalitionary killing" and, in creating a name, he creates a phenomenon. When comparisons are made between human and animal behavior and an assumption is posited that behaviors similar in appearance must have similar functions and evolutionary histories, a basic principle of biology is being violated. Form alone does not provide information about function nor shared genetic or evolutionary history. Referring to "rape" in dragonflies, "slavery" in ants, or "coalitionary killing" in chimpanzees and humans may sound like science but, to paraphase Marks' (2002) reprimand, science is concerned with biological connections, not metaphorical descriptions.

Another part of the demonic male theory is that an imbalance of power must be an incentive to coalitionary killing. Are we to suspect that whenever a group of chimpanzees or humans perceives weakness in an individual or another group, they will attack and kill? In fact, neither chimpanzees nor humans attack in all circumstances of imbalance of power, and coalitionary killing is extremely rare in both species (see Fry, 2006; Sussman; Garber, 2007). One major question pervades all observations of lethal chimpanzee attacks: What is the underlying motivation and what types of stressors prompt lethal attacks to occur in some cases and not in others? Also, in chimpanzees, how much do severe habitat encroachment, harassment, provisioning, crowding, hunting, and even constant surveillance affect the lives of these highly intelligent animals that are now in danger of extinction in almost every forest in which they occur ...and, how do many of these same stressors in the modern world affect humans?

Yet another part of the demonic male theory—that dominance drives are present—needs clarification. Robert Hinde (1970), one of the most respected animal behaviorists of our time, has considered the concept of psychological and behavioral "drives" at length. He emphasizes that the word itself can make for difficulties because it has been used in so many different ways. Where measures of behavior can be directly correlated, such as drinking leading to a cessation of thirst, the proposition of an intervening drive variable may be a valuable tool for research. However, when correlations between behaviors are not perfect, Hinde cautions, "such a concept is misleading and can be a positive hindrance" (1970: 196). The use of the concept of drive in relation to the extremely complex set of behavioral and contextual phenomena related to dominance seems to us to be entirely inappropriate.

Our detailed analysis of alleged "demonism" of chimpanzees and early humans does not mean we argue that chimpanzees or humans are not violent under certain circumstances, but simply that the claims of inherent demonism may be as greatly exaggerated as were earlier claims of noble savages and peaceable kingdoms. And furthermore, research seems to indicate that the neurophysiology of aggression *between* species (in other words, predation) is quite different from the spontaneous violence linked to *intra*specific aggression by humans (i.e., murder) (Scott, 1971; Blanchard et al., 1999). Even if hunting was a common subsistence technique among early hominins, this does not necessitate uncontrolled aggressiveness in human interactions.

What About Violence and War?

Why is there an acceptance that humans are innately aggressive and that we characterize our aggressive feelings through violent actions? The general primate physiology does not support this view and leads instead to a belief that cooperation is innate to primates, both human and nonhuman (Cloninger, 2004; Sussman and Garber, 2007). Why the disconnect? Sometimes putting things into perspective helps. There are more than six billion humans alive today—all are social animals having constant hour-by-hour interactions with other humans. We're willing to bet that the overwhelming majority of our six billion conspecifics are having days, weeks, and even entire lives devoid of violent interpersonal conflicts. This is not to naively underplay crimes, wars, and state-level aggression found in modern times, but it puts them in the domain of the *anomalous*. Who reads news report of an outbreak of terrible ethnic violence or genocide and thinks "What's so unusual about that?— perfectly normal, happens every day to everyone." War happens ... crime happens, but what is the context in which they happen? Why do murder rates vary so greatly from country to country, from culture to culture? Are war, crimes, and violence the genetic, unalterable norm ... or are they specific to stresses that occur when too many people want too few resources?

After an exhaustive examination of ethnographic research on modern societies ranging from nomadic foragers to urban industrialized societies, Fry (2006, 2007) documented the human potential for cooperation and conflict resolution in two groundbreaking volumes. Fry stresses that virtually all early studies defining man by his capacity for killing appear to be flawed. As Fry states: "War is either lacking or mild in the majority of cultures!" (2006: 97). Counter to assumptions of hostility between groups and among individuals and recurring warfare over resources, the typical pattern is for humans to get along rather well, relying on resources within their own areas and respecting resources of their neighbors. After an examination of the primary ethnographic information on nomadic foragers, Fry found the proposition that human groups are pervasively hostile toward one another is simply not based on facts but rather on "a plethora of faulty assumptions and over-zealous speculation" (2006: 183). Individuals and whole societies deal with conflicts in nonviolent ways. Fry summarized his findings by acknowledging the human propensity to behave assertively and aggressively, but adamantly stating that just as inherent is the human propensity to behave *prosocially* and cooperatively, with kindness and consideration for others. Indeed, Fry's work has convinced him that the very existence of human societies is dependent on the preponderance of prosocial tendencies over assertive and aggressive ones.

We aren't trying to ignore the role of aggression and competition in understanding primate and human social interactions. Our perspective, however, is that affiliation, cooperation, and social tolerance associated with long-term mutual benefits form the core of social group living. Our earliest ancestors lived in a world populated by large, fearsome predators. Strong indications from the fossil record and living primate species lead to the conclusion that hominins were regularly hunted by large predators and required social organization that promoted inconspicuous behaviors, minimal internal conflicts, and coordinated vigilance (Treves and Palmqvist, 2007; Hart and Sussman, 2009).

Getting Out of Our Genes

For the sake of argument, what if the portrait of us and our chimp cousins in *Demonic Males* is correct and we are both inherently violent? Are we doomed to be violent forever because this pattern is genetically coded? After millions of years of human evolution, can we rid ourselves of our inborn evils—get out of our genes, so to speak? Wrangham believes so, and it's fairly easy. We look at chimpanzees to see the worst aspects of our past, and we look at bonobos for the path of escape from it. In other words humans can learn how to behave by watching bonobos. But—we can't resist asking—if humans can change our inherited behavior so simply, why haven't we been able to do so before the authors of the demonic male theory enlightened us? Surely, there are variations in the amount of violence in different human cultures and individuals. If we have the capacity to change by learning from example, then our behavior is determined by socialization practices and by our cultural histories and not solely by our biological nature. This is true whether the examples come from benevolent bonobos or from pacifists and conscientious objectors during a war.

The theory of the demonic male, although it includes chimpanzees as our murdering cousins, is very similar to Man the Hunter theories proposed in the past. Further, it does not differ greatly from early Euro-Christian beliefs about human ethics and morality. We are forced to ask: Are these theories generated by good science, or are they just "good to think" *because* they reiterate our traditional cultural beliefs? Are the scientific facts being interpreted in such a way as to reinforce our traditional Euro-Christian myths of morality and ethics? Is the theory generated by the data, or are the data manipulated to fit preconceived notions of human morality and ethics? Since data supporting these theories are extremely weak, and yet the stories continue to repeat themselves, we are forced to believe that Man the Hunter—the myth—may continue in Western European views on human nature long into the future.

A similar theory to Wrangham and Peterson's on the nature of human hunting and killing has been proposed by chimpanzee researcher, Craig Stanford. Stanford (1999) believes that it is not hunting per se that is important for chimps or early humans but the sharing of meat. It is this meat-sharing that, according to Stanford, has led to the development of the human brain (however, not the chimpanzee brain), sophisticated tool use, our complex patterns of social interaction and structure, and the power of men to manipulate and control women. He portrays the roots of human behavior as manipulation and social cunning that arose from the use of meat by our ancestors. Stanford states: "This is very different than saying that because of a meat-eating past, we have an innately aggressive nature ... Humans are not demons by nature ... in spite of the attention that we focus on human violence" (1999: 217). Thus, from Wrangham and Peterson's and from Stanford's chimpanzee-based scenarios, we are left with completely different conclusions. What is missing from these "just so" stories of human evolution based on chimpanzee analogies is a careful analysis of the actual fossil evidence of our earliest human relatives. We have to agree with an earlier statement by Stanford that current models of hominin evolution are "either implicitly chimpanzee-referent models or restatements, updated and improved, of the "man-the-hunter" hypotheses of the 1950s and '60s" (Stanford and Allen, 1991: 58).

The Other Fifty Percent

Demonic males! Man the hunter! What about the other fifty percent of the species? Female hominins—were they killer apes, too? Obtaining meat may have been significant in later human evolutionary history, but there is considerable debate concerning the importance of hunting versus scavenging or scavenging versus gathering, during the entire hominin record and even the latter stages of human evolution. Many feminist anthropologists emphasize a Woman the Gatherer scenario of human evolution over the Man the Hunter scenario (Tanner and Zihlman, 1976).

Adrienne Zihlman proposes a markedly different view in opposition to the concept of Man the Hunter. Zihlman (1997, 2000) has been a pioneer in the attempts to understand the role of women in human evolution. Studying the behavior, anatomy, and ecology of the bonobos—and of modern-day foraging cultures, Zihlman has constructed a tenable characterization of the way earliest hominins might have exploited savanna or woodland edge environments. She envisions a flexible early hominin society in which women carried their offspring, conducted most of the socialization of the young, were repositories of group knowledge, had cognitive maps of the home range and its resources, were the center of society and the core of group stability, spread innovations, techniques, and knowledge through the group and onto the next generation, and were the main tool users and makers. Finally, she poses the theory that female choice of sexual partners existed, rather than sex through male coercion or aggression. Successful male mating behavior involved being appealing to females, which translates into females choosing less, rather than more, aggressive males with whom to mate.

Zihlman was among the first to address male-biased theories in human evolution and has provided a feasible alternative theory—one that best fits *all* the evidence. But her theory of Woman the Gatherer is still ignored, misunderstood, and underappreciated by many contemporary paleontologists, and sex-biased theories of killer apes and killer humans still pervade the popular literature. She states: "The role of women in evolution has undergone a number of permutations, but paradoxically, in spite of challenges to the contrary, the outcomes have resulted in little change ... anthropologists reach a wide audience through textbooks, television specials, and museum exhibits [but] women in evolution are rendered either invisible nonparticipants or as the handmaidens to men in prehistory" (Zihlman, 1997: 91).

The traditional view of passive handmaidens or compliant harem girls accurately reflects the first descriptions of female nonhuman primates studied in the wild by Sherwood Washburn and Irven DeVore (1961), as they undertook the intital field studies of baboons in the early 1960s. They took one look at the larger size of the males with their impressive shoulder mantles and huge canines and became fixated on male behavior. The rather innocuous looking females were dismissed completely while males were bestowed with the power to hold the baboon troop together through sheer force.

Ironically, when one of Washburn's female graduate students, Shirley Strum, went to the field, she looked past the imposing appearance of male baboons that had so captivated her mentor. Strum (2001) was baffled at first by why her own observations were at odds with previous research on baboons. After years of field studies and rigorous analyses, she could not dismiss the fact that the male researchers before her had gotten it all wrong. Females, not males, were the core of baboon society; they stayed with their mothers, sisters, aunts, and grandmothers from birth to old age.

Each lineage of baboon females (the matriline consisting of several generations of females) could be placed in a discernable dominance hierarchy.

On the other hand, males left as adolescents and entered new troops as often as every five years. While this had been known before Strum's field study,
she discovered that dominant, aggressive behavior got the males nowhere with
the females they encountered in their new social group. The "successful"
males—the ones who got to mate with females—finessed themselves into female society through friendship and amicable behavior. The unsuccessful males
were the ones who threw their considerable weight around and scared both
females and young offspring. Here's the way Strum describes those findings:

> As I recapitulated my years of male baboon studies, I grew more and more
> sure that social strategies, not aggression, were the ingredients of male
> success. ... Social strategies had to be engineered and learned, and that
> was why the long-term males [who had emigrated into the troop several
> years earlier] were the most successful. Newcomers had few options be-
> cause they lacked both social ties and experience.
> Their aggression—one of the few options they *did* have—made them feared,
> and thus dominant, but neither dominance nor aggression gave them access to
> much of what they wanted .... it was the long-term residents who showed
> how much time and experience was needed in this male world. They were
> the lowest-ranking, least aggressive and most successful. They had wisdom,
> friendships and an understanding of the subtle tactics necessary (2001:126).

Like Zihlman's portrait of early hominin lifestyle, in baboons it is female
choice of sexual partners and not male coercion or aggression that is important in successful mating behavior (see also Silk et al., 2003). Females choose
less, rather than more, aggressive males with whom to mate, and as field research has shown, female choice is the most common mating pattern among
species in the primate order (Quiatt and Reynolds, 1995; Swedell, 2005).

Were our ancestors gentle savages or bloodthirsty brutes? They were
social animals; they were primates; they were trying to adapt to their environment and reproduce successfully; they were complex beings in their
own right who were not necessarily headed in a foreordained direction.
What seems particularly pertinent to answering the question is the fact that
most primate societies and individuals exhibit cooperation as the dominant
social tool, not aggression (Fry, 2006; Sussman and Garber, 2007).

Conventional Wisdom as Science

How can we evaluate the recurring and popular Man the Hunter and Demonic Male theories? How do theories or new paradigms in science get ac-

cepted or, on the other hand, ignored? Are we dealing with scientific or political areas when we talk about paradigms? In 1962 a philosopher of science named Thomas Kuhn wrote a classic book, *The Structure of Scientific Revolution*. In it he argued that scientists examine the evidence related to their questions and come up with the most parsimonious explanation (or theory, or paradigm) that fits the data and techniques currently available at the time. However, the evidence is also filtered through a scientist's own background and theoretical orientation by his or her world view and cultural milieu. Changing popular, engrained paradigms that have become "conventional wisdom," such as Man the Hunter, is very difficult. This is especially so if the theory also fits conventional cultural views of the world. Scientists, like most people, are generally conservative in their ability to adopt new paradigms.

Once a paradigm becomes established within a scientific community, most practitioners become technicians working within the parameters of the theory but rarely questioning the validity of the theory itself. In fact even questioning the theory is often thought of as unscientific because the new theory and the old are incompatible and the internal logic of each paradigm differs. Proponents of each paradigm are often talking past one another—speaking a different language. As expressed by Strum when she was trying to get primatologists to accept her observations that aggression was not as pervasive or important an influence on the evolution of baboon behavior as had been previously thought: "In science, according to Kuhn, ideas do not change simply because new facts win out over outmoded ones. Many more social, cultural and historical variables make up the complete picture. Since the facts can't speak for themselves, it is their human advocates who win or lose the day" (2001: 164).

Science is an accumulation of better and better evidence to fit a theory ... or of finding that the old and new evidence are better accommodated by a completely new theory. And, in the end, even with new evidence and a better way of explaining it, ultimately, the politics of science must take its course. It is up to the audience to weigh the evidence. Discrepancies among the theories and the evidence must be evaluated. Once these discrepancies are seen to be overwhelming, the new paradigm will be accepted in favor of the old.

Science is not always truth. Science is just the best way to answer a particular question given the available evidence and technology at a particular time and place. We believe that the evidence indicates that humans have the "propensity" to be both peaceful and violent, that being peaceful is the norm, and that culture, life history, and context are more important in determining the outcome of social interaction than is heredity.

References

Ardrey, R. (1961). *African Genesis: A Personal Investigation into Animal Origins and Nature of Man.* New York: Atheneum.

Ardrey, R. (1976). *The Hunting Hypothesis.* New York: Atheneum.

Bahn, P. (1992). "Cannibalism or ritual dismemberment," in Jones, S.; Martin, R.; Pilbeam, D., Eds., *The Cambridge Encyclopedia of Human Evolution.* Cambridge: Cambridge University Press, p. 330.

Bercovitch, F. (1991). "Social stratification, social strategies, and reproductive success in primates," *Ethology and Sociobiology,* 12:315-333.

Bernstein, I. (1981). "Dominance: The baby and the bathwater," *Behavior and Brain Sciences,* 4:419-457.

Bernstein, I. (1997). "One man's view," *American Journal of Primatology,* 41:151-154.

Blanchard, C.; Hebert, M.; Blanchard, R. (1999). "Continuity versus (political) correctness: animal models and human aggression," in Haug, M, Whalen, R., Eds., *Animal Models of Human Emotion and Cognition.* Washington, D.C.: American Psychological Association.

Boaz, N.; Ciochon, R.; Xu, Q.; Liu, J. (2000). "Large mammalian carnivores as a taphonomic factor in the bone accumulation at Zhoukoudian," *Acta Anthropologica Sinica* (Suppl.), 19:224-234.

Bock, K. (1980). *Human Nature and History: A Response to Sociobiology.* New York: Columbia University Press.

Bock, K. (1994). "Hunting strategies of Gombe and Tai chimpanzees," in Wrangham, R.; McGrew, W.; de Waal, F.; Heltne, P., Eds., *Chimpanzee Cultures.* Cambridge: Harvard University Press, pp. 77-92.

Boesch, C.; Boesch, H. (1989). "Hunting behavior of wild chimpanzees in the Tai National Park, Ivory Coast," *American Journal of Physical Anthropology,* 78(4):547-574.

Boesch, C.; Crockford, C.; Herbinger, I.; Wittig, R.; Moebius, Y.; Normand, E. (2008). "Intergroup conflicts among chimpanzees in Tai National Park: lethal violence and female perspective," *American Journal of Primatology,* 70:519-532.

Brain, C. K. (1981). *The Hunters or the Hunted?* Chicago: University of Chicago Press.

Brown, D. (1991). *Human Universals.* Philadelphia: Temple University Press.

Cartmill, M. (1993). *A View to a Death in the Morning: Hunting and Nature Through History.* Cambridge: Harvard University Press.

Cartmill, M. (1997). "Hunting hypothesis of human origins," in Spencer, F., Ed., *History of Physical Anthropology: An Encyclopedia.* New York: Garland, pp. 508-512.

Cloninger, C. R. (2004). *Feeling Good: The Science of Well-being.* Oxford: Oxford University Press.

Dart, R. (1953). "The predatory transition from ape to man," *International Anthropological and Linguistic Review,* 1:201-217.

Degler, C. (1991). *In Search of Human Nature.* New York: Oxford University Press.

Ellis, L. (1995). "Dominance and reproductive success among nonhuman animals: A cross-species comparison," *Ecology and Sociobiology,* 16:257-333.

Fedigan, L. (1992). *Primate Paradigms.* Chicago: University of Chicago Press.

Ferguson, B. (2009). "Born to live: challenging killer myths," Paper presented at *Man the Hunted: Sociality, Altruism and Well-Being Conference.* St. Louis, March 12-14, 2009.

Fourrier, M.; Sussman, R.; Kippen, R.; Childs, G. (2008). "Demographic modeling of a predator-prey system and its implication for the Gombe red colobus (*Procolobus badius*) population," *International Journal of Primatology*, 29:497-508.

Fry, D. (2006). *The Human Potential for Peace: An Anthropological Challenge to Assumptions About War and Violence.* New York: Oxford University Press.

Fry, D. (2007). *Beyond War.* New York: Oxford University Press.

Ghiglieri, M. (1984). *The Chimpanzees of Kibale Forest: A Field Study of Ecology and Social Structure.* New York: Columbia University Press.

Ghiglieri, M. (1999). *The Dark Side of Man: Tracing the Origins of Male Violence.* Reading: Perseus Books.

Goodall, J. (1965). "Chimpanzees of the Gombe Stream Reserve," in De Vore, I., Ed., *Primate Behavior: Field Studies of Monkeys and Apes.* New York: Holt, Rinehart, and Winston, pp. 425-473.

Goodall, J. (1968). "The behaviour of free-living chimpanzees in the Gombe Stream Reserve," *Animal Behaviour Monographs*, 1:165-311.

Goodall, J. (1971). *In the Shadow of Man.* Boston: Houghton Mifflin.

Goodall, J. (1986). *The Chimpanzees of Gombe: Patterns of Behavior.* Cambridge: Harvard University Press.

Hart, D. (2000). *Primates as prey: Ecological, morphological, and behavioral relationships between primate species and their predators* [Ph.D. dissertation]. St. Louis Washington University.

Hart, D.; Sussman, R. W. (2009). *Man the Hunted: Primates, Predators and Human Evolution,Expanded Edition.* Boulder: Westview Press.

Hausfater, G. (1975). *Dominance and Reproduction in Baboons (Papio cynocephalus).* Basel; New York: S. Karger.

Hinde, R. (1970). *Animal Behavior: A Synthesis of Ethology and Comparative Psychology,* Second Edition. New York: McGraw Hill.

Klein, R. (1999). *The Human Career: Human Biological and Cultural Origins,* Second Edition. Chicago: University of Chicago Press.

Klein, R.; Edgar, B. (2002). *The Dawn of Human Culture.* New York: John Wiley & Sons.

Kuhn, T. (1962). *The Structure of Scientific Revolutions.* Chicago: Chicago University Press.

Johanson, D. C.; Edey, M. A. (1981). *Lucy: The Beginnings of Humankind.* New York: Simon and Schuster.

Marks, J. (2002). *What It Means to Be 98% Chimpanzee: Apes, People, and Their Genes.* Berkeley: University of California Press.

Monge, J.; Mann, A. (2007). "Paleodemography of extinct hominin populations," in Henke, W.; Tattersall, I., Eds., *Handbook of Paleoanthropology: Principles, Methods, and Approaches*, Vol. 1. Berlin: Springer, pp.673-700.

Nishida, T.; Hiraiwa-Hasegawa, M.; Takahata, Y. (1985). "Group extinction and female transfer in wild chimpanzees in the Mahale National Park, Tanzania," *Zeitschrift für Tierpsychologie*, 67:281-301.

Power, M. (1991). *The Egalitarians, Human and Chimpanzee: An Anthropological View of Social Organization.* Cambridge: Cambridge University Press.

Quiatt, D.; Reynolds, V. (1995). *Primate Behaviour: Information, Social Knowledge, and the Evolution of Culture.* Cambridge: Cambridge University Press.

Reynolds, V.; Reynolds, F. (1965). "Chimpanzees of Budongo Forest," in DeVore, I., Ed., *Primate Behavior: Field Studies of Monkeys and Apes.* New York: Rinehart and Winston, pp. 368-424.

Ruse, M. (1993). "Evolution and ethics: The sociobiological approach," in Pojman, L., Ed., *Environmental Ethics: Readings in Theory and Application.* Boston: Jones and Bartlett, pp. 91-109.

Sanz, C. (2004). *Behavioral ecology of chimpanzees in a central African forest: Pan troglodytes troglodytes in the Goualougo Triangle, Republic of Congo* [Ph.D. dissertation]. St. Louis: Washington University.

Scott, J. P. (1971). "Theoretical issues concerning the origin and causes of fighting," in Eleftheriou, B. E.; Scott, J. P., Eds., *The Physiology of Aggression and Defeat.* New York: Plenum, pp. 11-41.

Silk, J.; Alberts, S.; Altmann, J. (2003). "Social bonds of female baboons enhance infant survival," *Science*, 302:1231-1234.

Small, M. (1997). "The good, the bad, and the ugly," *Evolutionary Anthropology*, 5:143-147.

Smuts, B. (1987). "Gender, aggression, and influence," in Smuts, B.; Cheney, D.; Seyfarth, R.; Wrangham, R.; Struhsaker, T., Eds., *Primate Societies.* Chicago: University of Chicago Press, pp. 400-412.

Stanford, C. (1999). *The Hunting Ape: Meat Eating and the Origins of Human Behavior.* Princeton: Princeton University Press.

Stanford, C.; Allen, J. (1991). "On strategic storytelling: Current models of human behavioral evolution," *Current Anthropology*, 32(1):58-61.

Strum, S. (2001). *Almost Human: A Journey into the World of Baboons.* Chicago: University of Chicago Press.

Sugiyama, Y. (1972). "Social characteristics and socialization of wild chimpanzees," in Poirier, F., Ed., *Primate Socialization.* New York Random House, pp. 145-163.

Sussman, R. (2000). "Piltdown man: The father of American field primatology," in Strum, S.; Fedigan, L., Eds., *Primate Encounters: Models of Science, Gender, and Society.* Chicago: University of Chicago Press, pp. 85-103.

Sussman, R. (2003a). *Primate Ecology and Social Structure, Volume I: Lorises, Lemurs and Tarsiers.* Needham Heights: Pearson Custom Publishing.

Sussman, R. (2003b). *Primate Ecology and Social Structure, Volume II: New World Monkeys.* Needham Heights: Pearson Custom Publishing.

Sussman, R.; Garber, P. (2007). "Primate sociality," in Bearder, S.; Campbell, C.; Fuentes, A.; MacKinnon, K.; Panger, M., Eds., *Primates in Perspective.* New York: Oxford University Press, pp. 636-651.

Swedell, L. (2005). *Strategies of Sex and Survival in Female Hamadryas Baboons.* Upper Saddle River: Prentice-Hall.

Takahata, Y.; Huffman, M. A.; Suzuki, S.; Koyama, N.; Yamagiwa, J. (1999). "Why dominants do not consistently attain high mating and reproductive success: A review of longitudinal Japanese macaque studies," *Primates*, 40:143-158.

Tanner, N.; Zihlman, A. (1976). "Women in evolution: Innovation and selection in human origins," *Signs*, 1:585-608.

Treves, A.; Palmqvist, P. (2007). "Reconstructing hominin interactions with mammalian carnivores (6.0-1.8 ma)," in Gursky, S.; Nekaris, K., Eds., *Primate Anti-Predator Strategies*. New York: Springer, pp. 355-381.

Trinkaus, E. (2000). "Hard times among the Neanderthals," in Angeloni, E., Ed., *Annual Editions: Physical Anthropology 00/01*. Guilford: Dushkin McGraw-Hill, pp.131-135.

Tsukahara, T. 1993. Lions eat chimpanzees: The first evidence of predation by lions on wild chimpanzees. *American Journal of Primatology* 29(1):1-11.

Walters, J.; Seyfarth, R. (1987). "Conflict and cooperation," in Smuts, B.; Cheney, D.; Seyfarth, R.; Wrangham, R.; Struhsaker, T., Eds., *Primate Societies*. Chicago: University of Chicago Press, pp. 306-317.

Waser, P.; Wiley, R. (1980). "Mechanisms and evolution of spacing in animals," in Marler, P.; Vandenbergh, J., Eds., *Handbook of Behavioral Neurobiology*, Volume 3. New York: Plenum Press, pp. 159–233.

Washburn, S.; DeVore, I. (1961). "Social behavior of baboons and early man," in Washburn, S. L., Ed., *Social Life of Early Man*. Chicago: Aldine, pp. 91-105.

Washburn, S.; Lancaster, C. (1968). "The evolution of human hunting," in Lee, R.; DeVore, I., Ed., *Man the Hunter*. Chicago: Aldine, pp. 293-303.

Wilson, E. O. (1975). *Sociobiology: The New Synthesis*. Cambridge: Harvard University Press.

Wilson, M.; Wrangham, R. (2003). "Intergroup relations in chimpanzees," *Annual Review of Anthropology*, 32:363-392.

Wrangham, R. (1974). "Predation by chimpanzees in the Gombe National Park, Tanzania," *Primate Eye*, 2:6.

Wrangham, R. (1995). "Ape culture and missing links," *Symbols* (Spring): 2-9, 20.

Wrangham, R. (1999). "Evolution of coalitionary killing," *Yearbook of Physical Anthropology*, 42:1-30.

Wrangham, R.; Peterson, D. (1996). *Demonic Males: Apes and the Origins of Human Violence*. Boston: Houghton Mifflin.

Wrangham, R. W.; Wilson, M. L.; Miller, M. N. (2006). "Comparative rates of violence in chimpanzees and humans," *Primates*, 47:14-26.

Zihlman, A. (1997). "The Paleolithic glass ceiling: Women in human evolution," in Hager, L., Ed., *Women in Human Evolution*. London: Routledge, pp. 91-113.

Zihlman, A. (2000). *The Human Evolution Coloring Book*, Second Edition. New York: HarperCollins.

Chapter Two

Not Killing Other People
The Origin and the Only Future of *Homo sapiens*

Piero P. Giorgi
University of Queensland and European Centre

Introduction

At a first glance the idea of a nonkilling society may sound alien to most people habituated to history books punctuated by wars. However, if we stretch our mind in time and space a revealing picture appears in front of us. This holistic view of the human adventure covers three time periods: nonkilling societies that existed in the past, those existing now (here we must move our mind in space as well) and the nonkilling societies of the future. This paper is based on the suggestion that killing other human beings is a recent (the last 7,000-8,000 years) cultural aberration and our chance of surviving as a species depends on understanding this phenomenon and eliminating structural violence in our societies.

We will briefly analyse human societies in the Palaeolithic (100,000-12,000 years ago), in the so-called historical times (late Neolithic - present) and in the foreseeable future, in order to attempt an answer to the questions: Why in recent millennia have humans beings been engaged in so much violence? What is contributing to the continuation of violence? Will violence be sustainable in the future? Answers to these questions will guide us toward the design of future nonviolent societies based on the re-humanisation of people, not simply on moral codes.

We suggest that the period of historical times (the period dominated by violence) is locked in between of two events whose importance is currently underestimated: *the invention of food production* (12,000-6,000 years ago, depending on the region) (see second section) and *the failure of violent/military solutions* (conflicts of the last sixty years) (see the first part of the fifth section). The nonviolent future is therefore being prepared in this beginning of the 21st century (see the fifth section of this chapter).

After a brief review of the origins of violence, the main aim of this paper is to analyse the current cultural strategies adopted to channel children and adolescents toward competition and various forms of violence. This analysis leads to the conclusion that the very future of humanity depends upon a refusal to continue such violent training of young people. The outcome will be a future dominated by nonkilling cultures, the only solution to interrupt such an inhuman period of violence and avoid a rapid extinction of human beings.

Nonkilling Societies in the Palaeolithic

The literature on the origins of violence and war is heavily affected by mythologies and popular beliefs that find no correspondence in modern scientific knowledge.[1] The image of a brutish caveman holding a club with one hand and dragging a woman by her hair with the other dominates the popular imagination. The origins of such a myth go back to 17th century ideas about "man in nature" (Thomas Hobbes), the scientific distortions of social Darwinism (Herbert Spencer), the pop literature on human evolution (Robert Ardrey, Carl Sagan), the innativism of Konrad Lorenz, radical sociobiology, and the persistent inadequacy of high school human biology. The popular mythology about brutish prehistoric humans also affects our views of human nature and, specifically, the discipline of Peace Studies. What chances have we of reducing and eliminating violence in a culture that believes in innate human violence?[2]

Data from modern anthropology strongly suggest that during the first 90,000 or so years of their existence human beings displayed a nonviolent culture (Fry, 2007; Giorgi, 2001; 2008; 2009). Briefly, 40,000 years of rock art throughout the world essentially lack indications of duels or war as an important aspect of prehistoric cultures (Giorgi and Anati, 2004; Giorgi, 2008: 67-74), while classical art is dominated by warriors and war from the late Neolithic onward. The reports of anthropologists who lived with and studied con-

---

[1] The lack of communication and osmosis of ideas between academic disciplines is a recent deleterious trend in universities. Multidisciplinary studies toward a holistic view of human beings are often advocated but practically impeded by disciplinary specialisation and the close club mentality of intellectuals.

[2] Most academic textbooks of sociology and political science still reserve an important place in the theoretical presentation of their disciplines to the outdated ideas of Machiavelli, Hobbes, Rousseau, Freud and Lorenz, not to modern authors in anthropology and neurobiology. Nor do they mention authors supporting an optimistic idea of human nature (Kropotkin, Montague, Fromm, etc.). This contributes to maintaining the idea of human congenital violence; it keeps us, at best, at the level of negative peace (reducing inevitable violence) and impedes the development of positive peace (preventing violence).

temporary hunter-gatherers (the nearest available model of Palaeolithic cultures) describe nonviolence as the dominating trend in social life (Lee, 1984; Bonta, 1993; Fry, 2007; Giorgi, 2001: 105-130; 2008: 59-66; 2009). Moreover, basic textbooks of human developmental neurobiology state that specific social behaviour (such as violence and war) is defined after birth by specific cultural models, not by congenital information (Giorgi, 2008: 32-49) thanks to the extraordinary plasticity of postnatal and adult human brains (Doidge, 2008).

If violent behaviour and war appeared only in the last few thousands years and are the product of cultural conditioning, the persistence of the mythology of brutal prehistoric humans and congenital violence must be surreptitiously sustained by those who have a vested interest in maintaining violence and killing in society (see second part of the fifth section). We are probably facing a most effective phenomenon of social disinformation, whose mechanisms should be investigated to protect democracy.[3]

Nonkilling Societies in Historical Times

As indicated in the previous section, we suggest marking the beginning of historical times with the invention of food production, not that of the later invention of writing.[4] This means about 12,000 years BP (before present) in the Middle East, about 9,000 BP in Southern China and about 6,000 BP in Central America (three independent events that gradually spread around by cultural transfer). The transition from hunter-gathering (food collection) to domesticating plant and animals (food production) has not been

---

[3] Elsewhere we have suggested that most societies are currently oppressed by a commercial-media system (see notes 9, 10) that makes us egoist, ignorant, fearful and violent (thus vulnerable to manipulation). The 1986 Seville Statement that denied congenital human violence has been effectively barred from public exposure (Giorgi, 2001: 78-80). Books that support the idea of human unavoidable violence are liberally reviewed and promoted. The last example is a book of limited literary value, which was reviewed by the author in three pages of the prestigious *Newsweek* (May 17, 2010: 44-46) entitled "Why men love war". No answer to the rhetorical question, just a list of war-lusty famous leaders with truly silly comments. At the same time a media wall is built around good publications that are critical about war love and promote nonviolent solutions. Joseph Goebbels would have dreamed of having such an effective public control system, a shame for contemporary democratic countries.

[4] So far the beginning of history is considered to coincide with the existence of written documents. Modern findings in anthropology and archaeology have demonstrated that well-interpreted Palaeolithic rock art and early Neolithic artifacts are equally valid historical documents (Anati, 2003; Giorgi, 2007b, Giorgi, 2008: 67-74).

just an other technological advance; it had an enormous consequence on humanity, as it represented a rapid, purely cultural change in a species that emerged, instead, through a slow, harmonious biocultural process of natural selection.[5] Anthropology textbooks tend to represent this event as yet another clever achievement of the glorious march of humans toward civilisation, failing therefore to highlight the extraordinary discontinuity unwittingly introduced into the human adventure. Human beings found themselves with a Palaeolithic brain operating in a Neolithic culture, which exposed it to alien life conditions: large settlements, hierarchical social organisation and structural violence.[6] Structural violence[7] then generated direct violence (psychological and physical damage to others) and war. The malaise of civilisation—first denounced but wrongly explained by Sigmund Freud (Giorgi, 2007c)—appeared very early with its symptoms of unhappiness, poor health and poverty among the vast majority of "civilised" people. Jean Jacques Rousseau had an intuition of this problem, but, like Freud, lacked modern knowledge to formulate a correct criticism, as explained below (see also note 8).

Violent food producing cultures gradually pushed hunter-gatherers to the hedges of fertile lands and into harsh regions where they survived demonstrating their extraordinary ability to adapt through cooperation and solidar-

---

[5] Briefly, biocultural evolution is an evolutionary mechanism common to mammalian social species that has found its most sophisticated expression in *Homo sapiens*. It consists of an harmonious parallel evolution of neurological predispositions (not specific behaviour) transmitted by congenital information, and specific social practices transmitted by cultural transfer (Giorgi, 2008: 27-49). The current popular view of human behaviour being the result of interaction between genes and learning is not scientifically correct. Genes may carry behavioural predispositions, not specific social behaviour, while the latter is defined only by specific social models. Predispositions just regulate the time necessary to acquire behaviour, not "what" people do (specific behaviour).

[6] Elsewhere (Giorgi, 2001: 149-170; 2008: 77-102) we have presented a hypothesis on how structural violence, direct violence and war emerged in food producing societies. Very briefly, it was a chain of causes and effects that unwittingly took those communities from job specialisation, to large increase in number, social stratification, a minority in power, the need to maintain law and order, and to defend fields and herds from nomadic cultures that hunted and gathered ignoring the concept of property.

[7] Structural violence, a concept introduced by Galtung (1969), consists of *all the ideas and institutions that prevent people from expressing their human potentialities*. It is a powerful definition that goes beyond that of social injustice, because it contains an ontogenetic factor: human brain development, which is completed after birth. One is not born a human being; one becomes one after birth if the right conditions are available (Giorgi, 2001: 75-92).

ity, the very human qualities that were rapidly substituted by competition and greed in violent cultures. During the centuries of colonialism many nonkilling societies still existed in the world, but most of them have been exterminated or forcibly acculturated by invading foreign farmers and shepherds.

About ten years ago Bruce Bonta was able to list twelve peaceful cultures still living on the Earth (Bonta, 1993), while the study of nonviolent people is becoming an important topic of anthropological research (Van der Dennen, 1990; Sponsel and Gregor, 1994; Sponsel and Good, 2000; Fry, 2007). Are nonviolent people lonely idiots unable to do any harm, as described by J. J. Rousseau about 200 years ago,[8] or are they the closest model of clever cooperative human beings, as finally designed by biocultural evolution about 50,000 year ago? Are we to listen to the fantasies of 17-18th century philosophers or to the hypotheses of modern neurobiologists and anthropologists? The sad truth is that public knowledge and imagination is now oppressed by a commercial-media system with a vested interest that we are ignorant, distracted by trash entertainment, fearful, violent and slightly ill in order to make us vulnerable and obedient consumers.[9] The mythology of inevitable violence and media biases are part of this imposed scenario.[10]

The nonkilling societies currently studied by anthropologists are of two types: the few contemporary hunter-gathering cultures not yet acculturated or exterminated (12 listed by Bonta, 1993)[11] and cultures inspired by alternative religious and/or philosophical principles (Bonta, 1993 listed 11). Bruce Bonta

---

[8] Rousseau never described a "noble savage" (for a criticism see Giorgi, 2001: 14, note 7). So why do we keep perpetrating such a silly expression? When citing an author one should make sure we read his/her work, not second hand reports.

[9] Commercial-media oppression is a new form of structural violence rapidly emerging in the last 30 years or so. When *production* was of great economic concern, we were oppressed by an industrial system that tried to obtain most work in exchange for the least salary. Now that *consuming* is of great economic concern, we are oppressed by a commercial system that wants us to consume beyond our spending capacity (the essential cause of the current financial crisis).

[10] Commercial oppression (see previous note) is combined with a powerful media, which control our fundamental beliefs (the idea of human congenital violence, for example) and what and how much we should consume. It is not a coincidence that big financial groups compete for the ownership of television channels and newspapers. Very few people of course are aware of being oppressed in this way, as the new dictatorship has also convinced us that we are free, a diabolical plan indeed, almost an Orwellian dystopia.

[11] Recent anthropological studies of additional nonviolent cultures can be found in the web site <http://www.peacefulsocieties.org> and in other chapters of this book.

also listed 22 basically nonkilling cultures that have been partially acculturated or are producing food and trading with neighbouring violent cultures.[12]

Very briefly, the basic traits that characterise a nonviolent hunter-gatherer society are: small size, kindness toward small children, initiation of adolescents, adult nonviolent models, skill in conflict prevention (not management), solidarity, cooperation, sharing of food and resources, equalitarian social structures, tolerance, culture of being rather than having,[13] spirituality,[14] active entertainment,[15] and sense of humour. Also very briefly, the basic traits that characterise a nonviolent religious/philosophical society are: small size, strong collective identity, hard working, adult nonviolent models, skill in conflict resolution, control of youth, solidarity, hierarchical social structure but operating by consensus, ethical rules, protection from outside influence, and strong righteousness.

The differences and resemblances between these two approaches to nonviolence raise the question about the construction of violence and nonviolence in children, adolescents and adults (the main topic of this paper). We are convinced that it is impossible to stop the culture of killing and the practice of war without first understanding the way of reducing and eliminating structural violence. *We are also convinced that new ideas on how to construct a nonviolent society in modern times do not come from simply studying the few contemporary food-gathering cultures that never developed violence,[16] and even less from studying the social behaviour of Pri-*

---

[12] These contemporary nonviolent cultures would find themselves in a situation similar to that of some nonviolent agricultural people who lived in small townships of Malta and Crete during the Early Neolithic (Giorgi, 2007b).

[13] The important question discussed by Erich Fromm (1976).

[14] The difference between spirituality and religion is discussed in Giorgi (2008: 103-106). Briefly, spirituality is a functional potentiality of all human beings (mostly mediated by the prefrontal region of the frontal lobe). It deals with a set of metaphysical questions concerning origins and relationships with nature and other human beings. Religion is spirituality expressed within a new social framework emerging, interestingly, in the Neolithic that introduced the concept of divinity, priesthood, moral rules, and rituals. Religion sometimes helped to reduce violence, but it adopted aspects of structural violence.

[15] Pastimes can be passive (listening to and watching cinema, television, sports, theatre, concerts, etc.) or active (dancing, singing, playing music, telling stories). Excessive passive entertainment is degrading and sometime dangerous for the spectator (see note 18).

[16] These studies are indeed useful to realise that violence is not part of human nature, but not to understand how violence emerged in the Late Neolithic.

mates.[17] We think that it is necessary to study how structural violence, direct violence and war originated in food-producing cultures, in order to gradually remove the social mechanisms that have sustained them for thousands of years. As the unwitting introduction of violence was purely cultural, we can keep the advantages brought about by social injustice and violence (technology, art, knowledge, etc.) and culturally regain the human advantages of nonviolence (solidarity, cooperation, social justice, spirituality, etc.).

Cultural Strategies to Promote Violence

On April 25, 2010 a 44 year-old lorry driver in Northern Italy took his registered gun, many bullets and left by car for a well planned tour of killing: he shot his former wife and two persons with whom he had had various conflicts about money. He was nicknamed Rambo, known for his lonely life and his passion for weapons and muscle building. Journalist interviewing neighbours and acquaintances reported conflicting statements: from knowing him as a normal kind man or as a potential killer. Interestingly, on that occasion a criminologist recommended keeping an eye on lonely men, while educators stressed the need to teach boys nonviolent behaviour. Nobody even mentioned the pervasive violent entertainment (films, television and electronic games) and the need to curb it, rather than teaching good behaviour after having constructed a violent mind.[18] There is obviously a great deal of work to be done about understanding causes and mechanisms of violent behaviour in these "normal kind men"[19] generated by a diseased, violent culture.

---

[17] These studies are indeed useful to realise how pragmatic and variable adaptive social solutions are among Primates, but not to understand the unique selective mechanisms that led to the emergence of human brain and behaviour about 100,000 years ago. Primate brain and behaviour (as that of all higher Mammals) did not evolve by piling up new regions above older ones (as pop evolution suggested), but by experimenting with new associational connections in the cerebrum to match the functional need required by social inventions (biocultural evolution, see note 5).

[18] Violent entertainment contributes to the construction of specific neuronal connections during the first 6-7 years of life (subconscious deep culture) and reinforces them by directing specific neuronal connections in adolescence and adult life (conscious culture). Even in adulthood "mirror neurons" transform fiction into real motor activity in our brain. This "behaviour" settles in subcortical regions and becomes a true postnatal experience and behavioural models to be retrieved in future situations of stress (Giorgi, 2008; Doidge, 2008).

[19] In this case the use of the term "man" is literally correct. About 90% of prison inmates are men. If antisocial and violent behaviour were a part of human nature,

One specific feature of modern training in violence is our subconscious love for handguns. Let's start by considering the posters of films and noting how often the image that "sells" the product is a man (rarely a woman) who holds a pistol, his expression intense but self confident and calm. The weapon is not pointed against the observer, but held near the man's face, pointed upward, as "our heroes" do when lurking in pursuit of the "bad guys". The intimate association hero-pistol substitutes the cheek-to cheek of past posters of love films, as now violence sells better than romance. Let's see how violent entertainment and the secret love for pistols are being imposed to the public, an important case of structural violence of which we are not aware.

How To Ruin a Good Little Boy

When entering a toy shop it looks as if time has stopped: there still is a clear cut division between toys for girls and toys for boys, with a few exceptions of educational toys in between. In spite of the recent struggle for gender equality, girls must be still play with dolls, miniature houses and tools for various domestic chores. Boys must instead chose between vehicles (model motorbikes, cars and lorries) and a rich variety of violent tools, with real-size plastic pistols and guns dominating the scene. When challenged, parents tend to justify the purchase of toy weapons with the fact that we live in a violent society and boys must learn to adapt and defend themselves.[20]

Weapon toys are the first forms of subconscious habituation to violence, before moving toward the acceptance of and attraction to true weapons and real war. Toys are even more dangerous than television cartoons with terrific science fiction worriers, because toys are associated with the affective and reassuring relationship with parents giving presents. Electronic games with battle scenes where guns dominate the scene further reinforce the pistol-power relationship in older children, who now become active protagonists in realistic acts of violence. This developmental preparation is later confirmed by hours and hours spent watching violent films in adolescent and adult life; here the two genders finally join hands becoming diligent

---

one should find there 50% of women, unless this behaviour was defined (not just facilitated) by the Y chromosome or testosterone, which has been disproved.

[20] It is worth noting the two typologies of popular attitudes: non-critical adaptation to the *status quo* (conservative) and critical view of the *status quo*, but often unable to imagine an alternative (progressive).

consumers of war, police and hospital thrillers, where blood and death enter in their minds through the false illusion of "it is just fiction".[21]

Importantly, infant subconscious acquisition of violent social models can easily be interpreted as evidence of congenital violent instinct. This erroneous idea is supported by psychologists trained in old-fashioned Freudian concepts and without a preparation in modern developmental neurobiology. In 2010 we know instead that violence is a sophisticated example of social behaviour, which is not defined by genes but acquired during construction of subcortical connections in the first 6-7 years of life (deep culture) and then learned in later years during construction of cortical cognitive associational connections (Giorgi, 2001; 2008).

A crazy psychologist determined to ruin the mind of human beings would have hardly designed a better scheme to introduce an alien trait such as violence into our daily life. Who has a vested interest in human beings developing a violent social environment and habituation to violence, in opposition to the parallel process of biocultural evolution that designed the original brain and society of *Homo sapiens*? Promoters of positive peace will have to find an answer in order to suggest a slow, nonviolent project of disobedience to the logic of violence (see part 2 of the fifth section).

Strange Behaviour of Men Deprived of Humanity

Other methods exist to prevent a good boy from expressing all his human potentialities.[22] The early nonverbal models of deep culture and the later verbal ones made available for growing males are poorer than those offered to growing females. Briefly, we expect from a boy that he simply becomes strong, competitive and a winner in social conflicts; to this end we forgive overbearingness, arrogance, aggressive behaviour and low school results. From a girl we generally expect that she helps in the house, is diligent at school, and assists those in need. As a consequence, girls develop better human qualities: the art of communication, skill in negotiation, collaborative behaviour, and the dialectics of reciprocal help. In the Palaeolithic our brain has been selected for this very type of human relationships, in both men (cooperation in hunting) and women (cooperation in gathering), with the ultimate aim of sharing resources, not competing for them (Giorgi 2008: 62-65). With the emergence of structural violence (see third section) men have gained power, but have also lost a great deal of their humanity;

---

[21] See notes 15 and 18.

[22] This expression corresponds to the definition of structural violence (note 5).

women have retained it to a larger extent. The recent conquests in equal opportunity between genders have therefore resulted in girls becoming more intelligent and better citizens.[23]

In daily life, as well as in contemporary literature, one can observe a clear malaise among men, who are losing their traditional dominance and must find ways of reassuring themselves, often with destructive and aggressive behaviour particularly against women.[24]

A Society Drugged With Adrenaline

We are analysing how structural violence operates in today's society, in order to propose a project of nonviolent transformation toward the establishment of a future nonkilling society. One last important item proposed here is passive entertainment and a phenomenon almost unknown to the public: the danger of fiction.

Telling each other fantastic stories, gossip and news in the evening around fireplaces or inside stables is a trait common to all cultures, a communication need of all human beings. But, as with good wine, wisdom is in sobriety. During the last fifty years or so *we have become uncritically drunk with fictional passive entertainment through audiovisual systems.* Pastimes are not dialectic and collective anymore: at cinemas, concerts, sporting events, etc. there are passive consumers on one side and the show industry on the other. By spending too many hours just watching and listening we have lost the skills of telling stories, dancing, singing, playing an instrument, practising a sport, courting a person; we only look at other people doing it.

This tragic human castration and serious intellectual paralysis would be bad enough by itself,[25] without two more complicating factors. Fiction producers often promise strong emotions and outright "injections of adrenaline", but the need to compensate for a generally boring life prevents us from hearing the alarm bell: we are drugging ourselves with adrenaline. Good articles in physiology journals have already reported the phenomenon of habituation to the ar-

---

[23] The definition and the quantification of intelligence is a complex and controversial topic. In this case we refer simply to scholastic marks allocated by examiners and to the statistics of civic involvement of women.

[24] Interestingly, destructive and aggressive children are often those who lack social skills.

[25] Passive entertainment contributes to the disuse and wasting of the body: muscles not exercised and the brain not challenged by creative thoughts and problem solving (see Giorgi, 2007a, section "Body").

tificial excitement of fiction and the need for higher levels of adrenaline to obtain the same degree of excitement: the very definition of drug dependency.

In this context direct violence, blood and killing occupy a central role. A very significant proportion of passive entertainment (films, television series, printed fiction) concerns armed violence, criminology, police investigations, hospital emergencies or combinations of them. Who has a vested interest that we spend a great deal of our free time fantasising about guns, dynamite, crimes, wounds, hospitals, policemen, judges, physicians, and prisons? One can argue that this genre of fiction is not exactly driven by consumers' free choice.

The process of habituation to the presence and use of weapons and violence—which starts with apparently innocent toys at a very early age, is reinforced in adolescence with proactive electronic games, and is stabilised in adulthood with a systematic exposure to violent fiction—proceeds in parallel with the dependence on passive entertainment and adrenaline: this locks us into an acceptance of and even attraction to violence, weapons and war. Operators for a nonviolent transformation of society (see part two of the fifth section) will have to use convincing arguments to reduce and then eliminate dangerous objects and unhealthy practices with which we have become familiar, unwittingly dependent on and probably affectively attached to.

Future Nonkilling Societies

As suggested above nonkilling cultures have been the norm since the emergence of *Homo sapiens* about 100,000 BP and its migration throughout the world about 50,000 BP. Structural violence, direct violence and war appeared only in large settlements of the Late Neolithic. We now suggest that, after a relatively short interlude of violence (7-8,000 years), nonkilling cultures will soon develop in some regions of the earth and their superior life style and level of humanity will become a model to imitate by neighbouring cultures, just as violence was imitated a few thousand years ago.

The End of Violent Historical Times

To emphasise the negative importance of violence in human cultural evolution we have redefined the beginning of historical times (invention of food production, instead of writing) as indicated in the third section of this chapter. Now we identify the approaching end of it.

The bloodshed of the second world war surpassed even that of the first one and prompted in both cases the (unsuccessful) attempt to establish an international seat of arbitration (Society of Nations, United Nations). Both wars also set the scene for internal purges and extermination of unwanted civilians and political opponents in the dictatorial regimes of Joseph Stalin (about 20 million people) and Adolf Hitler (about 10 million people).

However something so utterly new began to happen in the years 1945-65 that we suggest that this post-war period should be considered the beginning of the end of historical times, although only a few scholars are aware of this important cultural turning point for humanity, that is characterised by *truly nonviolent revolutionary trends*, after thousands of years of violent solutions.

During these years a consistent cultural trend began to *question violence and war* as a way of resolving conflicts of interest between individuals, ideologies and nations. The United Nations issued the *Universal Declaration of Human Rights* (December 1948). Following the teaching of Mohandas K. Gandhi, *nonviolence emerged as a new theory and successful practice*. The *discipline of Peace Studies* was established by Johan Galtung and others in Norway and elsewhere. Gene Sharp documented, promoted and inspired *strategic nonviolent action* as a substitute for war and *civilian-based defence* as a substitute for national armies. Costa Rica abolished its army in 1949 and enjoyed a stable democracy ever since.

Two other trends are very important and little known. In these post-war years a consistent military trend has emerged characterised by *unsuccessful wars of aggression* launched by powerful nations against local popular armed forces. Examples: the Korean war, the French war in Indochina, the Vietnam war, the Soviet Union war in Afghanistan, the second Gulf war, and international "peace" interventions in Somalia, Yugoslavia, Lebanon, Afghanistan, etc.[26]

In these years a consistent political trend also emerged characterised by *successful nonviolent popular movements* that obtained substantial political changes without weapons. Examples: the Danish resistance to persecution of Jews by Nazi Germany, the independence of India from British occupation, the end of Franco's regime in Spain, the Solidarnosc movement for democracy in Poland, the end of the Marco regime in the Philippines, the fall of the Berlin Wall, the unification of Germany, the Ukraine movement for democracy, etc.[27]

These important trends have heralded *a new era of unsuccessful violence and successful nonviolence*, which we consider the beginning of the end of historical times, those characterised by violence and war. Only a bi-

---

[26] For the sake of brevity we omit the necessary discussion about special circumstances in each case. But the general character of selected cases is essentially correct.
[27] See previous note.

ased media[28] and an old-fashioned education system are delaying the public awareness of the obvious advantages of nonviolence and the new failures of the killing culture, both nationally and internationally.

The next necessary step is to study structural violence in daily life, the poorly understood mechanism that maintains the culture of violence and the tradition of war and prevents a speedy transformation into nonkilling cultures.

The Neotopia Project in Italy

As indicated above, eliminating violence and war is not a utopia anymore. We are facing a realistic possibility of transforming structurally violent communities into structurally nonviolent communities, through a nonviolent, slow and legal revolution based essentially on civic education and active citizenship. We have called this project Neotopia[29] from the Greek terms for "new" and "place". It has been proposed that such experimental places can only be small townships or, perhaps, city suburbs in a sufficiently democratic country.

The general rationale for such a nonviolent revolution has been presented by Giorgi (2007a),[30] while each township will have to adapt it to its own human, economic and physical context.

The general approach of Neotopia is quite simple: use active citizenship and participatory democracy to stop the violent training of children, disobey the subliminal orders of the commercial-media oppression, apply good existing laws in democratic countries, and nurture our natural predisposition for spirituality (not religion).[31] One can see that, unlike other social projects, this does not need financial and structural resources, because it consists essentially of changes in awareness, attitudes and behaviour. It requires, how-

---

[28] See notes 3,9,10.

[29] The term "neotopia" was first proposed ten years ago (Giorgi, 2001). The idea of a social project was proposed on the 60th anniversary of Gandhi's assassination (30 January 2008) and the Association Neotopia was established by Federico Fioretto in 2009 (<http://www.neotopia.it>).

[30] The Italian updated version of the English article Giorgi (2007a) can be downloaded at the web site <http://www.neotopia.it/area_download.html>. The aspects of structural violence analysed in daily life and their nonviolent alternatives are: citizenship, family, education, media and passive entertainment, the body, environment, commercial-media oppression, politics, antisocial behaviour, direct violence and self-defence, money and spirituality.

[31] For a review about our congenital spirituality, see Giorgi (2008: 104-105) and Urgesi et al. (2010). Gandhi often pointed out that nonviolence cannot be realised without a good degree of spirituality (not religion).

ever, a great deal of preparation, planning and collective determination, as it needs a critical mass of population agreeing to participate—the most enthusiastic ones being young couples with babies.

The first advantages of this nonviolent revolution will probably become apparent after one generation and a nonviolent culture will probably emerge after two generations. This sounds like a long time, but cultural changes are slow and after 8,000 years of violence, it is worthwhile enduring such an elaborate cure to become happy, healthy and with sufficient resources; that is, human beings.[32] The most effective strategy will be to distinguish short-term solutions for adults, medium-term solutions for adolescents and long-term solutions for babies, all three of them to be, however, initiated together.

The first experiments in training local social improvement groups[33] have proved very difficult and time consuming. For this reason we are preparing a Master in Applied Nonviolence to be offered at a university in Lombardy, to train future trainers. The handbook for this course is in preparation (September 2010); it will also be adapted as an educational tool for the public.

Conclusion

Nonkilling has been the natural strategy selected by biocultural evolution[34] for human beings since their emergence. It was unwittingly lost after the invention of food production and the consequent establishment of large hierarchical societies. Now that modern anthropology, neurobiology and evolutionary sciences have explained what happened in the Late Neolithic (a purely cultural

---

[32] Again, commercial-media oppression hides from the public the pandemic increase of chronic depression, the increase in morbidity (incidence of diseases) in spite of the decrease in mortality (causing longer periods of diseased life) and the increasing level of poverty in the lower and middle classes of "wealthy" nations. These are clear signs of the social malaise caused by structural violence. A nonviolent revolution would make us happier, healthier and richer.

[33] So far we have offered training in five communities and found an initial great interest in the idea, but problems in entering a new way of thinking and practical living. A consensus was found about the initial need to develop citizenship, participatory democracy and a strong family-school axis.

[34] See note 5. If biocultural evolution is well understood, it is clear that we are not genetically violent (as generally believed) nor genetically nonviolent (as implied by J. J. Rousseaux), because neurological predispositions do not define specific social behaviour (Giorgi, 2001; 2008) nor the victims of the widely accepted idea of interactionism (behaviour due to 50% nature and 50% nurture), because biological inheritance works differently from cultural inheritance (apples and pears cannot be added together).

selection for violence), we can acknowledge violence as a by-product of plant and animal domestication and culturally re-establish our natural nonviolent communities without giving up the technological advantages obtained during our brief spell of involvement in structural and direct violence.

This brief summary of years of study is the basis for concluding that nonkilling cultures have always been with us: for 90,000 years before agriculture as part of the natural setting of human beings, for 8,000 years after agriculture with a few persisting hunter-gathering peoples, and now as a logical conclusion drawn from scientific knowledge and the disasters recently caused by uncritical acceptance of violence.

The prediction of nonkilling societies as the future normal human condition is the main contribution of this paper. The other original approach is the importance allocated to structural violence as the origin of all forms of violence. In the short term, opposing war is a worthy pursuit, but it will not, alone, eliminate the culture of killing. This will occur with a nonviolent, slow revolution in life style, which is already heralding a new era of peace and, probably, the only way of escaping our extinction.

References

Anati, E. (2003). *40,000 ans d'art contemporain (40,000 years of contemporary art)*. Capo di Ponte: Edizioni del Centro

Bonta, B. D. (1993). *Peaceful People - An annotated bibliography*. Metchen: The Scarecrow Press.

Doidge, N. (2008). *The brain that changes itself - Stories of personal triumph from the frontiers of brain sciences*. Carlton North: Scribe Publications.

Fromm, Erich (1976). *To have or to be?* New York: Harper & Row.

Fry, D. P. (2007). *Beyond war*. New York: Oxford University Press.

Galtung, J. (1969). "Violence, peace and peace research," *Journal of Peace Research*, 6:167-191.

Giorgi, P. P. (2001). *The origins of violence by cultural evolution*. 2nd ed. Brisbane: Minerva E&S. Available at: <http://www.pierogiorgi.org>.

Giorgi, P. P. (2007a). "Countering with nonviolence the pervasive structural violence of everyday life - The case of small Italian townships," in Summy, Ralph V., Ed., *Nonviolent alternatives for social change*, in *Encyclopaedia of Life Support Systems (EOLSS)*. Oxford: Eolss Publishers.

Giorgi, P. P. (2007b). "A new interpretation of female symbols and figures produced in prehistoric Europe - The hypothesis of the centrality of women," in Bloom, M.; Giorgi, P. P.; Pietroboni, G., Eds., *Rock art in the framework of the cultural heritage of humankind*. Capo di Ponte: Edizioni del Centro, pp. 185-192.

Giorgi, P. P. (2007c). "The origins of violence - New ideas and new explanations affecting terrorism," in Ram, Senthil; Summy, Ralph, Eds., *Nonviolence - An alternative for defeating terror(ism)*. Hauppauge: Nova Science Publishers, pp. 11-27.

Giorgi, P. P. (2008). *La violenza inevitabile - Una menzogna moderna* (Inevitable violence - A modern lie). Milan: Jaca Book.

Giorgi, P. P. (2009). "Nonkilling human biology," in Evans Pim, Joám, Ed., *Toward a nonkilling paradigm*. Honolulu: Center for Global Nonkilling.

Giorgi, P. P.; Anati, E. (2004). "Violence and its evidence in prehistoric art - A comparison of ideas," in Anati, E., Ed., *Arte preistorica e tribale - Nuove scoperte, interpretazioni e metodi*. Capo di Ponte: Edizioni del Centro, pp. 263-269.

Lee, R. B. (1984). *The Dobe !Kung*. London: Holt, Rinehart & Winston.

Sponsel, L. E.; Good, K. R. (2000). "Anthropologists Debate Future of War," *Anthropology News*, 41(2):19-20.

Sponsel, L. E.; Gregor T., Eds. (1994). *The anthropology of peace and nonviolence*. London: Lynne Rienner.

Urgesi, C. et al. (2010). "The spiritual brain," *Neuron*, 65: 309-319.

Van der Dennen, J. M. G. (1990). "Primitive wars and ethnological inventory project" in Dennen, J. Van der; Falger, V., Eds., *Sociology and conflict - Evolutionary perspectives in competition, cooperation, violence and welfare*. London: Chapman & Hall, pp. 247-269.

Chapter Three

Nonkilling as an Evolutionary Adaptation

Douglas P. Fry, Gary Schober, Kaj Björkqvist
Åbo Akademi University in Vasa

In the word nonviolence, violence is the root, subtly implying the normal state of affairs, whereas the prefix "non" is special, tacked-on, unusual. Violence as a word stands alone, but by itself "non" is nonsensical, not even a word in its own right. By the same reasoning, the use of the word nonkilling might imply that killing is the norm. In this chapter, we will suggest just the opposite: Nonkilling is the normal state of affairs. Across many species, nonkilling is the default and killing is the exception, the oddity, the unusual. This thesis is derived from evolutionary theory and gains support from a consideration of data from biology, anthropology, and psychology.

There are exceptions such as infanticide in some species, which has its own evolutionary explanations, but for the most part intraspecific killing is rare in the animal kingdom. Many competitive interactions do not involve any physical contact so this pretty much precludes killing. In other cases, injuries and deaths within a species are avoided via a variety of different mechanisms.

Among humans, rates of killing vary markedly from one society to the next (Fry, 2006, 2007). As in other species, conflict and competition find numerous means of expression in humans that do not involve physical altercations, let alone killing. People tolerate differences and avoid confrontations by leaving the scene or moving elsewhere. People also discuss calmly or in anger, find solutions, make up, or just forget about a problem. People share, compromise, haggle, problem solve, debate, manipulate, give up, and reconcile. Meanwhile, no one is killed. People help others with their disputes as allies, advocates, or arbitrators. If we are going to try to assess which is more normal, killing or nonkilling, it behooves us to keep in mind all the murders that never occur in response to all the disputes and grievances that really do occur in human societies everyday.

An evolutionary orientation coupled with a consideration of biological, anthropological, and psychological data lead to certain propositions. The evidence and reasoning will follow, but here are some of the propositions for which we find support.

- In intraspecific competition, nonkilling has been favored by natural selection in humans.
- The Darwinian concept of sexual selection elucidates sex differences regarding human killing and physical aggression more generally.
- As in nonhuman animals, humans (especially males) use a great deal of restraint during intraspecific aggressive interactions.
- Selection pressures that favor restraint during physical aggression, paradoxically, have operated more strongly on men than on women due to male physical aggression being more dangerous than female physical aggression.
- An additional selection pressure, that would seem to be unique to humans, involves revenge-seeking by the family members of homicide victims; this selection pressure favors nonkilling.

The chapter consists of three main sections. First we consider ritualization and restraint across various species including humans. Anthropological sources reveal some intriguing similarities in humans to the patterns of restrained intraspecific competition in other species. Second, we consider sex differences related to intraspecific physical aggression and discuss their evolutionary origins. It would seem that men and women have different natures related to the expression of intraspecific physical aggression. Third, we explore three selection pressures that would seem to favor nonkilling over killing in humans. One of these selection pressures involves the psychology of payback killings and appears to be uniquely human.

The Costs and Benefits of Physical Aggression to Individual Fitness

Bernstein (2008: 60) writes that "The potential costs of fighting are such that natural selection has favored individuals that avoid taking risks when the cost to themselves is likely to exceed the benefits of anything obtained by engaging in that interaction." What are some of the "costs" and "benefits" of aggressive behavior if viewed in evolutionary terms? Costs include physical injuries, mortality, harming one's own kin if they are opponents, losing friends and allies by damaging relationships, taking time and energy away from important pursuits such as finding food, watching for predators, or seeking mates, and being expelled from the social group as a trouble-maker (Archer and Huntingford, 1994: 10; Bernstein, 2007, 2008; Björkqvist, 1994; Björkqvist and Österman; Lagerspetz, 1994; Boehm, 1999; Hamilton, 1971; Riechert, 1998: 82; Service, 1966; van Schaik and Aureli, 2000).

Evolutionary benefits of aggression vary from one species to the next and from one context to another, but include obtaining resources such as food, territory, and mates; safeguarding one's offspring and oneself from attack; and achieving or maintaining dominance in a social hierarchy, which in turn correlates with access to resources or mates (Alcock, 2005; Archer, 1988; Wilson, 1975: 242-243). Thus aggression serves a variety of evolutionary functions that vary from species to species (Alcock, 2005; de Waal, 1989, Wilson, 1975). The take-home message is that although aggression can be risky it also can be beneficial to individual fitness in certain circumstances. From an evolutionary perspective, we would expect that natural selection over many generations shapes the aggressive behavior of a species so as to maximize fitness benefits and minimize risks to fitness. This proposition would apply to humans as well as other animals.

Across species, most intraspecific aggression is nonlethal (Alcock, 2005; Hinde, 1974: 268; Kokko, 2008; Maynard Smith and Price, 1973). Nonetheless, death can result from injuries sustained during a fight, as reported, for example, among some primates, hyenas, and lions (Alcock, 2005; Schaller, 1972; Wilson, 1975: 246). Blanchard (1989: 104) points out that "In evolutionary terms…successful individuals will be those with techniques which enable them to avoid agonistic situations involving serious possibilities of defeat or injury, while leaving them to continue in more promising situations."

Consideration of intraspecific competitive and aggressive behavior in nonhuman animals reveals a variety of mechanisms through which individuals minimize risks. First, noncontact displays are used in place of actual fighting. For example, among elephant seals, threats outnumber fights by about sixty-to-one (Le Boeuf, 1971). Second, when fighting does occur, it tends to consist of ritualized aggression, wherein serious injuries and death are rare, such as in the type of head butting contests for which ungulates are renowned. Third, in territorial species, once boundaries have been established, threats and fights markedly decrease among neighbors (Kokko, 2008). Fourth, dominance hierarchies within social groups greatly reduce fighting on a daily basis as each individual knows their place relative to the other group members (Preuschoft and van Schaik, 2000). Fifth, animals practice avoidance and hence eliminate the possibility of confrontations. For instance, the members of one lion pride simply maintain a distance from lions of other prides (Schaller, 1972).

Most of the intraspecific aggression in the animal kingdom occurs between males and later in this chapter we will consider why this is so. Intraspecific male-male aggression usually does not entail all-out fighting, but rather reflects various types of restraint (Archer and Huntingford, 1994; Bernstein, 2007; Eibl-Eibesfeldt, 1961; Kokko, 2008; Le Boeuf, 1971; Riechert, 1998: 65). "There is an optimal level of aggression, rather than more being always better" (Kokko, 2008). In other words, animal aggression rarely involves "total war," as Maynard Smith and Price call it (1973: 15), "but instead intraspecific conflicts are usually of a 'limited war' type, involving inefficient weapons or ritualized tactics that seldom cause serious injury to either contestant." It is in the survival interests of both parties to "follow the rules" of ritualized fighting so as not to expend unnecessary energy or to increase the risk of injury. In illustration of this point, over the same observation period a team of researchers observed 1,308 ritualized sparring matches between pairs of male caribou who followed the restrained rules of engagement compared to six escalated fights (Alcock, 2005). That is a ratio of one serious fight to every 218 ritualized contests.

Display and Tournament Contests in Nonhuman Animals

Maynard Smith (1974) distinguishes two kinds of ritualized contests: displays and tournaments. Displays reduce the chances of physical injury to nil because they involve no physical contact. "Rather than bludgeoning a rival, males of many bird species settle their conflicts over a territory or a mate with much singing and feather fluffing, but without ever touching one another" (Alcock, 2005: 307). Side-blotched lizards direct push-up displays toward their rivals, and male tarantula hawk wasps compete over a territory by engaging in a series of rapid aerial ascents, flying upward side-by-side for many meters before they both dive back to earth, only to repeat the process over and over (Alcock, 2005). The average display contest, devoid of physical contact, lasts 25 minutes, but can go on for almost an hour before one wasp gives up. From a distance, red dear stags during the rut engage in bouts of reciprocal roaring as they compete for mating privileges. Researchers have found that roaring rate correlates with fighting ability and after a roaring contest, the male with the lesser roar often yields to the other stag (Archer, 1988; Archer and Huntingford, 1994).

The same species of red deer also illustrates the concept of tournament contests. Reciprocal roaring displays may escalate to parallel walking as each deer visually assesses the size and strength of his opponent, still without making physical contact, and if neither animal has yielded to the other by this point, the final stage of stag competition involves a tournament of antler wrestling

(Archer and Huntingford, 1994). Tournaments are energetically expensive and the possibility of injury does exist. However, Riechert (1998) cites research showing that serious injuries remain unlikely for this type of ritualized tournament, occurring one time in fifty among red deer stags, for example.

Examples of relatively safe tournament contests abound in the animal kingdom. For the most part, animals follow the rules of restraint and do not escalate to more serious forms of fighting. Rattlesnakes neutralize their prey by injecting them with deadly venom and may also attack predators with their fangs in self-defense. However, when two male rattlesnakes compete for a mate they do not use their lethal fangs on each other but instead wrestle with intertwined necks, each attempting to pin the other's head to the ground (Eibl-Eibesfeldt, 1961; Wilson, 1975: 243). Once this goal has been achieved by one of the snakes, the victor of the serpentine wrestling match releases the loser unharmed.

Giraffe males slam each other with their necks and heads (Alcock, 2005). Male mule deer "fight furiously but harmlessly by crashing or pushing antlers against antlers, while they refrain from attacking when an opponent turns away, exposing the unprotected side of its body" (Maynard Smith and Price, 1973: 15). At the point where one animal signals submission or attempts to flee, continuation of the fight merely increases the risks to both contestants and wastes energy without any gain to either individual (Bernstein, 2007; Roscoe 2007).

In summary, studies show that *nonlethal, restrained* intraspecific competition, in contrast to escalated serious fighting, has evolved as the typical pattern in many species (Alcock, 2005; Archer and Huntingford, 1994; Bernstein, 2007; Hinde, 1974: 269; Kokko, 2008: 49; Riechert, 1998: 65; Roscoe 2007). In other words, regarding intraspecific competition, natural selection tends to favor nonkilling over killing. "If aggression is elicited, then it must be limited, controlled, and regulated in such a way that it terminates with minimal risk of injuries," explains Bernstein (2008: 59). By evolutionary reasoning, the widespread appearance in the animal world of *displays* instead of contact aggression and *ritualized tournaments* instead of "total war" between two opponents suggests that *restraint* is a more successful strategy than engaging in unbridled aggression. "The 'fight no matter what' types would eventually encounter a superior opponent who would administer a serious thrashing. The 'fight only when the odds are good' types would be far less likely to suffer an injurious defeat at the hands of an overwhelmingly superior opponent" (Alcock, 2005: 309). As we shall next consider, the same evolutionary logic can be applied to explain patterns of restraint observed across cultural contexts among humans as well.

Display and Tournament Contests in Human Societies

Humans are perhaps the most behaviorally flexible species on the planet. Humans are learners *par excellence*. Yet natural selection has operated on human beings as it has on all species. If we turn to a consideration of human conflict behavior with knowledge about animal conflict in mind, we find some striking parallels. Humans engage in both types of intraspecific contest noted in the animal world: displays and tournaments. Just as engaging in serious aggression can be dangerous in other species, the same certainly holds true when two human males engage in physical aggression. As in many other species, the use of displays in place of actual fighting and the use of ritualized forms of competition as alternatives to escalated fighting make sense for humans when viewed from an evolutionary perspective. Clearly not all intraspecific aggression in humans is ritualized or restrained. However, humans may engage in more display, ritualization, and restraint than might immediately come to mind. These practices contribute substantially to nonkilling.

The Trumai are from the Upper Xingu River basin of Brazil. When a man became angry with another man, often due to suspected or real adultery, "malice was expressed either by a verbal interchange with the opponent or with angry speech" (Murphy and Quain, 1955: 58). Disputes of this nature generally took the form of harangues and shouted argument, usually during an evening gathering of the men in the Trumai village. Another example of verbal displays of anger and hostility comes from the Ainu of Japan (Hilger, 1971). Two men would engage in a haranguing contest. In one case, two men harangued each other in a verbal debate called *charange* continuously for three days without pausing to eat or sleep. Finally, one man gave up. The winner of the *charange* was then entitled to some of the property of the man who had capitulated due to physical and mental exhaustion.

Another interesting form of competition occurred among the Micmac of North America between two rivals over political leadership. Again, this contest involved no physical fighting. It was proposed instead that each man would go hunting and the winner of the contest would be the one who killed the most beavers and moose (Le Clercq, 1910). Among the Saulteaux of North America, a bully three times threw another man to the ground. The victim did not retaliate physically, but said: "All right. I know you have been looking for it a long time. I know you think you are a great *midé* [sorcerer]. You are nothing. If I point my finger at you, you will become a dead man" (Hallowell, 1974: 289). So the two men agreed as a ground rule to leave each other's family members out of the dispute and to practice sorcery only against each other. Eventually, the bully became ill and the other man proclaimed that he was clearly the stronger sorcerer.

The next form of contest is widely practiced by Canadian Inuit groups and generally referred to as a song duel. Hoebel (1967) points out how song duels resolve disputes and normalize strained relationships between members of a community. According to the rules of song dueling, two men had free range to insult and criticize each other in verse. In some cases, both antagonists were fully satisfied to have been able to insult and deride their rival publicly, so the song duel brought the dispute to a close (Balikci, 1970; Eckert and Newmark, 1980). Eckert and Newmark (1980: 206) provide an example of song duel lyrics:

> It is said that you, Utahania,
> Came stealthily creeping
> In to your little sister
> Qahatlovaq
> To go-whoring with her!
> And then, when she asked you
> 'What is it you want?'
> You looked rather foolish, did you not?

A final type of display contest that is functionally analogous to those observed among various other species has been dubbed a "wealth contest" by DuBois (1960) in reference to the Alorese of Indonesia. In one instance, a wealth contest was ignited between two men after one of them shouted at the other man's sons: "I'll hit you if you don't wish me to go with you. Go copulate with a dog" (DuBois, 1960: 123-124). The general idea is to see which contestant can amass the most pigs by drawing upon the contributions from their social networks. After a man named Mangma won such a contest, his supporters began to gloat:

> "Sapakiek! The rooster's tail droops! You are a voiceless night bird. Our lineage house's taproot goes down deep. You were mistaken." Then they all danced [a] challenge, saying "Hik, hik! My friend Maliseni [the loser of the contest] sit quietly; don't talk. We are the ones to talk. We are a bird with a bell-like voice; you are a silent night bird." (DuBois, 1960: 123)

Among the Siuai on Southern Bougainville on the Solomon Islands, any man who can give away more than he receives gains social status. A Siuai social-climber will carefully estimate another man's ability to accumulate wealth and then invite the rival to a competitive feast. The host then presents his guest of honor with an amount of pigs and shell money that he estimates cannot be paid back within a year or two. If in fact the guest cannot pay back, "matching pig for pig and money for money, the guest is 'killed' socially, and the host looks around for a worthier rival" (Oliver, 1949: 61).

In terms of highlighting a few points, in the foregoing examples winners and losers were determined without recourse to physical aggression. Like competing wasps that race in tandem to the heavens and back without any physical contact, the men in these cases competed through displaying their most clever lyrics, haranguing endurance, hunting prowess, sorcery skills, and wealth amassment abilities. These competitions were serious yet not physically dangerous. Status and other rewards were at stake but not life and limb.

We will now turn to ethnographic examples of tournament contests which do involve physical contact between opponents. The typical pattern involves wrestling between two men. The contests vary in intensity from one society to the next, but the first generalization is that they involve struggles between two rivals (Fry, 2005). The next generalization is that the winner of a contest gains status and sometimes a tangible reward such as a wife. Hence tournament contests, like displays, are serious business. Third, the curtailed aggression evident in human tournament contests parallels the ritualized fighting of some animal species. As among animals, the key point is that restrained aggression allows the establishment of dominance or access to resources with substantially less risk to the rivals than would result from all-out fighting. Thus tournament contests in humans are serious but less risky to the participants than unbridled aggression with its many costs and, ultimately, fitness-lowering potential (Fry, 2005).

We have seen that the Trumai of Brazil engage in display contests in the form of haranguing each other, usually at the evening men's circle. The Trumai and neighboring tribes in the Upper Xingu River basin also wrestle, often for sport and sometimes as a form of conflict resolution. "The closest approximation to the use of force was a mock wrestling match between the disputants in which light slaps and holds were mixed with talk" (Murphy and Quain, 1955: 57). For the neighboring tribes of the Upper Xingu, expressing anger through wrestling matches allows it to subside: "When our bellies are 'hot with anger' we wrestle and the anger is gone" (Gregor and Robarchek, 1996: 180).

Among the Siriono of Bolivia an angry man may "go hunting" to cool off. Disputes between men may be settled through wrestling at periodic drinking feasts (Holmberg, 1969). There are wrestling rules that limit aggression, and usually participants use self-restraint and follow the rules. Holmberg (1969: 156) explains that "aggression at drinking feasts is limited to wrestling matches; any other type of fighting is frowned upon and is usually stopped by nonparticipant men and women. On one occasion Eantándu when drunk, struck an opponent with his fists. Everyone began to clamor that he was fighting unfairly, 'like a white man.' He stopped immediately." Holmberg (1969: 152) reports that among the Siriono homicide is "almost unknown," suggesting that disputes rarely escalate into the realm of serious aggression.

The Netsilik Inuit utilize contests to settle disagreements with minimal danger to the participants. According to the rules, two rivals face off and take turns striking each other using blows directed at the forehead or shoulders. Eventually, one man gives up. A Netsilik informant explains that "After the fight, it is all over; it was as if they had never fought before" (Balikci, 1970: 186).

The Ona of Tierra del Fuego had wrestling contests for sport and also as a form of dispute resolution. The contests provide a relatively safe context for aggressive competition and the assertion of dominance of one man over another.

> It is carried on, to be sure, in the same way as ordinary wrestling for sheer fun, but here it proceeds with increased exertion and more malice. The occasions are insult, defamation of honor, or slighting another man, who will not put up with such things. ... [The wrestling] happens only if each believes he is a match for his opponent; otherwise the weaker one avoids challenging the other to fight. ...The two move toward each other and seize each other tightly. The previous irritation and the heightened jealousy cause each to attack boldly; they summon their utmost strength and plant themselves against each other in desperate rage, until finally one must succumb, either by being pressed against a tree or thrown on the ground. With this the existing disagreement has been settled to some extent, at least for today, namely, to the disadvantage of the one defeated (Gusinde, 1931: 645-646).

Northeastern Athabascan societies such as the Slave and Dogrib had a custom through which a challenger could "legally" acquire another man's wife by out-wrestling him (Helm, 1956). Osgood (1958: 204) explains how the Ingalik practiced a similar custom. A married woman might agree to leave her husband for another man, and off they would go together. The husband would then go looking for his wife. She might hide in the woods while the two men wrestled over her. Sometimes the husband was successful in getting his wife back and sometimes not.

When two Nama men from South Africa had a dispute, a council would attempt to settle the matter. If this was not possible, a contest with or without weapons could take place. Schapera (1930: 342) describes the procedure:

> When the councilors were unable to secure harmony between the liti-
> gants, the oldest of them took some sand in the palm of his hand, which
> he held out before the two men, or else he poured a little sand on to their
> shoulders. If the challenge was accepted, the sand was brushed away; but
> if one of the men refused it, he was branded as a coward and held to be in
> the wrong. Where both accepted the challenge, the councilors formed a
> ring around them. They then attacked each other with their fists, kicked,
> wrestled, and bit until one of them was overpowered. Reconciliation fol-
> lowed. The victor slaughtered a fat sheep, which was eaten by him and his
> opponent, with the councilors as guests.

Schapera (1930) notes that fighting with weapons was a more serious affair
and could have a lethal outcome.

Contests are a form of socially institutionalized restraint. Hoebel (1967:
92) concludes that contests serve as a means for handling conflict without
the loss of life in many Inuit societies, and this conclusion applies to other
societies as well. "Homicidal dispute, though prevalent, is made less frequent in many Eskimo groups by recourse to regulated combat—wrestling,
buffeting, and butting...The object of the boxing and butting contests is not
annihilation, but subjection." In this assessment we see an exact parallel to
animal tournaments. The ritualization of aggression in many species prevents injuries among contestants (Archer and Huntingford, 1994; Maynard
Smith and Price, 1973). Among humans, contests with rules that limit aggression can allow for the resolution of differences with less risk of injury
than might occur during less ritualized forms of fighting (Fry, 2005).

Thus contests have rules that promote restraint, and spectators take a
role in enforcing the rules if necessary, as we saw in the Siriono case when a
wrestling man was chided by onlookers not to fight "like a white man." The
metacommunicative context of contests is that they are simultaneously *serious yet not dangerous*, or at least not as dangerous as unbridled aggression.
Winning a contest by the rules enhances esteem and status, but winning
through cheating—that is, by fighting unfairly—may have an opposite effect
when the spectators and the social group are one and the same (Fry, 2005).

Sex Differences in Physical Aggression

The cross-cultural evidence shows an overall pattern. Men tend to engage in more *frequent* and more *severe* physical aggression than do
women. One way to document this difference between the sexes is to consider homicide from a culturally comparative perspective.

With cross-cultural regularity across a broad spectrum of cultures ranging from nomadic band societies—the social type with the most similarity to
those of the evolutionary past—to a range of relatively more complex social
forms such as tribes, chiefdoms, kingdoms, and nation-states, men commit
more homicides than do women (Balikci, 1970; Brown, 1991: 137; Burbank, 1992; 1994: 202; Daly and Wilson, 1988; Lee, 1979).

Fry (in press) examines information on homicide for a sample of 21 nomadic forager societies. Although the occurrence of homicide varies from
one nomadic forager society to the next, a clear pattern is apparent in the
descriptions of homicides in the forager ethnographic material: Men are
usually the killers and also the victims. Occasionally a woman may be a victim, but only rarely does a woman commit homicide (Fry, 2006: 221-222;
Lee, 1979). The Pintupi of Australia, as described by Myers (1986: 253), illustrates this nomadic forager pattern of sex differences regarding homicide: "Though fights including women are common, I have no record of
deaths inflicted by women's weapons. Men, on the other hand, are responsible for the deaths of women as well as men."

Among the 21 forager societies, the reasons for homicide include revenge
for a previous killing (15 societies), over a woman/adultery/sex (12 societies),
miscellaneous crimes such as theft, rape, and trespass (7 societies), and
community sanctioned executions (6 societies). Other less frequently mentioned reasons for killing include self-defense (3 societies), insults or "quarrels" (3 societies), punishment for a taboo violation (2 societies), and due to
starvation leading to cannibalism (1 society). Accidental killings are mentioned
as occurring among seven of the 21 societies (Fry, in press).

We also should bear in mind that most disputes in these societies are
nonlethal, and many conflicts involve no physical aggression at all. For 7 out
of these 21 nomadic band societies, or one third of the sample, ethnographers assessed homicides to be uncommon, being described as: rare, very
rare, never mentioned to occur, none known, and unknown.

Lee (1979) reports that for 22 homicide cases among the Ju/'hoansi of Bot-
swana, all of the killers were men. Hoebel (1967) reviewed ethnographic
sources looking for homicide cases committed among the Arctic Inuit and
found that 26 of the 27 killers were men. It is not only in nomadic band societies that men engage in more killing than do women. To provide a few diverse
examples, the Uniform Crime Statistics compiled by the FBI for 2008 show
that for murder cases where the sex of the perpetrator was known, only
1,176 of the killers were female, compared to 10,568 male offenders (United
States Department of Justice, 2009). Going back in time, historical archival re-

search for two areas of Colonial Mexico revealed that women constituted a mere three percent of the murderers (Taylor, 1979: 84). On Bellona in the Solomon Islands over a 600 year period, the number of persons who either killed or attempted murder was 195 males versus 2 females (Kuschel, 1992). In Buenos Aires, Argentina, in 1985, the number of homicides committed by men outnumbered those committed by women by a ratio of about nine-to-one (Hines; Fry, 1994). In comparing data on male-male homicides and female-female homicides across many societies, Daly and Wilson (1988: 161) conclude that, "intrasexual competition is far more violent among men than among women in every human society for which information exists."

Moreover, behavioral findings and crime statistics repeatedly show that nonlethal physical aggression also is both *more frequent* and *more severe* in men than in women (e.g., Archer, 2009; Björkqvist, 1994; Burbank, 1987; 1994; Campbell, 1999; Daly and Wilson, 1988; Fry, 1992; 1998; Hines and Fry, 1994; Kuschel, 1992; Lee, 1979; Maccoby and Jacklin, 1974: 368; Schober, Björkqvist and Somppi, 2009; Taylor, 1979; U.S. Department of Justice, 2008).

Although male violence, comparatively speaking, surpasses female violence, nonetheless it is important to keep in mind that there is great cultural variation in the amounts and kinds of physical aggression. Some societies have extremely low rates of homicide and other kinds of physical aggression, and some societies do not engage in feuding or warfare (Bonta and Fry, 2006; Fry, 2006). The Paliyan of India, for instance, have a nonviolent ethos (Gardner, 2004). Engaging in physical aggression is incompatible with their core values of respect and equality. Gardner (2004: 58) found no evidence of murder and notes "a complete absence of feuding within Paliyan society and a corresponding total lack of war." Of the Jahai of Malaysia, Sluys (1999: 307) reports that they "are known for their shyness toward outsiders, their non-violent, non-competitive attitude, and their strong focus on sharing." However, in societies that do engage in intergroup violence, with rare exceptions it is men who participate in feuds, and where war is practiced, meet on the battlefields (Adams, 1983; Burbank, 1987: 71, 1994: 202). In summary, it is important to keep in mind that whereas the generalization that human males engage in more frequent and more severe physical aggression than human females is strongly substantiated, this does not mean that men are everywhere-and-always violent (Fry, 2006).

Accounting for Sex Differences in Physical Aggression

In *The Descent of Man*, Darwin (1998) introduced the concept of sexual selection as a special kind of natural selection that acts on variation among individuals in their capacities to acquire mates. Darwin (1998) envisioned two mechanisms through which sexual selection operates. First, the members of one sex can favor sexual partners that have particular traits over other individuals lacking such traits. Second, the members of one sex can compete amongst themselves for mating access to the other sex. The first kind of sexual selection explains the evolution of ornamentation—for example, the huge and colorful tail feathers of the male peacock, sage grouse, and Central American quetzal (Alcock, 2005: 331; Darwin, 1998). The second form of sexual selection accounts for the evolution of fighting structures and behaviors. Usually the male of a species exhibits behavioral and structural fighting adaptations, which may include larger body size, greater muscle mass, and fighting anatomy specialized for intraspecific competition such as antlers and horns. Darwin (1998: 229) writes, "It is the males that fight together and sedulously display their charms before the females; and the victors transmit their superiority to their male offspring." Why is it usually the males that compete more actively for females rather than vice-versa?

Trivers (1972) suggests that the answer lies in the unequal amounts of *parental investment* typically made by females and males in offspring. Darwin (1998: 214-215) realized that: "The female often differs from the male in having organs for the nourishment or protection of her young, such as the mammary glands of mammals, and the abdominal sacks of the marsupials." Among mammals, at the minimum a male can contribute sperm in a matter of minutes, whereas the female contribution goes well beyond the act of fertilization as she must "invest" in her offspring through pregnancy and subsequent lactation. Parental investment consumes time and energy. The concept has been explained by Trivers (1972: 139) as any contribution "by the parent in an individual offspring that increases the offspring's chance of surviving (and hence reproductive success) at the cost of the parent's ability to invest in other offspring."

Darwin (1998: 583) proposed that to a large extent the secondary sex differences in humans, as in many other species, could be attributed to the operation of sexual selection: "There can be little doubt that the greater size and strength of man, in comparison with woman, together with his broader shoulders, more developed muscles, rugged outline of the body, his greater courage and pugnacity, are all due in chief part to inheritance from his half-human male ancestors." Symons (1979: 142; also see Archer 2009) points out that on the average, female body weight in humans is 80 to 89 percent of male body weight. Application of sexual selection and parental investment theory explains why men, to a greater extent than women, compete amongst themselves for members of the opposite sex (Archer, 2009; Symons, 1979: 153). This is the evolutionary thinking that lies behind the observation that human males engage in more frequent and more severe physical aggression, on the average, than do human females.

We must mention two important caveats at this point. First, the different potential for physical aggression between the sexes does not mean that male aggression is always frequent or that male aggression must be expressed (Fry, 2006). Peaceful societies manifesting very low levels of aggression by both sexes do exist and are well documented (Bonta, 1993, 1996, 1997; Bonta and Fry, 2006; Fry, 2006; Howell and Willis, 1989; Kemp and Fry, 2004; Montagu, 1978; Sponsel and Gregor, 1994).

Second, the suggestion that certain sex differences in humans including body size, muscular strength, and fighting ability are attributable to sexual selection in the form of same-sex competition, does not imply that *warfare* is a direct result of sexual selection. After all, larger male body size, strength, and other fighting attributes have evolved in numerous other animal species that lack any type of aggression remotely resembling warfare (Alcock, 2005; Fry, 2006, 2007; Maynard Smith and Price, 1973). Warfare in humans is a rather recent development, not an evolutionary adaptation. This topic is discussed thoroughly by Fry (2006, 2007).

Sex Differences in Restraint during Physical Aggression: A Theoretical Proposition

Female physical aggression is generally perceived to be less lethal than its male counterpart. Zapotec women from Mexico opined, for example, that quarrels are more dangerous between men than between women "because men are the ones that kill" (Fry, 1992: 189). Argentines from Buenos Aires perceive women's physical aggression to be "relatively harmless compared to men's aggression" (Hines and Fry, 1994: 232). Myers (1986: 253) explains that whereas some Pintupi men from Australia's Western Desert have killed, he knows of no case of a woman having done so, and Pintupi women are perceived as "harmless." On the basis of cross-cultural data on female aggression from 137 societies, Burbank (1987: 95) concludes that "female aggression involves little injury, even when it is physical."

Lorenz (1966) noted that restraints against injuring or killing conspecifics tend to be strongest and most consistent among social species and predatory animals that possess lethal weapons. "And so we find the strangely moving paradox that the most blood-thirsty predators, particularly the

Wolf, called by Dante the *bestia senza pace*, are among the animals with the most reliable killing inhibitions in the world" (Lorenz, 1966: 124).

Applying Lorenz's observation *within* the human species, the well documented differences between men and women regarding the frequency and severity of physical aggression including the potential to commit homicide, apparent across numerous cultural contexts, leads to a theoretical proposition: Natural selection has led to the evolution of greater *restraint* among human males regarding physical aggression because they have the capacity to more readily inflict serious injury and death than do human females. The same paradox noted by Lorenz (1966) is also evident in this proposition: Men are more dangerous and therefore practice more restrained patterns of fighting than do women. When men fight with restraint, in parallel to ritualized patterns of competition that have evolved in many other species, the risks of serious injury or death are reduced compared to "no holds barred" fighting.

Although the ethnographic data related to sex differences in restraint during intraspecific fighting are sporadic, men are rarely noted to employ their teeth and nails against their opponents whereas women are regularly reported to use biting and scratching when fighting. Based on a cross-cultural study of female aggression using the Human Relations Area Files, Burbank (1987: 88) reports that "a great part of female fighting consists of such actions as hair pulling, scratching, wrestling, kicking, biting, and hitting or punching with the bare hands."

Fry and Fry (2010) found that for 21 nomadic forager societies that constitute a subsample of the worldwide Standard Cross-Cultural Sample (SCCS), information regarding female physical aggression was available for ten societies. Co-wives and female rivals were frequent recipients of female physical aggression in these societies. Osgood (1958: 215-216) recounts for the Ingalik: "The husband goes to his girl friend's house but his wife is right behind him. She says to the girl, 'Why did you take my husband? I know you have been fooling around with him for a long time,' and she starts to kick the girl and tear off all her clothes." Osgood (1958: 219) describes how Ingalik women "call each other names and may attack each other physically—pulling hair, scratching, tearing off clothes, and so on." Whiting (1950: 77) recounts how a Paiute wife delivered a beating to a woman who had fooled around with her husband: "Handfuls of hair lay around on the ground when they got through."

The most common motive for female attacks was jealousy. Women were described as biting, scratching, hair-pulling, slapping, hitting, kicking, pushing, beating with sticks, and in one case shooting their victims (Fry and Fry, 2010). For instance, Aranda women fight with clubs and digging sticks, smashing each other on the head. Compared to Yahgan men, "women, after a brief battle of words, flare up more quickly, seize each other more brutally, bite some part of the body, strike with their fists against mouth and nose and scuffle while pulling very painfully and convulsively on a thick bunch of hair" (Gusinde, 1937: 889). Osgood (1958: 207) reports his Ingalik informants' warning that "An infuriated woman is as dangerous as a lynx and she does not hesitate to use her teeth and nails on an aggressor."

In comparing male and female aggression in nomadic band societies, the first generalization is that male aggression is more likely to cause serious injury or death than is female aggression. However, in both sexes, a great deal of aggression does not involve serious injuries at all. When women use weapons, more often than not, they tend to be clubs or their readily available digging sticks that are used during food gathering. Men employ a greater variety of weapons: spears, bows and arrows, clubs, knives, and so forth. Not surprisingly, regarding homicide, men are usually the killers and also the victims.

Both men and women punch, kick, and wrestle. Interestingly, nomadic forager women use some types of physical aggression that are rarely, if ever, reported for the men (Fry and Fry, 2010). Nomadic forager women pull each others' hair when fighting, scratch with their fingernails, and bite, in addition to aggressive behaviors that are also used by males, such as hitting and beating.

A set of data on sex differences in physical aggression was collected at the University of Ballarat in Victoria, Australia, and when analyzed reveal intriguing parallels to the anthropological observations on female fighting behavior. A sample of university students consisting of 56 females and 28 males responded to three inventories dealing with physical aggression. The inventories measured physically aggressive behaviors such as punching, kicking, biting, and slapping. The first inventory measured a respondent's likelihood of engaging in certain aggressive actions under conditions of anger and conflict with another person. The second and third inventories shifted the referents, first, to how a respondent thought a member of their own sex and, second, a member of the opposite sex, would usually react during anger or conflict.

Data from the three inventories were subjected to separate factor analyses using a generalized least squares method with orthogonal varimax rotation. For the three data sets, the total amount of variance explained by the factor solution were 53.83 percent for the self-assessment inventory and 62.95 and 61.03 percent for the same-sex and opposite-sex inventories, respectively. All three sets of inventory data yielded two-factor solutions.

Table 1. Results for factor analyses on three inventories on physical aggression.

Behavior	Self-Assessment Factor 1	Factor 2	View of Own Sex Factor 1	Factor 2	View of Opposite Sex Factor 1	Factor 2
Pull Hair	.72		.89		.94	
Scratch	.66		.73		.75	
Slap	.57		.59		.68	
Bite	.61		.78		.66	
Punch		.85		.81		.92
Wrestle		.78		.93		.69
Push		.74		.76		.87
Kick		.52		.48		.53
α =	.72	.84	.81	.85	.84	.85

As shown in Table 1, one factor for each data set corresponds with behaviors that are recurrently reported across ethnographies from different parts of the world as female aggression. The second factor includes behaviors regularly reported during male physical aggression and also sometimes during female aggression as well. We could consider Factor 1 as consisting of distinctively female elements of physical aggression and Factor 2 as typically male behaviors, while keeping in mind, based on ethnographic accounts, that women also engage in the male pattern (but that males rarely engage in the female pattern).

Interestingly, all three inventories, whether oriented toward a respondent's own behavior or toward what they view as the usual behavior of the sexes, yielded the same type of two-factor solutions. Across all three inventories, Factor 1 consists of pulling hair, scratching, slapping, and biting. We label this factor as Distinctively Female Physical Aggression, because men are rarely described as engaging in these behaviors while fighting. Factor 2 emerged from all three data sets consisting of punching, wrestling, pushing, and kicking. We label Factor 2 as Typically Male Physical Aggression, while acknowledging that women also engage in such behaviors. With the exception of only one item, *kick* as assessed in the own-sex inventory, none of the items have ambiguous factor loadings.

Analysis of variance results are presented in Table 2. Significant sex differences were found for all the comparisons with the exception of the Distinctly Female factor on the own sex inventory, where only a moderate trend is observed. The general pattern across the three inventories is that both male and female respondents tend to rate women higher for Distinctly Female Physical Aggression items and tend to score men higher for Typically Male Physical Aggression items. Thus the ethnographic and survey inventory data are in correspondence with each other. Some types of physically aggressive behaviors such as hair pulling and scratching are distinctively female.

Table 2. Male and Female Self-Assessments and Ratings Compared.

Inventory Type and Kinds of Aggression	Male Respondents		Female Respondents		df	F
	Mean	SE	Mean	SE		
Self Assessment						
Typically Male Items	7.45	.52	5.91	.35	1,81	6.13*
Distinctively Female Items	4.32	.27	4.99	.18	1, 81	4.15*
Ratings of Own Sex						
Typically Male Items	10.61	.44	7.04	.31	1, 84	44.40***
Distinctively Female Items	5.66	.40	6.53	.28	1, 84	3.18^
Ratings of Opposite Sex						
Typically Male Items	9.17	.53	13.32	.37	1, 84	41.52***
Distinctively Female Items	10.66	7.85	7.85	.38	1, 84	18.62***

^ $< .08$
* $< .05$
*** $< .001$

Selection Pressures Favoring Nonkilling in Humans

We suggest that three types of natural selection pressures have favored nonkilling over killing in human intraspecific aggression. Two of these also would apply to animal species, generally speaking, but the third can be considered uniquely human.

First, it is clear that natural selection tends not to favor lethal fighting among members of the same species (Alcock, 2005; Hinde, 1974: 268; Kokko, 2008; Maynard Smith and Price, 1973; Maynard Smith, 1974; Roscoe 2007). We have already considered that among various species, nonkilling is the rule, not the exception, during intraspecific aggression. A variety of mechanisms have evolved to reduce the chance of death during intraspecific competition, including use of displays, ritualized fighting, respect for submission signals, dominance hierarchies, avoidance, and so forth. It seems highly likely that evolutionary selection pressures have also favored restraint and other such mechanisms in humans. One line of support for this point of view is to note how human males, like their animal counterparts, make regular use of display and tournament contests in place of escalated interpersonal aggression. Gusinde (1937: 887) provides one example of restraint for the Yahgan of South America: "A person will literally foam with rage....Nevertheless, he can muster astonishing self-control when he realizes that he is too weak to stand against his opponent." Tonkinson's (1978: 124) observation pertaining to the Mardu of Australia also illustrates a system of restraint: "When men fight each other, the unstated aim...is to allow maximum opportunity for the dispute to be aired *verbally*. This takes place in an atmosphere of great public drama and menace, so that honor is seen to be satisfied, but with a minimum of physical violence." Restraint saves lives.

A second selection pressure that would favor nonkilling involves the concept of inclusive fitness. As a general evolutionary principle, Hamilton (1964, 1971) proposed that the degree of genetic relatedness between individuals affects how they interact. Hamilton (1964: 19) reasoned that "the social behaviour of a species evolves in such a way that in each behaviour-evoking situation the individual will seem to value his neighbours' fitness against his own according to the coefficients of relationship appropriate to that situation." On the one hand, helping relatives serves to enhance one's own fitness since relatives have alleles in common. On the other hand, serious aggression should be minimized among close genetic relatives for exactly the same reason. Hamilton was not implying that individuals consciously calculate the degree to which they are related before behaving altruistically or aggressively, but rather that natural selection performs this analysis over evolutionary time. Behavioral adaptations are thus designed through these selective processes. It can be hypothesized that in social-living species such as humans and their ancestors, most of the persons with whom a person regularly interacts would be related to some degree. When an individual protects and cares for close relatives, thereby increasing their chances to survive and reproduce, the actor enhances simultaneously his or her own inclusive fitness due to the fact that kin have multiple alleles in common. Killing and injuring relatives has the opposite effects on inclusive fitness and should be selected against. As the Gilyak believe, brothers should not fight brothers (Shternberg, 1999: 63).

We hypothesize the action of another powerful selection force that has favored nonkilling in humans. This third selection pressure involves the uniquely human tendency, which is noted in many forager band societies as well as in some other types of societies, for the close family members of a homicide victim to avenge the death of their relative by killing the killer. We find no such cases of revenge homicide among other animals. This means that killers in nomadic forager society often sign their own death warrant by committing a homicide, and given that the nomadic band social organization is the social type under which humans evolved, the fitness ramifications favoring nonkilling may be significant. In other words, the tendency for family members to avenge killings may constitute a powerful supplementary evolutionary selective force against intraspecific killing in humans in addition to the two previously discussed factors.

Recall that revenge was found to be the most common motive for committing homicide among the sample of 21 nomadic forager societies in the SCCS (Fry in press). Westermarck (1924) noted that humans have a psychological tendency to pay back an act of kindness with a corresponding good deed and also to repay abuse received with a matching punishment. Revenge homicide is but one manifestation of this reciprocity principle (Fry, 2006). When someone is killed in a nomadic band society, usually a male, the recurring pattern is for the family of the victim to attempt to kill the killer, motivated by feelings of revenge. If the victim's family succeeds, this payback killing typically ends the matter in nomadic band societies because the two killings cancel each other (Fry, 2006: 230).

This reciprocity principle is illustrated by the Micmac belief that "If thou killest, thou shalt be killed" (Le Clercq, 1910: 286), as well as in the observation for the Chukchee of Siberia that "a murder rarely remains unavenged" (Bogoras, 1975: 663). Similarly, the Montagnais-Naskapi of Canada's Labrador Peninsula believed that the appropriate payback for murder was the execution of the killer by a close male relative of the victim (Lips, 1947: 470). Among the Yukaghir of Siberia, traditionally the brother or another close relative of a murder victim could exact revenge. Jochelson (1926: 132) points out that "He does not kill directly, but requires from the murderer an explanation of his act, not infrequently letting him off with a ransom."

Among the Ingalik, revenge for a killing may be exacted by the victim's father, son, brother, grandfather, grandson, or uncle, but not by more distant relatives. Once, in the heat of passion, a friend of a murdered man stabbed his friend's killer. His friend had had no living relatives to avenge his death. Osgood (1958: 54) recounts how a couple of days after the killing of the murderer, the new victim's uncle, brother, and father arrived at the avenger's door and said: "You had no business to kill that boy."

"I know that," he answered, "but he talked to me without politeness and having already killed my friend, it made me mad and I killed him. You would do the same in the circumstances."

The words struck a chord with the relatives. "After considering the character of the one who had just been killed, they concluded that perhaps it was better he was dead" (1958: 54) In this case, there was no further killing.

It is also most relevant to note that one sure fire way to get killed in nomadic band society is to become a repeat offender, either by establishing a reputation as a trouble-maker or by committing a couple of murders (Boehm, 1999; Fry, 2006). The execution of overly violent men and bullies is a theme in ethnographic accounts. Damas (1991: 78), writing about the Copper Inuit, explains that "Certain men were feared for their aggressiveness or violent tendencies, but they almost invariably met with violent ends themselves." Hoebel (1967: 88) explains the typical fate of a recidivist killer:

> As a general menace, he becomes a public enemy. As a public enemy, he becomes the object of public action. The action is legal execution: a privilege-right of the executioner. The single murder is a private wrong redressed by the kinsmen of the victim. Repeated murder becomes a public crime punishable by death at the hands of an agent of the community.

Hoebel's interesting observation is that a recidivist killer is targeted for execution not only due to a desire for revenge on the part of his victims' families but more generally by the community due to his status as a public enemy. Lee's (1979: 394) description of how a Ju/'hoansi group jointly executed a recidivist killer illustrates Hoebel's point. "He had killed two people already, and on the day he died he stabbed a woman and killed a man. …No one came to his aid because all those people had decided he had to die. …They all fired on him with poison arrows till he looked like a porcupine." In a similar case, a Ju/'hoansi man called Gau had killed three people and was looked upon as a "lion" who "ate people" (Lee, 1979: 393). One night as he slept, Gau was stabbed in his chest. Based on a thorough survey of nomadic forager ethnographies, Boehm (1999: 82, italics added) concludes that "reports of execution of individuals who behave too aggressively are available for Eskimos, North American Indians, Australian Aborigines, and African foragers. …My suspicion is that the *pattern* may be generalized to nomadic foragers in general."

This observable pattern across widely-separated forager societies reflects Westermarck's (1924) second type of reciprocity, which stems not from gratitude felt for good deeds but from resentment felt for bad deeds. In band society, bullies, overly aggressive persons, serious trouble-makers, and especially recidivist killers, because they endanger everyone, sooner or later receive their just desserts in accordance with this reciprocity principle. In other words, the community overall views the killings of overly aggressive or recidivist offenders to be morally justified. For these various reasons, it is not surprising that restraint in the use of aggression, which is apparent in much animal aggression, also is a theme in various nomadic hunter-gatherer contexts. Exercising restraint regarding aggressive encounters may well be the outcome of strong selective forces operating over evolutionary time (Fry, 2006; 2007).

Conclusions

Regarding physical aggression, there are two human natures: female and male. In some contexts, females make greater use of noncontact indirect forms of aggression than do males (Archer, 2009; Björkqvist, 1994; Björkqvist, Österman and Kaukiainen, 1992; Lagerspetz, Björkqvist and Peltonen, 1988). On the other hand, females are less often physically aggressive than men, and, group-for-group, women cause less severe injuries than men. As we have seen, the cross-cultural evidence pertaining to homicide supports these conclusions. So, women are even more inclined toward nonkilling than men. Women are less dangerous.

This does not mean that women never engage in physical aggression. They obviously do (Burbank, 1987). One implication of the observation that female nature is less violent than male nature is that, paradoxically, selection may have favored more ritualized, rule-based, restrained physical aggression among men than among women. Women are described as fighting furiously, yanking hair from each other's scalps, scratching with their nails, and biting their opponents on the face and elsewhere. Of course some male fights escalate, but at the same time, much male-male competition takes more restrained paths. Ethnographic descriptions portray men as following the rules of limited engagement, in other words, as they wrestle, grapple, punch, or hit.

It is documented that boys have a tendency to rough-and-tumble play fight more than girls (Fry, 1987, 1990, 2005). One lesson learned during play fighting is the use of restraint (Bernstein, 2007, 2008; Fry, 2005; Korpela and Sandnabba, 1994; Pennisi, 2000). Bernstein (2008: 60) points out that "monkeys reared in social isolation seem to lack the social skills required to assess the willingness of a rival to engage in escalated aggression, the ability of the rival to inflict aggressive costs, and even the meaning of signals that a rival uses when conceding access to a contested resource." The lessons learned during play fighting in youth about assessing opponents, fighting with restraint, and reading signals about escalation or capitulation may have had more survival value for males than for females over the evolutionary history of our species (Fry, 1987, 1990, 2005).

Even though human males commit more homicides than do human females, killing is not the norm. A comparison of physical aggression across species including humans suggests that selection pressures rarely favor intraspecific killing (Hamilton, 1964, 1971; Maynard Smith and Price, 1973; Maynard Smith, 1974). A consideration of homicide among nomadic forager societies suggests that an additional selective force may have operated to favor nonkilling in humans: Killers tend to be targeted for execution by the families of their victims. Whereas violence appears to come more easily to male nature than to female nature, we suggest that human males also have been selected for nonkilling. In any case, the existence of peaceful societies demonstrates that humans, both female and male, can construct social worlds that are virtually free of lethal violence.

Acknowledgment

Some of the data reported in this chapter were collected during research funded by the National Science Foundation (Grant number 03-13670 to D. Fry), whose financial support is gratefully acknowledged.

References

Adams, David B. (1983). "Why there are so few women warriors," *Behavior Science Research*, 18:196-212.

Alcock, John (2005). *Animal Behavior: An Evolutionary Approach*, eighth edition. Sunderland: Sinauer.

Archer, John (1988). *The Behavioural Biology of Aggression*. Cambridge: Cambridge University Press.

Archer, John (2009). "Does sexual selection explain human sex differences in aggression?" *Behavioral and Brain Sciences*, 32:249-266.

Archer, John; Huntingford, Felicity (1994). "Game theory models and escalation of animal fighting," in Potegal, M.; Knutson, J., Eds., *The Dynamics of Aggression: Biological and Social Processes in Dyads and Groups*. Hillsdale: Lawrence Erlbaum, pp. 3-31.

Balikci, Asen (1970). *The Netsilik Eskimo*. Garden City: The Natural History Press.

Bernstein, Irwin (2007). "Social mechanisms in the control of primate aggression," in Campbell, C.; Fuentes, A.; MacKinnon, K.; Panger, M.; Bearder, S., Eds., *Primates in Perspective*. New York: Oxford University Press, pp. 562-571.

Bernstein, Irwin (2008). "Animal behavioral studies: Primates," in Kurtz, L., Ed., *Encyclopedia of Violence, Peace, and Conflict, Vol. I*, second edition. New York: Elsevier/Academic Press, pp. 56-63.

Björkqvist, Kaj (1994). "Sex differences in physical, verbal, and indirect aggression: A review of recent research," *Sex Roles*, 30:177-188.

Björkqvist, Kaj; Österman, Karin; Kaukiainen, Ari (1992). "The development of direct and indirect aggressive strategies in males and females," in Björkqvist, K.; Neimelä, P., Eds., *Of Mice and Women: Aspects of Female Aggression*. Orlando: Academic Press, pp. 51-64.

Björkqvist, Kaj; Österman, Karin; Lagerspetz, Kirsti (1994). "Sex differences in covert aggression among adults," *Aggressive Behavior*, 20:27-33.

Blanchard, D. Caroline; Blanchard, Robert J. (1989). "Experimental animal models of aggression: What do they say about human behaviour?" in Archer, J.; Browne, K., Eds., *Human Aggression: Naturalistic Approaches*. London: Routledge, pp. 94-121.

Boehm, Christopher (1999). *Hierarchy in the Forest: The Evolution of Egalitarian Behavior*. Cambridge: Harvard University Press.

Bogoras, Waldemar (1975). *The Chukchee*. (Reprint Series: Memoirs of the American Museum of Natural History, volume 7). New York: American Museum of Natural History Press.

Bonta, Bruce D. (1993). *Peaceful Peoples: An Annotated Bibliography*. Metuchen: Scarecrow Press.

Bonta, Bruce D. (1996). "Conflict resolution among peaceful societies: The culture of peacefulness," *Journal of Peace Research*, 33:403-420.

Bonta, Bruce D. (1997). "Cooperation and competition in peaceful societies," *Psychological Bulletin*, 121:299-320.

Bonta, Bruce D.; Fry, Douglas P. (2006). "Lessons for the rest of us: Learning from peaceful societies," in Fitzduff, M.; Stout, C., Eds., *The Psychology of Resolving Global Conflicts: From War to Peace, Volume 1: Nature vs. Nurture*, Westport: Praeger, pp. 175-210.

Brown, Donald E. (1991). *Human Universals*. New York: McGraw-Hill.

Burbank, Victoria K. (1987). "Female aggression in cross-cultural perspective," *Behavior Science Research*, 21:70-100.

Burbank, Victoria K. (1994). *Fighting Women: Anger and Aggression in Aboriginal Australia*. Berkeley: University of California Press.

Campbell, Anne (1999). "Staying alive: Evolution, culture and women's intra-sexual aggression," *Behavioral and Brain Sciences*, 22: 203-252.

Daly, Martin; Wilson, Margo (1988). *Homicide*. New York: Aldine de Gruyter.

Damas, David (1991). "Copper Eskimo," in Levinson, D., Ed., *Encyclopedia of World Cultures, Volume 1, North America*. Boston: G.K. Hall, pp. 76-79.

Darwin, Charles (1998 [1871]). *The Descent of Man*. New York: Prometheus Books.

De Waal, Frans (1989). *Peacemaking among Primates*. Cambridge: Harvard University Press.

Du Bois, Cora (1960). *The People of Alor: A Social-Psychological Study of an East Indian Island*. New York: Harper and Brothers.

Eckert, Penelope; Newmark, Russell (1980). "Central Eskimo song duels: A contextual analysis of ritual ambiguity," *Ethnology*, 19:191-211.

Eibl-Eibesfeldt, Irenäus (1961). "The fighting behavior of animals," *Scientific American*, 205:112-122.

Fry, Douglas P. (1987). "Differences between playfighting and serious fighting among Zapotec children," *Ethology and Sociobiology*, 7:285-306.

Fry, Douglas P. (1990). "Play aggression among Zapotec children: Implications for the practice hypothesis," *Aggressive Behavior*, 16:321-340.

Fry, Douglas P. (1992). "Female aggression among the Zapotec of Oaxaca, Mexico," in Björkqvist, K.; Niemalä, P., Eds., *Of Mice and Women: Aspects of Female Aggression*. Orlando: Academic Press, pp. 187-199.

Fry, Douglas P. (2005). "Rough-and-tumble social play in children," in Pellegrini, A.; Smith, P. K., Eds., *The Nature of Play: Great Apes and Humans*. New York: Guilford.

Fry, Douglas P. (2006). *The Human Potential for Peace: An Anthropological Challenge to Assumptions about War and Violence*. New York: Oxford University Press.

Fry, Douglas P. (2007). *Beyond War: The Human Potential for Peace*. New York: Oxford University Press.

Fry, Douglas P. (in press). "Human nature: The nomadic forager model," in Sussman, R.; Cloninger, R., Eds., *Sociality, Altruism, and Well-Being*. New York: Springer.

Fry, Nina Ekholm; Fry, Douglas P. (2010). "Aggression and conflict resolution among females in nomadic band societies," in K. Österman (ed.) *Research in Aggression and Conflict Resolution*. New York: Peter Lang, pp. 345-355.

Gardner, Peter (2004). "Respect for all: The Paliyans of South India," in Kemp, G.; Fry, D., Eds., *Keeping the Peace: Conflict Resolution and Peaceful Societies around the World*. New York: Routledge, pp. 53-71.

Gregor, Thomas; Robarchek, Clayton A. (1996). "Two paths to peace: Semai and Mehinaku nonviolence," in Gregor, T., Ed., *A Natural History of Peace*. Nashville: Vanderbilt University Press, pp. 159-188.

Gusinde, Martin (1931). *The Fireland Indians, Volume 1: The Selk'nam, on the Life and Thought of a Hunting People of the Great Island of Tierra del Fuego*. In the electronic Human Relations Area Files, Ona, Doc. 1. New Haven: HRAF, 1996.

Gusinde, Martin (1937). *The Yahgan: The Life and Thought of the Water Nomads of Cape Horn*, translated by Frieda Schütze. In the electronic Human Relations Area Files, Yahgan, Doc. 1. New Haven: HRAF, 2003.

Hallowell, A. Irving (1974). "Aggression in Saulteaux society," in Hallowell, A. I., Ed., *Culture and Experience*. Philadelphia: University of Pennsylvania Press, pp. 277-290.

Hamilton, William D. (1964) "The genetical evolution of social behaviour, II." *Journal of Theoretical Biology*, 7:17-52.

Hamilton, William D. (1971). "Selection of selfish and altruistic behavior in some extreme models," in Eisenberg, J. F.; Dillon, W. S., Eds., *Man and Beast: Comparative Social Behavior*. Washington: Smithsonian Press.

Helm, June (1956). "Leadership among the Northeastern Athabascans," *Anthropologica*, 2:131-163.

Hilger, M. Inez (1971). *Together with the Ainu*. Norman: University of Oklahoma Press.

Hinde, Robert A. (1974). *Biological Bases of Human Social Behaviour*. New York: McGraw-Hill.

Hines, Nicole J.; Fry, Douglas P. (1994). "Indirect modes of aggression among women of Buenos Aires, Argentina," *Sex Roles*, 30:213-236.

Hoebel, E. Adamson (1967). *The Law of Primitive Man: A Study in Comparative Legal Dynamics*. Cambridge: Harvard University Press.

Holmberg, Allan (1969 [1950]). *Nomads of the Long Bow: The Siriono of Eastern Bolivia.* New York: American Museum of Natural History.

Howell, Signe and Willis, Roy (1989). *Societies at Peace: Anthropological Perspectives.* London: Routledge.

Jochelson, Waldemar (1926). *The Yukaghir and the Yukaghirized Tungus* (The Jesup North Pacific Expedition Memoir of the American Museum of Natural History, Volume IX). New York: G. E. Stechert.

Kemp, Graham; Fry, Douglas P., Eds. (2004). *Keeping the Peace: Conflict Resolution and Peaceful Societies around the World.* New York: Routledge.

Kokko, Hanna (2008). "Animal behavioral studies: Non-primates," in Kurtz, L., Ed., *Encyclopedia of Violence, Peace, and Conflict, Vol. 1*, second edition. New York: Elsevier/Academic Press, pp. 47-56.

Korpela, Sirpa; Sandnabba, Kenneth (1994). "Gender-specific social experiences and the development of aggressive and sexual behavior in male mice," *Aggressive Behavior*, 20:123-134.

Kuschel, Rolf (1992). "'Women are women and men are men': How Bellonese women get even," in Björkqvist, K.; Niemalä, P., Eds., *Of Mice and Women: Aspects of Female Aggression.* Orlando: Academic Press, pp. 173-185.

Lagerspetz, Kirsti; Björkqvist, Kaj; Peltonen, T. (1988). "Is indirect aggression typical of females? Gender differences in 11- to 12-year old children," *Aggressive Behavior*, 14:403-414.

Le Boeuf, B. J. (1971). "The aggression of the breeding bulls," *Natural History*, 80:83-94.

Le Clercq, Chrétien (1910). "New Relation of Gaspesia," in Ganong, W. F., Ed., *Publications of the Champlain Society, Volume 5.* Toronto: Champlain Society, pp. 1-452.

Lee, Richard B. (1979). *The !Kung San: Men, Women, and Work in a Foraging Community.* Cambridge: Cambridge University Press.

Lips, Julian (1947). *Naskapi Law.* Philadelphia: American Philosophical Society.

Lorenz, Konrad (1966). *On Aggression.* New York: Bantam.

Maccoby, Eleanor; Jacklin, C. (1974). *The Psychology of Sex Differences.* Stanford: Stanford University Press.

Maynard Smith, John (1974). "The theory of games and the evolution of animal conflicts," *Journal of Theoretical Biology*, 47:209-221.

Maynard Smith, John; Price, G. R. (1973). "The logic of animal conflict." *Nature*, 246:15-18.

Montagu, Ashley, Ed. (1978). *Learning Non-Aggression: The Experience of Non-Literate Societies.* Oxford: Oxford University Press.

Murphy, Robert F.; Quain, Buell (1955). *The Trumai Indians of Central Brazil.* Seattle: University of Washington Press.

Myers, Fred R. (1986). *Pintupi Country, Pintupi Self: Sentiment, Place, and Politics among Western Desert Aborigines.* Berkeley: University of California Press.

Oliver, Douglas (1949). "Studies in the Anthropology of Bougainville," *Papers of the Peabody Museum of Archaeology and Ethnology, Harvard University* 29(4):1-97.

Osgood, Cornelius (1958) "Ingalik social culture." *Yale University Publications in Anthropology* 53:1-289.

Pennisi, Elizabeth (2000). "The snarls and sneers that keep violence at bay," *Science*, 289:576-577.

Preuschoft, Signe; Schaik, Carel P. van (2000). "Dominance and communication: Conflict management in various social settings," in Aureli, F.; Waal, F. de, Eds., *Natural Conflict Resolution*. Berkeley: University of California Press, pp. 77-105.

Riechert, Susan E. (1998) "Game theory and animal contests," in Dugatkin, L.; Reeve, H., Eds., *Game Theory and Animal Behavior*. New York: Oxford University Press, pp. 64-93.

Roscoe, Paul (2007). "Intelligence, coalitional killing, and the antecedents of war," *American Anthropologist*, 109:485-495

Schaller, George (1972). *The Serengeti Lion*. Chicago: University of Chicago Press.

Schapera, Isaac (1930). *The Khoisan Peoples of South Africa*. London: Routledge.

Schober, Gary; Björkqvist, Kaj; Somppi, Sari (2009). "Identifying a new subcategory of aggression: Sex differences in direct non-verbal aggression," *Journal of Aggression, Conflict, and Peace Research*, 1:58-70.

Service, Elman R. (1966). *The Hunters*. Englewood Cliffs, NJ: Prentice-Hall.

Shternberg, Lev I. (1999). *The Social Organization of the Gilyak* (Anthropological Papers of the American Museum of Natural History, 82). Seattle: University of Washington Press.

Sluys, Cornelia M. I. van der (1999). "Jahai," in Lee, R.; Daly, R., Eds., *The Cambridge Encyclopedia of Hunters and Gatherers*. Cambridge: Cambridge University Press, pp. 307-311.

Sponsel, Leslie E.; Gregor, Thomas, Eds. (1994). *The Anthropology of Peace and Nonviolence*. Boulder: Lynne Rienner.

Symons, Donald (1979). *The Evolution of Human Sexuality*. New York: Oxford University Press.

Taylor, William B. (1979). *Drinking, Homicide, and Rebellion in Colonial Mexican Villages*. Stanford: Stanford University Press.

Tonkinson, Robert (1978). *The Mardudjara Aborigines: Living the Dream in Australia's Desert*. New York: Holt, Rinehart, and Winston.

Tonkinson, Robert (2004). "Resolving conflict within the law: The Mardu Aborigines of Australia," in Kemp, G.; Fry, D. P., Eds., *Keeping the Peace: Conflict Resolution and Peaceful Societies around the World*. New York: Routledge, pp. 89-104

Trivers, Robert L. (1972). "Parental investment and sexual selection," in Campbell, B., Ed., *Sexual Selection and the Descent of Man, 1871-1971*. Chicago: Aldine, pp. 136-179.

United States Department of Justice (2008). "Arrests by Sex, 2007," Available at (accessed May 5, 2010): <http://www.fbi.gov/ucr/cius2007/data/table_42.html>.

United States Department of Justice (2009). "Murder Offenders by Age, Sex, and Race, 2008," Available at (accessed May 3, 2010): <http://www.fbi.gov/ucr/cius2008/offenses/expanded_information/data/shrtable_03.html>.

Van Schaik, Carel P; Aureli, Filippo (2000). "The natural history of valuable relationships in primates," in Aureli, F.; Waal, F.B.M. de, Eds., *Natural Conflict Resolution*. Berkeley: University of California Press, pp. 307-333.

Westermarck, Edward (1924). *The Origin and Development of the Moral Ideas*, in two volumes, second edition. London: Macmillan.

Whiting, Beatrice (1950). "Paiute sorcery," *Viking Fund Publications in Anthropology*, 15:1-110.

Wilson, Edward O. (1975). *Sociobiology: The New Synthesis*. Cambridge: Harvard University Press.

Chapter Four

Nonkilling Social Arrangements

Robert Knox Dentan
University of Buffalo

...violence and nonviolence are only human potentials... (Nanda, 1988: 422)

...the question for both politics and economy... was of tendencies, rather than of constitutions; ...before all else, it was for us to find out whither we are going, not to dogmatise... (Proudhon, 1989 [1851]: 77)

This essay argues that humans naturally form a particular social arrangement that tends to inhibit homicide. While they construct other social forms as well, their tendency in moments of stress or when those other forms collapse is revert to this primordial form. The social formation in question consists of egalitarian mutual-aid groups, functionally although often not consciously or ideologically focused on raising children to become childbearing adults. These groups are small, usually less than sixty people, so that members interact on a face-to-face basis with each other more often than they interact with outsiders. (Small group theorists call such social formations "primary groups"). These "primary groups" are local because, although intellection is useful in adapting to novel situations, thinking takes time and energy. It is more efficient to deal with a familiar environment more or less by rote, so that habit can take the place of reflexes among less cerebral species. The benefits of "familiarity" in this sense extend to people, the kinsmen and neighbors who make up local primary groups, so that these people practice what Kropotkin (2006 [1902]) calls "mutual aid." The relative comfort this familiarity and the associated mutual aid produces is, along with child-rearing, the glue that keeps small egalitarian groups together (Dentan, in press; Macdonald, 2009a; in press, a; in press, b). This paper attempts to demonstrate that 1) unlike most other social formations, such groups occur spontaneously at every level of human biological and social evolution and 2) that, since nonkilling ideology is a cultural universal, whatever the practice of a particular society, the only hope of nonkilling practice must lie in conditions that favor the spontaneous formation of such groups. In "modern" societies, those conditions are normally personal or societal disasters.

I open with a brief overview of human evolution, primarily informed by the work of Owen Lovejoy (e.g., 2009). The second section deals with the acephalous egalitarian groups that foragers and some swiddeners seem to form spontaneously; here my references are mostly to Semai, with whom I lived for a half dozen years, and other Southeast Asian peoples. The magisterial overviews of Douglas Fry (2006) and Charles Macdonald (in press, a) inform this ethnographic investigation. The third section deals with acephalous egalitarian groups that create "autonomous zones," often temporary, within postNeolithic societies. Here I rely primarily on the work of Thomas Lechner, Michael Niman (e.g., 2010), Rebecca Solnit (2009) and my own experiences in Alcoholics Anonymous. The conclusion of this section concerns communities that form during disasters. A final section deals with the possible implications of this assemblage of facts.

Essentialized "human nature" is not a useful concept, since it presupposes fixity in an area where flexibility is the most salient characteristic. This caveat applies especially in the area of human behavior. There have always been humans who kill people, due to brain damage, etc., but most killers who are not under state control simply act impulsively and foolishly. The question is not whether people are "by nature" (non)violent but what conditions make people tend to behave (non)violently. So this chapter (like Fry, this volume) begins by examining what human tendencies tend to be more successful than others.

Human Tendencies

Introduction

Evolution is stochastic. Fitness is relative. A fit organism leaves more fertile offspring than its competitors, without using much more energy. Minimaxing (game theory) provides useful models for fitness: minimize expenditure of energy, maximize number of offspring that survive to reproduce (Barash, 2003). In this sense, students can talk about "reproductive strategies." The language is unfortunately anthropomorphic: it implies not that organisms think about how to be fit, but that their anatomical and behavioral tendencies are more conducive to fitness than the tendencies of their competitors. Evolutionary success matches game theory models and thus looks like the product of conscious agency. It's hard, for example, to avoid anthropomorphizing "evolution" or "the environment" as if it "favored" or "selected" particular adaptations. Similarly, it is easy for people under the influence of the Enlightenmentto attribute adaptive human behavior to people's conscious rational choices, though in fact this sense of being rational is mostly illusory (e.g.,

Lemert, 2007: 3-16). Indeed, anyone who has taken public transportation in a large city or lectured to a large class recognizes that even waking people in postEnlightenment societies spend much of their time in light trance, not only not rational, but not even fully conscious. Explaining adaptive behavior by reference to ideological factors like ethos or values buttresses the illusion of conscious rationality but is in many cases simply a rationalization that actually obfuscates what is going on in the nonideological world.

In most cases, moreover, adding ideological elements as independent variables into an explanation of adaptive behavior also violates the principle of parsimony (Ockham's Razor); i.e., of two explanations of the same set of facts, the one that deploys the fewer independent variables is the better. I've argued elsewhere (Dentan, in press) in detail that, starting with early hominids, you can deduce a model of human behavior that looks a lot like East Semai society in 1962. Since Semai history is extremely complex, that model leaves out a lot of important variables and idiosyncratic ideology, but models are not to replicate the complexity of reality but to simplify it so that we can understand what we need to understand without working as hard as we have to do when grappling with the chaos of daily life. All we need to know is some basics and the principles of deduction. For other purposes, you need to know other things.

Hominid beginnings

About 4.4 million years ago, the oldest well-documented human ancestor, *Ardipithecus ramidus,* seems to have manifested a set of traits salient in this argument. "Ardi" apparently was incompletely bipedal, i.e., quadrupedal in the trees but standing bipedally upright on the ground, like all more recent humans (White et al., 2009). Still, *Ardipithecus* did not walk well bipedally. The legs of australopithecines, who appeared two hundred thousand years after *Ardipithecus,* were still short for long distance walking, a fact which, as discussed below, may indicate an ecological adaptation that did not facilitate mankilling.

Analyzing bipedalism in "Lucy," a later species (*Australopithecus afarensis*) that flourished about 3.2 million years ago, Owen Lovejoy developed a theory that he now applies to "Ardi" (2009). The theory runs like this. Among most terrestrial primates, males use one of two strategies to gain sexual access to females. For brevity's sake, I'll call these "dominance" and "seduction." A dominant male is, like most males, much larger and more robust than females. He has large canines (fangs) with which to drive off less well-endowed (subordinate) males. A subordinate male, however, may court a female when the dominant male is away, often using food as a seductive tool. Some of my physical anthropological colleagues refer to such males as "sneakyfuckers." Genetic evidence suggests that the two tactics are about equally effective, creating a (very rough) analogy with balanced polymorphism.

Lovejoy suggests that erect posture developed from a shift in female reproductive strategy to one that favored seduction. A male with two hands free can bring more snacks home to the female object of his desires. The concomitant shrinkage of the canines to a stubby diamond shape—part of a general "feminization" of males that sharply reduces sexual dimorphism—suggests that the new male tactic of providing a "targeted female" and her offspring with gathered foods and thus gaining her sexual loyalty supplanted the old one of asserting dominance through fighting (Suwa et al., 2009). These changes

> occurred within the context of a generalized nonspecialized diet. Comparisons of the *Ar. ramidus* dentition with those of all other higher primates indicate that the species retained virtually no anatomical correlates of male to male conflict. Consistent with a diminished role of such agonism, the body size of males was only slightly larger than that of females (Lovejoy, 2009).

Paleoanthropologists speculate that estrus (being "in heat") disappeared during this period, a process called "reproductive crypsis."

> If the female knew when she was fertile, she could basically cheat the system by taking all the food offered by her milquetoast of a provider, then cuckold him with a dominant male when she was ovulating...The food-for-sex contract thus depends on what Lovejoy calls "the most unique human character"—ovulation that not only goes unannounced to the males of the group, but is concealed even from the female herself" (Shreve, 2009).

Erect posture, which exposed female genitalia, could keep males interested in females even out of estrus. Since the males could not tell when females were fertile, they needed continuous sexual access and "bonded" with particular females. The three novel behaviors—"(i) regular food-carrying, (ii) pair-bonding, and (iii) reproductive crypsis....substantially intensified male parental investment" (Lovejoy, 2009).

> ...the almost continuous sexual receptivity of women is necessary to maintain pair bonding. Pair-bonding, in turn, may be a way of avoiding competition among men....Monogamous bonds [strengthened by male provision of food] allowed mothers to stay home with their progeny and take care of more than one dependent offspring at a time, which ape mothers cannot do (de Waal, 1989: 280).

Perhaps, like the bonobos they resemble in other ways, ardipithecines also used sex as a way to keep the peace.

Male parental involvement was also necessary to assure that *Ardipithecus* young survived long enough to reproduce. By itself, making more babies isn't enough to assure evolutionary "success." That's why rape isn't a successful male reproductive strategy: you get offspring but can't assure their survival. Large primates in general practice a "K reproductive strategy" which focuses on filling up the relatively few slots left in an environment near its carrying capacity (K) for the species—as opposed to an "r" one, which entails maximizing the number of young (r is the symbol for "reproductive capacity," i.e., the maximum possible number of offspring if all survive). K-strategy invests the available energy in enhancing the survivability of a few offspring. For most animals, the heavy investment is physiological, so that individual young are "precocial," capable of surviving on their own relatively early in their individual development. In r-strategy, the same amount of energy is dispersed among a relatively large number of offspring, which therefore tend to be "altricial," less mature and less likely as individuals to survive. For Ardi the main investment seems to have been in nurturing relatively altricial offspring: pairbonding and male food-carrying enhanced the survival of the young. The energy available goes to nurture rather than to precocity.

Band living, found among baboons and hominines alike, facilitates subsistence and, as part of K-reproductive strategy, safeguarding vulnerable children (Hrdy, 2009). It also facilitates "alloparenting," so that band members, usually kin, can look after youngsters when parents are absent (Taylor, 2002). The sort of peacemaking common to terrestrial primates (de Waal, 1989), and particularly to humans' closest surviving relatives, the bonobos, presumably played a large role in *Ardipithecus* social life, so that conflicts would not disrupt these mutually beneficial arrangements (e.g., Cords and Killen, 1998: 195-196). The reduction of sexual disparities in size and the shrinkage of male canines suggest that fighting, and thus killing, provided little or no survival advantage. It would have been difficult and dangerous to kill an adult of roughly equal size and strength. Moreover, the loss of a potential alloparent and coforager would be costly. Paradoxically, the commonest victims of what killing may have occurred were probably children, then as today (Shichor and Tibbetts, 2002: 77-79; Office for Victims of Crime, 2002: 81-82).

The result seems to have been, on a basic, early level, a human disinclination to killing other humans with whom one is familiar, if only because the risks usually outweigh the benefits. This disinclination may have spread to making war, since computer simulation indicates that warring egalitarian groups are less likely to survive than nonkilling ones (Younger, 2004). This nonkilling tendency shows up later in *Homo sapiens* in a number of ways. "Combat stress" ("battle fatigue") causes at least a third as many casualties in modern warfare as physical wounds—and sometimes as many (U.S. Marine Corps, 1992 : 1.1). Moreover, during actual combat, most soldiers and law enforcement officers—up to 90%—will not fire their weapons unless they have had special desensitization training. This proportion, according to a text widely used by the armed forces, the DEA and the FBI (Grossman, 2009), seems to have held as far back as the Bronze Age. To make fighting bearable, most soldiers rely on "Dutch courage," alcohol or other drugs. The aftereffects may include death by suicide: about a fifth of all U.S. suicides are combat veterans, who make up only 7.5% of the population (*Time*, 2010: 14). Most people are not wired for violence or killing.

Hominine Beginnings

The knee and the modern-style gut bucket pelvis appeared around three and half a million years ago, facilitating modern-style bipedal walking over long distances. About half a million years later, grassland began to replace forests on the savannahs, forcing our ancestors to travel farther, under hotter conditions, to extract subsistence from an increasingly inhospitable environment. A new human species appeared, *Homo ergaster.* Walking and running long distances became increasingly important, especially for males. Loss of body hair and changes in sweat glands facilitated staying cool, while a pad of head hair shielded people from the sun. By 1.6 million years ago, people were gracile and longlegged, according to North African and Spanish petroglyphs, looking a lot like the thin long-legged Nilotes who inhabit the human heartland today and remain the world's best distance runners (Jablonski, 2010; Lieberman and Bramble, 2007). By then, running after large animals seems to have been an important component of hunting.

The change in pelvic shape, shrinking the birth canal, made bringing the increasingly large brained babies to term difficult. The main physiological adaptation seems to have been bearing the children at an earlier stage in their individual development. The resultant neoteny (fetalization) kept babies "altricial" (physically dependent on adults) longer, forcing an intensification of K-reproductive strategy and diminishing the mobility of women.

The harsher environment increased the importance of meat in the diet, increasing the accessibility of calories and also stimulating the development of tool-making. At first, people probably threw rocks at game and clubbed wounded animals to death. The dominant tool in archeological sites is the simple Olduwan hand ax, a water-polished cobble small enough to fit comfortably in one's hand, with 2-3 flakes knocked off to give it an edge. Give one to any adult human today, and the person will hold it properly. These tools allowed people to smash the larger bones that they collected as they drifted from foragers to hunters-and-gatherers.

In K-reproductive cost-benefit strategy females are more valuable than males, because the female role in reproduction takes about nine months and the male from a few seconds to a few minutes. Therefore, if circumstances require the death of adults to ensure the survival of offspring, young males not yet bonded with particular females make the most cost-effective sacrifice. An increasingly dry period and the resultant scarcity forced people to consider larger animals as desirable prey. The resultant increasing danger and difficulty of the hunt increased the role of young males. As prey size increased, people developed tools and skills that made killing the quarry—and other people—easier, especially for groups of young men (Bingham, 2000). The intensification of hunting large animals, often herd ruminants, was forcing males to travel farther and to coordinate their activities more than before.

These changes forced the first split in human social and intellectual organization, between those who followed the traditional foraging tendency, in which the contributions of men and women were roughly balanced, and those tending increasingly to stress big game hunting by young men (Dentan, 2008b; Otterbein, 2004: 10-15). As remarked in the first paragraph of this essay, familiarity facilitates cooperation, so that bands of hunters began to form recognized subgroups in the local communities. Sociologists call such groups FIGs, fraternal interest groups, localized groups of mutually related males. Csilla Dallos' (in press) study of the development of hierarchy among Lanoh Semang foragers demonstrates how the response of older men to the increased economic importance of younger ones leads to the development of patriarchy. Crossculturally, the relative salience of FIGs correlates positively with the incidence of violence and ultimately with killing, particularly after the development of tools (e.g., atlatls) that permitted killing large creatures at a distance (Bingham, 2000; Otterbein, 2004: 56-59).

The next section of this paper examines the two traditions, foraging/small scale shifting agriculture ("egalitarian anarchists" for short) and FIG-dominated big game hunting/pastoralist ("patriarchal democrats" for short). Because the main focus of the paper is on facilitating nonkilling, most of the discussion will be about the anarchs, whose relative nonviolence has generated an enormous literature (for compendia of crosscultural references to which, see Bonta, 1993; Dentan, 1992; 1994; Erchak, 1994; Fry,

2006; Howell and Willis, 1989; Kemp and Fry, 2004; Kropotkin 2006[1902]: 62-125; Lye, 2001; Prescott, 1975; Sponsel and Gregor, 1994).

Two Basic Patterns in Human Communal Life

> The disciplining force of society is at its most effective when its human origins are denied or covered up. The admission that society - with all its prescriptions and proscriptions, rewards for obedience and punishments for veering off the line—rests ultimately on man-made choices and decisions invites critical scrutiny, dissent and resistance: What has been done by humans can be undone by humans. No wonder that throughout the modern era, attempts were made and continue to be made to represent the grounds for the demands of power-holders as beyond human capacity. (Bauman, 2010)

> Warfare developed along two separate paths. The hunting of large game animals was crucial to…the first…. At the origin of the second path were foragers who did little hunting but depended largely on gathering for subsistence, became sedentary, and then domesticated plants. Intergroup aggression was absent among these early agriculturists… Of all the varieties of human societies, the least likely to engage in warfare are the hunting and gathering [=foraging] bands. (Otterbein, 2004:10, 81)

Introduction

The traditional subsistence-based breakdown of societies into hunter-gatherers, horticulturalists, pastoralists, agriculturalist and modern (industrial capitalist) undercuts the reliability of hologeistic studies generally and of studies of (non)violence specifically (Dentan, 2008b; Fry, 2006; Otterbein, 2004). This paper disaggregates societies often classified together as "hunter-gatherers," a category that includes, e.g., Plains Indians and Siberian reindeer-hunters with tropical rainforest Semang peoples and maritime Inuit. It lumps big game hunters with pastoralists (as "patricentric democrats") and foragers with egalitarian swiddeners (as "anarchic egalitarians") (cf. Otterbein, 2004). Otterbein's usage seems more useful in the "nonkilling" context than Fry's (2006) distinction between "simple" and "complex" foragers, because it explicitly involves a criterion, the presence or absence of male fraternal interest groups, which seems to be involved in making the patriarchal democrats significantly more violent than the anarchs.

The rise of big game hunting described in the first section of this chapter split human foraging bands into killing and nonkilling social formations. Otterbein (2010: 37) divides them into four kinds of nonkillers (foragers, big game hunting microbands, incipient tillers and symbiotics) and four kinds of killers (big game hunting macrobands, mounted hunters, Australians and settled fisherfolk). Australians and settled fisherfolk in Otterbein's construal are violent peoples and thus (except for the Onge discussed above [cf. Kelly, 2000]) beyond the scope of this already pythonic chapter.

Table 1. Anarchs and Democrats

EGALITARIAN ANARCHS	PATRIARCHAL DEMOCRATS
<u>Examples</u>	
Semang, East Semai, central Inuit	Aboriginal Siberians, Nilotes, Pashtun, Abrahamic peoples
<u>Economy</u>	
Foraging → simple swiddening immediate return	Big game hunting → pastoralism delayed return
Low population density	Increasing population density
Smaller settlements	Larger settlements
Sharing	Sharing and redistribution
<u>Social Ties</u>	
voluntary	→ involuntary (kin-based)
fluid	structured
Monogamous nuclear family	Fraternal interest group (FIG) → polygynous family > patrilineage →
Ambilocal residence	virilocal → patrilocal postmarital residence
Informal → bride service	bride service/bride capture → bridewealth
high infant indulgence	low overall infant indulgence
loose supervision of kids	tough corporal discipline of kids, esp. boys
Locality (neighbors) primary	Locality → patrilateral kinship → patrilineage primary
Hierarchies:	
Age	Age, rank
Gender equality→ nominal g.e.	Nominal gender equality→ patriarchy
Neutral *re* homosexuality	→ covert homophilia + overt homophobia
<u>Values</u>	
Individual autonomy	Freedom + loyalty to leader
Egalitarianism of outcome	Egalitarianism of opportunity
Killing usually scary & dumb	Killing rivals/enemies manifests manliness

Table 2. Intersticial Anarchs and State Capitalists

ENCLAVED ANARCHS	STATE CAPITALISTS
Examples	
AA, Rainbows, spontaneous disaster groups	American "mainstream" (c. 2000 AD)
TAZ	
church basements, state parks, disaster areas	Home, workplace, commuting, resorts
Economy	
Immediate return	Delayed return
Sharing	Selling, lending, renting
Social Ties	
Small homogeneous groups	Enormous diverse groups
Voluntary membership	Voluntary → involuntary
Personalism (fellowship)	Meritocracy
No standard treatment of kids	Strict physical discipline of poor kids,
Tendency toward indulgence	constant supervision of others
Hierarchies	
Experience ("age")	Class, wealth, guanxi, ethnicity, language, etc.
Gender equality	Decaying patriarchal bias
Neutral re homosexuality	Persistent but weakening homophobia
Assuring conformity	
Personal social pressure	Punishment
e.g., "omming"	e.g., death penalty, "Biblical chastisement"
Values	
Individual autonomy	Freedom + loyalty to boss or leader
Egalitarianism of outcome	Egalitarianism of opportunity

Nonkilling "egalitarian anarchies" in this chapter would include foragers, with egalitarian swiddeners and incipient tillers as later developments out of foraging. I will later discuss spontaneous voluntary groups that form in the interstices of the state, and thus resemble "symbiotes," foragers surrounded by farmers (Wrangham, 2010: 39). The more warlike "patriarchal democrats" would include big game hunting macrobands; mounted hunting and pastoralism would be later specializations of big game hunting.

This chapter takes no position on the question of whether modern foragers, swiddeners, big game hunters and pastoralists socially resemble or differ significantly from people who subsisted in the same way before the onset of agriculture. In fact, there is evidence—discussed later in this chapter—that at least some of the swiddener anarchs have participated in defensive warfare. The point is that, as of today or recently, patricentric democrats like Dakota, Pashtun or Sudanese Nilotes seem to have significantly less trouble killing people than anarchic egalitarians like Semai, "Semang," Palawan or Paliyan, according to recent or current observations. Killing people seems significantly less compatible with egalitarian anarch lifestyle and significantly more compatible with how patriarchal democrats organize their societies.

Table I contrasts the two lifestyles. Since big game hunting originally develops out of foraging, I want to re-emphasize that the contrast is between emphases and tendencies, not between absolutes. The arrows in Table I indicate developments that tend to occur within the categories as time goes on, and particularly as population density and local group size increase. For example, East Semai swiddeners seem about as unlikely to kill people as their foraging Semang neighbors. Of course, Semang have known how to swidden for centuries, and Semai continued to forage. Semang foraging is not random wandering but involves some planning and preparation ("delayed return") although not as much as swiddening. Indeed, there is a Semai epic poem (Dentan, 2006) about how becoming swiddeners changed people's conception of time; the poem could be titled "Delaying Returns." Paliyan foragers may oscillate in and out of the culture of their agricultural neighbors (Gardner, 1985). And both Semai and Semang are also agro-foresters (talk about delayed returns!) and dealers in forest products (Dallos, 2010; Dunn, 1975).

Therefore, I think that the difference between "immediate return" activities, like foraging, and "delayed return activities" like big game hunting, agroforestry and pastoralism may not shed much light on killing and nonkilling. After all, the most violent segment of industrial capitalist society, regardless of "culture," is the urban lumpenproletariat, whose life is as hand-to-mouth ("immediate return") as it gets (Banfield, 1970; Gilsenan, 1993). And the formation and deployment of armed forces is a good example of a "delayed return" strategy.

Autonomy among Anarchs

> ...the closest approximation to equality known to any
> human societies. (Woodburn, 1982: 17)

Perhaps the most salient feature of anarch life is individual autonomy (Dentan, 1979: 63-70; Gardner, 1991; Griffin and Griffin, 1997; Robarchek, 1989). This autonomy precludes long term commitments and thus maximizes flexibility in social groupings, so that access to territory is open to any people who hang around long enough, whatever their ethnic identity or linguistic affiliation. In interpersonal relationships it manifests itself in a way that one might characterize as "symmetric respect" (Gardner, 1966; Prescott, this volume) or restraint (Fry, this volume) though usually accompanied by enough joking or backbiting that no one gets to act uppity (e.g., Dentan, 2004: 180). The flexibility, coupled with low population density, minimizes conflicts and thus killing. You can just move away from

> obnoxious people... Egalitarianism emerges from autonomy rather than from an abstract notion of equality: all are equally free to stay or leave, to hunt or rest, within the limits of their abilities and needs (Rousseau, 2006: 48; cf. Woodburn, 1982: 431).

As a result, there is no authoritative locus for knowledge, which tends to be idiosyncratic and "memorate" (Gardner, 1966), i.e. based largely on personal experience (e.g., Dentan, 2006; Dunn, 1975; Gardner, 1976) and always subject to revision, usually by adding on new bits (Lye, 2008: 41; Dentan, 1979: 93-95). To outsiders, the ideology seems incoherent (Guenther, 1979). Still, the acquisition of memorate knowledge assures that older people will, normally, know more than young ones, simply by virtue of piling up experiences, so that people like Temiar and Semai will often "listen to" them, the term they use for "respect their opinions" (Hood, 1989).

Autonomy frees up all people over the age of 2-3 years from control by adults. For East Semai, *saingnyent paay,* "new children" too young to toddle or talk, are foci of attention. Adults cuddle and play with them. As Charles Macdonald (personal communication, 2010) reports from among Palawan people, adults treat children as toys.

East Semai extend the term *saingnyent* sometimes in a derogatory sense to nor *litaaw* and *mnaleeh* (adolescents up to the age of about 25—when, incidentally, neurologists currently assure us, the forebrain is finally "mature"); the slur stresses the youngsters' supposed immaturity, impulsivity, vanity and obsession with sex (Dentan, 2008a: 210-213; 224-226). Still, although Palawan adults sometimes awkwardly berate teenagers who show signs of sexual libertinism (Macdonald, 2010), East Semai adults let *litaaw* and *mnaleeh* do what they expect *litaaw* and *mnaleeh* to do, most notably engage in irresponsible and promiscuous sex (Dentan, 1989: 102-107), like Paliyans of the same age (Gardner, 2010). And, even among anarchs who have recognized mates,

> In the old days...they did not stay married for very long. Sometimes they just went into the jungle at night [says one Lanoh woman; adds a man:] I married one there, left... I went all over the place...married and left, married and left....In those days it was our life to marry many and never stay in one place (Dallos, 2010).

Crossculturally, this sort of sexual freedom is associated with low levels of violence and killing (Erchak, 1994; Prescott, 1975). There is less reason to fight about sex, perhaps the commonest cause of violence among anarchs, if sex is freely available and women have as much of a say about it as men.

Because authority is diffuse, East Semai apply social sanctions as individuals, ad hoc (cf. Barclay, 1990; Purchase, 1996). A contrast with patriarchal democratic praxis may be instructive; East Semai routinely apply all the sanctions Athapascans, Inuit and Algonkians do, except for corporal punishment, banishment or death (but see below). The ideal in both cases is restorative justice (Amster, 2003: 15).

> Gossip, mockery, derision, and shunning are among the more informal sanctions employed in traditional [Canadian] Aboriginal communities. Formal sanctions include song or dream duels, banishment, various corporal punishments and, in rare instances, death. For Aboriginal peoples, the primary objectives of social controls and the imposition of sanctions are resolution of the conflict, restoration of order and harmony in the group or community, and healing of the offender, victim, and community (Griffiths and Hamilton, 1996: 180-181).

Learning Anarch Social Skills: "The Feeling's Much Deeper Than That"

> LBD *(middleclass Euroamerican grandmother, watching TV of the Haitian earthquake of 2010).* I'd like to volunteer to help.
> RKD *(her husband).* But you don't have any of the skills they want.
> LBD *(smiling).* I could always hold a baby.
> KD But you don't buy any religious values that say you should help.
> LBD The feeling's much deeper than that…

Several times I've tried to account for how Semai children learn the social skills they need to live autonomously (e.g., Dentan, 1978; 2008a: 177-199; Dentan and Edo, 2008: 7-10). But East Semai deny emphatically they teach their kids anything, which would be in their view a form of coercion (Dentan, 1978: 96). "The kids just learn," they say, typically by tagging along after adults and mimicking adult behavior.

I dismissed as play-acting the response of a Temiar headman among East Semai to a Malay official who urged him to settle down in a permanent settlement and plant rubber "for the sake of your children." The headman snorted and said, "Hey, man, we just jungle savages here. We don't look after our children. We look after ourselves, they look after themselves." The impression he left was deceptive—and worked to baffle the Malay development official—

but, like all good lies, it contained a kernel of truth. Although Semai life can be construed as focused on the welfare of children, i.e., on K-reproductive strategy (Dentan, in press), children do not play much of a role in normal Semai conversations nor do Semai pay a lot of overt attention to children who are no longer babies, unless the kids show signs of losing self-control, especially if they seem to be getting angry. I should have remembered Piaget, who

> theorized that adult-child interactions, which are asymmetrical and character-ized by constraint, inhibit the child's ability to construct fairness and reciproc-ity. In contrast, peer interactions, which are symmetrical and characterized by cooperation, promote the child's understanding. In particular, peer conflict forces children to take another's perspective and, by a process of reciprocity and abstraction, ... to develop moral judgment (Cords and Killen, 1998: 196).

Because this moral judgment develops out of practice, it is less articulate and formulaic than the codes of conduct that adults often seek to impose on children, sometimes by *force majeure* (Dentan, 2008a).

> The real moral sense which guides our social behavior is...based on the sympathy and unity inherent in group life. Mutual aid is the condition of successful social living (Baldwin, 1970: 79).

East Semai children learn what presumably their ancestors had learned for millenia before them, that successful justice is not a verbalized abstraction, the goal is not *fiat justitia ruat caelum*, "Let [impersonal] justice be done, though Heaven collapse." Instead the equivalent of justice is a set of ad hoc practical measures adopted in particular circumstances to restore the comity and serenity that allows the smaller members of a small community to continue their Daily routines in peace. East Semai children learn nonkilling skills by practice. For example, they conduct elaborate battles in which no one gets hurt, learning the importance of self-control and the difference between posturing and violence, little kids sometimes getting coaching from big ones on how to hold their "swords" (Dentan, 1978: 132; 1989: 116n2; photos in Alland, 1981: 146; Dentan, 1989: 101, pl. 2). Whether their peacekeeping is part of human genetic wiring or the product of their unarticulated cost-benefit assessment of particular situations, or both, is beside the point (but see Carrithers, 1989; Trevarthen and Logotheti, 1989). Semai children learn these skills, not because their parents teach them, but because their parents for the most part do not (cf. Fry, 1987; 1990).

Absence of Nonkilling Ideology

As "egalitarianism emerges from autonomy rather than from an abstract notion of equality" (Rousseau, 2006: 48), so autonomy, mutual aid and the consequent egalitarianism and antipathy to killing seem to emerge from unsupervised child's play. In daily routines "freedom" and "equality" do not seem to exist as verbalized abstract values, the way they do in many less free and more inegalitarian societies, e.g. the "patriarchal democrats." Of course, Semai who learn other languages are competent to talk about freedom, e.g., "...we don't like to work for others. We like to be free and live off the jungle. We don't fight among ourselves over the trees because we can identify which tree belongs to whom" (Yen, quoted by Man and Hoh 1987 in Dentan et al., 1997: 114). However, the Malay word for "free" that Yen used was probably *bebas,* which has strongly negative connotations (Dentan, 1997: 109-111). Except in the context of a "contrast culture," the subject does not arise.

Nor do Semai talk much about loving one's neighbor, though familiarity with the people in one's band, with whom one shares on a daily basis, produces a "fellowship" which people acknowledge by accepting them as "neighbors" (Semai *kawaad*), i.e., fellow band members, for the nonce (Macdonald, in press, a; Dentan, in press)

> ...human ethics based upon love and personal sympathy only have contributed to narrow the comprehension of the moral feeling as a whole. It is not love to my neighbour ...which induces me to seize a pail of water and to rush towards his house when I see it on fire; it is a far wider, even though more vague feeling or instinct of human solidarity and sociability which moves me.... It is the unconscious recognition of the force that is borrowed by each man from the practice of mutual aid; of the close dependency of every one's happiness upon the happiness of all; and of the sense of justice, or equity, which brings the individual to consider the rights of every other individual as equal to his own (Kropotkin, 2006 [1902]: xv-xvi).

The feeling is deeper than "values," as LBD suggests, and often less conscious than Kropotkin suggests. The children aren't aware of "learning skills" or the associated responses. Adults everywhere disrespect children's ability to understand their own world. Schooling quite consciously sets out to obliterate what the children have learned and the ways in which they learned it (e.g., Dentan and Juli Edo, 2009). The often unconscious feelings and behavior patterns that maintain anarchic egalitarianism feel like the products of unconstrained individual choice—as, in a sense, they are. Csilla Dallos (2010) remarks her surprise that a group of settled foragers do not seem to regret the rise of inequality among them. But how and why would you regret losing something you were never aware of having?

Indeed, the whole complex of autonomy, equality, mutual aid and nonkilling fits uneasily into "values" discourse. A corollary of autonomy is the absence of an authoritative locus of correctness; people do not even agree on the names for birds, let alone the nature of good behavior or of God (e.g., Dentan, 1975:93-95; 2006; Gardner, 1966, 1976; Guenther, 1979).

Scholars are probably better off talking about this complex as a set of "tendencies," the way Proudhon suggests in the epigraph of this chapter.

And, of course, any set of tendencies—in this case associated with nonkilling—coexists with other and sometimes opposite tendencies, to which this essay now turns.

Patriarchal Democrats, FIGs and Coalitional Violence

Hunting large animals (1) is much more dangerous than ordinary foraging and (2) requires teamwork, especially in the case of herd ruminants. The first condition requires physical strength and robust anatomy. Even Neanderthal hunters, with their much greater robustness, suffered numerous broken bones and died in their early thirties. It is not so much their relative physical strength that makes a strategy of deploying men in dangerous activities more cost-efficient than deploying women, but also the fact that men's role in reproduction requires much less of an investment of energy than women's: it takes a woman about nine months to produce a baby; a man's part in gestation is over in a few minutes. While a particular man's involvement in postnatal parenting is important for the differential survival of his offspring, alloparenting and other communal involvement in raising kids makes fathers less significant than mothers. Still, as men age, they tend to settle down with a particular wife and children. In other words, young men are ideal for hunters (and warriors) not so much because they are stronger than other people, but because they are cheaper and thus more disposable. "Women and children first."

The teamwork required of young male hunters probably arose out of environmental happenstance, as indicated in the preceding section of this chapter. But as hunters grow older, they gain more experience and skill, always important in as risky an enterprise as big game hunting. Older hunters are better hunters, until age impairs their physical ability. After that, as Dallos suggests, they try to retain their authority and prestige even after they have to give up hunting. A parallel phenomenon is that of coaches in the NFL, who are often retired players respected for their experience.

The NFL suggests another parallel: teams of players (hunters) who have played (hunted) together for a long time are better at the game (the hunt) than those who have not. You know what your teammate will do and wants you to do without having to ask. Thus keeping the band together as a "fraternal interest group" increases the efficiency of hunting. A FIG is also "a nascent military organization" (Otterbein, 2004: 86). The presence of FIGs is the best predictor of violence and killing within and between egalitarian bands (Otterbein, 2004: 50-68), presumably because of the bravery, bellicosity and physical strength that characterize young men. (For theories of young male violence, see Fry, 2006: 220-224; National Research Council, 1996: 51-54, 58-61; Wrangham, 2010.) Note: bellicosity and impulsive bravery are impediments to successful "modern" warfare.

Another thing happens as a result of this shift. Big game hunters "give" meat to nonhunters in classic Maussian style, expecting a reciprocal reward in terms of prestige or other recompense. According to the Oxford English Dictionary, the settlers in eighteenth century Massachusetts Bay Colony coined the term "Indian giver" to describe how their Algonquian neighbors would reclaim such gifts if the expected reciprocity was not forthcoming. "Sharing," the definitive mode of distribution among other foragers, withers.

I suspect that what happens is that aging hunt leaders, like Dallos' sedentized Lanoh elders, seek to retain young men's allegiance by controlling their access to women. But this tactic would be only a stop-gap that would lead to the eventual subordination of women. Fathers could generate their own hunting bands and guarantee their support in their dotage by producing sons, controlling their access to women and mandating virilocal postmarital residence. The subordination of women is central to this process. Dominant male values become those associated with big game hunting: courage, male bonding, stoicism in the face of pain, *esprit de corps*. The Sanskrit word that gave rise to English "virtue" and "hero" reflects these values, although less clearly than Spanish *machismo*. The alienation produced by subordinating women assigns them complementary and inferior roles. Controlling their wombs, the source of hunters becomes a central concern. Male homophilia sometimes, especially in pastoralism, shades into pederasty, a practice that may simultaneously run up against the heroic virtues and incur condemnation or denial (e.g., PBS "Frontline," 2010).

These characteristics also make young men a burden on most societies. The United States, for example, could save money by simply incarcerating all young men between puberty and middle age, so great is the cost of their recklessness and violence (Stephenson, 1995). Any society which values young men's talents is likely to suffer from their other tendencies. FIGs are facultative: they allow young men (and others) to celebrate aggressive characteristics which under other circumstances they might have deplored (but cf. Dentan, 2008a: 209-230, 238-24).

At this point the analogy with "coalitional violence" among chimpanzees (e.g., Wrangham, 2010) becomes instructive. I say "analogy" because, although people share a huge percentage of their genes with chimpanzees, and patriarchal democrat feuding and raiding resembles the coalitional violence of chimps, *Ardipithecus* marks a sharp anatomical break with chimps, and people also share a huge percentage of their genes with bonobos, which exhibit "no deadly warfare, little hunting, no male dominance, and enormous amounts of sex" (de Waal, quoted in Horgan, 2010: 77). The shrinkage of sharing and the rise of wheedling and begging is another way in which big game hunters seem more like chimpanzees than bonobos. The connection between the genetic overlap and the behavioral one is therefore unclear. Still, one can agree with Wrangham (2010: 30) that men tend to be "more dangerous than women, and that massive imbalances of power among hostile entities tend to induce violence."

The dominant explanation of coalitional violence relies on a subset of the social exchange theory introduced in the first section of this chapter, "the imbalance of power hypothesis" (Wrangham, 2010: 37, 40), which recapitulates the findings of sociologists that people are more likely to be violent when they are less likely to suffer unwanted consequences (cf. Dentan, 2008a; 2008b)—a major reason that children are the most frequent victims of violence, with women in second place (Gelles and Straus, 1998). Or, in the chilling Malay proverb, "Soft ears are the ones get pinched." Chimpanzees and patriarchal democrats are likely to attack significantly weaker outsiders. The homophilia that marks bands of young male killers strengthens in-group ties and makes neighboring "outsiders" seem like a challenge.

And cost-effective big game hunting requires weapons that kill large animals at a distance, relatively safely. In the reflexive cost-benefit calculus of killing, hand-to-hand assault runs a usually unacceptable risk of being seriously injured or hurt oneself—and, as human population increases, the chances of encounters between neighboring bands and competition for scarce resources increases the potential for killing (Dentan, 2008a; Wrangham, 2010: 35), in part by generating notions of "ethnicity" alien to anarchs. Under these circumstances, young men tend to become killers, more than in egalitarian anarchies—and, analysts sometimes forget, are more likely to suffer the deleterious consequences of violence.

Lip service to autonomy and equality can continue in FIG-run societies. Take the Ilongot of Luzon, where teams of men armed with spears and dogs communally hunt down deer, wild buffalo, pigs and wild cats at least twice a week; group hunts without dogs, lasting 3-5 days, provide meat for negotiations about bride-price (Rosaldo and Rosaldo, 1975: 104). The Rosaldos continue that "Ilongot society is an ordered anarchy; ideologically all men are equal, and no political specialist or leader exists" (Rosaldo and Rosaldo 1975:105). But men have more *liget* than women—anger, passion, energy, vitality, qualities Ilongot attribute to successful local groups (Rosaldo, 1988: 167). So men get to *tuydek* women, order them around. And adults get to boss kids. "In practice, community leadership tends to reside in sets of male siblings [=FIGs]..." (Rosaldo and Rosaldo, 1975: 105). Ilongot are famous for headhunting and feuds. The conjunction of FIGs, anarchist ideology and killing fits this paper's argument that peaceable anarchies are not the products of conscious nonkilling egalitarian ideologies ("values"). It should not be surprising that the presence of such ideologies produces neither peace nor (for women and children) autonomy. The persistence of such ineffectual ideologies in hierarchical societies is testimony to the hold egalitarian feelings have on humans, whether due to the evolutionary biology sketched in the last section of this paper or the often unconscious cost/benefit calculation that may underlie mutual aid among traditional anarchs.

Anarchs as Killers

> Violence is typically a young man's vice; it has been said that the most effective crime-fighting tool is a 30th birthday. (Drehle, 2010: 34)

> Killing people, shooting arrows at one another, cutting each other up withknives. That's how we are so little now, this is how we have been so quickly finished off....All the Onge of one *bera* [territory] would...go at night, and ambush the Onge of another....Everybody would be killed off, then piled up inside the *bera*, and then set on fire. They would cut off a piece of the little finger, or [the hand] from the wrist and then take these as trophies to show to the women, see how many I've killed. (Venkateswar, 2004: 45)

There seem to be three circumstances in which anarchic egalitarians kill people without pressure from outsiders:

1. young men quarreling over sexual access to particular women,
2. self-defence against perceived threats to personal or communal welfare,
3. euthanasia.

1. By far the most common agents of killing, between bands and within bands, are young men fighting over women (e.g., Dentan, 2008a: 209-213, 224-226, 238-240; Fry, 2006; Gardner, this volume; Knauft, 1987; Otterbein, 2006; Venkateswar, 2004: 45, 69). For example, in the case just cited, Onge fighting was usually over a woman, people from one bera refusing to give a girl in marriage to another bera, so that the frustrated suitor's people kidnapped her (Venkateswar, 2004: 69). Nothing about autonomy and anarchy prevents the characteristics that people attribute to young men (e.g., Wrangham, 2010) from becoming valuable; nothing prevents young men from allying with each other even more than they ally with other neighbors. The change from anarchy to democratic patriarchy is not "evolutionary" in the sense of being irreversible. For instance, in West Malaysia, between 4,000 and 3,000 years ago "hunting in coordinated groups and ambushing the relatively dangerous ungulates apparently gave way to very small hunting parties less likely to disturb the ever-watchful arboreal prey" (Bulbeck, 2003: 148). East Semai, Batek Semang and Lanoh Semang—among whom peaceability is marked—tended to follow the latter pattern (e.g., Dallos, 2010; Dentan, 1962-1963; 1979: 31-32; Endicott and Endicott, 2008: 72-80); Temiar and west Semai, somewhat less peaceable, the former pattern (Dallos, 2010). A similar change from democratic patriarchy to foraging and farming marked a return to peace in the Neolithic near east (see third section of this chapter). Otterbein's data strongly suggest positive correlations on the one hand between dependence on big game hunting and violence and, conversely, between dependence on gathering or swiddening and peace (2004: 87-90).

As noted, dependence on sometimes violent men to hunt dangerous animals seems to create the conditions for the development of patriarchal gender relationships. Among rainforest foragers sexual relations tend to be free and easy (Dentan, 1979: 62-63; Gardner, 2010; this volume; Macdonald, 2010), a situation that tends to be associated with nonkilling and nonviolence in general (Prescott, 1975).

2. The other main reason that otherwise peaceable anarchs engage in violence is in individual or collective self-defense. In general, the preferred method of handling attack is to flee and scatter (Dentan, 1992). The open and optional character of band affliation allows multiple asyla for refugees from personal or collective attack and thus facilitates a fission-fusion style of settlement pattern, as long as population density remains low (Fix, 1977).

> We can't sustain being tied down to one place. Malays will come and take our [band territories]…Or, there'll be a war, and we'll lose everything…If

we keep moving, people will have a hard time getting at us. We don't like killing people, and we hate being killed. Settling down is just asking for trouble [East Semai (Temiar) headman quoted by Juli Edo, Williams-Hunt and Dentan (2009: 223)].

Attack from outside can make anarchs wage defensive guerilla warfare, usually by ambush (e.g., Dentan, 1992, 1999), especially if increasing population density or genocidal invasion decreases the opportunity for successful flight. Young men and their supporters can then deploy the skills acquired by attacking outsiders against their neighbors, bringing the war back home, as seems to have happened with the Onge mentioned above (Cipriani, 1966: 3-10; for Semai, cf. Dentan, 2008a: 209-211; Juli Edo, Williams-Hunt and Dentan, 2009: 220-222).

Attack from inside, by people who should be friends and neighbors, can have the same results. To his surprise, Keith Otterbein's classic hologeistic study of capital punishment found it a cultural universal (1986; cf. 2004: 41-42, 74, 78). Semai deny in principle that they execute people, but Williams-Hunt and I documented in detail what may be a west Semai case in a congested regroupment zone, in which an incorrigibly bellicose drunk who had raped a couple of women died "by accident" in a nighttime brawl (Dentan and Williams-Hunt, 1999). There were also a couple of alleged but not confirmed cases of incorrigibly violent people who seemed to suffer from brain damage (e.g., had grand mal seizures) and who apparently died by poison given them by family members; the man who told me the story said, with typical Semai casuistry, that the poisoner didn't actually kill the victim, since the victim had a choice whether or not (unknowingly) to drink the poison.

The "threat" may be a social construct, like the threat of criminal killers or "stranger danger" in current Angloamerican societies (Leyton, 1997 [1995]; Dentan, 2001a). Without scanting the role of "warrior religions" like Thuggee, "Passages," Shinto or Sikhism (e.g., Eller, 2006: 195-202), one must note that the rise of patriarchal Abrahamic religions from the wreckage of Sumer has spawned an enormous amount of supererogatory killing. Despite an overt nonkilling ideology, Abrahamism generates killing cults and frenzies, inquisitions, pogroms, jihads, hate crimes and crusades. The "moral panic" (Leyton, 1997) that often accompanies these killings has its equivalent among egalitarian anarchs in witch-killings (Knauft, 1987), which make up a significant proportion of the cases of "capital punishment" in both societies (Otterbein, 1986). Students of peaceable anarchies made the connection between witchcraft belief and killing early on (e.g., Kropotkin, 2006: 76-77). Temiar, much like their Semai neighbors in many ways, express witchcraft beliefs, and accusations of witchcraft may have fueled the threat of feuds (Benjamin, 1968: 33).

But belief in witches is not universal among egalitarian anarchs. Mary Douglas argues, largely from her wonderful African studies, that

> if we have social units whose external boundaries are clearly marked, whose internal relations are confused, and which persist on a small scale, then we should look for the active witchcraft type of cosmology (1996: 111-112).

In tropical Southeast Asia, most egalitarian anarchies are small-scale, with extremely flexible internal relations, but external boundaries are fluctuating and permeable (Gibson; Sillander, in press). For example, Semang and Semai kinship terminology is "confused" in what seems to be Douglas' sense, i.e., ad hoc and optional (Dentan, 1970, 1975, 1976, in press). Local communities are "small scale" in her sense, especially among Semang (e.g., Dallos, 2010) and East Semai in the mid-twentieth century (Dentan, 1971). But external boundaries are also flexible and optional. Instead of saying that members of one's group may become inimical as a result of mutating into witches, Semai say that they do so by dying and becoming "ghosts" (*kcmooc*), a subclass of shapeshifting demons. Ghosts still yearn to be part of the community, are drawn back into it by the scent of familiar and beloved people, whose souls they then devour. External groups, Malays and Temiar, in contrast to whom Semai traditionally define themselves, are the ones who may practice witchcraft, not Semai, say Semai (Robarchek, 1988), not Jahai, say Jahai Semang (van der Sluys, 2006: 47). This construction fills many of the same needs as belief in internal witchcraft, without rationalizing and justifying killing (Robarchek, 1988).

In the 21st century, the penetration into west Semai life of fundamentalist Christianity and Malay beliefs in black magic, *ilmu,* has spread belief in witches. An apparently west Semai member of a parapolice force allegedly boasted a few years ago that he had killed a Semai man by *ilmu.* The dead man's son then murdered the self-styled killer.

Finally, increasing scarcity of resources, sometimes as a result of increasing population density, also, increases quarreling and the potential for violence (Otterbein, 1985):

> We don't fight and squabble like other peoples because we're all spread out. There aren't many of us, and we live scattered around. Those other peoples, there're lots of them. If we all lived crowded together like them, we'd fight too (young Semai man, quoted by Juli Edo, Williams-Hunt and Dentan, 2009: 228).

The introduction of valued items can set normally peaceable anarchist peoples to fighting, just as does artificially feeding other primates. The novelties initially are scarce, the classic example being steel knives in South America and the fur trade in North America. Such wars may but need not create local leaders (Benjamin, 1968: 33); one version of the Semai war epic assigns leadership to a Malay shapechanging shaman (Dentan, 1999) while in another version the leader is a wise Semai man not unlike the narrator, but there is no killing (Juli Edo, 1990: 50-54).

3. East Semai, like central Inuit and San (Lee, 1979: 382), sometimes constructed a small residence for a person who was hopelessly sick or aged and abandoned them there. Semai, always super-punctilious about agency when talking about killing, deny that such abandonment is really killing. The person dies of natural causes.

Defeat and Surrender

Unlike the earliest foraging bands, recent and current egalitarian anarchs have a number of ties, e.g., trade, with their more hierarchical neighbors (e.g., Bailey et al., 1989; Dallos, 2010; Dentan, 2001b; Dunn, 1975; Gardner, 1985, 1988; this volume; Gibson, 1989: 69-71; Headland and Reid, 1989). These ties often change anarchies in a number of ways. One of the most significant is the extinction of violent resistance. The ideology of industrial capitalist imperialism tends to construct this extinction as purely the product of *force majeure,* rather than an active adaptation by surrendered people, one which resonates throughout their lives (but see Endicott, 1983).

Among such peoples "fear" is a virtue, using the word in its Hobbesian sense:

> ...a certain foresight of future evil; ...to distrust, suspect, take heed, provide so that they may not fear, is also incident to the fearful....It is through fear that men secure themselves by flight indeed, and in corners, if they think that they cannot escape otherwise (Hobbes, 1966 [1651]: 216n; see discussion of this passage in Dentan, 1992: 229-230).

Among other things, people have to accept relative powerlessness with equanimity (Dentan, 2008a). This abandonment of any struggle to make things work out the way one wants seems to intensify the mutual aid and fellowship that arise from mutual familiarity, and to create a context which tends even more than simple egalitarian anarchy to minimize killing, e.g., among San, Onge, Buid and Semai (Cipriani, 1966; Dentan, 1992, 2008a; Gibson, 1989; Thomas, 1959). San, for instance, seem in a short period of time to have gone from big game hunters to ferocious horseriding pastoralists to subdued hunter-gatherers and thence into the lumpenproletarian underclasses and paramilitaries that take so many once peaceable peoples (Denbow and Wilmsen, 1986; Gordon 1992).

I have argued elsewhere (1992, 1994, 2008a) that the experience of violent defeat and/or life in the vicinity of an unpredictably violent greater power tends to generalize, producing an attitude that Christians, Muslims and AAs call "surrender" or "letting go" (*Gelassenheit*); "Dying" is the Sufi and Christian mystical metaphor. In brief, this attitude involves accepting the fact that one is of little importance in the grand scheme of things and is unlikely to have the power to force things to turn out the way one wants. Living in the present ("right mindedness," as Buddhists say) is a reasonable adaptation to such powerlessness. This fatalistic complex meshes readily with traditional egalitarian anarch tendency to stress "immediate returns" and to avoid killing.

Hidden Within the Machinery of Babylon

> To overturn a government...is only the beginning of the social revolution. The machine of the State once out of gear, the hierarchy of functionaries disorganized and not knowing in what direction to take a step, the soldiers having lost confidence in their officers—in a word, the whole army of defenders of capital once routed—then it is that the grand work of destruction of all the institutions which serve to perpetuate economic and political slavery will become ours. The possibility of acting freely being attained, what will revolutionists do next? (Kropotkin, 2002: 237)

> The autonomous citizen and the autonomous polity are entangled in a chicken-and-egg relationship. They may only exist and survive together – which makes irresolvable the question of where to start to bring (both!) of them about. The genuine question of practical import is where to find the public site fit for their encounter and likely to become a new (or restored) meeting point. (Bauman, 2010)

One received truth in industrial capitalist societies is that, even if egalitarian anarchies actually do or did exist (a fact that the dominant ideology makes into a dubious proposition for many people) they are superannuated and, well, doomed (for better or worse) by "progress" (e.g., Alexiades, 2010; Kirsch, 1997; Fry, 2006: 114-145). Even some anarchist theorists denounce "lifestyle anarchism" as Rousseauvian romanticizing of "primitive peoples," "puerile rubbish" and "irrationalism" (e.g., Bookchin, 1999: 186-198), preferring a movement led by wise intellectuals. But many industrial capitalist states are not, or not yet, totalitarian. There are spatial and temporal interstices in the web of social control, where "civil society" flourishes, and, within that locus, peaceful egalitarian anarchies often maintain a foothold, however precarious (Bouvard, 1975; Dentan, 1994; Erasmus, 1981; Hakim Bey, 2010; Kahter, 1972; Veysey, 1973; Watson, 1997; cf. Graeber, 2007). The magazine *Communities* and its directory (Fellowship for Intentional Community 2007) list hundreds and hundreds of geographically localized "intentional"communities, many egalitarian and anarchist (Hakim Bey, 2010). Some, like Alcoholics Anonymous (AA) and the Rainbow Family of Living Light ("Rainbows"), join into quite large assemblages of local communities that set up temporary autonomous zones (TAZs) in limited areas, within which members interact peacefully with other people as equals and can for a while practice "lifestyle anarchism." Although Marxists classify these areas as those in which the state has no current interests, and the social formations therein as "beggars' democracies" (Wittfogel, 1958), members treat these zones as refuges from the enclaving society. Some members call the society from which they seek relief "Babylon." They take precautions to keep their boundaries clear (Dentan, 1992, 1994; Hakim Bey, 2010).

In America, where religiosity has a privileged status, a quasi-religious rationale offers these groups some further protection from Babylonian interference. For example, the origin of Alcoholics Anonymous and its offshoots like Narcotics Anonymous in the "primitive Christian" Oxford Group and its offshoots gave them a narrative and practice close enough to religion to permit them to function relatively freely, although group traditions identify AA and NA as "spiritual, not religious" and recall the fact that one of the founders of AA was head of the American Atheist Society. NA's "Basic Text," for example, refers to its "spiritual beliefs" (2008: viii). For many Babylonians, however, there is no distinction between "spirituality" and "religion," the former being a euphemism for the latter in secular contexts. The mystified disjunction in meanings helps protect the enclaved anarchies.

> Whether or not "primitive Christian" social organization resembled that of "band-level" societies, that of these modern [intentional peaceable anarch] groups does in some ways. [For example, people often join the organization as a result of preexisting ties like friendship or employment in the same workplace.] Affiliation with a particular local group usually rests on proximity. Membership in local groups is flexible, following the fission-fusion pattern characteristic of foraging or swiddening band societies. [All it takes to form a new AA group traditionally is a coffee pot and a resentment. An AA group is roughly equivalent to a Rainbow "Talking Circle."] Leadership often rests on persuasive ability. Distinctions based on age and

sex occur but are subordinate to the principle of egalitarianism within the group. Nonviolence is fundamental within the group, and members often become less prone to violence outside. Members should share "feelings," and often economic resources. Many social activities, such as dances and picnics, recruit only from within the group, and so on.

Readers who find the analogies between egalitarian... [intentional peace] groups and bands unconvincing should be aware that the former sometimes explicitly make the case that...they are replicating "primitive" social relations (Dentan, 1988:280).

For example, the Rainbow "origin myth" contains references to Native American traditions that Niman (2011, in press) characterizes as "fakelore." Similarly, congeners like Firedance hark back, vaguely, to Oceanic rituals. This mythopoeia earns them some scorn from anthropologists and other academics (e.g., Bookchin, 1999: 170-208).

Because there are so many nonkilling egalitarian anarchies in the U.S. alone, it seems useful to exclude those which do not precisely fit this egalitarian acephalous anarchist model. Thus this chapter ignores the cenobitic Christian pacifists—Amish, Mennonites and Hutterites—who originally inspired my notion that defeat was critical in producing nonkilling praxis, as opposed to peaceable pieties (Dentan, 1992, 1994). Like most Christian fundamentalists, they are patriarchal and brutal to children in the name of "discipline." They practice their version of "Biblical chastisement" (Pearl, 2009, 2010), a technique that recently made the news when members of the "NGJ Ministries" inadvertently chastised some kids to death (Harris, 2010). (NGJ stands for "no greater joy," as in "I have no greater joy than to hear that my children walk in truth" [III John 4]. Michael and Debi Pearl, who head NGJ, maintain a popular web site, publish many books and a slick magazine, full of photos of laughing blonde children, walking in well-chastised truth.) Not that only Protestant "educators" torture children (Anonymous, 2009; Ghosh, 2010).

Similarly, this chapter excludes the more violent "black" anarchist movements of the twentieth and twenty-first century (e.g., Dolgoff, 1974) and the "primitive Christian" anarchist medieval peasant revolts that culminated in the sixteenth century Volkssturm (Cohn, 1970). Although European peasant anarchist movements harked back to an imagined primordial peaceful and egalitarian anarchist past—"When Adam delved and Eve span/Who was then the gentleman?"—and, in its defeat, gave rise to the pacifist Hutterites, Amish and Mennonites, nevertheless the peasant revolutionaries and their opponents engaged in massive reciprocal killings (Dentan, 1994). The recent terrorist Hutaree ("Christian warrior") branch of the rightwing Michigan Militia mined the same vein of

Abrahamic violence, citing the imminence of the Apocalypse: "It started out as a Christian thing. You go to church. You pray. You take care\ of your family. I think David [Stone, her ex-husband and head of the militia] started to take it too far." (Donna Stone, quoted in Williams and Corey, 2010: 2) The militia plotted to kill a policeman and then attack his funeral party (Gray, 2010).

Finally, the chapter excludes the inchoate libertarian wing of the Tea Party movement, because of its alliance with such Christians, Confederate slavocratic revanchism and violent rightwing factions, like Christian Identity, the Aryan Nation and neoNazi groups. However important these groups are for anarchist theory—they show, for instance, that under hierarchical regimes, anarchism per se need not be particularly peaceable—they are inappropriate for a book on nonkilling.

Moreover, even the groups discussed here have to interact with Babylonian officialdom, and, like traditional anarchs in contact with states, may form the equivalent of "headmen." For instance, there is a titular AA hierarchy, which local groups call "New York" and to which some of them send delegates or money. "New York" finances publications, deals with Babylon and occasionally issues ukases that local groups may or may not ignore. "New York" expelled the "Syracuse group" in Buffalo from AA for reasons not clear to most Buffalo group members. Most locals know neither the rationale of the ostracism (misuse of the custom of "sponsorship") nor, in most cases, the fact of the expulsion. Practically, New York's disfavor has no consequences, much like the orders of a traditional anarch "headman." Finland is the only country with an "official" (state) AA; with the de-Sovietization of Finland, amicable competition with U.S.-style anarchic AA has begun.

The Twelve Steps in AA are explicitly only "suggestions," to which no member can claim "perfect adherence," according to the passage from the "Big Book," read at the beginning of each meeting. The basic stance is to "identify" with the speakers, not "compare," i.e., contrast your experience or views with theirs. While "Step Nazis" and "Big Book thumpers" may claim to advocate "true AA" (Lechner, 2002), in practice the custom is normally like that of the Rainbow Family:

> [If anyone tells you to do something] in a very authoritative voice that implies that his close relative founded the Rainbow...remember! This is only friendly advice, and no matter the tone of voice in which it is given, it should always be understood as such. Develop never-ending compassion and patience. Nobody then—with the tentative exception of a consensus reached in a Talking Circle—has any authority over your way of life (Israeli Rainbow pamphlet quoted byTavory and Goodman, 2009: 273).

These enclaved groups tend to form in moments of personal and/or sociopolitical crisis. Alcoholics join AA when they have "hit bottom," i.e., taken so much punishment as a result of drunken behavior that they have "a desire to stop drinking," the only requirement for membership. Initially, the criterion was "a sincere desire to stop drinking," but the founders decided that requirement was too onerous. Pacifists familiar with AA urge it as a model for "peace groups" (e.g., Brooks, 1987: 38).

Similarly, many Rainbows also find themselves under spiritual or psychological stress in their lives in Babylon. Many Rainbows regard Babylon as a disaster in and of itself, says an anthropologist who is personally familiar with Rainbow praxis (McClusky, 2010), impersonal, exploitative, unnatural and unsustainable:

> forests of buildings and rivers of concrete where other men and women missed the stars at night and tended small plants on windowsills and kept tiny dogs and took them for walks along corridors in the endless procession of boxes and intersections and lights; where they rented space in other people's property so they had somewhere to sleep so they could get up and perform profit-related tasks they neither understood nor cared about, simply so they would be given tokens of exchange they needed in order to rent the space in which they slept and snarled and watched television....a society that was itself trapped in fracture and betrayal and despair; ...a culture turning into a Christmas bauble, gaudy beauty wrapped around an emptiness coalescing faster and faster into parking lots and malls and waiting areas and virtual chat rooms—non-places where nobody knew anything about anybody anymore (Marshall, 2002: 284-85).

A few days' or weeks' relief every year in the woods lets Rainbows relearn the complex skills

> that life in egalitarian communities requires and that, Rainbows hope, will filter into Babylon. They don't form because cops shoot at them and think of them as a disaster. They Form because they think of Babylon as a disaster and because they have faced personal disasters similar to those that AA folks have faced (McClusky, 2010).

Both AA and the Rainbows are "occasional groups" (Pospisil, 1964) inhabiting temporary autonomous zones, TAZs (Lechner, 2002; Niman, this volume). As TAZs they can afford, like egalitarian foragers and swiddeners, to admit anyone who wants to join, despite anarchist theorists' anxiety that "'[o]pen-membership' communes invariably end up swamped with freeloaders and sex-starved pathetic creeps" (Hakim Bey, 2010). In fairness, west Semai, whose settlements have for hundreds of years offered asyla to Malays fleeing their own government, say "only ugly and stupid Malays come to live with us."

Members of these "occasional" anarchist enclaves claim to reap "spiritual" or "healing" benefits from belonging to these groups. Among these benefits is the radical transformation of the self into a more satisfying form through the construction of fellowship (Lechner, 2002; Tavory; Goodman, 2009; cf. Wallace, 1956). They reinvent tactics familiar to defeated peaceable egalitarian anarchist people, like "surrender"; e.g., Step One in AA or the warning that "righteous indignation" is an emotion best left for others. They stress "fellowship" (cf. Macdonald, in press, b), which includes traditional egalitarian anarchist mutual aid. Mutual aid, in turn, tends to inhibit violence and killing. For instance, attacked by government forces, Rainbows try to encircle them, humming "ommmmmm" to soothe the attackers' violent feelings and repeating "We love you" (Kalafer and Kalafer, 2009), thereby sometimes further spooking the forces of law and hierarchy.

Disaster and Dystopia

> What's so appealing to filmmakers about these postapocalypic tales [*The Road, The Book of Eli*] anyway? ...The dog-eat-dog lesson has been drilled into us again and again, and I'm beginning to wonder if filmmakers aren't using the world's end as a trope to license a neo-primitivist ethos. When people must scavenge just to survive, any kind of violence is justified. (Denby, 2010: 82)

> Anarchism does not mean bloodshed; does not mean robbery, arson, etc. These monstrosities are, on the contrary, the characteristic features of capitalism. Anarchism means peace and tranquility to all. (Spies, 1995: 44-45)

In fact, peaceable egalitarian mutual aid groups tend to form spontaneously wherever and whenever some disaster afflicts a localized population. Aside from "disaster sociologists" (e.g., Fritz, 1996; Solnit, 2009: 104-109), few people know about them (for five disaster case histories, see Solnit, 2009).

This ignorance reflects the vulgar Calvinist Hobbesianism that rationalizes the power of the state: left to their own devices, people will turn upon each other (Solnit, 2009: 309-310). Douglas Fry spends a good part of his magisterial *Human Potential for Peace* lambasting the equivalent vulgar Hobbesianism directed at traditional peaceable egalitarian anarchies (2006: 83-86, 162-183). Denby, the film critic quoted in the epigraph to this section, uses the word "neo-primitivist" to describe imaginary pervasive mindless violence, as if all "primitive" people behaved that way or, more generally, all people deprived of the benefits of the leviathan state. NGJ Ministries, the patriarchal Calvinist child-beating advocates, operate out of these assumptions, based on the doctrine of Original Sin, hoping that "Our personal mistakes and shortcomings can be corrected in our sons. We can give God a better childhood, youth, and manhood than our own" (Pearl, 2010a: 17).

This vulgar Calvinist Hobbesianism requires repressing the fact, well known and important to the Founding Fathers and statistically true today that

> If punishments be very severe, men are naturally led to the perpetration of other crimes, to avoid the punishment due to the first. The countries and times most notorious for severity of punishments were always those in which the most bloody and inhuman actions and the most atrocious crimes were committed; for the hand of the legislator and the assassin were directed by the same spirit of ferocity, which on the throne dictated laws of iron to slaves and savages, and in private instigated the subject to sacrifice one tyrant to make room for another (Beccaria, 1778: ch. 27).

Instead, almost any action that seems to defy or even simply ignore the titular authority of the state meets violent repression, to prevent a dreaded chaos. For instance, free speech, once a right, was, in the case of opposing World War I, likened to crying 'Fire!' in a crowded theatre, and banned. More recently, free speech, except by corporations, is confined to "free speech zones," TAZs segregated from the assemblages of powerful people whose actions are to be protested and surrounded by barriers—sometimes topped by razor wire—and heavily armed police, although, as McClusky comments (2010) you can also find some on (equally segregated) college campuses. Such violently imposed and often superfluous order, for children and citizens, takes precedence over more appropriate and practical measures, often at great human cost.

For instance,

> In the wake of an earthquake, a bombing or a storm, most people are altruistic, urgently engaged in caring for themselves and those around them, strangers and neighbors as well as loved ones. The image of the selfish, panicky, or regressively savage human being in times of disaster has little truth to it. Decades of meticulous sociological research on behavior in disasters…have demonstrated this. But belief lags behind, and often the worst behavior in the wake of a calamity is on the part of those who believe that others will behave savagely and that they themselves are taking defensive measures…[In many disasters] innocents have been killed by those who believed or asserted that their victims were the criminals and they themselves were the protectors of the shaken order.…The astonishing gap between common beliefs and actualities about disaster limits the possibilities (Solnit, 2009: 2-3).

A society which condones brutal force to destroy the children's culture which this paper, following Piaget, has argued is vital for learning how to preserve equality and autonomy (Akopsa, 2010; Pearl, 2009, 2010b; Dentan and Juli Edo, 2008; Gatto, 2003, 2006) is not one to tolerate the success of spontaneous egalitarian social formations at jobs the state normally monopolizes. Such successes undermine the legitimacy of the state. Vulgar Calvinist Hobbesian mythology rationalizes, justifies and mystifies crushing the anarch communities that arise in the wake of natural disasters. Indeed, some state organizations construe the communities themselves as "natural disasters" (Niman, 2011, in press), a belief reciprocal to the Rainbow construal of the Babylonian state.

When a disaster occurs the mass media launch a barrage of alarmist Hobbesian reports that deal not with the mutual aid that is actually occurring but with the "rape and murder [that] are the next grim reapers for the survivors," predictions that hurt relief efforts (Jarosz, 2010). On the "Today Show" on March 9, 2010, Karl Rove told Matt Lauer that false rumors about snipers slowed the Bush administration's response to Hurricane Katrina. The press construes raiding stores for food, medicine and other supplies as "looting," even when there is no alternative but death. Predictions of chaos and killing seem especially dire when the affected population is of African origin. Before the dust had time to settle in Haiti, CNN was calling for the immediate (re)establishment of "central authority," their experts warning of chaos, rape, murder and psychological disaster otherwise (e.g., Landau, 2010), despite the response from people on the ground that the newsreaders' response is "a little overblown." The army becomes the main arm of state intervention, with the primary goal of "restoring [hierarchical] order" and the secondary goal of distributing aid. Hence, when the troops, "the most visible portion of international support," depart as conditions worsen, the now self-helpless survivors are alarmed (A.P., 2010), though, as the chief program officer of an aid organization remarked, "The real solution is to deliver services… rather than turn Haiti into a military state" (*Time* / A.P., 2010).

In fact, Hobbesian vigilantes and the state itself commit far more violence during disasters than anyone else (Niman, 2011, in press; Solnit, 2009: 247-266). By contrast, one of the earliest and most effective responses in the wake of Hurricane Katrina came from the Rainbow Family of Living Light members, who showed up by individual initiative. They used their skills at cooperatively using locally available materials to feed and otherwise support Gatherings of thousands to feed and otherwise support thousands of refugees. They were so successful that even the Bush administration acknowledged their contribution, praising a "natural disaster" (Rainbows) for their work in mitigating another "natural disaster" (Katrina) (Niman, 2011, in press; Solnit, 2009: 295-302).

Like membership in other enclaved anarchies, e.g., AA and the Rainbow Family, membership in disaster anarchies also allows people to reconstruct their sense of self and its possibilities (Fritz, 1996; Solnit, 2009: 115-119). Quondam members of spontaneous egalitarian disaster mutual aid groups look back on their membership with almost painful nostalgia, as a time when their lives were vividly meaningful and they felt a deep connection to the other people in their lives, a mild version of which many Americans vaguely recall experiencing after the terrorist attacks of "9-11." Uncoerced mutual aid is something humans like doing. One of the most heartbreaking intentional egalitarian communities, explicitly dedicated to sharing resources and protecting the weak, was the one that unwanted former child soldiers and war orphans formed in their refuge from the adults who used and discarded them, the sewers of a southern African city (Nordstrom, 2004: 174-177).

I suggest that these positive emotions, which inhibit killing, are closely akin to the emotions experienced in battle, which may involve killing:

> The enduring attraction of war is this: Even with its destruction and carnage it can give us what we long for in life….purpose, meaning, a reason for living. Only when we are in the midst of conflict does the shallowness and vapidness of much of our lives become apparent. Trivia dominates our conversations and increasingly our airwaves. And war…allows us to be noble (Hedges, 2002: 3).

It is important to recall, as this chapter has already pointed out, that without special "desensitization training," the vast majority of soldiers, up to 90%, feel these sentiments but still do not try to kill anyone (Grossman, 2009). Hedge's paean to war sounds a lot like Solnit's to disaster.

> …disaster doesn't sort us out by preferences; it drags us into emergencies that require we act, and act altruistically, bravely, and with initiative in order to survive or save the neighbors, no matter how we vote or what we do for a living. The positive emotions that arise in these unpromising circumstances demonstrate the social ties and meaningful work are deeply desired, readily improvised, and intensely rewarding (Solnit, 2009: 7).

It's not the violence of war, not the killing, that makes it so attractive. "War" is just a subset of "disaster," and disaster brings out the "mutual aid" and egalitarian anarchism that lurks, always, just under the surface of routine hierarchy, repression, depression and mutual hatred. The intense joy rarely endures, though nostalgia does and the transformation of self seems to last, at least if contact with the transformative group continues. And, as in the case of war, the negative aftereffects of being involved in killing, as agent or target, seem far worse than those that follow being involved in other calamities (e.g., Grossman, 2009; Sherman, 2010, U.S. Marine Corps, 1992). Even Hobbesians put the figure for the latter at 10% suffering PTSD and 10% depression; the latter number includes people depressed by not being able to get a job after the crisis is over (Landau, 2010). Perhaps these strong emotions make young men better behaved, for a while, when disasters create a TAZ in which their strength and daring are praiseworthy, than in daily Babylonian routines under a punitive order-keeping regime that has no use for them (cf. Dentan, 2008a: 226). During the 2010 disaster in Haiti, for example, the gangs of young thugs endemic in quotidian Haitian life did not emerge as a threat (looting for profit instead of to survive) until after the arrival of US troops and the re-emergence of the local police.

By contrast with the post-traumatic stress syndrome that affects so many ex-warriors, members of enclaved anarchies report that routine group life remains more satisfactory than life in Babylon. The way Rainbows are in their TAZ, says a woman at a Rainbow Gathering, "is how people ought to be" (Kalafer; Kalafer, 2009), i.e., the way they were meant to be. In early 2010 the discussion topic for a group of a dozen or so Buffalo AAs was whether belonging to a "home group" was important to following "the Program." (A "home group" is a particular group one tries to attend at least weekly and where one may receive the annual tokens AA hands out for continuing membership without drinking.) Everyone said that a home group was vital. The word that came up most often was "comfort," which a couple of people attributed to "familiarity." Among Semai, I have argued in this paper and elsewhere (in press), familiarity is the basis of what Gibson and Sillander (in press) and Macdonald (in press, b) call "fellowship," a sense of solidarity that promotes "mutual aid" and thus works against killing. Atheist or agnostic AAs sometimes say that their "Higher Power" ("which keeps us sober") is G. O. D., "Group of Drunks," i.e., the local group and what AAs call "The Fellowship."

Summary

Evolutionary Adaptations

1. From the beginning, the hominid family's reproductive strategy has favored seduction and sharing by males over dominance by violence. The original survival strategy involved gathering, scavenging and small game hunting by both genders. Increasing neoteny (fe-

talization) required not only the "invention of fatherhood" but also the involvement of alloparents and more generally of mutual aid. Group living facilitated the effectiveness of these subsistence and childrearing techniques and undercut the utility of killing.

2. Individual autonomy, entailing an absence of restrictions on group membership, helped maintain a fission-fusion settlement pattern. The ability to flee stressful economic or communal situations undercut any attempts to assert dominance and limited the utility of killing. Thus autonomy led to equality and anarchy (lack of definitive authority). Intergroup killing works against the survival of egalitarian anarchies.

3. The hominine subfamily invented tools that allowed them to kill large animals, as Neanderthals did, and eventually to kill such animals at a distance, without suffering the devastating injuries that mark Neanderthal remains. This development increased the significance of young males in society (as FIGs) and facilitated homicide, especially by young men.

In short, raising children to reproductive adulthood was the central reproductive imperative for human survival. Peaceable cooperative living in small scattered anarchic mutual-aid groups is normal for humans. Killing is mostly by young men and mostly about access to women. Nevertheless, the "wired-in" imperatives of group living seem to make over 90% of humans loath to kill under any circumstances.

Traditional Egalitarian Anarchy

1. Traditional egalitarian anarchies are small primary groups, with no restrictions on membership and a stress on mutual aid. Subsistence involves gathering and small game hunting, with a few groups also involved in agroforestry or swiddening. Although these activities require awareness of seasonal changes in the resource base, they are mostly ad hoc and "immediate return." Activities involving killing-at-a-distance are male-dominated. Sharing is the main mode of distribution, with the idea of "property" often weak or almost absent.

2. The main disparity in power is between adults and children, with finer and vaguer disparities by relative age among adults. But, although adults offer children a refuge from trouble, they rarely intervene in children's activities. The children play in groups mixed by age and sex. In these groups they learn the skills necessary for life in an egalitarian anarchy.

While gender equality is elusive, these peoples come as close to equality between the sexes as human society attains.

3. Reliance on mutual aid raises the "cost" of killing to generally unacceptable levels. What killing occurs is generally by young men seeking sexual access to particular women, which may elicit retaliatory killing. The rise of FIGs increases this sort of killing.

4. Like almost all other societies, egalitarian anarchs tend to value nonkilling and, under particular circumstances, tend to practice capital punishment. Among ideological factors in (non)killing, belief in witchcraft, apparently common in societies with closed boundaries, seems to generate homicides, mostly in the form of capital punishment.

5. This type of social formation demonstrably produces less killing than any other.

Egalitarian Anarchies in the Interstices of the Machine

In the U.S. the liberal authoritarian hierarchies of Western capitalist industrialism couple with a vulgar Calvinist Hobbesianism that denies the viability of anarchist ideals or praxis to create an ideology that equates freedom from government with violent disorder. Still, "civil society" includes "temporary autonomous zones" in which state control is ineffective. Within these areas spontaneous mutual aid anarchies can form, e.g., AA and its offshoots, the Rainbow Family and numerous intentional peace communities. Under conditions of disaster and the collapse of local hierarchies, moreover, similar occasional mutual aid anarchies also tend to form.

Although these groups typically seek to avoid confrontation with outsiders, their existence seems to ipso facto challenge state hierarchy, especially in the U.S. (unless the groups operate under a quasi-religious rationale). Operating under the same Calvinist-Hobbesian assumptions as the state, mass media after a disaster tend to report as fact the vile and violent behavior their ideology predicts, at the same time downplaying positive mutual aid.

Inconclusion

These remarkable societies suggest that, just as many machines reset themselves after a power outage, so human beings reset themselves to something altruistic, communitarian, resourceful and imaginative after a disaster, that we revert to something we already know how to do. The possibility of paradise is already within us as a default setting. (Solnit, 2009: 18)

A Liberal Utopian Solution to Killing: Values under an "Overarching Authority"

> Just as the modern era lifted the agora from its Aristotelian city-state level and reconstituted it at the level of the nation-state, the only prospect of its reconstitution under the increasingly globalized human condition is at the *level of humanity*—the "cosmopolitan" level, to use the term persuasively argued and promoted with great force by Ulrich Beck. Admittedly, this is a daunting task—though perhaps, in an era equipped with information highways, not much more daunting than was the task of lifting [it] from the local to the nation-state level in the times preceding the installation of telecommunication networks.... Daunting or not, the task has to be sooner or later performed, if the present-day ambient uncertainty and ubiquitous fears, those un-detachable attributes of liquid modernity, are to stand a chance of mitigation, let alone a prospect of cure. (Bauman, 2010)

The persistent morality of peaceable anarchies manifests itself in the ideology of most peoples, no matter how violent their lives may be. Many mythologies look "back" to a Golden Age when people were gentle and shunned killing (e.g., Cohn, 1970: 187-280; Wallace, 1956). Although Chinese history is a bloodbath, when Daoists like Laozi praise the ancients (e.g., LeGuin, 1997: 20-21), they describe a people much like Semai or Buid (Dentan, 2004: 184). Almost all peoples value peace in the abstract. It's just that they make exceptions for particular circumstances. Capital punishment and war are near universals, children everywhere the most likely victims of violence.

The most often proffered solution for this killing is the inculcation of nonkilling values (e.g., Bonta, 1996: 416; Fry, 2004: 200-203; Gardner, this volume; Robarchek and Robarchek, 1996). This suggestion rests on the fact that most nonviolent peoples express a preference for a peaceful life, although none of them are pacifists except the defeated and enclaved Christian cenobites and pacifist intentional communities to whom this paper refers only in passing. The first step, presumably, would be to stop glamorizing killing (Grossman, 2009). Although the advocates of inculcating nonkilling values are experienced scholars whose work I follow closely and whom I admire greatly, I wonder whether glamorizing killing actually increases killing or merely reflects the amount of killing that takes place anyway. A social structure that features FIGs and patriarchy will facilitate something like "honor killings"; if it also includes segmentary patrilineages, killing is likely to be endemic (Boehm, 1987; Otterbein, 2004). Many such societies profess Abrahamic religions. Abrahamic religions preach peace. The word "Islam," which you can gloss as "submission" or "surrender," has the same root (SLM) as *salaam* or *shalom*, "peace." The current slaughterhouse in the Middle East indicates how preaching peace works out in practice in patriarchal democracies. Would glamorizing nonkilling work much better?

> Ideology is a specious way of relating to the world….As the repository of something suprapersonal and objective it enables people to deceive their conscience and conceal their true position and their inglorious *modus vivendi* both from the world and from themselves…. If ideology originally facilitated… the constitution of power by serving as a psychological excuse, then from the moment that excuse is accepted, it constitutes power inwardly, becoming an active component of that power. It begins to function as the principle instrument of ritual communication *within* the system of power (Havel, 1991: 133).

The argument here is not that avowed peaceable values, Abrahamic or not, are insincere, but that they are velleities riddled with systemic and ad hoc exceptions; and so make little difference in people's behavior. "We take almost all the decisive steps in our lives as a result of slight inner adjustments of which we are barely conscious" (Sebald, 2001: 134).

The flip side of this call for pushing "peaceful values" is that constantly representing violence, with or without glorification, desensitizes people to violence (Fry, 2004: 201; Gelles and Straus, 1988: 194). In fact, such repeated exposure is the method the U.S. government uses to overcome the human reluctance to engage in killing to which this chapter has referred (Grossman, 2009). The technique is not to glamorize killing, which doesn't work very well, but to make it reflexive and thoughtless—no big deal. But in capitalist societies anything which has the huge market that representations of violence enjoy responds to repression by going underground and becoming pornography. Take for example a favorite and approved violent method of childtraining in the U.S.: Google "spanking." The response overwhelms the capacity of the search engine and it has to ask plaintively for particulars: race? schoolgirls? bondage? B&D? S&M?

The final question that needs answering is the ancient one, *quis custodet ipsos custodies?* (Juvenal, 1918). Normally I find the notion of "structural violence" too vague and loaded to be useful, but the question "Whose Utopia?" (e.g., Hébert, 2002) needs answering. First, what entity will have the "overarching authority" (Robarchek and Robarchek, 1996) to inculcate or enforce nonkilling values? Historically, the answer has been ultimately the imperialist state, which claims a monopoly *on* killing that it often enforces *by* killing, e.g., in the pacification of San peoples in southern Africa (e.g., Denbow; Wilmsen,

1986; Guenther, 1976, 1980, 1986). Proximately, the chief state values-enforcer is schooling (e.g., Dentan and Juli Edo, 2009; Dentan, Williams-Hunt and Juli Edo, i.p.). Once "pacified," the supposed beneficiaries of state bureaucratic justice and schooling often initially express enthusiasm (Juli Edo, Williams-Hunt and Dentan, 2008; Fry, 2006: 113, 257-8; Robarchek, 1986).

Fry (2006: 259), calling for "creating greater global governance," is aware of imperialist history, but expresses the hope that a democratized UN will avoid "repressive peacemaking." His personal experience with the remarkable efficiency, professionalism and dedication to peace and nonviolence of the Scandinavian bureaucracy (e.g., Dobinson, 2004) must give him confidence in that possibility. But, as the American founding fathers knew, any government policy which depends on the goodwill and ethical standards of the governors is insecure: in World War II, Sweden and Finland had no difficulty cooperating with the Nazis, and Scandinavian popular culture is awash in imagined corrupt totalitarian fantasies (e.g., Larsson, 2010; Mankell, 2004, 2005; Nesser, 2009; Sjabo, 2006). Larsson was editor of *Expo,* a magazine that often covered rightwing, antidemocratic and neoNazi Swedish organizations. And Norway gave the world the word "quisling."

To create a nonkilling society

> ...one can try various measures: religious conversion, economic improvement through development projects, improvement of education... Indeed, these are exactly the measures suggested and implemented by government bodies... [to] assimilate the weaker with the stronger. For one reason or another, including resistance by the weaker ones, the measures have evolved into something completely unrecognizable from the original intention (Nobuta, 2008: 243-244).

Moreover, the dominant Hobbesian and/or imperialist ideology of the states in question tends to construct a lot more violence and killing beyond the boundaries of state authority than actually exists there, as this section of chapter has tried to show. Such self-serving perceptions are almost impossible to change by submitting evidence (e.g., Dove, 1983, 1985). The violence and killing beyond the boundaries become more salient to a state when the state has other interests in the area, so that dispossession, displacement and ethnic cleansing tend to accompany the intervention. "Pacification," like "liberation," has long rationalized, justified and mystified imperialist expansionism.

Finally, state schooling is formally difficult to distinguish from enslavement: state agents take children willy-nilly from their homes; eradicate their egalitarian child culture and undermine their ethnic one; substitute a posture of subordination to whatever class, caste or ethnic group controls the state; provide slaves/students whatever rudimentary skills they need to serve their new masters; and, in the proposed solution to killing, inculcate "nonviolent values," leaving violence to state experts—including, in Malaysia and the U.S., their teachers (Dentan and Juli Edo, 2009; Dentan, Williams-Hunt and Juli Edo, i.p.; Gatto, 2003). Killing, as usual, is a state monopoly. Unsurprisingly, "pacified" and "schooled" Semai seem considerably more likely to kill than their less surveilled ancestors were (Dentan, 2007, 2008a; Dentan and Williams-Hunt, 1999). They are also worse off by a number of measures than they used to be (e.g., Dentan, 2002; Dentan et al., 1997). The San case referenced above is similar, although the details differ.

There is no question that the people who do the "pacification" in almost all instances profit far more than the people pacified. It's not a zero-sum game, but there are many cases in which the latter seem to be net losers, moving from the complexity of more or less egalitarian rustic anarchy into the relative simplicity of subordination and depersonalization. There is a question as to whether mechanizing and industrializing killing and making it a monopoly of a culture like this represents much of an advance over leaving the killing to FIGs.

A Nihilist Utopia

> Let them then not complain of immaturity that dies about thirty; they fall but like the whole world, whose solid and well-composed substance must not expect the duration and period of its constitution… our ends are as obscure as our beginnings…
> That general opinion, that the world grow near its end, hath possessed all ages past as nearly as ours….[A time that will] reduce those seeming inequalities and respective distributions in this world to an equality and recompensive justice in the next… (Sir Thomas Browne, *Religio Medici*, apud Browne, n.d.: 75, 81)

> The possibility of paradise hovers on the cusp of coming into being, so much so that it takes powerful forces to keep such a paradise at bay. If paradise now arises in hell, it's because in the suspension ofthe usual order and the failure of most systems, we are free to live and act another way. (Solnit 2009: 7)

The dominant Abrahamic-Hobbesian ideology of Western industrial capitalism constructs anarchy either as violent chaos or, more sentimentally, as a kind of cute primitivism that cannot meet the demands of "real life" (e.g., Bookchin, 1999: 186-198). For example:

...what may usefully be said of the Semai is that they do not deny [Calvin-ist-Hobbesian] human nature, but do their very best to hobble it wherever necessary, in the interest of balance and human welfare. Their utopian so-lution, however, is a poor competitor in the open market. And as all ideas, all mutations, in the end all species, must be judged on their success in competing with others of their kind, the Semai experiment has to be judged a noble failure (Watson, 1995: 157).

From the also-Darwinian perspective of this chapter, it seems a little pre-mature to determine the relative success or failure of anarchies and states. Both, as this chapter has attempted to show, still flourish, the anarchies even within the body of the state. The anarchies have flourished for tens of thousands of years or perhaps a couple of hundred thousand (if you count only *Homo sapiens*), a couple of million if you count hominines, more than that if you count hominids. The state has lasted ten or twelve thousand years, industrial capitalism a few hundred. There are serious doubts whether capi-talism in its current form is sustainable, and reasonable doubt that the state can survive the disasters that would follow the ecological catastrophe that seems to be coming and which would overwhelm capitalist infrastructure.

Indeed, there's a good deal of doubt that the human species can survive the mass extinction that has already begun and that rivals in scope the ex-tinction of the dinosaurs, as a result of "[human] population growth, con-sumption of resources, carbon gas emissions and the mass extinction of [other] species" (Zizek, 2010: 327). The tardy, feeble and conditional re-sponse of human institutions so far does not suggest that salvation will come from state or corporations.

But let's take the sunny view, that some humans survive the massive population collapse. As things fall apart, the centers cannot hold. The failure of electronic information storage and the crumbling of acid-paper hard copies should delay the opportunity to rediscover lost technology, even if the system of schooling had trained a large enough segment of the population to use the relevant information if it were available. It seems likely that nation states will disintegrate into progressively smaller and smaller local social formations, as people revert to their usual response to disaster, as sketched above.

The upshot should be the blossoming of the two sorts of rural inten-tional communities currently flourishing in the civil society: the libertarian but patriarchal survivalist right (e.g., Coates, 1987) and the anarchist com-munard left, supplemented by a few patriarchal but pacifist cenobitic farm-ing communities (e.g., Niman 2011, in press, this volume). Both sectors should gain recruits from disaster communities (e.g., Solnit, 2009).

A similar situation occurred at the end of the Ice Ages. Two sorts of communities flourished: democratic but patriarchal big game hunters and relatively egalitarian and peaceful foragers. The former manifested rates of killing that were extremely high even by modern industrial state standards, due mostly revenge, raiding, etc. (Fry, 2004: 257-259; Gat, 2007; Keeley, 1995). But then came a further ecological change: "Big game hunting went into sharp decline following the end of the last Ice Age; in the Levant, the final disappearance of the largest animals was followed by the disappearance of once-bountiful gazelle herds" (Balakrishnan, 2007: 37-38). Perforce, the big game hunters drifted into a subsistence pattern congenial to egalitarian anarchy: "they did not have war because they had ceased to be hunters of big game" (Otterbein, 2004: 13). Even a Hobbesian like Keeley (1995: 120) acknowledges that from 11,000 to 9000 BCE, "Not only is there no indication of any increase in warfare in this period, there are no indications of warfare at all." Remember: computer simulation indicates that warfare diminishes the "survivability" of small egalitarian communities (Younger, 2004). The absence of warfare and big game would presumably diminish the salience of FIGs in daily routines.

American survivalists are banking proximately on storing enough supplies to get through the collapse and arming themselves well enough to defend those supplies against an expected influx of "mud people" (nonwhites) from the collapsing cities. Ultimately they hope for the restoration of a more libertarian America, the Rapture and/or the End of Days. Many of the men are deer hunters. A few are prepared to "live off the land" and have stored books to help them. The question is whether, should America not revive and the End of Days not come, enough big game will survive to support a big game hunting economy. The ethnic cleansing and "pacification" of Native Americans, the near-extinction of large predators and the clear-cutting of American primary forests have led to a deer population explosion, so that there are many more deer now than when the Europeans arrived. The moose, bison, wild sheep, musk ox, caribou and mountain goat populations are much smaller and concentrated. They are therefore likely to perish in an ecological catastrophe. There is therefore a question about whether even the deer populations can survive an all-out assault for two or three centuries by FIGs wielding weapons far more deadly than those deployed by indigenous big game hunters. The protoneolithic evidence suggests not. Anyway, the stored weapons will not last forever, and stone knapping projectile heads is a skill, once lost, not readily reacquired. And how many modern Americans have heard of an atlatl?

In that case, the intentional enclaves and disaster communities might predominate. People would become foragers or horticulturalists, much like the egalitarian anarchies this chapter has sketched. Warfare would cease, though young men would continue to fight over women and sometimes kill each other. Perhaps people would have learned to isolate young men and women from the rest of society, in separate age-based settlements like those of the Nyakyusa or Muria Gond. But that's probably too much to hope for.

Thanks!

Peter M. Gardner, Charles Macdonald, Laura J. McClusky, Charles Macdonald and Michael Niman, reliable colleagues and good friends, helped me compose this chapter.

References

Akopsa (2010). "History of Violence: Christian boarding schools and the March 10 trial of Jack Patterson," *The Seminal*, February 23. Available at: <http://seminal.firedoglake.com/diary/31378>

Alexiades, Miguel (2010). "Indigenous Peoples in the Popular Consciousness," in Lee, Julian C. H., Ed., *The Malaysian Way of Life*. Subang, Msia, and London: Marshall Cavendish Editions, pp. 69-71.

Alland, Alexander (1981). *To Be Human*. New York: John Wiley.

Amster, Randall (2003). "Restoring (Dis)Order: Sanctions, Resolutions, and 'Social Control' in Anarchist Communities," *Contemporary Justice Review*, 6(1):9-24.

Anonymous (2009). "The Wearin' of the Mean," *Harper's Magazine*, 319(1911): 20-21.

A[ssociated] P[ress] (2001). "As US Troops Depart, Concern about Support," *Buffalo News*, 8 Mar.: A3.

Bailey, R. C.; Head, G.; Jenike, M.; Owen, B.; Rechtman, R.; Zechenter, E. (1989). "Hunting and Gathering in Tropical Rainforest: Is It Possible?," *American Anthropologist*, 92:59-82.

Balakrishnan, Gopal (2007). "The Role of Force in History," *New Left Review*, 47:23-56.

Baldwin, Roger N. (1970). Note for "Anarchist Morality," in Kropotkin, Peter, *Anarchism: A Collection of Revolutionary Writings*. Mineola: Dover, p. 79.

Banfield, E. C. (1970). *The Unheavenly City*. Boston: Little, Brown.

Barash, David P. (2003). *The Survival Game: How Game Theory Explains the Biology of Cooperation and Competition*. New York: Times Books.

Barclay, H. (1990). *People without Government: An Anthropology of Anarchy*. Seattle: Left Bank.

Bauman, Zygmunt (2010). "The Disempowering," *Truthout*, Sunday 27 March.

Beccaria, Cesare Bonesana (1778 [1764]). *An Essay on Crimes and Punishments [Dei Dellitti e delle Pene]*. Philadelphia: R. Bell.

Benjamin, Geoffrey (1968). "Temiar Society," *Federation Museums Journal*, 13:1-43

Bingham, P. A. (2000). "Human Evolution and Human History: A Complete Theory," *Evolutionary Anthropology*, 9:248-257.

Boehm, Christopher (1987). *Blood Revenge: The Enactment and Management of Conflict in Montenegro and Other Tribal Societies*. Philadelphia: University of Pennsylvania Press.

Bonta, Bruce D. (1993). *Peaceful Peoples: An Annotated Bibliography*. Metuchen; London: Scarecrow Press.

Bonta, Bruce D. (1996). "Conflict Resolution among Peaceful Societies: the Culture of Peacefulness," *Journal of Peace Research*, 33:403-420.

Bookchin, Murray (1999). *Anarchism, Marxism, and the Future of the Left. Interviews and Essays, 1993-1998*. San Francisco: A. K. Press.

Bouvard, M. (1975). *The International Community Movement: Building a New Moral World*. Port Washington: Kennikat Press.

Brooks, D. (1987). "Good Vibrations: The New Peace Offensive," *National Review*, 39(21):36-39.

Browne, Sir Thomas (n.d. [1642]). *Religio Medici and Other Essays*. London: Chapman and Hall.

Bulbeck, F. David (2003). "Hunter-Gatherer Occupation of the Malay Peninsula from the Ice Age to the Iron Age," in Mercader, J., Ed., *Under the Canopy: The Archeology of Tropical Rain Forests*. New Brunswick: Rutgers University Press, pp. 119-161.

Carrithers, Michael (1989). "Sociality, not aggression, is the key human trait," in Howell, S.; Willis, R., Eds., *Societies at Peace: Anthropological Perspectives*. London: Routledge, pp. 187-207.   .

Cipriani, Lidio (1966). *The Andaman Islanders*. New York: Praeger.

Clark, Owen (2010). "DA: Deadly Child Abuse Case Linked To 'Biblical Chastisement,'" *khsltv.com*, Feb. 12.

Coates, J. (1987). *Armed and Dangerous: The Rise of the Survivalist Right*. New York: Hill and Wang.

Cohn, Norman (1970 [1957]). *The Pursuit of the Millenium: Revolutionary Millenarians and Mystical Anarchists of the Middle Ages*. New York: Oxford University Press.

Cords, Marina; Melanie Killen (1998). "Conflict Resolution in Human and Nonhuman Primates," in Langer, J.; Killen, M., Eds., *Piaget, Evolution and Development*. New Jersey: Lawrence Erlbaum Assocs, pp. 193-218

Dallos, Csilla (2010). *From Equality to Inequality: Social Change among Newly Sedentary Lanoh Hunter-Gatherer Traders of Peninsular Malaysia*. Manuscript in the possession of the author.

Denbow, James R.; Wilmsen, E. (1986). "The Advent and Course of Pastoralism in the Kalahari," *Science*, 234:1509-1515.

Denby, David (2010). "Wastelands," *The New Yorker*, 18 Jan.: 82-83.

Dentan, Robert Knox (1962-1963). *Catalog for Semai collection*. New York: American Museum of Natural History.

Dentan, Robert K. (1970). "Hocus Pocus and Extensionism in Central Malaya," *Notes on Semai Kinship Terminology. American Anthropologist*, 70 (2):358-362.

Dentan, Robert K. (1971). "Some Senoi Semai planting techniques," *Economic Botany*, 25: 136-159.

Dentan, Robert Knox. 1975. If there were no Malays, who would the Semai be? In Judith Nagata, ed., Pluralism in Malaysia: myth and reality. Contributions to Asian Studies 7:50-64.

Dentan, Robert Knox (1976). "Identity and ethnic contact: Perak, Malaysia, 1963," *Journal of Asian Affairs*, 1(1): 79-86.

Dentan, Robert Knox (1978). "Notes on childhood in a nonviolent context: the Semai case," in Montagu, Ashley, Ed., *Learning nonaggression*. London: Oxford University Press, pp. 94-143.

Dentan, Robert K. (1979 [1968]). *The Semai: a nonviolent people of Malaysia*. New York: Holt, Rinehart and Winston.

Dentan, Robert Knox (1988). "Band-level Eden: a mystifying chimera," *Cultural Anthropology*, 3:276-284

Dentan, Robert Knox (1989). "How Semai Made Music for Fun," *Echology*, 3: 100-122.

Dentan, Robert Knox (1992). "The rise, maintenance and destruction of peaceable polity," in Silverberg, James; Gray, J. Patrick, Eds., *Aggression and peacefulness in humans and other primates*. New York: Oxford University Press, pp. 214-270.

Dentan, Robert Knox (1994). "Surrendered men: Peaceable enclaves in the post-Enlightenment West," in Sponsel, Leslie E.; Gregor, Thomas, Eds., *The anthropology of peace and nonviolence*. Boulder: Lynne Rienner, pp. 69-108.

Dentan, Robert Knox (1997). "The Persistence of Received Truth: How the Malaysian Ruling Class Constructs Orang Asli," in Winzeler, Robert, Ed., *Indigenous Peoples and the State: Politics, Land, and Ethnicity in the Malaysian Peninsula and Borneo*. New Haven: Yale University Southeast Asia Studies, pp. 98-134.

Dentan, Robert Knox (1999). "Spotted Doves at War: the Praak Sangkiil," *Asian Folklore Studies*, 63(2):397-434.

Dentan, Robert Knox (2001a). "Ambivalences in Child Training by the Semai of Peninsular Malaysia and Other Peoples," *Crossroads*, 15(1):89-129.

Dentan, Robert Knox (2001b). "Semai-Malay Ethnobotany: Hindu Influences on the Trade in Sacred Plants, Ho Hiang," in Rashid, Razha; Karim, Wazir Jahan, Eds., *Minority Cultures of Peninsular Malaysia: Survivals of Indigenous Heritage*. Penang: Academy of Social Sciences (AKASS), pp. 173-187.

Dentan, Robert Knox (2002). "Ideas Redeem, but Political Memories Do Run Short: Islamiciztion among Malaysia's Orang Asli," *Social Justice: Anthropology, Peace and Human Rights*, 3(3-4):153-190.

Dentan, Robert Knox (2004). "Cautious, Alert, Polite and Elusive: The Semai of Central Peninsular Malaysia," in Kemp, Graham; Fry, Douglas, Eds., *Keeping the Peace: Conflict Resolution and Peaceful Societies around the World*. New York; London: Routledge, pp. 167-184.

Dentan, Robert Knox (2006). "How the Androgynous Bird God Brought Agriculture to Semai of West Malaysia: Discipline, Hard Work and Subordination to the Cycle of Time," in Le Roux, Pierre; Sellato, Bernard, Eds., *Les messagers divins: aspects esthetiques et symboliques des oiseaux en Asie du sud-est.* Marseille: IRASEC; and Paris: Editions Seven Orients/ Connaisances et Savoirs, pp. 295-356.

Dentan, Robert Knox (2007). "Arifin in the Iron Cap: Confessions of a Young Man, Drowning," in Waterson, Roxana Helen, Ed., *Southeast Asian Lives: Personal Narratives and Historical Experience.* Singapore; Athens: Singapore University Press and Ohio University Press, pp. 181-220.

Dentan, Robert Knox (2008a). *Overwhelming Terror: Love, Fear, Peace, and Violence among Semai of Malaysia.* Lanham: Rowman and Littlefield.

Dentan, Robert Knox. 2008b Recent Studies on Violence: What's In and What's Out. Reviews in Anthropology 37(1): 1-27.

Dentan, Robert Knox (in press). "Childhood, familiarity and social life among East Semai," in Gibson, Thomas; Sillander, Kenneth, Eds., *Anarchic Solidarity: Autonomy, Equality, and Fellowship in Southeast Asia.* New Haven: Yale University Southeast Asia Program Publication.

Dentan, Robert Knox; Williams-Hunt, Bah Tony (Anthony) (1999). "Untransfiguring death: Rape, drunkenness, development and homicide in an apprehensive void," in Gomes, Alberto, Ed., *Modernity and Indigenous Minorities in Malaysia and Indonesia,* RIMA [*Review of Indonesian and Malaysian Affairs*] 33(1): 17-66.

Dentan, Robert Knox; Williams-Hunt, Bah Tony (Anthony) (in press). "'They Do Not Like to Be Confined and...Told What to Do': Schooling Malaysian Indigenes," in Adams, Kathleen; Gillogly, Kathleen, Eds., *Everyday Life in Southeast Asia.* Bloomington; Indianapolis: Indiana University Press.

Dentan, Robert Knox; Endicott, Kirk Michael; Gomes, Alberto G.; Hooker, M. Barry (1997). *Malaysia and the Original People: A Case Study of the Impact of Development on Indigenous Peoples.* Boston: Allyn and Bacon.

Dentan, Robert Knox; Edo, Juli (2008). "Schooling vs. Education, Hidden vs. Overt Curricula: Ways of Thinking about Schools, Economic Development and Putting the Children of the Poor to Work," *Moussons,*12:3-34.

Dobinson, Kristin (2004). "A Model of Peacefulness: Rethinking Peace and Conflict in Norway," in Kemp, Graham; Fry, Douglas, Eds., *Keeping the Peace: Conflict Resolution and Peaceful Societies around the World.* New York: Routledge, pp. 149-166.

Dolgoff, Sam, ed. (1974). *The Anarchist Collectives: Workers Self-Management in the Spanish Revolution 1936-1939.* New York: Free Life Editions.

Dove, Michael R. (1983). "Theories of Agriculture and the Political Economy of Ignorance," *Agroforestry Systems,* 1: 85-99.

Dove, Michael R. (1985). "The Agroecological Mythology of the Javanese and the Political Economy of Indonesia," *Indonesia,* 39: 1-36.

Drehle, David von (2010). "Why Crime Went Away," *Time,* 22 Feb.: 32-35.

Dunn, Fred (1975). "Rain-Forest Collectors and Traders: A Study of Resource Utilization in Modern and Ancient Malaya," *Monographs of the Malaysian Branch of the Royal Asiatic Society,* 5.

Eller, Jack David (2006). *Violence and Culture: A Cross-Cultural and Interdisciplinary Approach.* Belmont: Thompson Wadsworth.

Endicott, Kirk Michael (1983). "The Effects of Slave Raiding on the Aborigines of the Malay Peninsula," in Reid, Anthony, Ed., *Slavery, Bondage and Dependency in Southeast Asia*. New York: St. Martin's Press, pp. 216-245.

Endicott, Kirk Michael; Endicott, Karen L. (2008). *The Headman Was a Woman: The Gender Egalitarian Batek of Malaysia*. Long Grove: Waveland Press.

Erasmus, Charles J. (1981). "Anarchy. Enclavement, and Syntropy in Intentional and Traditional Communities," in Castile, G. P.; Kushner, G., Eds., *Persistent Peoples: Cultural Enclaves in Perspective*. Tucson: University of Arizona Press, pp. 192-211.

Erchak, Gerald (1984). "Cultural Anthropology and Wife Abuse," *Current Anthropology*, 25:331-332.

Erchak, Gerald (1994). "Family Violence," in Ember, Carol; Ember, Melvin, Eds., *Research Frontiers in Anthropology*. Englewood Cliffs: Prentice Hall.

Fellowship for Intentional Community (2007). *Communities Directory, 5th ed*. Rutledge: Fellowship for Intentional Community.

Fix, Alan G. (1977). *The Demography of the Semai Senoi* (Anthropological Papers, Museum of Anthropology, 62). Ann Arbor: Museum of Anthropology.

Fritz, Charles (1996). "Disasters and Mental Health: Therapeutic Principles Drawn from Disaster Studies," University of Delaware Disaster Research Center. Available at: <http//www.udel.edu/DRC/preliminary/hande10.pdf>.

Fry, Douglas P. (1987). "Differences between Playfighting and Serious Fighting among Zapotec School Children," *Ethology and Sociobiology*, 8:285-306.

Fry, Douglas P. (1990). "Play Aggression among Zapotec School Children: Implications for the Practice Hypothesis," *Aggressive Behavior*, 16:321-340.

Fry, Douglas P. (1999). "Peaceful Societies," in Kurtz, L. R., Ed., *Encyclopedia of Violence, Peace and Conflict*, Vol. 3. San Diego: Academic Press, pp. 719-733.

Fry, Douglas P. (2006). *The Human Potential for Peace: An Anthropological Challenge to Assumptions about War and Violence*. New York: Oxford University Press.

Gardner, Peter M. (1966). "Symmetric Respect and Memorate Knowledge: the Structure and Ecology of Individualistic Culture," *Southwestern Journal of Anthropology*, 22: 389-415.

Gardner, Peter M. (1976). "Birds, Words, and a Requiem for the Omniscient Informant," *American Ethnologist*, 3:446-468.

Gardner, Peter (1985). "Bicultural Oscillation as a Long-term Adaptation to Cultural Frontiers: Cases and Questions," *Human Ecology*, 13: 411-432.

Gardner, Peter (1988). "Pressures for Tamil Propriety in Paliyan Social Organization," in Ingold, T; Riches, D.; Woodburn, J., Eds., *Hunters and Gatherers I: History, Evolution, and Social Change*. Oxford: Berg, pp. 91-106.

Gardner, Peter M. (1991). "Foragers' Pursuit of Individual Autonomy," *Current Anthropology*, 32:543-572.

Gardner, Peter (2010). "Lovers not fighters," personal communication, 02/17/10.

Gat, Azar (2007). *War in Human Civilization*. Oxford: Oxford University Press.

Gatto, John Taylor (2003). "Against School," *Harper's Magazine*, 307 (1840):33-38.

Gatto, John Taylor (2006). *The Underground History of American Education: An Intimate Investigation into the Prison of Modern Education.* New York: Oxford Village Press.

Gelles, Richard J.; Straus, Murray A. (1998). *Intimate Violence.* New York: Simon and Schuster.

Ghosh, Bobby (2010). "Papal Problem," *Time*, 175(12):34-37.

Gibson, Thomas (1989). "Symbolic Representataions of Tranquility and Aggression among the Buid," in Howell, Signe; Willis, Roy, Eds., *Societies at Peace: Anthropological Perspectives.* Londion; New York: Routledge, pp. 60-78.

Gibson, Thomas; Sillander, Kenneth, Eds. (in press). *Anarchic solidarity: Autonomy, Equality and Fellowship in Southeast Asia.* New Haven: Yale University Southeast Asia Program Publication.

Gilsenan, Michael (1993 [1982]). *Recognizing Islam: Religion and Society in the Modern Middle East.* London; New York: I. B. Tauris.

Gordon, Robert J. (1992). *The Bushman Myth: The Making of a Namibian Underclass.* Boulder: Westview Press.

Griffin, Marcus B.; Griffin, P. Bion (1997). "Agta Foragers: Alternative Histories and Culural Autonomy," *Australian Journal of Anthropology*, 8:259-269.

Graeber, David (2007). "There Never Was a West: Or, Democracy Emerges from the Spaces in Between," in Graeber, David, Ed., *Possibilities: Essays on Hierarchy, Rebellion, and Desire.* Oakland: A.K. Press, pp. 329-374.

Gray, Steven (2010). "Spotlight: The Hutaree Militia," *Time*,175(14):18.

Griffiths, C.T.; Hamilton, R. (1996). "Sanctioning and Healing: Restorative Justice in Canadian Aboriginal Communities," in Galaway, B.; Hudson, J., Eds., *Restorative Justice: International Perspectives.* Monsey: Criminal Jusrtice Press, pp. 175-191.

Grossman, Dave, Lt. Col. (2009). *On Killing: The Psychological Cost of Learning to Kill in War and Society.* New York: Little, Brown and Company.

Guenther, Matthias G. (1979). "Bushman Religion and the (Non)sense of Anthropological Theory of Religion," *Sociologus*, 29:102-132.

Hakim Bey [Peter L. Wilson] (2010). "Permanent TAZs," Institute for New Culture Thecnologies. Available at: <http://www.t0.or.at/hakimbey/paz.htm>.

Hancock, L.; Mitchell, C. (2007). *Zones of Peace.* Herndon: Kumarian Press.

Harris, Lynn (2010). "Godly discipline turned deadly - A controversial child 'training' practice comes under fire - this time from Christians themselves," Available at: <http://ww.salon.com/life/feature/2010/02/22/no_greater_joy>.

Havel, Vàclav (1992). *Open Letters: Selected Writings 1965-1990.* New York: Vintage.

Headland, Thomas; Reid, Lawrence (1989). "Hunter-Gatherers and Their Neighbors from Prehistory to the Present," *Current Anthropology*, 30:43-66.

Hébert, Martin (2002). "Whose Utopia? Development, Resistance, and Patterns of Structural Violence in a Mexican Indigenous Region," *Social Justice: Anthropology, Peace and Human Rights*, 3(3-4):99-138.

Hedges, Chris (2003). *War Is a Force That Gives Us Meaning.* New York: Anchor Books.

Hobbes, Thomas (1966 [1651]). "The State of Nature," in Hammer, L. Z., Ed., *Value and Man: Readings in Philosophy.* New York: McGraw-Hill, pp. 214-219.

Hood Salleh (1989). "Bases of Traditional Authority among the Orang Asli of Penin-
sular Malaysia," *Akademika*, 35 (Julai): 75-86.
Horgan, John (2010). "Reconciling Hawks and Doves: On the Possibility of Ending
War," *Ecotone*, 6(1):70-89.
Howell, Signe (2006). ·Chewong Women in Transition: The Effects of Monetization
on a Hunter-Gatherers Society," in Baer, Adela, Ed., *Orang Asli Women of Ma-
laysia: Perceptions, Situations and Aspirations*. Kuala Lumpur: Center for Orang
Asli Concerns, pp. 61-106.
Howell, Signe; Willis, Roy, Eds. (1989). *Societies at Peace: Anthropological Perspec-
tives*. London: Routledge.
Hrdy, Sarah B. (2009). *Mothers and Others: The Evolutionary Origins of Mutual
Understanding*. Cambridge: Harvard University Press.
Jablonski, Nina G. (2010). "The Naked Truth," *Scientific American*, 302(2):42-49.
Jarosz, Philip James (2010). "Negative Talk Hurts Haiti Relief Efforts," *Buffalo News*,
(23 Jan.): A7.
Juli Edo (1990). *Tradisi Lisan Masyarakat Semai. Monograf Fakulti Sains Kemasyara-
katan dan Kemanusiaan 16*. Kuala Lumpur: Universiti Kebangsaan Malaysia.
Juli Edo; Williams-Hunt, Anthony; Dentan, Robert Knox (2009). "'Surrender,' Peace-
keeping and Internal Colonialism," *Bijdragen tot de Taal-, Land- en Volken-
kunde*,165(2-3):216-240.
Juvenal (1918 [approx. 2nd c. AD]. *Ancient History Sourcebook: Satire VI*. Ramsay,
G. G., Ed. and Tr. London: Loeb Library.
Kalafer, Steve; Kalafer, Jonathan (2009). *We Love You*. New Jersey: New Jersey Pictures.
Kanter, R. M. (1972). *Commitment and Community: Communes and Utopias in So-
ciological Perspective*. Cambridge: Harvard University Press.
Keeley, Lawrence (1995). *War before Civilization*. Oxford: Oxford University Press.
Kelly, R. C. (2000). *Warless Societies and the Origins of War*. Ann Arbor: University
of Michigan Press.
Kemp, Graham; Fry, Douglas P. (2004). *Keeping the Peace: Conflict Resolution and
Peaceful Societies around the World*. New York: Routledge.
Kirsch, Stuart (1997). "Lost Tribes: Indigenous People and the Social Imaginary,"
Anthropological Quarterly, 70(2):58-67.
Knauft, Bruce (1987). "Reconsidering Violence in Simple Human Societies," *Current
Anthropology*, 28(4):457-500.
Kropotkin, Peter (2002 [1880s]). "Revolutionary Government," in Baldwin, R. N. ed.,
Anarchism: A Collection of Revolutionary Writings. Mineola: Dover, pp. 237-250.
Kropotkin, Peter (2006 [1902]). *Mutual Aid: A Factor of Evolution*. Mineola: Dove
Landau, Elizabeth (2010). "In Haiti, mental aftershocks could be far-reaching,"
CNN (Jan.19). Available at: <http://www.cnn.com/2010/HEALTH/01/15/haiti.
mental.psychological.effects/index.html>.
Larsson, Stieg (2010). *The Girl Who Played with Fire*. New York: Vintage Books.
Lechner, T. (2002). *Surrender without Subordination* [PhD thesis in anthropology].
SUNY University at Buffalo: <http://sites.google.com/site/drthomaslechner/>.

Lee, Richard Borshay (1979). *The !Kung San: Men, Women, and Work in a Foraging Society*. Cambridge: Cambridge University Press.

Lemert, Charles (2007). *Thinking the Unthinkable: The Riddles of Classical Theories*. Boulder and London: Paradigm Publishers.

Lewis, Wyndham (1989 [1926]). *The Art of Being Ruled*. Santa Rosa: Black Sparrow.

Lieberman, Daniel E.; Bramble, Dennis M. (2007). "The evolution of marathon running: capabilities in humans," *Sports Medicine*, 37(4-5):288-290.

Lovejoy, C. Owen (2009). "Reexamining human origins in the light of *Ardipithecus ramidus*," *Science*, 326(5949): 74.

Lye Tuck-Po, ed. (2001). *Orang Asli of Peninsular Malaysia: A Comprehensive and Annotated Bibliography*. Kyoto: Center for Southeast Asian Studies.

Lye Tuck Po (2008). "Being Forest Peoples: Globalizing Local Sustainability," *Moussons*, 12:35-48.

Lynd, Staughton; Lynd, Alice, Eds. (1995). *Nonviolence in America: A Documentary History*. Maryknoll: Orbis Books.

Macdonald, Charles J.-H. (2007). *Uncultural Behavior. An anthropological investigation of suicide in the Southern Philippines*. Kyoto: Monographs of the Center for Southeast Asian Studies, Kyoto University.

Macdonald, Charles J.-H. (2009a). "The Anthropology of Anarchy," *Occasional Paper from the School of Social Science, Institute for Advanced Study*, 35.

Macdonald, Charles J.-H. (2009b). "L'anthropologie du suicide. Interprétation ou explication? Reponse à Rozenberg," *L'Homme*, 191: 201-209.

Macdonald, Charles J.-H. (2010). "Lovers not fighters," personal communication, 02/13/10.

Macdonald, Charles J.-H. (in press, a). "A Theoretical Overview of Anarchic Solidarity," in Gibson, Thomas; Sillander, Kenneth, Eds., *Anarchic Solidarity: Autonomy, Equality, and Fellowship in Southeast Asia*. New Haven: Yale University Southeast Asia Program Publication.

Macdonald, Charles J.-H. (in press, b). "Kinship and fellowship among the Palawan," in Gibson, Thomas; Sillander, Kenneth, Eds., *Anarchic Solidarity: Autonomy, Equality, and Fellowship in Southeast Asia*. New Haven: Yale University Southeast Asia Program Publication.

MacMillan, Harriet L; Boyle, Michael H.; Wong, Maria Y.-Y.; Duku, Eric K.; Fleming, Jan E.; Walsh, Christine A. (1999). "Slapping and spanking in childhood and its association with lifetime prevalence of psychiatric disorders in a general population sample," *Canadian Medical Association Journal*,161(7):805-809.

Man Yuke Foong; Hoh, Amelia (1987). "Living in Fear of 'Outsiders'," *Sunday Star*, 5 July.

Mankell, Henning (2004 [2002]). *Before the Frost*. New York: Vintage.

Mankell, Henning (2007 [2005]). *Kennedy's Brain*. New York: New Press.

Marshall, Michael (2002). *The Straw Men*. New York: Jove.

McClusky, Laura J. (2010). Personal communication, 3/23/10.

Montagu, Ashley, Ed. (1978). *Learning Nonaggression: The Experience of Non-Literate Societies*. London: Oxford University Press.

Nanda, Serena (1988). "More dialogue on the "bloodthirsty" Semai," *American Anthropologist*, 90: 422-423.

N[arcotics]A[nonymous World Services] (2008). *Narcotics Anonymous*, 6th ed. Chatsworth: Narcotics Anonymous World Services.

National Research Council (1996). *Understanding Violence against Women*. Washington, DC: National Academy Press and American Psychological Association.

Nesser, Hakan (2009 [1996]). *Woman with Birthmark*. New York: Random.

Niman, Michael I. (2011, in press). *People of the Rainbow: A Nomadic Utopia*. Knoxville: University of Tennessee Press.

Nobuta, Toshihiro (2008). *Living on the Periphery: Development and Islamization among the Orang Asli*. Kyoto; Melbourne: Kyoto University Press; Trans Pacific Press.

Nordstrom, Carolyn (2004). *Shadows of War*. Berkeley: University of California Press.

Office for Victims of Crime (2002). "Children as Victims and Witnesses," in Shichor, D. Tibbetts, S. G., Eds., *Victims and Victimization*. Prospect Heights: Waveland Press, pp. 81-102.

Otterbein, Keith F. (1985). *The Evolution of War: A Cross-Cultural Study*, 2nd. ed. New Haven: Human Relations Area Files.

Otterbein, Keith F. (1986). *The Ultimate Coercive Sanction*. New Haven: Human Relations Area Files.

Otterbein, Keith F. (2004). *How War Began*. College Station: Texas A&M University Press.

Otterbein, Keith F. (2010). "The Relevance of the Anthropology of War to the Study of Small-Scale Wars Today," *Teaching Anthropology: SACC Notes*, 16(1): 37-39.

Pearl, Michael (2009). "Child Training Marathon (revised and updated)," *NGJ Ministries*, Nov.-Dec.: 3-5, 31.

Pearl, Michael (2010a). "Like Father, Like Son," *NGJ Ministries*, March-April:17.

Pearl, Michael (2010b). "Spank and Save a Child," *NGJ Ministries*, May-June:3-10.

Pospisil, Leopold (1964). "Law and Social Structure among the Nunamiut Eskimo," in Goodenough, W. H., Ed., *Explorations in Cultural Anthropology*. New York: McGraw-Hill, pp. 395-432.

Prescott, James W. (1975). "Body Pleasure and the Origins of Violence," *The Bulletin of the Atomic Scientists*, Nov.: 10-20.

Proudhon, Pierre-Joseph (1989 [1851]). *General Idea of the Revolution in the Nineteenth Century*. London: Pluto Press.

PBS [Public Broadcasting System] (2010). "Frontline: The Dancing Boys Of Afghanistan," Available at: <http://www.pbs.org/wgbh/pages/frontline/dancingboys/>.

Riches, David (2000). "The Holistic Person; Or, the ideology of egalitarianism," *Journal of the Royal Anthropological Institute*, 6(4):669-685.

Robarchek, Clayton A. (1988). "Ghosts and Witches: The Psychocultural Dynamics of Semai Peacefulness," Paper presented at the 87th national meeting of the American Anthropological Association.

Robarchek, Clayton A. (1989). "Hobbesian and Rousseauan Images of Man: Autonomy and Individualism in a Peaceful Society," in Howell, S.; Willis, R., Eds., *Societies at Peace: Anthropological Perspectives*. London: Routledge, pp. 31-45.

Robarchek, Clayton A.; Robarchek, Carole (1996). "Waging Peace: The Psychological and Sociocultural Dynamics of Positive Peace," in Wolfe, A. W.; Yang, H., Eds., *Anthropological Contributions to Conflict Resolution*. Athens: University of Georgia Press, pp. 64-80.

Rosaldo, Renato; Rosaldo, Michelle (1975). "Ilongot," in LeBar, F. M., Ed., *Ethnic Groups of Insular Southeast Asia*, Vol. 2. New Haven: Human Relations Area Files, pp. 103-106.

Rosaldo, Renato (1988). "Ethnic Concentrations: The Ilongots of Upland Luzon," in Terry Rambo, A.; Gillogly, Kathleen; Hutterer, Karl, Eds., *Ethnic Diversity and the Control of Natural Resources in Southeast Asia*. Ann Arbor: Center for South and Southeast Asian Studies, University of Michigan, pp. 161-172.

Rousseau, Jérôme (2006). *Rethinking Social Evolution: The Perspective from Middle-Range Societies*. Montreal: McGill-Queen's University Press.

Sherman, Nancy (2010). *The Ultimate War: Inside the Hearts, Minds, and Souls of Our Soldiers*. New York: W.W.Norton.

Sjabo, Jo (2006 [2000]). *The Red breast*. New York: Harper.

Sebald, W. G. (2001). *Austerlitz*. New York: Modern Library.

Shichor, David; Tibbetts, S. G. (2002). "Types of Victims," in Shichor, David; Tibbetts, S. G., Eds., *Victims and Victimization*. Prospect Heights: Waveland Press, pp. 77-80.

Solnit, Rebecca (2009). *A Paradise Built in Hell: The Extraordinary Communities That Arise in Disaster*. New York: Viking.

Spies, August 1995[1886]. "Speech in Court," in Lynd, Staughton; Lynd, Alice, Eds. *Nonviolence in America: A Documentary History*. Maryknoll: Orbis Books, pp. 43-45.

Sponsel, Leslie E.; Gregor, Thomas, Eds. (1994). *The Anthropology of Peace and Nonviolence*. Boulder: Lynne Rienner.

Stephenson, June (1995). *Men Are Not Cost-Effective: Male Crime in America*. New York: Perennial.

Suwa, Gen; Kono, Reiko T.; Simpson, Scott W.; Asfaw, Berhane; Lovejoy, C. Owen; White, Tim D. (2009). "Paleobiological implications of the *Ardipithecus ramidus* dentition," *Science*, 326 (2 Oct.):69.

Tavory, Iddo; Goodman, Yehuda C. (2009). "'A Collective of Individuals': Between Self and Solidarity at a Rainbow Gathering," *Sociology of Religion*, 70(3): 262-284.

Taylor, Shelley E. (2002). *The Tending Instinct: How Nurturing Is Essential to Who We Are and How We Live*. New York: Holt.

Thomas, Elizabeth Marshall (1959). *The Harmless People*. New York: Knopf.

Time (2010). "Briefing: The World," *Time*, 15 Feb.:14-15.

Time/AP (2010). "Ted Costan of Partners in Health, quoted in Verbatim," *Time*, 22 March:18.

Trevarthen, Colwyn; Logotheti, Katerina (1989). "Child in Society, and society in children: the nature of basic trust," in Howell, S.; Willis, R., Eds., *Societies at Peace: Anthropological Perspectives*. London: Routledge, pp. 165-186.

U.S. Marine Corps (1992). *Combat Stress. Fleet Marine Force Manual (FMFM) 4-55*. Quantico: U.S. Marine Corps.

Van der Sluys, Cornelia (2006). "Are the Jahai a Non-Violent People?" in Baer, Adela, Ed., *Orang Asli Women of Malaysia: Perceptions, Situations and Aspirations*. Kuala Lumpur: Center for Orang Asli Concerns, pp. 43-50.

Venkateswar, Sita (2004). *Development and Ethnocide: Colonial Practices in the Andaman Islands*. Copenhagen: International Work Group for Indigenous Affairs.

Veysey, L. R. (1973). *The Communal Experience: Anarchist and Mystical Counter-Cultures in America*. New York: Harper and Row.

Waal, Frans B. M. de (1989). *Peacemaking among Primates*. Cambridge: Harvard University Press.

Wallace, Anthony F. C. (1956). "Revitalization Movements," *American Anthropologist*, 58:264-281.

Watson, David (1997). *Beyond Bookchin: Preface for a Future Social Ecology*. Detroit: Black and Red.

Watson, Lyall (1995). *Dark History: A Natural History of Evil*. New York: Harper Collins.

White, Tim D.; Asfaw, Berhane; Beyene, Yonas; Haile-Selassie, Yohannes; Lovejoy, C. Owen; Suwa, Gen; WoldeGabriel, Giday (2009). "*Ardipithecus ramidus* and the paleobiology of early hominids," *Science*, 326 (2 Oct.): 64.

Williams, Corey; Barrett, Derlin (2010). "Christian Militia Tied to War on Police," *Buffalo News* (30 March):1-2.

Wilson, Monica (1951). *Good Company: A Study of Nyakyusa Age-Villages*. Long Grove: Waveland Press.

Wittfogel, Karl (1958). *Oriental Despotism: A Comparative Study of Total Power*. New Haven: Yale University Press.

Woodburn, James (1982). "Egalitarian Societies," *Man*, 17:431-51.

Wrangham, Richard (2001). "Chimpanzee Violence is a Serious Topic: A Response to Sussman and Marshak's Critique of *Demonic Males: Apes and the Origins of Human Violence*," *Global Nonkilling Working Papers*, 1:29-50.

Younger, Stephen M. (2004). *Leadership, Violence, and Warfare in Small Societies: A Simulation Approach*. Los Alamos; Manoa: Los Alamos National Laboratory; University of Hawai'i at Manoa.

Zizek, Slavoj (2010). *Living in the End Times*. London: Verso.

Chapter Five

How Can a Society Eliminate Killing? [1]

Peter M. Gardner
University of Missouri

Introduction

We are living in an age in which anthropologists tend increasingly to seek answers to their questions using materialist approaches. As powerful as these approaches may be, in some instances values also turn out to play an essential part in our explanations. A case in point is the explanation of south Indian Paliyans' notable success in avoiding intentional killing of humans. These hunter-gatherers are a quiet and peaceful people; they would number among the least violent folk ever described by anthropologists. But, what allows us to understand this accomplishment?

Paliyans are refuge-area hunter-gatherers in relatively dry forested hills in southeastern India. The author conducted general ethnographic research on their culture in 1962-64, followed up by brief visits in 1978 and 2000-01 (Gardner, 1966, 1991, 1993, 1995, 2000a, 2000b, 2004). Paliyans may be aloof, but they are not actually isolated (Gardner, 1978, 1982, 1985, 1988). They appear to have had at least 1,800 years of tangential contact with members of Tamil society (a vigorous society that traded with the Roman Empire in the second century AD) because classical south Indian poetry refers to familiar sounding yam and honey collecting people in the very hills Paliyans now occupy. We can at least say with certainty that Paliyans have engaged in sporadic trade in forest products with Tamils for centuries (Grierson, 1903: 46).

The Paliyans and their Environment

Paliyans dwell in a patchy environment on the lower slopes of ranges that rise to 2,555 m. Somewhat wetter northern faces of the hills support a

[1] This research was supported, during 1962-1964, by a fellowship from the Ford Foundation (administered by the Joint Committee of Social Science Research Council and the American Council of Learned Societies), then an extension of that fellowship; and, during 1978, by a Faculty Summer Fellowship from the Research Council of the University of Missouri plus a travel grant from the American Institute of Indian Studies. The author takes sole responsibility for all statements of fact and interpretation in this paper.

tropical moist forest with some bamboo; elsewhere, the main vegetation includes thorny trees and bushes or even cactus at lower elevations and tropical dry evergreen forest above (Puri, 1960: 147-150, 175-184, 246-248). Whether wet or dry, the lower forest abounds in diverse small game and several species of dioscorea yam (*D. oppositifolia* and *D. pentaphylla* in particular), their staple foods. Sago palms (*Caryota urens*), found about 1,000 m above the plain, are exploited in place of yams during prolonged droughts. It should be said that both sexes dig yams and, in small bands or work parties, women may be integral to hunts in which hardwood digging sticks double as lances. Normally people collect just for their own households. Self-reliance is expected. Only when people work cooperatively in killing a big deer or pig, or in netting a large run of fish, is there any sharing of the take by members of the work party. And adults are also quick to share food with siblings or other close kin who are ill or disabled.

Some Paliyans camp deep in quiet wooded valleys in settlements of 18 to 30 individuals, the inhabitants of which tend to come and go on a weekly basis. Others live near the edge of the forest in slightly larger communities, where enterprising or specially licensed people from Indian society, or forestry staff, can make contact with them and obtain their help in collecting more than 60 forest products, including honey, condiments, medicinal plants, sandalwood, and toiletries. They are paid for this labor with machete-like "bill hooks," cloth, tobacco, and rice (the rice intended to compensate them for gathering trade goods in place of their own foods).

Initially I saw these two kinds of settlement as being less acculturated and more so. Only after my initial fieldwork concluded did I appreciate the idea that groups dwelling for years in deep forest appeared to be Paliyans who had retreated there fairly recently due to difficulties with Tamils. Members of one such shy, reclusive band (to whom I had been able to pay a brief visit in the company of a trusted friend of theirs) confided about losing three members to a violent honey contractor several years before. He had become so enraged when they, his customary workers, refused to collect honey for him that he shot two of them and kicked another to death. Subsequent reexamination of all band movements corroborated this hunch; isolated groups lived simply, but they were not significantly less acculturated than their fellows. The apparent dynamics of Paliyan movements toward and away from their frontier with Tamils resembled those of the well documented 2,000-year-old oscillation Lattimore has mapped out for Mongols in their relations with Chinese in China's inner Asian borderlands (Gardner, 1985; Lattimore, 1951).

Paliyan Social Life

Several distinct aspects of Paliyan social interaction bear mention. Paliyan society is strictly egalitarian, by gender as well as by age. There is not even a subtle difference in rights or responsibilities. Quite early in my fieldwork I, with my sexist family upbringing, heard a 75-year-old man speak to others about his 10-year-old stepdaughter using terms indicative of great respect. I asked him in private later about why he had chosen the words he did. He failed initially to grasp the point of my question. Then, when he finally got what I meant, he grinned broadly and, with an exuberant flourish of his hands, said he did so "because she is a person!" Husband and wife have precisely the same rights as one another in regard to property, the fruits of their labor, divorce, sexual freedom, and so on. And each shows respect for the other by never uttering the spouse's name. Marital relations are symmetrical right down to the details. There is also occasional playful cross-dressing of spouses, at work or during evening dances, that makes light of gender distinctions (Gardner, 2006: 53-54). As for age, a child also has rights that must be protected by anyone handy, if its mother or any other person behaves in an unacceptable way toward it. I have previously covered all this in print and have described, as well, the ways in which children are groomed for both self-reliance in dealing with problems and independent decision-making at an early age (1966: 391-393, 2000a: 226).

Because many societies have, since the 1940s, been termed "individualistic" or "atomistic," with considerable emphasis on traits such as self-reliance and suspiciousness (Hallowell, 1946; Honigmann, 1946; Mason, 1946; Rubel and Kupferer, 1968), it is important to make clear that there is much warmth in personal interaction amongst Paliyans. People joke and tease amiably within work parties during rest breaks. There can be spirited male or female circle dances or dances between married couples under the full moon, with all participants and onlookers smiling. The quiet tone of normal life is anything but ominous. In sum, they bear no resemblance to the self-centered Ik of East Africa (Turnbull, 1972) or the isolated and alienated individuals in early Ingmar Bergman films.

Most bands have one to three people who are said to have "good heads," and who are able to step forward voluntarily to help when there is tension over social or ritual matters (such as when a god fails to respond to a shaman's call). They use word play, clowning, or soothing speech to distract and calm their fellows. They are not "heads" in the sense of holding authority. Indeed, no husband, parent, kin group elder, or anyone else holds a position of authority. We have here a smoothly functioning anarchy in the original Greek sense, with society "lacking a head,"[2] and it is far from being anarchic in the more recent sense of being chaotic.

Paliyan Conflicts

As quiet as their settlements are, Paliyans are not without conflicts. During 202 days when I had 24-hour contact with the two main bands I studied, 31 cases of interpersonal difficulties were witnessed and I was able to ascertain the causes and the handling of all but two. That sounds like a substantial amount of conflict, so just how "wild" and undisciplined *are* these hunter-gatherers whom our anthropological ancestors would have called "savages"? To begin with, let me emphasize that, rather than being undisciplined, they are highly restrained when upset. Some of the difficulties in my list were so minor that they would not be noticed in most Western communities, not even in well-monitored school playgrounds. Over a third of the cases were merely instances of adults, usually mothers, expressing annoyance at frustrating, tantrum-prone children and scurrying after them, swatting in the air with handfuls of soft shrubbery or grass. Other instances include mild blows between young playmates or verbal tiffs between spouses. All these cases have been summarized elsewhere (Gardner, 2000a: 225-228, 2004: 62-65). Even counting the mildest episodes of conflict, there was only about one every six or seven days. Twenty-one of the 31 cases eventuated in nothing more than the offended or "injured" party keeping silent or sobbing quietly, or else the persons in conflict going their separate ways. In the remaining 10 cases there was a rejoinder of some sort: four spouses who had been offended by their partners talked back briefly; four youngsters struck back lightly at age mates who had bothered them; and, in the two remaining cases, adults struck blows, once quite seriously.

These last two events warrant description. In both instances, a man expressed his concern inappropriately for his sister or for his wife and unborn child. In the first case, a man asked another, "Where did you go with my sister?" When the second man snapped back, "Why do you ask?" a brief fight broke out and, before it was over, the supposed lover also threatened the interfering brother. It was the brother who was out of line, for the alleged tryst should have been none of his business. No injuries were sustained.

---

[2] I follow here the usage of Birket-Smith (1929: 260), Labouret (1931: 215), Evans-Pritchard (1940: 5-6), Lowie (1948: 11, 14, 21), and Hoebel (1954: 294).

In the second case, a man learned that his very pregnant wife had fed their four children and him without holding back any food for herself. He upbraided and struck her for starving herself and the unborn child. Upset to the point of tears, he struck his mother and a neighbor, both of whom ran in to see the reason for the altercation. Trembling, acting as if he felt overwhelmed, he picked up a billhook, chased newcomers out of the house, and stood in his doorway with the blade upraised. His wife's brother asked a child to run and fetch me. Knowing virtually nothing about the cause of the disturbance, but theorizing that a distressed Paliyan could not actually swing the implement at anyone, I told him calmly that the billhook was not needed and wrapped my fingers around its blade. Still weeping, he released it at once and treated me like an ally as he led me into their house to show me the empty pot.

Competition for women has been shown to be a major source of violence in simple societies in South America, New Guinea, Africa, etc. (Gusinde, 1961[1937]: 988; Knauft, 1987: 477; Lee, 1984: 93). Although some of the Paliyan difficulties between spouses had to do with suspicions that the wife or the husband had an ongoing extramarital affair or hoped to establish one, this did not result in noticeable difficulty between supposed rivals. At most, the offended husband or wife voiced objections or simply walked out of the marriage. On the other hand, if the new relationship was more serious than a fleeting affair, some spouses just kept quiet and accepted being members of polygynous or polyandrous unions. I observed two Paliyan men opting to make the best of such a situation and going along with polyandrous arrangements, rather than terminating their marriages (as two other men had done just before my study began). There was actually a bit of cooperation between the co-husbands in one of those households and quite harmonious relations in the other. When the senior male in the first case talked about his wife's other sexual activities and said, "It is not my business," I went back over all my data on marital relations and came to the realization that neither spouse *owned* the other in this society. The same was true of children; they made their own decisions and parents never behaved as if they owned them, or sought to exert control over whether they made cooking fires at age five, whether they chose to move to an aunt's house at six, or whether they married a particular person as they approached puberty. If one does not own one's spouse or child, and if all people are deemed to have the right to plan independently the course of their own actions, this ought to interfere with seeing the spouse's lover or the child's preferred housemate as a rival.

Learning About a Key Value

Paliyans are extremely taciturn. In the morning, when people sat warming up in groups in small patches of sunlight, an hour might go by with fewer than 30 to 40 quiet words being spoken within the camp. This was not an expression of aloofness, however. The very sitting together was a measure of their feelings of emotional closeness. And, after a few minutes, they commonly moved on silently to sit with another little group. Chatter is not only unnecessary in the establishing of contact, it is undesirable. Proximity speaks in its place. Several times, I have seen one of the elders pack and leave a band without a word being said to his or her close relatives about the reason for the departure or the intended destination. These are personal matters that do not necessarily warrant discussion. If Paliyans in general speak little, those over 40 years of age are yet quieter. Can people get by with almost no use of farewells? Apparently they can.

You can understand that my formal interviews were neither liked nor tolerated at first. So, for weeks on end, I resorted to learning in the same way that their children do, simply by watching. Soon, though, I began going to work all day with collecting parties (pooling my take with the family that took me along—as if I was their child) and participating in the whole spectrum of nonsubsistence activities such as games, dance, and chasing venomous snakes. In these varied settings it seemed natural to them to guide my actions and provide me with at least some verbal explanations of what we were seeing and doing. It was through hundreds of hours of this watching, participating, and listening that I eventually gained my first insights about possible rules behind the behavior. As it was a number of months before I heard them put more abstract matters, such as their values, into words, I had, by that time, a preliminary sense of what those values were. As Paliyans were not prone to exaggeration when they did speak, this technique meant that I did not have to deal with the usual discrepancies between words and actions. I had gained a grasp on actualities.

The key Paliyan value is that one should avoid what I was eventually to hear them call "*tarakkoravaa*," a word that can be translated roughly as "disrespect." It actually refers to people being placed on different levels, with one lording over another person or becoming a dependent burden. Only children, the aged, and the infirm can be legitimate dependents but, when they are, this status is granted graciously. Disrespect, then, is a breach of equality, and it hurts. What were referred to earlier in this chapter (etically) as "conflicts" might more accurately have been phrased (in Paliyan emic terms) as "disrespectful acts and their results."

Heading Off Escalation

What does it take to actually eliminate violence from a society such as theirs? Life amongst humans eventually generates the whole range of negative emotions, whatever society we are talking about. Members will in time feel annoyance, resentment, hurt, envy, jealousy, and anger just by virtue of exposure to the behavior of others. How is it possible to cope with these emotions peacefully? I have seen business meetings in the Society of Friends (Quakers) becoming like overly stressed pressure cookers as members, all of whom were thoroughly committed to peace, tried to cope amicably with minor disagreements within their little community. In just the same way, the equally peaceful Paliyans become tense as they attempt to flex with the unwelcome acts of their fellows, and yet more tense when social problems are caused by outsiders. They may even grit their teeth when under pressure. In one memorable instance of the latter sort, a uniformed junior forestry officer ordered a Paliyan child to go over to a raggedy Paliyan elder (with whom I happened to be sitting and talking at that moment) and fetch something for him to chew. It was not phrased as a request; it was a blunt demand. The old man gave the child what the officer had so brusquely asked for and, audibly gritting his teeth, said, "Tell him anything I own is his." Negative feelings may lurk almost unnoticed behind nice words, but they are definitely there.

So, when I state that people who have had long and intimate contact with Paliyans in their work (a high ranking forestry officer who served under the British, a teacher at a tribal school, me, etc.) say with one voice that there is no murder within this society, how can I account for this achievement? The answer may well be by virtue of Paliyan adherence to the belief that one owes respect to all others. It is a key value for them. A disrespectful act by another person is no excuse for responding to it in a way that is, in turn, disrespectful. As they themselves view it, to reply in an annoyed manner is to create a situation in which two people are misbehaving. Paliyans hold that they accomplish nothing good by acting thus, for it only aggravates the problem.

Looking at the Paliyan way of handling feelings from a tactical perspective, it is possible to see that, by refusing to talk back, or by walking away from an offensive community member or outsider, one heads off escalation. An unwelcome utterance does not give rise to a yet more unpleasant one, or a clenched fist, or the act of picking up a weapon, or actual use of that weapon. While "avoiding escalation" is not how a Paliyan would express the outcome of be-having properly, from an objective standpoint that clearly is the actual result.

Some cultures harbor mutually contradictory values, an example being a culture in which religious leaders are praised for speaking in public about the value of loving or respecting one's neighbors, but in which listeners go out next morning seeking to establish themselves as valuable, respected members of the community by reaping all the profit they can from dealings with those very neighbors. With such battling values, almost any behavior could be regarded as justified. There was no obvious Paliyan value that counters valuing the avoidance of disrespect. That may serve to give it the degree of influence it has over behavior.

We have to appreciate what is going on from a Paliyan perspective. If spouses, close kin, and neighbors all handle their interpersonal problems this way, no Paliyan is going to interpret walking away as "backing down" or "being submissive"; those pejorative labels are ours. It is appropriate to view a Paliyan turning away from offensive actions, rather, as completely proper and socially approved behavior. There is no cost; there is no hu-miliation. That may be difficult to appreciate for those who have grown up in societies in which it is considered proper to defend oneself or else face a charge of cowardice. The Paliyan style of walking away from conflict *within their own egalitarian society* has an altogether different quality; it is an un-ambiguous act of strength, strength in controlling oneself.

Paliyans' neighbors are loud, vigorous, competitive Tamils who live in a stratified society in which it is normal to be aware of who rightfully occupies a superior position. Even twins have uneven statuses, depending on who was de-livered first. A 64-year-old Tamil friend of mine would not indulge in the pleas-ure of smoking in front of his 67-year-old brother, even though both were dig-nified senior teachers. He had to take a subordinate stance in order to express his respect for his senior. Power is one of the four aims of life in Hinduism, so that control and domination of subordinates is integral to the social blueprint. If only in their loud, pushy style of speaking, Tamils prove to be the most difficult possible neighbors for the peaceful and egalitarian forest dwellers. It is almost as if Paliyan culture is the direct opposite of that of south Indians.

Returning to the idea that values can do much to shape behavior, there remains the question of how the values came into existence. Years ago, I suggested that being subject to first hand contact with powerful and bullying neighbors might explain why enclaved peoples are among the world's nota-ble individualists (Gardner, 1966). Others have put forward similar argu-ments regarding the consequences of perennial acculturation pressure and humiliation (Horney, 1937; Gillin, 1942; James, 1961; Orans, 1965). And there are complementary theories, such as that of Foley (1988), who attributes emergence of the socially simple, egalitarian band, with its considerable reliance on female subsistence activities, to post-Pleistocene conditions. Whether or not any of these theories prove testable in the long run, it appears to be clear that the values that guide Paliyan actions are at least a proximate cause of their avoidance of escalation of human conflict.

References

Birket-Smith, Kaj (1929). *The Caribou Eskimo, Part I, Material and Social Life and their Cultural Position.* Copenhagen: Gyldendalske Boghandel, Nordisk Forlag.

Evans-Pritchard, E. E. (1940). *The Nuer.* Oxford: Clarendon Press.

Foley, Robert (1988). "Hominids, humans and hunter-gatherers: An evolutionary perspective," in Ingold, T.; Riches, D.; Woodburn, J., Eds., *Hunters and Gatherers I: History, Evolution, and Social Change.* Oxford: Berg, pp. 207-221.

Gardner, Peter M. (1966). "Symmetric respect and memorate knowledge: The structure and ecology of individualistic culture," *Southwestern Journal of Anthropology,* 22: 389-415.

Gardner, Peter M. (1978). "India's changing tribes: Identity and interaction in crisis," in Gupta, G. R., Ed., *Main Currents in Indian Sociology: Vol. 3, Cohesion and Conflict in Modern India.* Durham: Academic Press/Delhi: Vikas, pp. 289-318.

Gardner, Peter M. (1982). "Ascribed austerity: A tribal path to purity," *Man,* 17: 462-9.

Gardner, Peter M. (1985). "Bicultural oscillation as a long-term adaptation to cultural frontiers: Cases and questions," *Human Ecology,* 13(4): 411-32.

Gardner, Peter M. (1988). "Pressures for Tamil propriety in Paliyan social organization," in Ingold, T.; Riches, D.; Woodburn, J., Eds., *Hunters and Gatherers I: History, Evolution, and Social Change.* Oxford: Berg, pp. 91-106.

Gardner, Peter M. (1991). "Pragmatic meanings of possession in Paliyan shamanism," *Anthropos,* 86: 367-84.

Gardner, Peter M. (1993). "Dimensions of subsistence foraging in South India," *Ethnology,* 32: 109-44.

Gardner, Peter M. (1995). "Illness and response among South Indian foragers," *Medical Anthropology,* 16: 119-39.

Gardner, Peter M. (2000a). "Respect and nonviolence among recently sedentary foragers," *Journal of the Royal Anthropological Institute,* 6: 215-36.

Gardner, Peter M. (2000b). *Bicultural Versatility as a Frontier Adaptation among Paliyan Foragers of South India.* Lewiston: Edwin Mellen Press.

Gardner, Peter M. (2004). "Respect for all: The Paliyans of South India," in Kemp, G.; Fry, D. P., Eds., *Keeping the Peace: Conflict Resolution and Peaceful Societies around the World.* New York/London: Routledge, pp. 53-71.

Gardner, Peter M. (2006). *Journeys to the Edge: In the Footsteps of an Anthropologist.* Columbia: University of Missouri Press.

Gillin, John P. (1942). "Acquired drives in culture contact," *American Anthropologist,* 44: 545-54.

Grierson, Philip J. H. (1903). *The Silent Trade.* Edinburgh: William Green and Sons.

Gusinde, Martin (1961). *The Yamana* [trans. from German 1937 original by F. Schütze]. New Haven: HRAF

Hallowell, A. Irving (1946). "Some psychological characteristics of the Northeastern Indians," in Johnson, F., Ed., *Man in Northeastern North America.* Andover: R. S. Peabody Foundation for Archeology, pp. 195-225.

Hoebel, E. Adamson (1954). *The Law of Primitive Man.* Cambridge: Harvard University Press.

Honigmann, John J. (1946). *Ethnography and Acculturation of the Fort Nelson Slave.* New Haven: Yale University Press.

Horney, Karen (1937). *The Neurotic Personality of Our Time.* New York: W.W. Norton.

James, Bernard J. (1961). "Social-psychological dimensions of Ojibwa acculturation," *American Anthropologist,* 63: 721-46.

Knauft, Bruce M. (1987). "Reconsidering violence in simple societies," *Current Anthropology,* 28: 457-500.

Labouret, Henri (1931). *Les Tribus du Rameau Lobi.* Paris: Institut D'Ethnologie.

Lattimore, Owen (1951). *Inner Asian Frontiers of China,* 2 ed. New York: American Geographical Society.

Lee, Richard B. (1984). *The Dobe !Kung.* New York: Holt, Rinehart and Winston

Lowie, Robert H. (1948). "Some aspects of political organization among the American Aborigines," *Journal of the Royal Anthropological Institute,* 78(1-2): 11-24.

Mason, J. Alden (1946). *Notes on the Indians of the Great Slave Lake Area* (Yale University Publications in Anthropology, 34) New Haven: Yale University Press.

Orans, Martin (1965). *The Santal: A Tribe in Search of a Great Tradition.* Detroit: Wayne State University Press.

Puri, G. S. (1960). *Indian Forest Ecology, Vol. I.* New Delhi: Oxford Book and Stationary Co.

Rubel, Arthur J.; Kupferer, Harriet J. (1968). "Perspectives on the atomistic-type society: Introduction," *Human Organization,* 27(3): 189-90.

Turnbull, Colin M. (1972). *The Mountain People.* New York: Simon and Schuster.

Chapter Six

Into the Heart of Darkness
Rethinking the Canonical Ethnography on the Yanomamo

Leslie E. Sponsel
University of Hawai'i

> The most famous study of conflict in the ethnographic literature is Chagnon's work on the Yanomamo. Chagnon described Yanomamo warfare as a longstanding pattern of conflict attributable to particularities of social organization, ecological pressures, and the "fierce" personality type. (Heider, 2001: 335)

> They are probably not the kind of people you would invite over for afternoon tea. They are quick to anger, will bear a grudge for years and often launch violent attacks on members of their own tribe. (Allman, 1988: 57)

> Contemporary anthropology continues to invent other peoples to serve as vehicles to conceptualize important social and intellectual problems of the Western human self today. We have invented the Yanomamo of South America as a symbol to conceptualize human aggression and sexuality. (Pandian, 1985: 48)

> Historians, by centering violence, conflict and war have also, if counter to their intentions, contributed to their enduring legitimization, popularization and perpetuation by marginalizing nonkilling, nonviolence, and peace. (Adolf and Sanmartin, 2009: 206)

Introduction

In the early 1970s, in a graduate seminar called Ethnology of Lowland South America facilitated by Professor Thomas Gregor at Cornell University, I first read the then famous ethnography by Napoleon Chagnon (1968a) titled *Yanomamo: The Fierce People* based on his extensive fieldwork starting in 1964. My impression was that the Yanomamo are essentially Hobbesian savages with a nasty and brutish lifestyle wherein violence is ubiquitous. My reaction was that these were about the last people in the world that I would ever want to visit. But then in planning the research design for my doctoral dissertation I asked a former student of Professor Gregor, then already a leading Venezuelan anthropologist Dr. Nelly Arvelo-

Jimenez, which indigenous society in the Amazon would be the most appropriate for the fieldwork component of my dissertation focused on a biological
approach to indigenous hunting behavior and ecology (Sponsel, 1981). She responded that the Yanomamo would be best. She mentioned that she had met
them in the forest while working with the adjacent Yecuana, and found
them very friendly. She kindly agreed to serve as my sponsor where she
worked in the Department of Anthropology at the Venezuelan Institute for
Scientific Investigations (IVIC) near Caracas, and she proved most kind,
generous, and helpful with her expertise, advice, and time. There I also met
briefly with the French social anthropologist, Jacques Lizot, who by that time
had already lived and worked with Yanomamo for several years. He assured
me that there was violence among the Yanomamo, but volunteered that it
had been grossly exaggerated by Chagnon.

After traveling five days up river by motorized canoe with Yecuana and
then walking half a day into the forest I finally entered my first Yanomamo village, a northern subgroup known as the Sanema in the Erebato River region,
a tributary of the Caura River. From the outset and throughout my stay the
Sanema proved to be most kind, courteous, and helpful, like other indigenous
peoples I visited and worked with in the Amazon. Moreover, the Sanema, although a subgroup of Yanomamo, were not the "fierce people" at all as initially labeled by Chagnon in the subtitle of the first three editions of his book.
Nevertheless, there were three alarms of an incipient raid on the village although they turned out to be false, merely some strange noise alerting the village but later recognized as harmless. From the trembling women standing
next to me at the time of one alarm it was quite obvious that villagers took
the matter very seriously. However, my experiences with the Sanema made
me begin to wonder about Chagnon's depiction of Yanomamo as such a violent society, as had the previous remarks of Arvelo-Jimenez and Lizot.

Since my fieldwork in 1974-75 for six months sampling the behavioral
ecology of Sanema predator-animal prey interactions, I have never enjoyed
the opportunity to return to them, but worked elsewhere in the Venezuelan
Amazon with Yecuana and Curripaco in association with IVIC and on research grants from Fulbright and the UNESCO-Man and the Biosphere Programme. Then, in 1981, with my regular employment at the University of
Hawai'i and marriage to a Thai, I turned to Thailand instead of Venezuela
where I have worked ever since. Nevertheless, I have pursued any publication on the Yanomamo that I could find, over the decades reading most of the
more than 60 books and other literature on the Yanomamo (Sponsel, 1998).

By now I am convinced that Chagnon's representation of the Yanomamo as the primitive "fierce people" living in chronic endemic tribal warfare is problematic in numerous ways. Indeed, some anthropologists who have lived and worked with the Yanomamo for many years more than Chagnon view his ethnographic description of their aggression as grossly exaggerated, distorting, and misleading, as will be discussed later. This characterization of the Yanomamo has even proven dangerous for them (Albert, 2001; Davis, 1976; Martins, 2005; Ramos, 2001; Rifkin, 1994; Tierney, 2001: 328-331).

The above considerations combined with the emergence of the revolutionary research and other initiatives on nonkilling societies by Glenn Paige (2009), and his diverse collaborators (e.g., Evans Pim, 2009), leads to *the primary goal of this essay*, to rethink the Yanomamo by pursuing the basic question: Are the Yanomamo a killing society, a nonkilling society, or something in between? To answer this question the fifth edition of Chagnon's (1997a) own ethnographic case study will be scrutinized, following Paige's (2009: 85-87) suggestion to reconsider classic texts. Space does not allow a review of other publications by Chagnon or additional authors, but some will be cited as supporting documentation and to provide leads for readers who may wish to pursue some matters further. But, first, for those who are not familiar with the Yanomamo, a brief description will be provided which is summarized from one of my previous publications (Sponsel, 2006b). (For other surveys of Yanomamo culture see Chagnon, 1973; Hames, 1994; Lizot, 1988; Peters-Golden, 2009; Rabben, 2004; and Wilbert, 1972, and for the broader context see Sponsel, 1986a, 2008, 2010a).

Yanomamo

The Yanomamo are one of the most famous of all cultures in anthropology and beyond; they are truly ethnographic celebrities. More than 27,400 Yanomamo live in some 360 scattered communities that range in size from 30 to 90 individuals with a few reaching more than 200. They reside in a vast area of some 192,000 square kilometers in the Amazon rainforest. Their mostly mountainous territory overlaps the border between northwestern Brazil and southeastern Venezuela. [See Lewis (2009) for the population estimate.]

Reciprocity is one of the most outstanding attributes that distinguishes this unique culture. It is a pivotal social principle applied in almost every aspect of their daily life, and most frequently through kindness, sharing, cooperation, and camaraderie. However, this principle is also applied in resolving disputes, occasionally even through violence between individuals, groups, or villages, the focus of Chagnon's famous case study.

The Yanomamo live in an intensely intimate world, socially and ecologically. Traditionally they dwell together in a big, palm leaf thatched, communal, round house with a large open central plaza. Their egalitarian society is structured primarily through kinship. Each village is relatively autonomous politically. A charismatic headman can lead only by persuasion in developing a consensus; there is no chief or other authority uniting more than one community let alone Yanomamo society as a whole. However, alliances among several villages are common for economic, social, and political purposes. In their society the units of residence, kinship, and politics are not isomorphic, but they overlap in diverse, complex, and fluid ways.

This fluid dynamic is mirrored by a subsistence economy that entails almost daily forays into the surrounding forest for gardening, hunting, fishing, and gathering. Over two millennia the Yanomamo developed a sustainable society in terms of their low population density, limited interest in accumulating material culture, high mobility, subsistence economy, environmental knowledge, and world view, values, and attitudes. They practice a rotational system of land and resource use not only in their shifting or swidden horticulture, but also in their rotation of hunting, fishing, and gathering areas.

Since the mid-19th century more than three dozen anthropologists have worked with the Yanomamo in various areas and ways, but for widely different lengths of time. For instance, the French social anthropologist Jacques Lizot actually lived with them for about a quarter of a century. By now several dozen books have been published about the Yanomamo, although with diverse approaches, scope, foci, depth, quality, and accuracy. With so many different anthropologists publishing this much on the Yanomamo for over a century, it is feasible to compare accounts to identify points of agreement, presumably indicative of ethnographic "reality," and other points of disagreement, presumably reflecting the individual ethnographer's interpretations, idiosyncracies, biases, and other phenomena. The first comprehensive ethnography on the Yanomamo was published in Spanish by Louis Cocco in 1972 after living with them as a Salesian missionary for 15 years. Already at this time there was enough research on them by various investigators to allow Cocco (1972: 35-102) to include several chapters on the history of Yanomamo studies. (Also see Margolies and Suarez, 1978; Migliazza, 1972: 357-393.)

The Yanomamo are neither noble nor ignoble savages (Sponsel, 2005). They live in neither a utopia nor a dystopia, but in the real world. They are simply fellow human beings with a distinctive culture. As one observer of the Yanomamo, Greg Sanford (1997: 63) has written: "I have a hard time looking at the Yanomami as 'natives,' 'Indians,' 'aborigines' or whatever you may choose to call them. I see them as human beings, people who have the same emotions and feelings as you and I. After all, the word Yanomami simply means "human being." Must we look at them as some kind of exotic beings that exist only to satisfy our curiosity?"

In this essay the spelling used by Chagnon is followed only because the focus is on his ethnographic case study. However, there are numerous other spellings in the literature including Yanoama, Yanomama, and Yanomami. In the earlier literature they are also referred to as Guaika, Shiriana, Shirishana, and Waika, among other ethnonyms (Loukottka, 1968: 224-226; Olson, 1991: 411-412; Salazar Quijada, 1970). Yanomami is most commonly used by anthropologists who have worked most extensively with their society. Also, here diacritical markings are omitted.

First, the attributes of Yanomamo as a killing society will be surveyed, and second, those of Yanomamo as a nonkilling society, both based solely on Chagnon's (1997a) book. Finally, the numerous and diverse problems with his work will be explicated.

Killing

Chagnon (1997a: 206) asserts that resort to violence is the only possibility in a violent world like that of the Yanomamo; killing is the only practical alternative for their survival. However, in the fifth edition of his case study Chagnon presents a new model of "Bellicose and Refugee Strategies" that fits his description of geographical, ecological, social, political, and cultural variation. The model seems quite plausible, but remains hypothetical although the limited data he provides is suggestive (p. 91). The bellicose strategy characterizes the lowlands, while the refugee strategy characterizes the highlands, but this dichotomy may be too simple (cf. Sponsel, 1983: 207).

At the same time Chagnon asserts that war is the central and pivotal factor in Yanomamo life: "The fact that the Yanomamo have lived in a chronic state of warfare is reflected in their mythology, ceremonies, settlement pattern, political behavior, and marriage practices. Accordingly, I have organized this case study in such a way that students can appreciate the effects of warfare on Yanomamo culture in general and on their social organization and political relationships in particular..." (p. 8). He goes on to write: "And, the history of every village I investigated, from 1964 to 1991, was intimately bound up in patterns of warfare with neighbors that shaped its politics and determined where it was found at any point in time and how it dealt with its current neighbors" (p. 9).

Chagnon equates warfare with raiding: "Yanomamo warfare proper is to go on a raid. Most definitions of war emphasize that it is a 'military contest between two independent groups' with the intent of 'inflicting lethal harm.' Raiding between villages fits this definition...." (p. 185). He goes on to state that "it is sometimes more meaningful to look at their wars as contests between groups of kinsmen who collectively may live in several different villages over short periods of time..." (p. 185). Chagnon writes that: "Most wars are merely a prolongation of earlier hostilities, stimulated by revenge motives. The first causes of hostilities are usually sorcery, killings, or club fights over women in which someone is badly injured or killed.... The Yanomamo themselves regard fights over women as the primary causes of the killings that lead to their wars" (p. 190). A treacherous feast in which many guests are massacred is considered by the Yanomamo themselves to be the ultimate form of violence (p. 190). (See pages 191-204 for a detailed description of a specific war and settlement relocation.)

Aggressive behavior is highly ritualized, including vocalizations, postures, rattling arrows against a bow, and so on (pp. 175, 178). However, Chagnon asserts that Yanomamo warfare is not merely ritualistic because at least 25% of all adult males die violently in the area where he conducted field research (pp. 7, 205).

From Chagnon's perspective then, the Yanomamo are "the fierce people" (*waitiri*), not only in the subtitle of the first three editions of his book, but in his persistent characterization of their culture. Accordingly, the Prologue sets the tone for much of the remainder of Chagnon's book. It describes the brutal axe murder of Ruwahiwa while visiting in the Bisaasi-teri village, and the subsequently revenge killing of a dozen Bisaasi-teri while guests at a treacherous feast (pp. 1-3). Moreover, this event initiated a war between the Bisaasi-teri and Shamatari that lasted 20 or 25 years (pp. ix, 207).

Chagnon summarizes his controversial 1988 article in the journal *Science* (pp. 204-206). The "facts" place the nature and extent of violence among Kaobawa's people, the focus of much of the book, into regional perspective: 40% of the adult males participated in the killing of another Yanomamo, the majority of them, 60%, killed only one person. But some men participated in killing up to 16 other people. Moawa killed single-handedly a total of 22 people (pp. 205, 213).

Aggresssion is the primary theme which reoccurs throughout the entire book, but is concentrated in the Prologue and Chapters 5, 6, and 7. From the beginning aggression shapes Yanomamo culture (p. 9). The Yanomamo creation myth emphasizes that men are inherently fierce (p. 104). (For rather different versions of Yanomamo creation accounts consult Wilbert and Simoneau, 1990). Boys are socialized to be assertive, for example, returning blow for blow with a stick. Older men instruct them in war games (p. 131). Some men display deep scars on the shaved tops of their heads from club fights as a badges of endurance, courage, and fierceness (p. 52).

Unokais are adult males who have killed one or more individuals. They have two and a half times as many wives, and three times as many children. In other words, males who kill more people also have greater reproductive fitness. Chagnon implies that this is the pattern for Yanomamo in general, ignoring here the matter of variation that he discussed earlier. Moreover, *Chagnon asserts that this may be the pattern in the history of the human species as a whole*, but without citing any scientific evidence to substantiate such a claim (p. 205). However, Chagnon also mentions that males with a reputation for being fierce are sometimes killed before other males in a village, thereby leaving the village weakly defended (p. 195).

Chagnon identifies "a graded series of of aggressive encounters" from duels (chest-pounding, side-slapping, club fighting, and ax fighting) to raids. The treacherous feast in which several invited guests from another village may be massacred is another type of aggression. Another form is to shoot a volley of arrows into a village hoping to hit someone (pp. 185-189).

The main objective of lower levels of aggression seems to be to injure the opponent without drawing blood or killing him, and then withdraw from the contest. Thus, for example, the flat blade of a machete or axe is more likely to be used than the cutting edge. However, sometimes injuries are so severe that an individual dies. Also, the aggression may escalate to higher levels (p. 186).

Chagnon describes the raid: "The objective of the raid is to kill one or more of the enemy and flee without being discovered. If, however, the victims of the raid discover their assailants and manage to kill one of them, the campaign is not considered to be a success, no matter how many people the raiders may have killed before sustaining their single loss" (p. 189). Capturing women is a desired side benefit of a raid (p. 189). One village was raided approximately 25 times over the 15 months during Chagnon's first fieldtrip (p. 9).

Ten is the smallest number of raiders that can be effective (p. 202). When raiders approach an enemy village to stage an ambush they divide into subgroups of four to six individuals and then work in relays, one subgroup ambushing some individual from the village around dawn as they come down the main trail to fetch water at the river or perform some other morning routine. Then the raiders flee, and some split into a subgroup to wait in ambush for any males from the village that chase after them (p. 198). Most of the time the raiders manage to ambush a single individual, kill him, and retreat before they are discovered. This is considered to be the most desirable outcome of a raid" (p. 199). However, raiders will not attack a large well-armed group as they guard others leaving their village for their early morning activities (p. 199).

Feasts where one village invites another to visit, feast and trade usually cultivate friendly relationships and alliances thereby reducing duels and more serious forms of violence. However, of the six feasts that Chagnon witnessed during his first 18 months with the Yanomamo, two ended in fighting (p. 183).

A *himo* may be used in a club fight, a special palm-wood weapon made for that purpose with a sharp pointed end that can be used to spear if the fight escalates (pp. 106-107, 187). Chagnon mentions "war arrows" as lanceolate bamboo points coated with curare drug, but he does not describe these as distinctive from those used in hunting prey animals (pp. 49, 66, 181). Villages at war may also erect a defensive wooden wall or palisade around the back perimeter of their communal shelter (pp. 59, 194). The entrance of the village may be sealed off at night to make it more difficult for any intruders (p. 132). In addition, barking dogs serve as an alarm to alert villagers about the approach of strangers who may be raiders (p. 59).

Chagnon devotes a whole chapter to discussing alliances in general, next a particular feast in dramatic detail, and then the chest-pounding and side slapping duels, all against the background of intervillage hostilities and histories. Allies provide a safety net for up to a year when fissioning of a village occurs and the resulting refugees need a safe haven with food before their new gardens are productive (p. 159). The forest cannot supply sufficient wild foods to allow a large group to be sedentary; they depend on garden produce. However, a smaller group is vulnerable to hostile others (p. 160). Because of the risk of being driven from their gardens, no village can exist in isolation without some sociopolitical alliances with other villages as recourse for food and shelter (p. 160).

Chagnon asserts that there is no simple single cause of aggression within and among Yanomamo communities; instead, a somewhat different combination of factors may act in synergy varying in space and time with particular circumstances. The main proximate causes of fights among men within and between villages are women, including extramarital affairs, accusations of sorcery causing a death, and theft of food, although theft accusation is often aimed at provocation (p. 186). Chagnon rejects animal protein scarcity as a causal factor in Yanomamo aggression (pp. 91-97). [See Chagnon

(1997a: 93) and Sponsel (1986a, 1998: 100-101) for leads to most of the pertinent literature on the animal protein hypothesis. Also see Good (1989; 1995a, b) and Harris (1984). Wilbert (1972: 15) anticipated the animal protein hypothesis as an explanation of Yanomamo aggression.]

Yanomamo society is male dominated. Sex is a common motif in the oral literature of Yanomamo culture (p. 103, cf. Wilbert and Simoneau, 1990). Most fighting within a village stems from sexual affairs and failure to deliver a promised woman (pp. 7, 79). Competition for women stems in large part from the combination of preferential female infanticide and polygyny. Female neonates are more likely to be killed than male ones when a woman has another nursing infant to support. Preferential female infanticide leads to an unbalanced sex ratio which would otherwise be nearly the same; that is, about as many males as females in the population. Instead, there are more males than females in the population (pp. 94, 97). The imbalance is further aggravated by polygyny as some males have more than one wife. An extreme example is Matakuwa who had 11 wives and 43 children (p. 208). One result of competition among men for female mates is the role of women in exchange between villages (p. 160). Sometimes females are also abducted in a raid. Indeed, when raiding is a serious threat, women always leave the village with the danger of being abducted in their minds, and they may be guarded by men with one of their arrows already set in their bow ready for defense against any potential ambush by raiders (pp. 126, 129).

In general, the Yanomamo consider almost any death not caused by observing some kind of physical aggression to be the result of spiritual aggression. Furthermore, in principle, deaths require revenge by the closest relatives and allies. Thus, death from illness also fuels the cycle of blood revenge. This may be aggravated by introduced disease and epidemics from Western contact, a fact that Chagnon appears to downplay.

Apparently Chagnon has a deep understanding of intra- and inter-village sociopolitical dynamics; however, clearly he interprets these principally in terms of aggression (p. 79). He observes that villagers have to find a balance between village size for defense and village size growth which inevitably generates tensions, conflicts, and eventually violence (pp. 76-77). He notes that "... intervillage warfare was an indelible force that affected village size and village distribution..." (p. 31). The larger the village, the more fighting that occurs (p. 188). Villages are rarely able to exceed 300 individuals without fissioning into smaller new villages because of increasing tensions, conflicts, and violence (p. 152). The violent death of someone through aggression within a village leads to fissioning (p. 77).

Communities based solely on kinship cannot be maintained when they increase to a size of around 300. To hold a larger community together it needs to develop a new organizing principle, such as lineages or clans, or greater political authority, and the Yanomamo do not have such principles. In addition, a larger community would need more formal conflict resolution mechanisms. Chagnon mentions that the largest village is 400 (p. 211), although in the final chapter on cultural change he mentions that some mission villages range up to 600 Yanomamo (p. 229).

What Chagnon identifies as macro movements are motivated by politics and warfare, and he asserts that they must be understood in that context. The initial phase of a macro move is a response to the recognition of the potential of some killing, if people continue to reside in the same village (p. 75). A macro move may also be initiated in response to chronic raids by an enemy with their cumulative death toll (p. 76). Villages within walking distance of one another have to be either allies or enemies because neutrality is not any option (p. 185). The physical size of a communal dwelling is even related to warfare in terms of the space needed to house guests who are allies (p. 58). However, other factors may also influence movement, such as the presence of another indigenous culture, the Yecuana, epidemics, and the attraction of missions for trade goods, medical care, schooling, and security (pp. 63-64).

Chagnon asserts that there is a population explosion among Yanomamo (p. 64), and that a "demographic pump" is pivotal in helping to explain warfare (p. 89). This relates to growth in village size beyond the upper limit of around 300, and also to maintain intervillage spacing to exploit needed natural resources and to keep distance from enemies. [However, it should be noted that village size and population growth does not necessarily generate aggression among other indigenous societies (e.g., Sponsel, 1986b; Thomas, 1982).]

Yanomami male personalities vary in fierceness and bravery (pp. 25-31). An especially aggressive personality and also leadership style can be important determinants of the frequency of different levels of aggression within and between villages (pp. 191, 212-213). The personality of an individual male can generate or reduce violence. In particular, a headman may be a valiant warrior as well as a peacemaker, depending on the specifics of a situation. But Chagnon asserts that "Peacemaking often requires the threat or actual use of force, and most headman have an acquired reputation for being *waiteri* fierce" (p. 7). In some circumstances, a man can be fearful and avoid conflict. For instance, one of Chagnon's guides, Bakotawa, abandoned him and took his canoe to return home because of fear of an enemy village that Chagnon wished to visit in his research (pp. 36, 41).

There is a whole other dimension of aggression among the Yanomamo and that is very important to them. Chagnon alludes to it repeatedly, but does not pursue it in any depth. Physical aggression, including raids, can be generated by a belief that an enemy shaman from another village has caused death within one's own village (pp. 55, 70, 97). The religious component of Yanomamo culture and aggression might have been documented in much more detail, given its importance for Yanomamo (cf., Good, 1997; Lizot, 1985: 85-137; Peters, 1998: 151-161; Rifkin, 1994: 302-306, 310, 318; Wilbert and Simoneau, 1990). (For Chagnon's brief comments on shamanism and spirits see pp. 113, 116-119, 128, 131, 133, 196, and 216.)

Nonkilling

From Chagnon's ethnographic observations and interpretations as briefly summarized above it is clear that the Yanomamo are a killing society. Or, are they? Is aggression ubiquitous through space and time? The present author's answer is that, like many societies, while there are killers among the Yanomamo, most people do not kill. There are several reasons for this which are also embedded in Chagnon's ethnography, but not highlighted by him as of any significance.

First, there is the fact that Yanomamo villages lack food surplus, social specialization, and authority, and thus they lack anything that comes close to the common meaning of a military institution, unlike chiefdom and state sociopolitical systems. As Chagnon observes: "Much of the daily life revolves around gathering, hunting, collecting wild foods, collecting firewood, fetching water, visiting with each other, gossiping, and making the few possessions they own...." Men hunt almost daily (p. 5). In many villages there are several shamans who almost daily use hallucinogenic drugs to communicate with their spirits (p. 118). A feast for allies from another village requires a week of hunting in order to accumulate a sufficient quantity of meat for guests, and a day of preparing a banana soup as well, plus a surplus of ripe bananas from the gardens (pp. 170-173). Chagnon states that many activities do not really vary much seasonally (p. 133). Raiding can detract attention from the necessities of everyday survival and it can become intolerable to the point of necessitating a move to gain a modicum of peace and security (p. 76). *If the above factors are taken into consideration, then it would appear that the daily routine in which Yanomamo are usually engaged to sustain their lives is simply incompatible with any regular aggression at any level.* In this regard, a systematic and detailed time allocation study would be revealing to determine the time invested in different activities during the annual seasonal cycle, but such a quantitative inventory is lacking in Chagnon's publications. [See pp. 121-137 for a wealth of detailed information about daily village and social life, and also Peters (1998) and Smole (1976).]

A second factor is demographic. About 30-40% of a village population is comprised of children (p. 247), and children are not killers. Females do not participate in raiding, yet they comprise about half of the population of adults. Elderly males are not killers. Also, if 40% of adult males are killers, then 60% are not. *Clearly the majority of Yanomamo are not killers.* Chagnon (1997: 93) asserts that "The *group* is in a fundamental sense a sum of its *individual* parts." If this is so, then on Chagnon's own terms his characterization of the Yanomamo as "the fierce people" is a gross misrepresentation, because it does not reflect the proportions of killing and nonkilling individuals within Yanomamo society. Of course, the majority of the people even in a society engaged in full-fledged warfare are not killers, but Chagnon's focus on aggression tends to obscure this reality for the less cautious reader. (For demographic data see Chagnon, 1974: 158-159 and Early and Peters, 1990, 2000.)

If 25% of all adult males die from violence, then the remaining 75% of all adult males die from nonviolent causes. Usually women are not killed on a raid, except by accident if a volley of arrows is shot into a village (p. 24). Old women are highly respected, immune to raiders, and can safely serve as intermediaries between enemy villages. They have a unique position in intervillage politics and warfare (p. 126). Therefore, most Yanomamo are not killed by others, but die from diseases and other natural causes. (For some details about the causes of death see Chagnon, 1974: 160.)

A third factor is time, and in particular seasonality. The usual timing of raids is during the dry season and in the early morning hours (pp. 7, 46, 48, 129). The wet season which extends for about six months discourages raiding, among other things because many impassable swamps that inundate the forest in the lowlands require walking around them (p. 194). Also, snakes concentrate in the higher ground to escape flood waters in the forest (pp. 199, 204). In short, what Chagnon calls warfare is a seasonal activity mostly limited to a few months of the year wherever it occurs, and that is not everywhere.

A fourth factor is space. Neighboring villages are usually on at least trading terms and not actively at war (pp. 164, 183). Alliances serve to limit warfare (p. 160). Raiding between villages keeps them widely separated (p. 46). Also, there is far more aggression including warfare in the lowlands than in the highlands. Accordingly, there are extensive areas where relative peace prevails.

A fifth factor is conflict avoidance. Chagnon writes that: "The warfare pattern waxes and wanes in all Yanomamo areas. Years may go by in some regions, such as on the periphery of the tribe, where no intervillage conflicts occur…. Several years might pass without shooting difficulties with some neighboring group, but anything beyond that is not common" (p. 75). Yet one village remained in one area for 60 to 80 years (p. 72).

There are several other hints that at least in some situations some Yanomamo try to avoid conflict. Intervillage alliances provide a safe haven for refugees (pp. 80, 86-87). "The Yanomamo tend to avoid attacking those villages with which they trade and feast, unless some specific incident, such as the abduction of a woman, provokes them" (p. 160). Alliances between villages may stabilize with reciprocity in trading, feasting, and/or women exchange (p. 163). Some villages may retreat into the forest rather than pursue an enemy, and some men may fail to take responsibility to revenge some offense (p. 193). A special ritualistic visitor's pose symbolizes that he has come in peace, but if any host has reason they may shoot him then or not at all (p. 174). Headman Rerebawa sought peace between his village of Mishimishimabowei-teri and the village of Bisaasi-teri (pp. 215, 223). Some in Bisaasi-teri opposed and tried to prevent the ambush of Ruwahiwa (p. 222). A few individuals in the village of Mishimishimabowei-teri helped some of Kaobawa's people escape a massacre (p. 214). Some men avoid or refuse to participate in a massacre during a treacherous feast (p. 166). Some men avoid duels, and a headman opposes escalation of violence to the level of an ax fight (p. 180). Within hours of setting out on a raid some men turn back with excuses like having a sore foot or being sick (p. 198). Males are not always enthusiastic about raiding even though they feel the social pressure of the obligation to avenge the death of a relative (p. 203). A headman may attempt to keep a fight from escalating (p. 188). A headman may order individuals to leave in order to prevent further bloodshed (p. 189). Chagnon himself helped make peace by transporting a headman to another village in his canoe (p. 217). When these scattered points are considered together they undermine the characterization of the Yanomamo as the "fierce people."

A sixth factor is conflict reduction. Chagnon mentions that in some fights between two individuals others seem to join in to balance the sides out of a sense of fairness (pp. 186-187). He writes that: "Indeed, some of the other forms of fighting, such as the formal chest-pounding duel, may even be considered as the antithesis of war, for they provide an alternative to killing. Duels are formal and are regulated by stringent rules about proper ways to deliver and receive blows. Much of Yanomamo fighting is kept innocuous by these rules so that the concerned parties do not have to resort to drastic means to resolve their grievances. The three most innocuous forms of violence, chest pounding, slide slapping, and club fights, permit the contestants to express their hostilities in such a way that they can continue to remain on relatively peaceful terms with each other after the contest is settled. Thus, Yanomamo culture calls forth aggressive behavior, but at the same time provides a somewhat regulated system in which the expressions of violence can be controlled" (pp. 185-186).

Hallucinogenic drugs that are used in shamanic rituals can also contribute to the violence of an individual. Chagnon notes that ordinarily timid men may become fierce when on drugs, and people try to calm them down because they can become dangerous to others (p. 118). Also, women may apply a magical plant to try to make men less violent (p. 69). Apparently, fierceness is not always positively valued by every Yanomamo.

Chagnon says: "There are also more customary ways to resolve conflicts-each increasingly more violent and dangerous than the previous way" (p. 212). "But their conflicts are not blind, uncontrolled violence. They have a series of graded forms of violence that ranges from chest-pounding and club-fighting duels to out-and-out shooting to kill. This gives them a good deal of flexibility in settling disputes without immediate resort to violence." Also, alliances and friendships limit violence as does intervillage trading, feasting, and marriage (p. 7).

A headman may be engaged in nonviolent conflict resolution, negotiation, peace making, and related initiatives within and between villages to reduce tensions and conflicts or resolve disputes nonviolently, sometimes even intervening in fights or duels, disarming a dangerous individual high on drugs or just out of control, arranging safe conduct in hostile territory, and so on (pp. 134-135).

A man who has killed someone undergoes seclusion for a week during a process of a special purification ritual (p. 200). From Chagnon's description, it appears that killing another human is recognized as something quite extraordinary, personally disturbing to the killer and other villagers, and the aftermath is considered dangerous to the killer. But Chagnon does not elaborate on this matter (cf. Barandiarian, 1967; Grossman, 1995; McNair, 2009: 327, 345).

In conclusion, more than enough has been said about nonkilling based on Chagnon's own ethnography to demonstrate that *killing is not ubiquitous among the Yanomamo*. Furthermore, this raises the possibility that it might well have been very revealing if Chagnon had also considered nonkilling in systematic detail, and, perhaps, even inserted a whole chapter on it in his case study.

Problems

Chagnon mentions that "Some anthropologists argue that the Yanoma-mo I have studied are unusual or very different, not representative of the larger population. If the Yanomamo I have studied are 'special' or 'unusual' by comparison to Yanomamo studied by others, it should also be made clear that they represent 25 percent of all known Yanomamo. Until we know how large and representative other samples are, we at least know this one is not an insignificant one." However, while a quarter of a population is an impressive sample size, that alone does not automatically validate any scientific analysis and interpretations. For instance, one of the problems with Chagnon's argument that males who kill more have higher reproductive fitness is the likelihood that they may also be more likely to be killed themselves in revenge and that obviously ends their reproduction. Chagnon does not adequately address this problem (cf. Chagnon, 1997b).

Chagnon notes that at the time of his research there were 250-300 villages, and that each village is somewhat different, although commonalities exist as well (pp. 207-208). Furthermore, he mentions that much of his monograph is about the village of Bisaasi-teri in the Mavaca area, although he also worked in one other village called Mishimishimabowei-teri, and he places these in a larger regional context as well (pp. 2-3). Thus, Chagnon offers one explanation for possible differences in the observations of different researchers among the Yanomamo; namely, geographic and ecological variation within the immense territory of the Yanomamo may be related to large variations in warfare intensity and other forms of violence across regions (pp. xi-xii). Indeed, it is likely that Yanomamo villages in the highlands where there is less violence are more representative of traditional society than the villages in the lowlands where there is more violence and more influence from Westerners.

Another variable may be contact history, no less than 250 years of it to varying degrees (Cocco, 1972; Ferguson, 1995; Migliazza, 1972; Smole, 1976). Although Chagnon portrays the Yanomamo as a largely isolated, uncontacted, and traditional primitive tribal society, especially until the last chapter of his book, he notes that the first missionary, James Barker, had sustained contact beginning in 1951, 13 years before Chagnon first started his fieldwork (p. 3). However, Chagnon asserts that significant cultural change did not begin to occur until the 1990s (pp. ix-x, 1), one of the reasons for the new fifth edition of his book. Yet Brian Ferguson (1995) in a meticulous and penetrating ethnohistorical and ethnological study reveals with substantial documentation that the Yanomamo have been influenced to varying degrees by external forces for centuries, sometimes directly along the perimeter of their territory, but more often indirectly diffusing inward, especially by Western trade goods and diseases. Thus, Ferguson reaffirms Chagnon's claim that "past events and history must be understood to comprehend the current observable patterns" (p. 1). Had Chagnon himself considered in a scholarly manner the material of others as Ferguson did, then perhaps his characterization of the Yanomamo might be somewhat different. (Also, see Curtis, 2007; Ferguson, 1992a, b; Ramos, 2001; Wright et al., 1999: 367.)

Chagnon mentions assertions by critics that he invented data, exaggerated violence, and so on, and suggests that this may simply reflect researchers working in different areas given the spatial variation among the Yanomamo in terms of geography, ecology, culture, politics, conflict, and contact (pp. 82, 90-91). He writes that: "In Chapter 2 I discussed what is now beginning to look like a major difference in the degree to which violence, warfare, and abductions characterize different areas of Yanomamoland." He asserts: "... the known variations in warfare intensity and fighting over women are so extreme from one region of the Yanomamo to another" (p. 82). In an interview Chagnon states: "No serious scientist has ever doubted my data" (Wong, 2001: 28). (For the controversy over the allegation that Chagnon invented and/or manipulated his data and related problems see Albert, 1989; Beckerman et al., 2009; Carneiro da Cunha, 1989; Chagnon, 1988, 1989, 1990, 1995, 1997b, Early and Peters, 1990; 2000; Ferguson, 1989; Fry, 2006: 184-199, 2007: 135-139; Good and Lizot, 1984; Lizot, 1989, 1994a; Moore, 1990; Ramos, 2001; and Tierney, 2001: 158-180).

The above considerations regarding regional variation, however, do not effectively respond to two of Chagnon's most serious critics. Jacques Lizot (1985) who actually lived with Yanomamo for more than a quarter of a century starting in 1968, and Kenneth Good (1991) who lived with them from 1975-1988. According to Good (personal communication), Lizot's main base for most of his fieldwork was Tayari-teri which is located only about an hour farther up the Orinoco river, depending on water conditions, from Bisaasi-teri which was Chagnon's main base. Good's main village of Hasupuwe-teri was much farther up the Orinoco above the Guajaribo rapids, but he emphasizes that all of the communities are the same Yanomamo. Furthermore, spatial variation among Yanomamo does not explain why *almost all anthropologists who have worked extensively with the Yanomamo are critical of Chagnon's persistent depiction of them as the "fierce people"* long after he dropped that phrase from the subtitle in the fourth edition of his book. (See Lizot, 1985, 1988, 1994.)

Chagnon's whole emphasis throughout his book and elsewhere is on conflict, violence, and warfare, which can be a legitimate focus for any researcher (Chagnon, 1968a, b; 1996a; Ferguson, 1984; Lizot, 1977; Sponsel, 2000a; Sponsel and Good, 2000). His particular focus may be the result of some combination of factors such as personal and/or professional interests (aggression including warfare), individual personality, preoccupations of American culture and society, and historical context. For example, the first edition of Chagnon's book was published in 1968 during the extremely tragic and controversial Vietnam War. In contrast, French anthropologists like Bruce Albert and Jacques Lizot (1985), Brazilian anthropologist Alcida Ramos (1995), and Canadian anthropologist John Peters (1998) do not concentrate on aggression, although they do not deny by any means that aggression is one element in Yanomamo life, society, and culture. However, other American anthropologists who have worked with the Yanomamo, including Kenneth R. Good (1991) and Gale Goodwin Gomez do not concentrate on conflict, violence, and warfare either. (Incidentally, Chagnon does not mention Good's 1991 book, although he does cite the dissertation of his one-time student.) Accordingly, Chagnon's research focus on the subjects of conflict, violence, and warfare, in contrast to other anthropologists who have spent very substantial amounts of time in the field living with and studying the Yanomamo, some of them far longer than Chagnon, is not simply a product of his cultural, sociopolitical, and historical context alone.

Chagnon points out that high levels of violence and warfare are also found elsewhere as reported by Etorre Biocca (1970; 1996) and non-anthropologists Luis Cocco (1972), Margaret Jank (1977a), Mark Ritchie (1996, 2000), and Helena Valero (1984: 208). (Also, see Dawson, 2006; Jank, 1977b; Lizot, 1985: 141-185; and Peters, 1998: 207-220.) Consider the following data extracted from a careful reading of one of the sources that Chagnon cites as confirmation of his account of Yanomamo, Biocca (1996). This text certainly contains some shocking anecdotal accounts of brutal violence. An analysis reveals 46 episodes of aggression over a period of 24 years, about two annually on average. However, these episodes included only two homicides, six blood feuds, and six raids. Accordingly, Biocca does not provide very strong confirmation for Chagnon's representation of the Yanomamo as the fierce people. Furthermore, Biocca's account is based on the memory of a single informant who was a victim, Helena Valero, having been abducted by the Yanomamo at 11 years of age in 1932 and lived with them for 24 years. Biocca taped her recollections in 1962-1963 and cross-checked them with other informants. However, apparently

Valero was dissatisfied with Biocca's account since she published her own book later (Valero, 1984). Nevertheless, Steven A. LeBlanc (2003:152) and Smith (2007: 12-15) both cite an anecdote of an episode of brutal violence recounted in Biocca's book with the implication that violence and warfare are ubiquitous among the Yanomamo. It would appear that science is trumped by the ideology of the apologists for war. It would be interesting to systematically compare the accounts of Biocca and Valero, and also to compare them with a biography from the Waorani, another Amazonian indigenous society that is also infamous for its violence (Wallis, 1965). However, such comparisons are beyond the scope of this essay.

In the most extensive and sophisticated demographic study of any Yanomamo population, Early and Peters (2000: 230) point out that in the entire 66-year period covered by their research on the demography of the Xilixana Yanomami of the Mucajai River area in Brazil, there were only five raids. That is an average of one raid about every 13 years. They also note that there were no raids during Kenneth Taylor's 23 months of fieldwork among eight villages of the Auaris Sanuma subgroup of Yanomami. Early and Peters (2000: 203) conclude: "The Yanomami do conduct deadly raids, but the stereotype of all Yanomami as engaged in chronic warfare is false and resented by the Yanomami themselves" (cf., Salamone, 1997: 20). Peters lived with the Yanomamo in Brazil for a decade.

Lizot (1985: xiv-xv), who lived with Yanomamo starting in 1968 for more than a quarter of a century and virtually in the same area where Chagnon worked, writes: "I would like my book to help revise the exaggerated representation that has been given of Yanomami violence. The Yanomami are warriors; they can be brutal and cruel, but they can also be delicate, sensitive, and loving. Violence is only sporadic; *it never dominates social life for any length of time*, and long peaceful moments can separate two explosions. When one is acquainted with the societies of the North American plains or the societies of the Chaco of South America, one cannot say that Yanomami culture is organized around warfare. They are neither good nor evil savages. These Indians are human beings" (emphasis added).

Good (1991: 13), who lived with Yanomamo for 14 consecutive years mostly in the same general area as Chagnon, from 1975-1988, writes: "To my great surprise I found among them a way of life that, while dangerous and harsh, was also filled with camaraderie, compassion, and a thousand daily lessons in communal harmony." Furthermore, Good (1991: 73) says: "The more I thought about Chagnon's emphasis on Yanomama violence, the more I realized how contrived and distorted it was. Raiding, killing, and wife beating all happened; I was seeing it, and no doubt I'd see a lot more of it. But by misrepresenting violence as the central theme of Yanomama life, his *Fierce People* book had blown the subject out of any sane proportion." (Also, see pages 13, 55, 56, 73, 174-175 in Good's book.) Indeed, Good was far more impressed with the relative harmony within the intimate communities of the Yanomamo (pp. 13, 33, 69, 80, 82). It should be possible to reach some conclusion about such issues by pursuing a systematic comparison of the several dozen ethnographies on the Yanomamo; however, this may not be easy because the foci, depth, quantification, and other aspects of the contents of different books are very uneven.

Anthropological filmmaker Timothy Asch (1991: 35) who collaborated closely with Chagnon in most of his Yanomamo films wrote: "'The fierce people,' indeed, you can't call an entire society the fierce people or any one thing for that matter...." Asch (1991: 38) also mentions the "irresponsibly categorized and grossly maligned "fierce people'." Asch's different view of the Yanomamo are reflected in several short films he made that are available from the Documentary Educational Research such as "A Father Washes His Children." (Also see Asch, 1992.)

The above conclusions coincide with the observation by Bruce Albert, Alcida Ramos, Kenneth Taylor, and Fiona Watson (2001) who have all worked with Yanomamo, the first three for many years: "We have, between us, spent over 80 years working with the Yanomami. Most of us speak one or more Yanomami dialect. Not one of us recognizes the society portrayed in Chagnon's books, and we deplore his sensationalism and name-calling" (Albert et al., 2001). Ramos (2001) even refers to Chagnon's description of the Yanomamo as "character assassination."

Other factors which may explain the differences between depictions of the Yanomamo by Chagnon and almost all other anthropologists who have worked with the Yanomamo include personal differences. Indeed, Chagnon himself recognizes that "... the anthropologist's reactions to a particular people are personal and idiosyncratic...." (p. 10). Furthermore, Karl Heider (1997) mentions several reasons why ethnographers may arrive at different perspectives and interpretations about the same culture: someone is wrong; they are observing different subcultures; they are studying the same culture but at different times; and/or they are looking differently at the same culture. Perhaps some of these reasons apply in the case of different anthropologists who have conducted research with the Yanomamo. At the same time, almost all anthropologists who have worked extensively with Yanomamo are in agreement that Chagnon exaggerated and distorted the violence in

Yanomamo society. Even Chagnon's filmmaker, Timothy Asch (1991, 1992), eventually arrived at this same conclusion.

Something else that initially seems to be peculiar about Chagnon's ethnography is his assertion that nonviolent conflict resolution mechanisms are absent among the Yanomamo (p. 211). This is peculiar because such mechanisms are known to be well developed in numerous and diverse other sociocultural systems (Bonta, 1996; Fry and Björkqvist, 1997; Kemp and Fry 2004). Perhaps Chagnon simply wasn't interested in them, or just didn't look for them among his Yanomamo. But this is not necessarily unusual. Researchers and others tend to pay far more attention to killing than to nonkilling in many contexts, marginalizing nonviolence while privileging violence (e.g., Evans Pim, 2009). In trying to understand violence it might well be revealing to also consider nonviolence, as for example, why some men do not join raids or engage in other forms of aggression in Yanomamo society.

As Jacob Pandian (1985: 104) astutely remarks in a discussion about the Yanomamo: "In other words, the social and cultural reality constructed by the anthropologist is actually a portrait of his own psychological reality, as dictated by the ideas that are considered meaningful to him and his audience." (Also see Ramos, 1987; 2001.) Accordingly, further discussion of Chagnon's personality is merited here (cf. Dyer, 2006; Irons, 2004).

Chagnon's first person accounts of his ethnographic experience reveals his remarkable persistence, stamina, and courage in facing many difficult challenges, hardships, and dangers throughout the 60-63 months of actual fieldwork during some 25 fieldtrips stretching over a period of approximately about 30 years. Chagnon says that he risked his life, and it was endangered on several occasions (pp. 42, 209, 254-258). He learned to defend himself fiercely to gain respect (p. 17-19). Given the nature of his research problems, he needed to collect detailed genealogies which is extremely difficult and can even be dangerous in a society in which it is taboo to mention the personal names of individuals and especially deceased persons (cf. Wilbert, 1972: 51). Chagnon describes how he ignored Yanomamo customs and etiquette in pursuing personal names in spite of the taboo (pp. 13-21, 251-252). Also, he learned to manipulate and deceive informants to collect accurate genealogies (pp. 22-25). Chagnon mentions that the Yanomamo are not always truthful (pp. 221-222) and that he himself has lied in dealing with them (p. 252). He also states that among the Yanomamo "Strategically deployed, deception and self deception are survival enhancing social tools" (p. 222). [See Chagnon (1974) for more details about his field methods.]

Chagnon's personal presence throughout his book holds the attention of readers and helps to understand his fieldwork methods and experiences, an approach reminiscent to some degree of postmodernist reflexivity. Indeed, Chagnon is unusually candid in his book. For instance, he mentions that he facilitated a raid by providing transportation for ten raiders in his motorized canoe (pp. 201-202). However, it may be a weakness in revealing some of his ethical misconduct which an extraordinary number of individuals have questioned on that and other grounds (Albert, 2001; Albert and Ramos, 1989; Begley, 2000; Booth, 1989; Borofsky, 2005; Carneiro da Cunha, 1989; Chagnon, 1974, 1995, 1997b; Coronil, 2001; Davis, 1976; Fischer, 2001; Fluehr-Lobban, 2002; Geertz, 2001; Good, 1991; Gregor and Gross, 2004; Horgan, 1988; Hume, 2010; Johnston, 2010; Landes et al., 1976; Mann, 2001; Miller, 2001; Monaghan, 1994; Nugent, 2001; Padilha, 2010; Rabben, 2004; Ramos, 1987, 2001; Rifkin, 1994; Robin, 2004; Sahlins, 2001; Salamone, 1997; Salzano and Hurtado, 2003; Sponsel, 1998, 2010b; Sponsel and Turner, 2002; Stoll, 2001; Tierney, 2000, 2001; Time, 1976; Terrence Turner, 1994, 2001; Trudy Turner, 2005; Whiteford and Trotter, 2008: 5, 40; Wilson, 2001; Wolf, 1994; Wong, 2001).

Chagnon tries to take much of the credit for the visibility of the Yanomami that helped gain them recognition and assistance during the 1980s massive and catastrophic invasion of illegal gold miners into their territory in Brazil. Chagnon credits his publications and films with making the Yanomamo known to the world, although he admits that publications of other "knowledgeable anthropologists" contributed to their "international visibility" (p. 232, also pp. 253, 259, cf. 1997b). While Chagnon's books reached American audiences, Lizot (1976a, 1978) reached audiences in France and in Spanish speaking countries like Venezuela. Moreover, as mentioned previously, there is a long history of numerous and diverse anthropological accounts of the Yanomami extending back into the early 19th century. In addition, Chagnon discusses his personal heroism again in connection with the investigation of the massacre of Yanomamo by gold miners at Hashimu. However, he avoids mentioning the controversy that surrounded his role in the inquiry including being expelled from Venezuela by a judge and military officials on September 30, 1993 (Stoll, 2001: 37), even though he cites some of the literature in a footnote albeit without providing complete citations in the bibliography (pp. 233-235).

Chagnon concludes his book with the assertion that: "The Yanomamo are now a symbol for all tribesmen and their habitats, everywhere" (p. 259). However, many readers may not be clear about precisely what the Yanomamo actually symbolize in Chagnon's ethnography other than Hobbesian savages. In using his case study among others in teaching various anthropology courses for more than three decades it is clear to the present author that the main message which most readers acquire on their own reading is that the Yanomamo are Hobbesian savages who would be better if civilized (cf. Sponsel, 1992, 1994a). Another message is that as primitives the Yanomamo reflect the inherent aggressiveness of human nature (cf. Sponsel, 1996a, 1998, 2009). In short, without the benefit of informed and critical analysis this book may simply reinforce preconceived American cultural stereotypes and ethnocentrism. This is serious, because through the five editions that have been commonly used in anthropology courses since 1968, several million students have been exposed to what the Yanomamo symbolize for Chagnon.

The American cultural mindset appears to be influencing Chagnon's conceptual framework. In his ethnography about the Yanomamo he uses concepts reflecting American militaristic ideology such as credible threat and peace through strength (p. 158). A cold war mindset with its nuclear weaponry for mutually assured destruction as a credible threat to sustain peace between superpowers is mirrored in Chagnon's view of intervillage politics, as for example, when he mentions the "politics of brinkmanship," bluff, intimidation, and detante (pp. 160-161, 216). It appears that his conceptual framework is not totally devoid of ethnocentric conceptualizations and interpretations of the Yanomamo, although the same could be said of many other ethnographers. Science is not ahistorical, acultural, apolitical, and amoral, no matter how much one may attempt to be neutral and objective or claim to be so (e.g., Holmes, 2008).

Chagnon's (1996, 1997a) use of the concepts of war, peace, and military are problematic as well (Lizot, 1994b). The nature and scale of aggression among the Yanomamo include raids and massacres, but they hardly merit the designation of war, except by the broadest definition as a potentially lethal conflict between two political entities which can be villages in the case of the Yanomamo. Such a vague conception of war almost renders it a cross-cultural universal which is counter to the overwhelming bulk of evidence (e.g., Fry, 2006, 2007; Kelly, 2000; Sponsel, 1998: 106-109). Intervillage raids among the Yanomamo are more reminiscent of the famous blood feud between the extended families of the Hatfields and McCoys in the Appalachian mountains of Kentucky and Virginia from 1882 to 1890 that involved the killing of a dozen individuals (Rice, 1982; Waller, 1988). (For similar cases of blood feuding see Boehm, 1984; Keiser, 1991; Kelly, 2000; and Otterbein, 1985, 1994, 2004).

In the case of the Hatfields and McCoys, "yellow journalism" in the popular press focused on selected fragments of reality thereby exaggerating and sensationalizing them into a myth of savagery although there were feuds many times worse elsewhere. Some think that Chagnon's ethnography was a similar distortion, including most anthropologists who have spent any length of time working with the Yanomamo.

As Good (1991: 44) observes: "The Yanomama, I knew, never engage in anything like open warfare. They think it's absurd to risk your life that way and possibly get a lot of people killed. Instead, a raiding party will sneak up on an enemy village and hide in the bushes overnight, maybe on the trail leading to the village gardens. Then next morning they will wait until some-one passes, shoot him, then run off. *No heroics, no single combat, no massed battles.* Just hide, shoot, and run. You accomplish your purpose, and you don't get yourself killed in the process."

In response to Chagnon's (1968a,b) earliest publications on the Yano-mamo, Robin Fox (1969) and Elman Service (1968) both questioned his equa-tion of feuding and raiding as warfare. (Also see Fry, 2006, 2007; Sponsel, 1998.) David P. Barash (1991: 32, 82-83) in the first major textbook in peace studies defines war as armed aggression for political goals between or within nation-states involving a military sector separate from a civilian one with 50,000 troops and 1,000 combat dead. However, this definition is too narrow and exclusive for most anthropological students of warfare. What is sorely needed is a systematic and objective typology of warfare and other forms of aggression (Sponsel, 2000; Sponsel and Good, 2000). (Also, see Keegan, 1993: 97, 121; Kelly, 2000: 122-123, 139-142; LeBlanc, 2003: 57; Levinson, 1004: 63-66; Otterbein and Otterbein, 1965; and Smith, 2007: 15-17).

Likewise, Chagnon uses the concept of the military so loosely and care-lessly as to be meaningless (e.g., pp. 160-162). The term usually refers to full-time professionally trained armed combatants of a nation state. Levin-son (1994: 115) states: "A society is considered militaristic when it engages in warfare frequently; when it devotes considerable resources to preparing for war; when its soldiers kill, torture, or mutilate the enemy; and when pursuit of military glory is an objective of combat." (See also Eckhardt, 1973.) The Yanomamo do not conform to the normal conception of the military. Fur-thermore, among the Yanomamo, there is nothing comparable by any stretch of the imagination to the military of the Venezuelan state based in the vicinity of some of their communities (Chagnon, 1997a: 238). But reference to war and military among the Yanomamo connects Chagnon's work with the broader discourse on these subjects, thereby lending him notice and pres-tige. (On American militarism see Andres, 2004; and Hedges, 2002.)

The negative concept of peace is implicated in Chagnon perspective; namely, peace is no more than the absence of war (pp. 168, 216). Adherence to such a simple and myopic concept of peace may help explain why Chagnon focuses on killing to the neglect of nonkilling in Yanomamo society. However, *peace is not rare, it is just rarely studied*, contrary to Chagnon in the case of the Yanomamo, and also to some of his partisans like Thomas Gregor more generally (1996:xii-xiv, cf., Sponsel, 1996a). As Kelly (2000: 75) observes: "Warfare is not an endemic condition of human existence but an episodic feature of human history (and prehistory) observed at certain times and places and not others." Furthermore, empathy, cooperation, and altruism are no less a part of Yanomamo character than they are part of animal nature in general (Bekoff and Pierce, 2010; Good, 1991). [For further explication of the distinction between negative and positive peace see Sponsel (1994b: 14-16), and for an elaboration of the problems with Chagnon's conceptual framework regarding warfare, military, and other concepts see Sponsel (1998).]

In Yanomamo society women appear to be passive rather than active agents, only laborers, producers of children, sex objects, and items of exchange (Chagnon, 1997a: 210). Yanomamo culture is "decidedly masculine—male chauvinistic" (p. 122) and Chagnon is male; thus, these two factors may help explain why he has relatively little to say about the role of women in intra- and inter-village politics among other matters related to gender. Nevertheless, some anthropologists have accused him of male sexist bias (Tiffany and Adams, 1994, 1995, 1996). Research is sorely needed on all aspects of women in Yanomamo society, culture, economy, politics, violence, and nonviolence. For instance, Chagnon does not consider the reproductive fitness of women, only that of men.

Evolution as cumulative change through time is certainly a scientific fact, but evolutionism is a political ideology; that is, viewing so-called primitive cultures as survivals from some prior stage of cultural evolution (e.g., Fabian, 1991). When Chagnon asserts that Yanomamo reflect some aspects of "our entire history as humans" (p. 154), he is not referring to cross-cultural or pan-human universals shared by humanity. Instead he is referring to the Yanomamo as representing an earlier stage of cultural evolution rather than merely an alternative lifestyle among our contemporaries. Obviously Chagnon views the Yanomamo as some kind of primitive survivals from the Stone Age; that is, foot Indians with minimal horticulture at an early stage of the Neolithic (p. 45, cf. Wilbert, 1972). He mentions the term primitive throughout his book (pp. 5, 10, 11, 19, 31, 79, 121, 139, 144, 145, 164, 211, 243, 247, 248). However, the concept of primitive was challenged as derogatory stereotyping and went out of fashion among professional anthropologists several decades ago, unless very carefully qualified in special contexts (e.g., Montagu, 1968; cf. Roes,

1997). One of Chagnon's collaborators, James V. Neel (1970), also viewed the Yanomamo as "primitive," as did Wilbert (1972: 4, 13-15). However, Chagnon (1997) persists in applying the term in the fifth edition of his book (cf. Fabian, 1991). The Yanomamo are not anachronistic, but Chagnon's continuing use of the term primitive is (Wong, 2001: 26-28). Nevertheless, this adds to the attraction of his book for many naïve readers (cf. Chagnon, 1973, 1997b; Fischer, 1969). Yet using the term primitive without appropriate qualification in the media may serve to reinforce negative stereotypes of the Yanomamo held by the general public (Wong, 2001: 26-28).

Chagnon has spent a total of 63 months (p. viii) or 60 months (p. 1, 8) actually living with Yanomamo during his field research, this stretched out over a period of about 30 years (p. vii, xii). He made 20 (p. 8) or 25 (p. viii) separate fieldtrips, and visited some 60 villages (p. 27). Chagnon says that "… I have been studying the Yanomamo now for nearly 30 years" (p. 204), states that he has been studying the Yanomamo for 32 years (pp. 248, 257), and claims that he has "25 years of field data" (p. 213). Whichever the correct numbers, given the nature of his research Chagnon has likely visited a greater number of villages than any other field researcher. However, his fieldwork was curtailed during various periods by the refusal of the Office of Indian Affairs of the government of Venezuela to issue further research permits. Chagnon (1997b: 101) attributes curtailment during 1975-1984 to professional jealousy and nationalism of Venezuelan anthropologists. However, many Venezuelan anthropologists have their own achievements that are widely recognized nationally and internationally, thus no reason to be jealous. In addition, any Venezuelan nationalism did not prevent other foreigners from conducting long-term field research in the Amazon, such as the American Kenneth R. Good and the Frenchman Jacques Lizot. In short, it is likely that other reasons were involved for the Venezuelan government's refusal of his application to return to the Yanomamo. The government rejected his applications at least three times (Wong, 2001: 27).

Chagnon asserts that he has studied 25% of his estimated some 20,000 individuals among the Yanomamo (p. 83). At the same time, he writes that: "Only two of the seven population blocs shown in Figure 2.14 are the focus of most of the discussion in this book…." (p. 80). He resided mainly in two communities, Kaobawa's village of Bisaasi-teri (pp. 3, 83-84), and to a much lesser degree Mishimisimabowei-teri (p. 209). Both of these two villages are within the sphere of contact influences from missionaries and other Western forces, and were so even before Chagnon started. The Venezuelan Malaria Control station was located near the Mavaca mission for over 25 years (p.

246). Bisaasi-teri was a base of the New Tribes Mission, and a Salesian mission was directly across the river (Kenneth R. Good, personal communication). Chagnon emphasizes the necessity to not limit ethnographic observation to one community at a single point in time (p. 207). However, he initially spent some 15 months in the village of Bisaasi-teri (p. 208). [For more on the context of Chagnon's fieldwork, see Cocco (1972) and Ferguson (1995: 277-306).]

Another dimension of his research sample is his recognition of five distinct ecological zones within the territory of the Yanomamo (pp. 83-88). Moreover, he asserts that: "These ecological and geographical differences seem to lie behind social, political, demographic, and historical differences when villages from the two areas are compared" (p. 87). "The most startling difference is the degree to which violence and warfare—and the consequences of these—distinguish highland and lowland groups from each other. Warfare is much more highly developed and chronic in the lowlands. Men in the lowland villages seem 'pushy' and aggressive, but men from the smaller, highland villages seem sedate and gentle. Not unexpectedly, alliance patterns are more elaborate in the lowlands and dramatic, large, regular feasts are characteristic, events in which large groups invite their current allies to feast and trade. Larger numbers of women in the lowland villages are either abducted from or 'coerced' from weaker, smaller neighbors—including highland villages.... In addition, fewer of the adult men in the highland villages are *unokais*, i.e., men who have participated in the killing of other men...." (p. 87). (Also, see pp. 88-91.) But these zonal differences are not systematically, quantitatively, and statistically demonstrated; he offers mostly qualitative assertions instead (Table 2.1, p. 88). Regional differences need to be far more carefully pursued and documented. For instance, Chagnon suggests that resources in the highlands are less abundant than in the lowlands, thus perhaps protein capture from animal prey may be more of a problem in the former (p. 94).

Chagnon depicts Yanomamo as traditional primitives little influenced by external forces, yet he was led into his first village called Bisaasi-teri by missionary James P. Barker who started in 1950 (p. 11) or 1951 (p. 3), and had lived there for five years (p. 11). The Venezuelan Malaria Control Service had their first permanent field station next to the village and had been in the area for decades (p. 17). He arrived in the village shortly after a serious fight and was confronted by men with drawn arrows (pp. 11-12). He set up temporarily in Barker's hut (p. 13) and Bisaasi-teri remained his base of operations for many years (p. 17).

Chagnon notes that it is difficult to generalize about contact because there is much regional variation in its degree and kind (p. 228). He mentions that Kaobawa's community, Bisaasi-teri, had direct contact with missions for over four decades by the time of the fifth edition of his book (p. 228). He identifies gradual change in contrast to catastrophic change. But, other than a page or so on gold miners, he focuses almost exclusively on the impact of the Catholic Salesian missionaries, and affords almost no consideration to the Protestant New Tribes missionaries. He discusses mainly the impact of guns from the Salesians on raids of weaker villages and on diseases from contact, especially in intermediate villages that are not isolated, but do not have regular access to medical care from the missions. It becomes obvious that the Salesians and Chagnon have some kind of dispute (pp. 257-258). [Also see Capelletti (1994), Salamone (1997), Tierney (2001: 315-326), and Wong (2001: 27). In 1974, Chagnon released films on both of the missionary organizations, "Ocamo Is My Town," and "New Tribes Mission" (pp. 271-272).]

Yanomamo village size at missions varies from 400-600, a result of the mis-sionization process of centralization for access and administration, plus the at-traction of the Yanomamo to missions for trade goods, medical care, schools, and security (p. 229). Warfare is diminishing in the vicinity of missionaries be-cause shotguns afford an advantage against any potential raiders. However, guns may also be used by Yanomamo living in or close to missions as an advan-tage to raid more distant villages (pp. 238-239). In 1964, there were no shot-guns in Mavaca, but by 1975 missionaries had introduced them to some mem-bers of at least 8-10 villages and this impacted on warfare patterns (p. 60). [Note that ten villages is a fraction of the estimated total of 360 villages in Yanomamo territory]. Chagnon is preoccupied with the introduction of guns by the missionaries as complicating Yanomamo aggression (pp. 190-191, 204, 215, 224, 226) (cf. Chagnon, 1996b; Ferguson, 1995; Tierney, 2001: 18-35).

Chagnon uses quantitative data and graphs to reveal that the Salesian mis-sions are responsible for disease and deaths, up to 25% in some of 17 vil-lages, but he doesn't consider Protestant missions (pp. 234-254). He writes that: "Contact with foreigners at the Salesian Mission in Venezuela is the most likely explanation of the higher mortality patterns in these groups" (p. 250), and that "we [Westerners] initiated contacts and brought new sick-ness" (p. 258, cf., Tierney, 2001: 53-82, 334-337).

The forces of culture change or acculturation are mentioned throughout the book. Crude clay pots were still used in 1965, but were replaced by aluminum containers from Western trade by the late 1970s (pp. 49, 172). Matches replaced wooden fire drills (pp. 50-51). Airplanes were rare until after 1964 (p. 101). Chagnon says that we [Westerners] caused the Yano-mamo to crave trade goods (pp. 16-19, 242, 250, cf., Ferguson, 1995).

Culture change raises the question of just how traditional were some of the Yanomamo communities that Chagnon visited, and especially his main village of Bisaasi-teri which is the basis for much of his case study. Ferguson (1995) has argued in a meticulous systematic survey of ethnohistorical and ethnological literature that the society that Chagnon views as engaged in primitive, endemic, and tribal warfare has been influenced directly on the periphery of its territory and indirectly in the interior by Westerners of various kinds for centuries. For instance, the first European contact with Yanomamo appears to have been in 1787 with the Portuguese Boundary Commission. (Also see Chagnon, 1996b; Chernela, 1997; Cocco, 1972; Ferguson, 1992a, b, 1995; Migliazza, 1972; Peters, 1998.)

Ferguson raises the possibility that at least some of Yanomamo aggression is a product of contact influences, especially competition for trade goods. In a whole chapter on Chagnon, Ferguson (1995: 277-306) even notes that the aggression in the areas where he worked may be influenced by his distribution of trade goods. But in his book Chagnon only mentions Ferguson in a footnote of one sentence (p. 208, cf. Chagnon, 1996b). Again, perhaps Chagnon's focus in his book on the Salesians is an attempt to deflect attention from Ferguson's critical analysis and its ethical implications. [For another example of Chagnon's response to critics, and to Ferguson in particular, see Curtis (2007).]

The use of literature that fits one's observations and interpretations, and the avoidance of literature that does not is a common tactic of an advocacy argument, but does not advance science and scholarship. For example, Chagnon's critique of the animal protein hypothesis formulated by Marvin Harris (1984) to try to explain aggression among the Yanomamo totally ignores the dissertation by Good (1989) even though it directly addresses that very issue. He only cites that dissertation in a completely unrelated matter (p. 230). Also, he ignores Good (1995a,b), and Good and Lizot (1984).

In discussing the illegal invasion of gold miners into Yanomamo territory in Brazil in the 1980s, Chagnon ignores the critical role of the Pro-Yanomami Commission, the Yanomami Commission of the American Anthropological Association, Survival International, and other organizations (pp. 231-233). In discussing the controversy surrounding the investigation of the massacre of Yanomamo by gold miners at Hashimu Chagnon cites four publications including those of three critics in a footnote, but the full citations are not provided in the bibliography (p. 234). He does not cite an important report on the massacre by the French anthropologist who was part of the official investigation team, Bruce Albert (1994). (Also see other documentation by Ramos et al., 2001; Rocha, 1999; and Turner, 1994.) The reader begins to wonder how much other relevant information is ignored in Chagnon's book and other publications. (On the tragic consequences of the mining invasion in Yanomamo territory see Albert, 1994; Berwick, 1992; Pro-Yanomami Commission; Rabben, 2004; Ramos, 1995; Sponsel, 1979, 1994a, 1995, 1996b, 1997, 2010c; Survival International, 2010; Tierney, 2001; and Turner, 1991.)

There is also selectivity in quantification. Chagnon's use of quantification and statistical analysis is uneven, not always systematic and clear. For example, he mentions that: "At this time the Patanowa-teri were being raided by a dozen different villages" (p. 135) Also, Chagnon mentions "... the several clubs fights that took place while I was in the field on my first trip...." (p. 136). Episodes of fighting are described throughout the book with varying degrees of detail, but often in anecdotal fashion; for example, "Club fighting is more frequent in large villages..." (p. 188). Again, "The Patanowa-teri then became embroiled in new wars with several villages...." (p. 192). In one year at least eight individuals were killed by raiders. The Pantanowa-teri were raided 25 times during Chagnon's initial fieldwork (p. 194). Chagnon writes that sporadic intervillage raiding may endure a decade or more (p. 204). In addition, serious physical abuse of a wife appears to be rather common among the Yanomamo. Wife abuse occurs, including beating, serious injuries, and even killing (pp. 124-126, 135). In short, Chagnon's quantification of phenomena is not systematic, thorough, and precise; some numbers are specified while others are not. *It is impossible to obtain a clear idea of the frequency and intensity of each of the different levels in the hierarchy of aggression for a single village during a particular period of time*, even for the most studied village of Bisaasi-teri, this in spite of Chagnon's apparent wealth of knowledge and data. This belies Chagnon's seeming scientific rigor including instrumentation for measurements and for some subjects statistical and computer analysis. Numbers are magic to many readers in the sense that they impart the appearance of real science, but this can be deceptive. (Also, see Chagnon, 1974; and his films "Yanomama: A Multidisciplinary Study" in 1971, and "A Man Called Bee: Studying the Yanomamo" in 1974.)

The Yanomamo also need to be considered in cross-cultural perspective (Sponsel, 1998: 109-110). Types of aggression that are present among the Yanomamo are found in the following percentage of societies for various sample sizes: violence as a means of solving problems (54%), female infanticide (17%), wife beating (84.5%), bride raiding (50%), rape (50%), anger and aggression over the death of a loved one (76%), blood feuding (53.5%), village fissioning (78%), and sorcery as a cause of illness and death (47%) (data extracted from Levinson, 1994). Types of aggression that are rare to absent in

Yanomamo society but found in a percentage of other societies for various sample sizes include physical punishment of children (74%), suicide (47%), gerontocide (25%), capital punishment (96.2%), human sacrifice (17%), cannibalism (34%), internal warfare (67%), external warfare (78%), and torturing enemies (50%) (data extracted from Levinson,1994). Thus, from a cross-cultural perspective the Yanomamo are not such an extraordinarily violent society.

Chagnon's violentology with its distorting focus on the Yanomamo as essentially a killing society, and the problematic nature of some of his fieldwork, data, analysis, and interpretations raise another very serious issue. His "fierce people" characterization of the Yanomamo is parroted by many apologists for war and others as reflecting primitive tribal warfare and even human nature in general. Logically, either the authors who uncritically broadcast Chagnon's work to an unsuspecting public are ignorant of the broader literature on the Yanomamo and the criticisms of other anthropologists with extensive experience among the Yanomamo, or they purposefully ignore them. In either case, their indiscriminant use of Chagnon's construction of the Yanomamo as the "fierce people" does not reflect quality science and scholarship. Considering that the criticisms of Chagnon's work have been made for decades by numerous and diverse anthropologists, many of them Yanomamo experts (Sponsel, 1998: 114), one might well suspect that the apologists for war utilize Chagnon's work simply because it conveniently fits and reinforces their political ideology (cf., Kegley and Raymond, 1999: 20-21, 245; Lewontin, 1993).

Just to mention a few, among the apologists for war who seem to uncritically use Chagnon's work as if it were canonical are Ghiglieri (1999), Keeley (1996), LeBlanc (2003), Smith (2007), Watson (1995), and Wrangham and Peterson (1996). However, even more politically neutral scholars of violence and war also use Chagnon's work indiscriminately (eg., Eller, 2006, Keegan, 1993; Otterbein, 2004). The same applies to the authors of numerous introductory textbooks in cultural anthropology. However, Richard H. Robbins (2009: 291-293, 300-305) is more cautious than most when he recognizes Chagnon's representation of the Yanomamo as Hobbesian. Of course, if the raiding and other forms of aggression which occur in some places and times among the Yanomamo do not merit the term war, then the relevance of Chagnon's work to the apologists for war and the study of war in general is reduced if not eliminated. In any case, some of these scientists and scholars would do well to learn how to distinguish truth and its opposite (Frankfurt, 2005, 2006). They might also consider some of the literature that has been accumulating for decades on the anthropology of peace and nonviolence which most neglect entirely (Bonta, 2010; Howell and Willis, 1996;

Montagu, 1978; Sponsel and Gregor, 1994). (For more on assessing ethnographic texts in general see Atkinson, 1992; and Hammersley, 1990.)

It is unlikely that the apologists for war and others of various persuasions are totally unaware of the criticisms, controversies, and scandals that have periodically erupted around Chagnon's work at least since the mid-1970s (e.g., Landes et al., 1976; Time, 1976). They have appeared not only in specialized scientific and academic publications, but also in the broader public media, including periodicals such as the *Chronicle of Higher Education, Guardian Weekly, Natural History, New York Review of Books, Newsweek, Scientific American, The New Republic, The New Yorker, Time, and U.S. News & World Report*.

The net effect of the publications of Chagnon and his disciples has been to stigmatize the Yanomamo as "the fierce people" focusing attention on their internal aggression and deflecting it from the aggression impacting on them from outside influences, including introduced Western diseases that have repeatedly precipitated devastating epidemics (Sponsel, 1994a, 1997, 2006a, b, 2010c).

Smole (1976: 14-15) writes that: "Unfortunately, most explorers have been unable to appreciate the humanness of the Yanoama. Instead, adventurers helped give them a reputation for being more 'wild' (bravo or salvaje in Spanish), violent, and potentially dangerous than most other Indians of South America. Over the years they have become legendary." The fierce characterization by Chagnon has negatively impacted on the Yanomamo in various ways. As just one example, the famous British social anthropologist, Sir Edmund Leach, refused to lend his name as a sponsor for a campaign by Survival International in London to raise funds to develop educational programs for the Yanomamo in the 1990s (Albert et al., 2001).

In spite of the numerous and diverse problems with Chagnon's work revealed above and in the supporting literature cited, his loyal partisans act as if they believe that only Chagnon is right and instead all of his critics are wrong, an improbable scenario to say the least (e.g., Borofsky, 2005; Gregor and Gross, 2004). This scenario is obviously improbable, given the extraordinarily large number of critics of Chagnon's work, among them many with extensive field experience living and working with the Yanomamo. Chagnon (1997b) and his partisans have attempted to frame his critics as simply a matter of individuals who are anti-science, anti-evolution, anti-biology, postmodernists, or jealous. Any examination of the resumes of the varied critics would not sustain such simplistic attempts at dismissal.

An observation from Linda Tuhiwai Smith (1999: 7-8) applies here: "Research is one of the ways in which the underlying code of imperialism and colonialism is both regulated and realized. It is regulated through the formal rules of individual scholarly disciplines and scientific paradigms, and the institutions that support them (including the state). It is realized in the myriad of representations and ideological constructions of 'the Other' in scholarly and 'popular' works, and in the principles which help to select and recontextualize those constructions in such things as the media, official histories and school curricula."

There is no scientific reason for privileging internal aggression over external aggression from culture contact influences when the latter actually threatens the very survival of the vulnerable population of the Yanomamo, except, perhaps, a lingering colonial mentality fixated on the primitive tribal other and its supposed endemic and chronic tribal warfare. Myths have their uses, ideological and otherwise (cf., Albert et al., 2001). In his critique of Chagnon's work Rifkin (1994: 320) goes to the extreme of asserting that: "This anthropology is, then, not an anthropology at all but a deformed social science in the service of the engineering sciences of destruction." [For the broader Cold War context of Chagnon's research see Johnston (2007), Tierney (2001), and Wax (2008).]

Conclusions

The Yanomamo are especially relevant to the subject of nonkilling societies because they have been celebrated as the most famous ethnographic case of essentially Hobbesian savages, yet this canonical representation is seriously flawed on many counts as demonstrated above using Chagnon's own main book. *The pivotal point of this whole essay is that thinking in terms of nonkilling can open up an entirely new dimension in studying sociocultural systems, and also it can expose the biases and distortions from whatever source that is focusing so much on killing.* Certainly there is considerable aggression among Yanomamo, there is no doubt about that from Chagnon's documentation and that of many other anthropologists and non-anthropologists. However, killing is not ubiquitous in time and space, and not everyone is a killer, indeed only a minority of the population kills. To generalize in the subtitle of his book, and to persistently characterize them after the subtitle was dropped from the fourth edition as "the fierce people," is a misleading oversimplification and overgeneralization that distorts the nature of Yanomamo daily life, society, and culture. Moreover, this derogatory stereotype may influence others in ways that harm, or at least do not help, the Yanomamo as a vulnerable indigenous population in the Amazon (Chagnon, 1997a, b; Davis, 1976; Lizot, 1976; Martins, 2005; Rabben, 2004; Ramos, 1995; Ramos; Taylor, 1979; Rifkin, 1994).

The nonkilling perspective reveals that the Yanomamo case as depicted by Chagnon is problematic in several respects, and, in turn, *that renders the arguments of the apologists for war who rely on it uncritically problematic as well.* Their reliance on this case without taking into consideration more of the literature including by other anthropologists, and especially critics of Chagnon, is careless scholarship and scientifically unreliable and even misleading. If their use of Chagnon's case reflects the quality of their science and scholarship in general, then the entire edifice of their work may be problematic as well. Ironically, individuals, many of whom purport to be hard core scientists and accuse others of being anti-science, reveal their own work as shoddy, unreliable, and irresponsible. Many are the same individuals who accuse critics of Chagnon's work and advocates of the study of nonviolence and peace of being ideological when their own work evinces ideologically driven bias and advocacy in argumentation. *Most of all, science, scholarship, and society cannot advance by ignoring the largest part of reality in any society; namely, nonkilling* (cf., Paige, 2009; Evans Pim, 2009). Yanomamo sociocultural reality is grossly distorted when this dimension of their life is neglected, and that can have very serious negative consequences for them.

In conclusion, the Yanomamo are neither a killing society nor a nonkilling society, but exhibit some attributes of each, and this varies regionally. Chagnon and his partisans have exaggerated aggression among the Yanomamo to the point of distortion in the view of almost all of the anthropologists who have lived and worked extensively with this society. Ultimately, the Yanomamo are our contemporary fellow human beings with a distinctive lifestyle, not an exemplar of some primitive stage of cultural evolution or of an inherently violent human nature. For cultural anthropologists, the challenge is to document and publicize the humanity of the so-called Other, not to stigmatize and dehumanize them. The former can contribute to peace, the latter to just the opposite.

Acknowledgements

While researching and writing this essay I benefited greatly from email communications and telephone conversations with Kenneth R. Good who generously shared some of his wealth of profound knowledge and understanding of the Yanomamo after living with them for 14 consecutive years. However, I am solely responsible for any deficiencies in this essay.

References

Adolf, Antony; Sanmartin, Israel (2009). "How to Historicize What Did Not Happen (But Makes the Past, Present and Future Possible)," in Evans Pim, Joam, Ed., *Toward a Nonkilling Paradigm*. Honolulu: Center for Global Nonkilling, pp. 203-216.

Albert, Bruce (1989). "Yanomami "violence": Inclusive Fitness or Ethnographer's Representation," *Current Anthropology*, 30(5):637-640.

Albert, Bruce (1994). "Gold Miners and the Yanomami Indians in the Brazilian Amazon: The Hashimu Massacre," in Johnston, Barbara Rose, Ed., *Who Pays the Price? Sociocultural Context of Environmental Crisis*. Washington: Island Press, pp. 47-55.

Albert, Bruce, Ed. (2001). *Research and Ethics: The Yanomami Case*. Brasilia: Comissão Pró-Yanomami, Documentos Yanomami 2.

Albert, Bruce; Ramos, Alcida (1989). "Yanomami Indians and Anthropological Ethics," *Science*, 244(4905):632.

Albert, Bruce; Ramos, Alcida; Taylor, Kenneth I.; Watson, Fiona (2001). *Yanomami: The Fierce People?* London: Survival International. Available at: <http://www.survivalinternational.org/material/87>

Allman, William F. (1988). "A Laboratory of Human Conflict," *U.S. News & World Report*, 104(14):57-58.

Andreas, Joel (2004). *Addicted to War: Why the U.S. Can't Kick Militarism*. Oakland: A. K. Press. Available at: <http://www.addictedtowar.com>.

Asch, Timothy (1991). "The Defense of Yanomami Society and Culture: Its Importance and Significance," *La Iglesia en Amazonas*, XII:35-38.

Asch, Timothy (1992). "Book Review: *Into the Heart: One Man's Pursuit of Love and Knowledge among the Yanomama*, Kenneth Good (with David Chanoff)," *American Anthropologist*, 94(2):481-482.

Atkinson, Paul (1992). *Understanding Ethnographic Texts*. Newbury Park: Sage.

Barandiaran, Daniel de (1967). "Vida y Muerte Entre Los Indios Sanema-Yanoama," *Antropologica*, 21:1-43.

Barash, David P. (1991). *Introduction to Peace Studies*. Belmont: Wadsworth.

Beckerman, Stephen; Erickson, Pamela I.; Yost, James; Regalado, Jhanira; Jaramillo, Lilia; Sparks, Corey; Ironmenga, Moises; Long, Kathryn (2009). "Life Histories, Blood Revenge, and Reproductive Success among the Waorani of Ecuador," *Proceedings of the National Academy of Sciences*,106(20):8134-8139.

Begley, Sharon (2000). "Into the Heart of Darkness," *Newsweek*, Nov. 27: 70-75.

Bekoff, Marc; Pierce, Jessica (2010). *Wild Justice: The Moral Lives of Animals*. Chicago: University of Chicago Press.

Berwick, Dennison (1992). *Savages: The Life and Killing of the Yanomami*. London: Hutchinson.

Biocca, Ettore (1970). *Yanomamo: The Narrative of a White Girl Kidnapped by Amazonian Indians*. New York: E.P. Dutton & Co.

Biocca, Ettore (1996). *Yanoama: The Story of Helena Valero, a Girl Kidnapped by Amazonian Indians*, 2nd Edition. New York: Kodansha America.

Boehm, Christopher (1984). *Blood Revenge: The Enactment and Management of Conflict in Montenegro and Other Tribal Societies*. Philadelphia: University of Pennsylvania Press.

Bonta, Bruce D. (1996). "Conflict Resolution among Peaceful Societies: The Culture of Peacefulness," *Journal of Peace Research*, 33:403-420.

Bonta, Bruce D. (2010). *Peaceful Societies*. <http://www.peacefulsocieties.org>.

Booth, William (1989). "Warfare Over the Yanomamo Indians," *Science*, 243(4895): 1138-1140.

Borofsky, Robert F., Ed. (2005). *Yanomami: The Fierce Controversy and What We Might Learn From It*. Berkeley: University of California Press

Cappelletti, E.J. (1994). "Fighting the Common Enemy in the Amazon," *Anthropology News*, 35(5):2.

Carneiro da Cunha, Maria Manuela (1989). "Letter to the Editor/the AAA Committee on Ethics," *Anthropology News*, 30(1):3.

Chagnon, Napoleon A. (1968). *Yanomamo: The Fierce People*. New York: Holt, Rinehart and Winston.

Chagnon, Napoleon A. (1968). "Yanomamo Social Organization and Warfare," in Fried, Morton; Harris, Marvin; Murphy, Robert, Eds., *War: The Anthropology of Armed Conflict and Aggression*. Garden City: Doubleday & Company, pp. 109-159.

Chagnon, Napoleon A. (1973). "Yanomamo," in *Primitive Worlds: People Lost in Time*. Washington: National Geographic Society, pp. 141-183.

Chagnon, Napoleon A. (1974). *Studying the Yanomamo*. New York: Holt, Rinehart and Winston.

Chagnon, Napoleon A. (1988). "Life Histories, Blood Revenge, and Warfare in a Tribal Population," *Science*, 239(4843):985-992.

Chagnon, Napoleon A. (1989). "Response to Ferguson," *American Ethnologist*, 16(3): 656-570.

Chagnon, Napoleon A. (1990). "On Yanomamo Violence: Reply to Albert," *Current Anthropology*, 31(1):49-53.

Chagnon, Napoleon A. (1992). *Yanomamo*. New York: Harcourt Brace Jovanovich.

Chagnon, Napoleon A. (1995). "L'ethnologie du deshonneur: Brief Response to Lizot," *American Ethnologist*, 22(1):187-189.

Chagnon, Napoleon A. (1996a). "Chronic Problems in Understanding Tribal Violence and Warfare," in Bock, Gregory R.; Goode, Jamie A., Eds. *Genetics of Criminal and Antisocial Behaviour*. New York: John Wiley & Sons, pp. 202-236.

Chagnon, Napoleon A. (1996b). "Book Review: Yanomami Warfare: A Political History, R. Brian Ferguson," *American Anthropologist*, 98(3):670-672.

Chagnon, Napoleon A. (1997a). *Yanomamo*. Fort Worth: Harcourt Brace.

Chagnon, Napoleon A. (1997b). "Sticks and Stones," Betzig, Laura, ed. *Human Nature: A Critical Reader*. New York: Oxford University Press, pp. 100-102.

Chernela, Janet M. (1997). "Book Review: Yanomami Warfare: A Political History, R. Brian Ferguson," *American Ethnologist*, 24(1):227-229.

Cooco, Luis (1972). *Iyewei-Teri: Quince anos entre los Yanomamos*. Caracas: Libreria Editorial Salesiana.

Coronil, Fernando, et al. (2001). "CA Forum on Anthropology in Public: Perspectives on Tierney's Darkness in El Dorado," *Current Anthropology*, 42(2):265-276.

Cultural Survival (2010). *Cultural Survival, Inc.* Cambridge: <http://www.cs.org>.

Curtis, Adam (2007). *The Trap: What Happened to Our Dream of Freedom?* London: BBC, British Broadcasting Corporation (2C 2:17). Available online at: <http://www.youtube.com/watch?v=JMw4ISOK2nU> and =T5vTODv_rGU).

Dawson, Michael (2006). *Growing Up Yanomamo*. Enumclaw: WinePress Publishing.

Davis, Shelton H. (1976). "The Yanomamo: Ethnographic Images and Anthropological Responsibilities," in Davis, S. H.; Matthews, R. O., Eds., *The Geological Imperative: Anthropology and Development in the Amazon Basin of South America*. Cambridge: Anthropology Resource Center, pp. 1-23.

Documentary Educational Research (2010). *Documentary Educational Research*. Available at: <http://www.der.org>.

Dyer, Elizabeth A. (2006). "Chagnon, Napoleon (1938-)," in Birx, H. James, Ed., *Encyclopedia of Anthropology*, Vol. 2. Thousand Oaks: Sage, pp. 477-478.

Early, John D.; Peters, John F. (1990). *The Dynamics of the Mucajai Yanomama*. New York: Academic Press.

Early, John D.; Peters, John F. (2000). *The Xilixana Yanomami of the Amazon: History, Social Structure, and Population Dynamics*. Gainesville: University of Florida Press.

Eckhardt, W. (1973). "Anthropological Correlates of Primitive Militarism," *Peace Research*, 5:5-10.

Eller, Jack David (2006). *Violence and Culture: A Cross-Cultural and Interdisciplinary Approach*. Belmont: Thomson Higher Education.

Evans Pim, Joam, Ed. (2009). *Toward a Nonkilling Paradigm*. Honolulu: Center for Global Nonkilling. Available at: <http://www.nonkilling.org>.

Fabian, Johannes (1991). *Time and the Other: How Anthropology Makes Its Object*. New York: Columbia University Press.

Ferguson, R. Brian (1984). "Introduction: Studying War," in Ferguson, R. B., Ed., *Warfare, Culture, and Environment*. Orlando: Academic Press, Inc., pp. 1-81

Ferguson, R. Brian (1989). "Do Yanomamo Killers Have More Kids?" *American Ethnologist*, 16(3):564-565.

Ferguson, R. Brian (1992a). "Tribal Warfare," *Scientific American*, 266(1):108-113.

Ferguson, R. Brian (1992b). "A Savage Encounter: Western Contact and the Yanomami War Complex" in Ferguson, R. Brian; Whitehead, Neil L., Eds., *War in the Tribal Zone: Expanding States and Indigenous Warfare*. Santa Fe: School of American Research, pp. 199-227.

Ferguson, R. Brian (1995). *Yanomami Warfare: A Political History*. Santa Fe: School for American Research Press.

Fischer, A. (1969). "The Personality and Subculture of Anthropologists and Their Study of U.S. Negroes," in Tyler, S.A., Ed., *Concepts and Assumptions in Contemporary Anthropology*. Athens: Southern Anthropological Proceedings, 3, pp. 12-17.

Fischer, Michael J. (2001). "In the Science Zone: The Yanomami, Science and Ethics," *Anthropology Today*, 17(3):19-36, 17(4):9-14, 17(5):16-19.

Fluehr-Lobban, Carolyn (2002). "Darkness in El Dorado: Research Ethics, Then and Now," in Fluehr-Lobban, Carolyn, *Ethics and the Profession of Anthropology: Dialogue for Ethically Conscious Practice*. Walnut Creek: AltaMira Press, pp. 85-106.

Fox, Robin (1969). "Book Review: War: The Anthropology of Armed Conflict and Aggression, Fried, Morton, Harris Marvin, and Robert Murphy, eds.," *American Anthropologist*, 71:314-315.

Frankfurt, Harry G. (2005). *On Bullshit*. Princeton: Princeton University Press.

Frankfurt, Harry G. (2006). *On Truth*. New York: Alfred A. Knopf.

Fry, Douglas (2006). *The Human Potential for Peace: An Anthropological Challenge to Assumptions about War and Violence*. New York: Oxford University Press.

Fry, Douglas (2007). *Beyond War: The Human Potential for Peace*. New York: Oxford University Press.

Fry, Douglas; Bjorkqvist, Kaj, Eds. (1997). *Cultural Variation in Conflict Resolution: Alternatives to Violence*. Mahwah: Lawrence Erlbaum Associates, Publishers.

Geertz, Clifford (2001). "Life Among the Anthros [review of Tierney 2001]," *New York Review of Books*, Feb, 8: 18-22.

Ghiglieri, Michael P. (1999). *The Dark Side of Man: Tracing the Origins of Male Violence*. Reading: Perseus Books.

Good, Kenneth R. (1989). *Yanomami Hunting Patterns: Trekking and Garden Relocation as an Adaptation to Game Availability in Amazonia, Venezuela*. Gainesville: University of Florida Doctoral Dissertation.

Good, Kenneth R. (1997). "Amazing Grace," *Natural History*, 106(2):44-45.

Good, Kenneth R. (1995a). "Hunting Patterns and Village Fissioning among the Yanomami: A Cultural Materialist Perspective," in Murphy, Martin F.; and Margolis, Maxine L., Eds., *Science, Materialism, and the Study of Culture*, Gainesville: University of Florida Press, pp. 81-95.

Good, Kenneth R. (1995b). "Yanomami of Venezuela: Foragers or Farmers- Which Came First?," in Sponsel, Leslie E., Ed., *Indigenous People and the Future of Amazonia: An Ecological Anthropology of an Endangered World*. Tucson: University of Arizona Press, pp. 113-120.

Good, Kenneth R.; Chanoff, David (1991). *Into the Heart: One Man's Pursuit of Love and Knowledge among the Yanomama*. New York: Simon & Schuster.

Good, Kenneth R.; Lizot, Jacques (1984). "Letter to Science," in Ferguson, R. Brian, Ed., *Warfare, Culture, and Environment*. Orlando: Academic Press, pp. 133-135.

Gregor, Thomas A., Ed. (1996). *The Natural History of Peace*. Nashville: Vanderbilt University Press.

Gregor, Thomas A.; Gross, Daniel (2004). "Guilt by Association: The Culture of Accusation and the American Anthropological Association's Investigation of Darkness in El Dorado," *American Anthropologist*, 106(4):687-698.

Grossman, D. (1995). *On Killing: The Psychological Cost of Learning to Kill in War and Society*. Boston: Little, Brown and Company.

Hames, Raymond C. (1994). "Yanomamo," in Wilbert, Johannes, Ed., *Encyclopedia of World Cultures: South America*, Vol. 7. Boston: G.K. Hall, pp. 374-377.

Hammersley, Martyn (1990). *Reading Ethnographic Research: A Critical Guide*. New York: Longman.

Harris, Marvin (1984). "A Cultural Materialist Theory of Band and Village Warfare: The Yanomamo Test," in Ferguson, R. Brian, Ed., *Warfare, Culture, and Environment*, Orlando: Academic Press, pp. 111-140.

Hedges, Chris (2002). *War is a Force that Gives Us Meaning*. New York: Public Affairs.

Heider, Karl G. (1997). "The Rashomon Effect: When Ethnographers Disagree," *American Anthropologist*, 90:73-81.

Heider, Karl G. (2001). Seeing *Anthropology: Cultural Anthropology Through Film*. Boston: Allyn and Bacon.

Holmes, Bob (2008). "How Warfare Shaped Human Evolution," *New Scientist*, 2682 (Nov.) 12. Available at: <http://www.newscientist.com/article/mg20026823.800-how-warfare-shaped-human-evo>.

Horgan, John (1988). "The Violent Yanomamo," *Scientific American*, 258(5):17-18.

Howell, Signe; Willis, Roy, Eds. (1989). *Societies At Peace: Anthropological Perspectives*. New York: Routledge.

Hume, Douglas W. (2010). "Darkness in El Dorado," *Antropological Niche*, Available at: <http://www.nku.edu/~humed1/index.php/darkness-in-el-dorado>.

Irons, William (2004). "Chagnon, Napoleon A.," in Amit, Vered, Ed., *Biographical Dictionary of Social and Cultural Anthropology*. New York: Routledge, pp. 88-89.

Jank, Margaret (1977a). *Mission: Venezuela*. Stanford: Brown Gold Publications.

Jank, Margaret (1977b). *Culture Shock*, Chicago: Moody Press.

Johnston, Barbara Rose, Ed. (2007). *Half-Lives and Half-Truths: Confronting the Radioactive Legacies of the Cold War*. Santa Fe: School for Advanced Research Press.

Johnston, Barbara Rose (2010). "Anthropologists in the Amazon: Secrets of the Tribe," *Counterpunch*, March 19-21<http://www.counterpunch.org/johnston03192010.html>.

Keegan, John (1993). *A History of Warfare*. New York: Random House/Vintage Books.

Keeley, Lawrence (1996). *War Before Civilization: The Myth of the Peaceful Savage*. New York: Oxford University Press.

Kegley, Jr., Charles W.; Raymond, Gregory A. (1999). *How Nations Make Peace*. New York: St. Martin's Press.

Keiser, Lincoln (1991). *Friend by Day, Enemy by Night: Organized Vengeance in a Kohistani Community*. Fort Worth: Harcourt Brace.

Kelly, Raymond C. (2000). *Warless Societies and the Origin of War*. Ann Arbor: University of Michigan Press.

Kemp, Graham; Fry, Douglas P., Eds. (2004). *Keeping the Peace: Conflict Resolution and Peaceful Societies Around the World*. New York: Routledge.

Landes, S.; Berreman, Gerald D.; Zaretsky, Kathleen; Leonardo, Michael; Michalak, Lawrence L.; Newman, Katherine S.; Boster, James S.; Villalon, Maria Eugenia;

Scheper-Hughes, Nancy; Paris, Teresa J.; Granpierre, Kathleen (1976). "Time Criticized for Yanomamo Characterization," *Anthropology Newsletter*, 17(7):28.

LeBlanc, Steven A. (2003). *Constant Battles: The Myth of the Peaceful, Noble Savage.* New York: St. Martin's Press.

Levinson, David (1994). *Aggression and Conflict: A Cross-Cultural Encyclopedia.* Santa Barbara: ABC-CLIO.

Lewis, M. Paul, Ed. (2009). *Ethnologue: Languages of the World,* 16th Edition. Dallas: SIL International. Available at: <http:www.ethnologue.com>.

Lewontin, Richard C. (1993). *Biology as Ideology.* London: Penguin.

Lizot, Jacques (1976a). *Le Cercle des Feux: Faits et dits des Indiens Yanomami.* Paris: Editions du Seuil.

Lizot, Jacques (1976b). *The Yanomami in the Face of Ethnocide.* Copenhagen: International Work Group for Indigenous Affairs Document No. 22.

Lizot, Jacques (1977). "Population, Resources, and Warfare among the Yanomami," *Man,* 12:497-515.

Lizot, Jacques (1978). *El Circulo de Los Fuegos: Vida y Costumbres de los Indios Yanomami.* Caracas: Monte Avila Editores.

Lizot, Jacques (1985). *Tales of the Yanomami: Daily Life in the Venezuelan Forest.* New York: Cambridge University Press.

Lizot, Jacques (1988). "Los Yanomami," in Coppens, Walter, Ed., *Los Aborigines de Venezuela.* Caracas: Fundacion La Salle de Ciencias Naturales, pp. 479-583.

Lizot, Jacques (1989). "Sobra la Guerra: Una Repuesta a N.A. Chagnon (Science 1988)," *La Iglesia en Amazonas* 44:23-24.

Lizot, Jacques (1994a). "Of Warfare: An Answer to N.A. Chagnon," *American Ethnologist,* 21(4):845-862.

Lizot, Jacques (1994b). "Words in the Night: The Ceremonial Dialogue - One Expression of Peaceful Relationships Among the Yanomami," in Sponsel, Leslie E., Gregor, Thomas A., Eds., *The Anthropology of Peace and Nonviolence.* Boulder: Lynne Rienner Publishers, pp. 213-240.

Loukottka, Cestmir (1968). *Classification of South American Indian Languages.* Los Angeles: UCLA Latin American Center.

Margolies, Luise; Suárez, Maria Matilde (1978). *Historia de la Etnología Contemporánea en Venezuela.* Caracas: Universidad Católica Andrés Bello.

Mann, Charles C. (2001). "Scientific Community: Anthropological Warfare," *Science,* 291(5503):416, 419-421.

Martins, Leda (2005). "On the Influence of Anthropological Work and Other Ethical Considerations: The Impact of Chagnon's Work in Brazil," in Borofsky, Robert F., Ed. *Yanomami: The Fierce Controversy and What We Might Learn From It.* Berkeley: University of California Press, pp. 189-195.

McNair, Rachel M. (2009). "Psychology of Nonkilling," in Evans Pim, Joam, Ed., *Toward a Nonkilling Paradigm.* Honolulu: Center for Global Nonkilling, pp. 327-347.

Migliazza, Ernst Cesar (1972). *Yanomama Grammar and Intelligibility* [Ph.D. dissertation, Indiana University]. Ann Arbor: University Microfilms International.

Miller, D.W. (2001). "Academic Scandal in the Internet Age," *The Chronicle of Higher Education*, Jan. 12: A 14.

Monaghan, Peter (1994). "Bitter Warfare in Anthropology," *Chronicle of Higher Education*, Oct. 26, XLI Section A: 11, 18-19.

Montagu, Ashley, Ed. (1968). *The Concept of Primitive*. New York: Free Press.

Montagu, Ashley, Ed. (1978). *Learning Non-Aggression: The Experience of Non-Literate Societies*. New York: Oxford University Press.

Moore, J. (1990). "The Reproductive Success of Cheyenne War Chiefs: A Contrary Case to Chagnon's Yanomamo," *Current Anthropology*, 31(3):322-330.

Neel, James V. (1970). "Lessons from a 'Primitive' People," *Science*, 170(3960):815-822.

Nugent, Stephen (2001). "Anthropology and Public Culture: The Yanomami, Science, and Ethics," *Anthropology Today*, 173:10-14.

O'Connor, Geoffrey (1990). *Contact: The Yanomami Indians of Brazil*. New York: Filmakers Library.

Olson, James Stuart (1991). *Indians of Central and South America: An Ethnohistorical Dictionary*, Westport: Greenwood Press.

Otterbein, Keith F. (1985). "Feuding - Dispute Resolution or Dispute Continuation," *Reviews in Anthropology*, 12:73-83.

Otterbein, Keith F., Ed. (1994). *Feuding and Warfare: Selected Works of Keith F. Otterbein*. Langhorne: Gordon and Breach.

Otterbein, Keith F. (2004). *How War Began*. College Station: Texas A&M University Press.

Otterbein, Keith F.; Otterbein, Charlotte S. (1965). "An Eye for an Eye, a Tooth for a Tooth: A Cross-Cultural Study of Feuding," *American Anthropologist*, 67:1470-1482.

Padilha, Jose (2009). *Secrets of the Tribe*. Watertown: Documentary Educational Resources. Available at: <http://www.der.org/films/secrets-of-the-tribe.html>.

Paige, Glenn D. (2009). *Nonkilling Global Political Science*. Honolulu: Center for Global Nonkilling. Available at: <http://www.nonkilling.org>.

Pandian, Jacob (1985). *Anthropology and the Western Tradition: Toward an Authentic Anthropology*. Prospect Heights: Waveland Press.

Peters, John F. (1998). *Life Among the Yanomami: The Story of Change Among the Xilixana on the Mucajai River in Brazil*. Orchard Park: Broadview Press.

Peters-Golden, Holly (2009). "The Yanomamo: Challenges of the Rainforest," in Peters-Golden, Holly, Ed., *Culture Sketches: Case Studies in Anthropology*, 5th edition. New York: McGraw-Hill Higher Education, pp. 260-279.

Pro-Yanomami Commission (2010). *Pro-Yanomami Commission*. Brasília; Boa Vista. Available at: <http://www.proyanomami.org.br>.

Rabben, Linda (2004). "Savage Anthropology," in Rabben, Linda, *Brazil's Indians and the Onslaught of Civilization: The Yanomami and the Kayapo*. Seattle: University of Washington Press, pp. 132-149.

Ramos, Alcida Rita (1987). "Reflecting on the Yanomami: Ethnographic Images and the Pursuit of the Exotic," *Cultural Anthropology*, 2:284-304.

Ramos, Alcida Rita (1995). *Sanuma Memories: Yanomami Ethnography in Times of Crisis*. Madison: University of Wisconsin Press.

Ramos, Alcida Rita (2001). "Old Ethics Die Hard: The Yanomami and Scientific Writing," Paper read at the Townsend Center for the Humanities, University of California, Berkeley, October 22, *Series Antropologia*, 302. Available online at: <http://www.unb.br/ics/dan/Serie302empdf.pdf>.

Ramos, Alcida Rita; Albert, Bruce; Oliveira, Jo Cardoso de (2001). *Haximu: Foi Genocídio!* Brasília: Comissão Pró-Yanomami (CCPY), Documentos Yanomami, 1.

Ramos, Alcida Rita; Taylor, Kenneth I. (1979). *The Yanoama in Brazil 1979.* Copenhagen: International Work Group for Indigenous Affairs Document No. 37.

Rice, Otis K. (1982). *The Hatfields and McCoys.* Lexington: University of Kentucky Press.

Rifkin, Jeffrey (1994). "Ethnography and Ethnocide: A Case Study of Yanomami," *Dialectical Anthropology*, 19(2/3):295-327.

Ritchie, Mark A. (1996). *Spirit of the Rainforest.* Chicago: Island Lake Press.

Ritchie, Mark A. (2000). *Spirit of the Rainforest: A Yanomamo Shaman's Story*, 2nd edition. Chicago: Island Lake Press.

Robbins, Richard H. (2009). *Cultural Anthropology: A Problem-Based Approach.* Belmont: Wadsworth.

Robin, Ron (2004). "Violent People and Gentle Savages: The Yanomami Controversy," in Robin, Ron, *Scandals and Scoundrels: Seven Cases That Shook the Academy.* Berkeley: University of California Press, pp. 138-165.

Rocha, Jan (1999). *Murder in the Rainforest: The Yanomami, the Gold Miners and the Amazon.* London: Latin American Bureau.

Roes, Frans (1997). "Napoleon Chagnon: Then You Are In Bad Luck," in *Speak, Darwinists!* Available at: <http://www.froes.dds.nl>.

Salamone, Frank (1997). *The Yanomami and Their Interpreters: Fierce People or Fierce Interpreters?* Lanham: University Press of America.

Salazar Quijada, Adolfo (1970). *Onomástica Indígena Actual de Venezuela.* Caracas: Universidad Católica Andrés Bello.

Sahlins, Marshall (2001). "Jungle Fever," [review of Tierney 2001] in *Guardian Weekly*, Nov. 17: 33.

Salzano, Francisco M.; Hurtado, A. Magdalena, Eds. (2003). *Lost Paradises and the Ethics of Research and Publication.* New York: Oxford University Press.

Sanford, Greg (1997). "Who Speaks for the Yanomami? A New Tribe's Perspective," in Salamone, Frank, Ed., *The Yanomami and Their Interpreters: Fierce People or Fierce Interpreters?* Lanham: University Press of America, pp. 57-65.

Service, Elman R. (1968). "War and Our Contemporary Ancestors," in Fried, Morton; Harris, Marvin; Murphy, Robert, eds., *War: The Anthropology of Armed Conflict and Aggression*, New York: Doubleday & Company, pp. 160-167.

Smith, David Livingstone (2007). *The Most Dangerous Animal: Human Nature and the Origins of War.* New York: St. Martin's Press.

Smith, Linda Tuhiwai (1999). *Decolonizing Methodologies: Research and Indigenous Peoples.* New York: Zed Books.

Smole, William J. (1976). *The Yanoama Indians: A Cultural Geography.* Austin: University of Texas Press.

Sponsel, Leslie E. (1979). "A Note on the Urgency of Research among the Yanomami of the Brazilian Amazon," *Review of Ethnology* (Wien), 7(1-9):72.

Sponsel, Leslie E. (1981). *The Hunter and the Hunted in the Amazon: An Integrated Biological and Cultural Approach to the Behavioral Ecology of Human Predation* [Ph.D. dissertation, Cornell University]. Ann Arbor: University Microfilms Int.

Sponsel, Leslie E. (1983). "Yanomama Warfare, Protein Capture, and Cultural Ecology," *Interciencia* (Caracas), 8(4):204-210.

Sponsel, Leslie E. (1986a). "Amazon Ecology and Adaptation," *Annual Review of Anthropology*, 15:67-97.

Sponsel, Leslie E. (1986b). "Book Review: Order Without Government: The Society of the Pemon Indians of Venezuela by David John Thomas," *New Scholar*, 10(1-2):318-321.

Sponsel, Leslie E. (1994a). "The Yanomamo Holocaust Continues," in Johnston, Barbara Rose, Ed., *Who Pays the Price? Examining the Sociocultural Context of the Environmental Crisis*, Washington: Island Press, pp. 37-46.

Sponsel, Leslie E. (1994b). "The Mutual Relevance of Anthropology and Peace Studies," in Sponsel, Leslie E.; Gregor, Thomas, Eds., *The Anthropology of Peace and Nonviolence*. Boulder: Lynne Rienner Publishers, pp. 1-36.

Sponsel, Leslie E. (1995). "Relationships Among the World System, Indigenous Peoples, and Ecological Anthropology," in Sponsel, Leslie E., Ed., *Indigenous Peoples and the Future of Amazona: An Ecological Anthropology of an Endangered World*. Tucson: University of Arizona Press, pp. 263-293.

Sponsel, Leslie E. (1996). "The Natural History of Peace: A Positive View of Human Nature and Its Potential," in Gregor, Thomas A., Ed., *The Natural History of Peace*. Nashville: Vanderbilt University Press, pp. 95-125.

Sponsel, Leslie E. (1996). "History, Conservation, and Human Rights: The Case of the Yanomami in the Amazon of Brazil and Venezuela," in Lewis, Connie, Ed., *Managing Conflicts in Protected Areas*. Gland: IUCN, pp. 62-62.

Sponsel, Leslie E. (1997). "The Master Thief: Gold Mining and Mercury Contamination in the Amazon," in Johnston, Barbara Rose, Ed., *Life and Death Matters: Human Rights and the Environment at the End of the Millennium*. Thousand Oaks: Altamira Press, pp. 99-127.

Sponsel, Leslie E. (1998). "Yanomami: An Arena of Conflict and Aggression in the Amazon," *Aggressive Behavior*, 24(2):97-122.

Sponsel, Leslie E. (1999). "Book Review: Life Among the Yanomami: The Story of Change among the Xilixana on the Mucajai River of Brazil, by John F. Peters," *American Anthropologist*, 101(3):35-36.

Sponsel, Leslie E. (2000). "Response to Otterbein," *American Anthropologist*, 102(4):837-840.

Sponsel, Leslie E. (2005). "Noble Savage and Ecologically Noble Savage," in Taylor, Bron, Ed., *Encyclopedia of Religion and Nature*, Vol. 2. New York: Thoemmes Continuum, pp. 1210-1212.

Sponsel, Leslie E. (2006a). "Darkness in El Dorado Controversy," in Birx, H. James, Ed., *Encyclopedia of Anthropology*, Vol. 2. Thousand Oaks: Sage, pp. 667-673.

Sponsel, Leslie E. (2006b). "Yanomamo," in H. James Birx, Ed., *Encyclopedia of Anthropology*, Vol. 5. Thousand Oaks: Sage, pp. 2347-2351. (Reprinted in Angeloni, Elvio, Ed., 2010, *Annual Editions Anthropology* 10/11, New York: McGraw-Hill).

Sponsel, Leslie E. (2008). "Amazon: Environment and Nature," in Selin, Helaine, Ed., *Encyclopedia of the History of Science, Technology, and Medicine in Non-Western Cultures*, Vol. 1. The Netherlands: Springer, pp. 757-762.

Sponsel, Leslie E. (2009). "Reflections on the Possibilities of a Nonkilling Society and a Nonkilling Anthropology," in Evans Pim, Joam, Ed., *Toward a Nonkilling Paradigm*. Honolulu: Center for Global Nonkilling, pp. 35-72. Available at: <http://www.nonkilling.org/node/18>.

Sponsel, Leslie E. (2010a). "Yanomami," *Homepage*. Available at: <http://www.soc.hawaii.edu/Sponsel/Yanomami/Yanomami/MP_Yanomami.htm>.

Sponsel, Leslie E. (2010b). "El Dorado Controversy," *Homepage*. Available at: <http://www.soc.hawaii.edu/Sponsel/El%20Dorado%20Controversy/MP_ElDorado.html>.

Sponsel, Leslie E. (2010c, in press). "The Master Thief: Gold Mining and Mercury Contamination in the Amazon," in Johnston, Barbara Rose, Ed., *Life and Death Matters: Human Rights and the Environment at the End of the Millennium*, 2nd edition. Walnut Creek: Left Coast Press.

Sponsel, Leslie E.; Good, Kenneth R. (2000). "Anthropologists Debate Future of War," *Anthropology News*, 41(2):19-20.

Sponsel, Leslie E.; Gregor, Thomas, Eds. (1994). *The Anthropology of Peace and Nonviolence*. Boulder: Lynne Rienner Publishers.

Sponsel, Leslie E.; Turner, Terence (2002). "Charges of Wrong Doing by Anthropologists," *Chronicle of Higher Education*, Aug. 9, Section 2: B13.

Stoll, David (2001). "Science Attacks Amazon Tribe," *The New Republic*, 496(4):34-39.

Thomas, David John (1982). *Order without Government: The Society of the Pemon Indians of Venezuela*. Urbana: University of Illinois Press.

Tierney, Patrick (2000). "The Fierce Anthropologist," *The New Yorker*, 76(3):50-61.

Tierney, Patrick (2001). *Darkness in El Dorado: How Scientists and Journalists Devastated the Amazon*. New York: W.W. Norton and Co.

Tiffany, S.W.; Adams, K.J. (1994). "Anthropology's "fierce" Yanomami: Narratives of Sexual Politics in the Amazon," *National Women's Studies Association Journal* 6:169-196.

Tiffany, S.W.; Adams, K.J. (1995). "Feminists Re-Reading the Amazon: Anthropological Adventures into the Realm of Sex and Violence," East Lansing: *Michigan State University Women and International Development Program Working Paper*, 253.

Tiffany, S.W.; Adams, K.J. (1996). "Housewives of the Forest: Representations in Ethnographic Film," *Women's Studies*, 25:169-188.

Thomas, David John (1982). *Order Without Government: The Society of the Pemon Indians of Venezuela*. Urbana: University of Illinois Press.

Time (1976), "Beastly or Manly? *Time*, 107(10):69.

Turner, Terrence (1991). *Report of the Special Commission to Investigate the Situation of the Brazilian Yanomami*. Arlington: American Anthropological Association Available at: <http://www.aaanet.org/committees/cfhr/docshist.htm>.

Turner, Terrence (1994). "The Yanomami: Truth and Consequences," *Anthropology Newsletter*, 35(5):48, 46.

Turner, Terrence (2001). *The Yanomami and the Ethics of Anthropological Practice*. Ithaca: Cornell University Latin American Studies Program Occasional Paper, 6.

Turner, Trudy, Ed. (2005). *Biological Anthropology and Ethics: From Repatriation to Genetic Identity*. Albany: State University of New York Press.

Valero, Helena (1984). *Yo Soy Napeyoma: Relato de una Mujer Raptada por los Indigenas Yanomami*. Caracas: Fundación LaSalle de Ciencias Naturales.

Waller, Altina L. (1988). *Feud: Hatfields, McCoys, and Social Change*. Chapel Hill: University of North Carolina Press.

Wallis, Ethel Emily (1965). *The Dayuma Story: Life Under Auca Spears*. New York: Harper.

Watson, Lyall (1995). *Dark Nature: A Natural History of Evil*. New York: Harper-Collins Publishers.

Wax, Dustin M., Ed. (2008). Anthropology at the Dawn of the Cold War. AnnArbor: Pluto Press.

Whiteford, Linda M.; Trotter II, Robert T. (2008). *Ethics for Anthropological Research and Practice*. Long Grove: Waveland Press.

Wilbert, Johannes (1972). "The Hunters: The Yanoama of Territorio Amazonas," in Wilbert, Johannes, *Survivors of Eldorado: Four Indian Cultures of South America*. New York: Praeger, pp. 13-64.

Wilbert, Johannes; Simoneau, Karin, Eds. (1990). *Folk Literature of the Yanomami Indians*. Los Angeles: UCLA Latin American Center Publications.

Wilson, Samuel M. (2001). "Informed Consent: A Muckraking Book Spotlights the Ethics of Anthropological Fieldwork," *Natural History*, 110(2):90.

Wolf, Eric R. (1994). "Demonization of Anthropologist in the Amazon," *Anthropology Newsletter*, 35(3):2.

Wong, Kate (2001, March). "Fighting the Darkness in El Dorado," *Scientific American*, 284(3):26-28.

Wrangham, Richard; Peterson, Dale (1996). *Demonic Males: Apes and the Origins of Human Violence*. Boston: Houghton Mifflin Company.

Wright, Robin; Cunha, Mauela Carneiro da (1999). "Destruction, Resistance, and Transformation - Southern Coastal, and Northern Brazil (1580-1890)," in Salomon, Frank; Schwartz, Stuart B., Eds., *The Cambridge History of the Native Peoples of the Americas: Volume 3, South America*. Cambridge: Cambridge University Press, pp. 287-381.

Chapter Seven

Menraq and the Violence of Modernity

Alberto Gomes
La Trobe University

The various bands live at peace with one another....War, or any other form of hostility, is absolutely unknown, not only between the different bands and tribes of the Semang themselves, but also with the Sakai, and even with the Malays, by whom they are not infrequently harassed. They never react to ill-treatment with treachery, much less with open violence. They merely withdraw and avoid their oppressors. As a result, self preservation has developed in them a marked timidity and suspicion of all strangers. (Murdock, 1934: 94-95)

Today, the Negritos are an extremely peace-loving people, shy to a fault, and reluctant to take any part in disputes and dissension. Their immediate reaction to any threat, real or imaginary, is one of flight... (Carey, 1976: 49)

3 killed, 2 hurt in fight with Orang Asli By Shamsul Akmar
KOTA BARU, Mon—Three men were killed and two others were injured in a fight, believed to be over land matters, with a group of Orang Asli men in Sungai Rual, Jeli, about 100km from here. Police have detained 11 Orang Asli men in connection with the killings. (*New Straits Times*, 27/04/1993)

Introduction

The epigraphs relate to the Menraq, better known in anthropological literature and/or official or bureaucratic parlance as Semang or Negritos. I prefer calling them Menraq because it is an inclusive autonym meaning human or people in most of the dialects spoken in the Rual settlement (hereafter shortened to Rual) where I did my fieldwork[1] and because the other

---

[1] This chapter is mostly drawn from Gomes (2007) which was based on ethnographic data I collected during my several field visits to Rual since 1975. I have had the privilege of meeting and living with the Rual Menraq during a period spanning 30 years (1975 to 2006). I first visited Rual Resettlement in August 1975 and since then visited the settlement in 1976, 1978, 1979, and 1988. Between 1999 and 2006, I made four short visits of a few days to a week to Rual; my last visit was in September 2006. The time

ethnonyms are inappropriate for a number of reasons; the official term, Negrito, which derives from Spanish meaning 'short black' is unquestionably a racist ethnic label. The statements were made at different times in the past: 1934, 1976, and 1993. The first by an anthropologist, the second by a former head of the Malaysian Department of Aboriginal Affairs, also an anthropologist and the third by a Malaysian journalist reporting the killing of three Malays allegedly by Menraq from Rual.

Murdock's portrayal of Menraq as peaceful people with an aversion to aggressive behaviour is derived from earlier work by Skeat and Bladgen (1906), Schebesta (1928, 1954), and Evans (1937), among others. Carey's depiction of the Menraq is reiterated in all subsequent ethnographical work on this group of people (Kirk and Karen Endicott, Alberto Gomes, Terry Rambo, Razha Rashid, Shuichi Nagata, Lye Tuck Po, Csilla Dallos and Corry van der Sluys). All in all, the Menraq are represented in all these accounts as an irrefutably peaceful and nonviolent people. In the words of Robert Dentan (1992: 219):

> Nonviolence is so salient in Aslian everyday life that all the ethnographers who have worked there—whatever their nationality, gender, theoretical biases, or original scientific "problem"—have wound up grappling with peaceability and its relationship with Aslian egalitarianism, ethnopsychology, and religious ideology.

Then the question is what turned Menraq into killers in 1993? Someone imbued with a Hobbesian perspective may jump to the conclusion that the Menraq killing, albeit purportedly, is proof of the innateness of human aggression, contending that even peaceable humans may and do kill at times. It is my argument that peaceability is the norm (or innate predisposition) and violence or aggressive behaviour is an aberration (see Sponsel, 2009; and Dentan in this volume). So the question ought to be posed differently: why did this aberration or abnormality take place in the Menraq settlement in 1993?

The precise details of what transpired in April 1993 are unclear as people are naturally reticent to elaborate what actually happened. This reticence is

---

depth in my field research allows for a longitudinal or diachronic analysis but the short field visits may imply a lack of ethnographic depth, as the time spent on the key anthropological research tool of participant observation is relatively short. However, for almost three decades I have carried out research among the Orang Asli at large, visiting about 100 or so villages. In 1982–84, I conducted my doctoral study on economic change among the Semai (another Orang Asli group), for which I lived for a period of 14 months in a village as a participant observer (Gomes, 2004).

natural for a people like the Menraq who adhere to a nonviolent sociability. They find it extremely hard to speak about incidents of violent behaviour, particularly if they are implicated as perpetrators of such violence. It is also possible that this reluctance to speak about violent events could be a psychological coping mechanism so that people can come to terms with the traumatic effects of the event. It could also very much have been an attempt to erase this event from their collective memory.

During my visit a few months after the event, I was able to piece together what had occurred from conversations with people, including the eleven men accused of killing. I was told that a non-Menraq man, a Malay, turned up at a hamlet at Rual, belligerently demanding the people move out by the next day. He insisted that the land the Menraq were occupying belonged to him as he had bought the land from the State land office. The Menraq had just returned from a temporary settlement as their hamlet had been quarantined after a cholera outbreak that killed six villagers. The next day the man turned up with five other Malay men, reportedly brandishing machetes and speaking aggressively, to chase the Menraq away. The Menraq headman told the Malays of his people's decision to stay put, indicating that they were residing on their ancestral land. The Malays abused the Menraq and physically threatened the people with their machetes. The situation turned tense, and after a Malay man assaulted the village headman, a scuffle broke out which ended in fatalities. One Malay man succumbed to injuries purportedly inflicted by the Menraq, and two Malay men were found dead a kilometer or so away in the van they travelled in, allegedly killed by blowpipe-propelled poisoned darts. Three Malays who bolted from the scene escaped unhurt. The incident was reported to the authorities and eleven Menraq were arrested. Subsequently nine men were charged with culpable homicide not amounting to murder. The court trial went on for months and eventually the accused were acquitted. To a question by the defence lawyers as to which one of the accused was the owner of the blowpipe believed to be the murder weapon, the police officer in court replied that he was uncertain because "they all look alike." With such an element of doubt, the presiding judge requested the charges against the accused be dropped and the case was dismissed.

While the accused were freed, this event had left deep scars in the collective psyche of the Menraq. When eleven of the men were initially arrested and incarcerated in the police lock-up, the whole settlement was in a state of shock. The NGO and defence lawyers engaged to represent the accused in the court trial were initially unable to get the Menraq to cooperate. A defence lawyer told me that when he first approached them the people appeared terrified and extremely frightened and were distrusting of outsiders. It was only after one of the members of the NGO mentioned the names of anthropologists, including myself, who had befriended them did they break their silence and reticence to speak about the incident.

In this chapter, I hope to show how the violence that took place in Rual in 1993 is linked to the growing despair and discontentment among the Menraq emanating from their experiences of displacement, dispossession, and deprivation. The chapter will shed light on how changing social and economic conditions stemming from modernization projects can lead to violent conflict. I begin with a brief ethnographic overview.

The Rual Menraq

The Menraq belong to a category of tribal people called Orang Asli (Original Peoples), the Aborigines of Peninsular Malaysia. On the basis of their language, linguists surmise the Menraq to be descendents of an ancient people who inhabited the Malay Peninsula. The pre-historian, Peter Bellwood (1997: 128) asserts that "the Negritos and their traditional hunting and gathering lifestyle must be considered as autochthonous to the Indo-Malaysian Archipelago."

Established in 1972 as a result of a government-sponsored resettlement programme, Rual is a small Menraq settlement in Kelantan, a northeastern state of Peninsular Malaysia. Menraq living in the vicinity were enticed to leave their home territories and settle at the site as part of the government's modernization programme for the Orang Asli. Before they were resettled, the Menraq eked out a living by foraging the tropical forests for game, wild tubers, and vegetables. They also engaged in some collecting of forest products such as rattan, bamboo, honey, and bean pods (such as petai and kerdas) which they exchanged for such food and goods like rice, salt, machetes, and cloth.

While the Menraq are renowned in anthropological circles as a tropical forest hunting and gathering people, Rual Menraq hardly engage in foraging these days as government-sponsored and directed development has transformed them into sedentary cultivators of cash crops and occasional wage workers. In other words, they have become simple commodity producers who depend on the market for most of their necessities of life which they have to pay for with income they earn from the sale of rubber and palm oil and so on as well as from their wages gained from mostly menial labour.

They have also been converted to Islam, although they are yet to become devout Muslims. In 2006 the settlement had 475 residents and in many aspects, it has become almost indistinguishable from a Malay kampong.

Traditional Normative System

Menraq nonviolence and peaceability are shaped by several of their social and cultural precepts and practices, namely egalitarianism, individual autonomy and social flexibility, and generalized reciprocity. These in turn are conditioned by their economic pursuits and ecological adaptation. Pre-resettlement Menraq fit well with Woodburn's characterization of "immediate-return" foraging societies, which are "societies that do not store food or engage in protracted production processes" (quoted in Endicott, 1988: 121). Woodburn (1982: 435) observed that immediate-return foraging groups tend to be egalitarian primarily because of their nomadism, which allows people "to move away without difficulty and at a moment's notice from constraint which others may seek to impose on them" and because of the relative personal autonomy of individuals who are not dependent on others for basic survival:

> Whatever the system of territorial rights, in practice in their own areas and in other areas with which they have ties, people have free and equal access to wild foods and water; to all the various raw materials they need for making shelters, tools, weapons and ornaments; to whatever wild resources they use, processed or unprocessed, for trade (Woodburn, 1982: 437).

Nomadism also allows people to move away from troublesome others and escaping from conflict-prone situations and concomitantly minimizing the potential for conflict which could escalate into violence.

As is common in egalitarian foraging societies, no individual or a group of individuals in traditional Menraq society possesses the power or authority to control or manipulate consensus. Individuals may make decisions, whether political, economic or jural, through consultations, deliberations and negotiations with other members of the band. The opinions and ideas of older, usually male, are given more weight but not without some open discussion. Deciding on where to forage or set camp is a good and intriguing example of this process. Instead of people getting together to talk about this matter, they remain in their respective shelters and simply loudly call out prospective sites and reasons for the choice. The band members present arrive at a decision upon weighing the pros and cons of the various suggestions. Women do take part in this consultative process but they play their role in a rather inconspicuous manner.[2] They express their views, sometimes in whispers, to their

---

[2] Kirk Endicott (personal communication) notes that Batek women do speak for themselves in camp-wide discussions.

husbands who will then repeat them loudly for the benefit of the others in the camp. The male spouse, it appears, acts on these occasions as a spokesperson for the conjugal family. Any form of coercion or physical threatening is viewed with disdain and Menraq would simply avoid such confrontations by flight. Furthermore, as van der Sluys (1999: 310) notes, Menraq strongly believe that forcing someone to do one's bidding will raise "hot" emotions and in the process weaken the person's *ruway* (soul) causing him or her to fall ill or even die. But obviously such a direct decision-making process can be carried out only in a camp-like situation where shelters are arranged in a semicircle allowing for the people to communicate in the manner described above. The modern arrangement of houses that are separate and well spaced out from one another makes such communication difficult, if not impossible.

While strong egalitarianism within the band may suggest an absence of political leadership, in reality Menraq do adhere to a system of headmanship which appears to be partly adopted from the Malays, especially in reference to the title of the leader, *penghulu* (Malay: village headman).[3] As Kirk Endicott (1974: 245) has suggested, this system of headmanship may have existed for a long time in "Semang" society. However, the roles of the headmen, which in the past may have been loosely defined, have become more important or authoritative; they are primarily facilitated by state officials' insistence on arranging matters through an acknowledged leader. The official selects an individual from the band to assume the role of *penghulu*, although the selection is usually legitimized locally by a presumption that the band members have elected their own headman. An important criterion for headmanship is a good ability to converse and negotiate in Malay (*Bahasa Malaysia*), the national language of Malaysia, as his primary duty is to act as a go-between for the state officials and agencies, particularly the JHEOA. Endicott (1974: 245) has also noted this criterion in his study of the Batek:

> In fact, the main duty of a *penghulu* is to deal with outsiders, including government agencies. He acts as a kind of foreign minister for his group, a spokesman and communicator of information from outside. What little authority he has internally, qua *penghulu*, is derived from his role as intermediary between the J.O.A. and the Batek.

---

[3] "Penghulu" usually refers to a government-appointed and salaried position as compared to "Ketua" which means "Head" in Malay. In Malay villages (*Kampong*), one may find a Penghulu and a Ketua Kampong, the former a civil servant or representative of the government responsible for the village administration and the latter plays a more traditional role of village leader or headman.

Headmen also often assume the role of mediator in commercial exchanges between Menraq and traders. In arranging for the supply of forest products, traders contact the band headmen and place orders for specific products. The traders also negotiate with the headmen the terms of trading like price of the products and time and place of the eventual commercial exchange. Headmen then pass this information on to the members of their band. Previously, the headmen did not receive any payment or gratuities for this role but these days they demand a payment from the trader. They refer to this payment as their "cut" or commission.

It is not always easy for headmen to secure overwhelming support from their band members who generally value their personal autonomy and independence. This is in spite of the headman's position being government-authorized; he is provided with an official letter of appointment and a nominal salary. In the early years of the Rual Resettlement, only the headmen of the respective band were given special timber houses as a mark of their headmanship. The government's act of installing and recognizing a headman and establishing a rather elaborate system of leadership among the Menraq have certainly sown seeds of inequality in a community noted for its egalitarianism.[4]

Egalitarianism works well in curbing or eliminating the potential for grievance, considered in several studies as a source of conflicts,[5] by ensuring that everyone has almost equal access to power, status and prestige in the traditional Menraq society. To prevent or avert grievance that may arise from inequalities emanating from differential abilities, talents and access in relation to economic activities, production or access to resources, Menraq advocate and practice generalized reciprocity. In generalized reciprocity, sharing occurs within a group of people and the obligations to make a return gift are shared by the members of the group. A donor does not expect to receive a return gift from his or her recipient. Instead the donor's generosity is likely to be reciprocated by someone else in the group of people involved in reciprocal exchanges. Such reciprocity drives the sharing of food and resources as well as cooperative labor, especially in gathering, fishing, and forest collecting. There is also a great deal of labor cooperation among band members in most of their subsistence pursuits. In this way they represent Kropotkin's ideal "mutual aid" society (Kropotkin, 1972 [1914]).

---

[4] See Shuichi Nagata (2004) for an extended discussion of the implications of government policy on leadership in a "Semang" Resettlement in Kedah.
[5] Much has been written about the nexus of greed and grievance as a source of armed violence. See, for example, Collier and Hoeffler (2002), Gurr (1993) and Korf (2005).

For the traditional hunter-gatherer Batek people, Endicott declares that food sharing is "...an absolute obligation to the Batek, not something that the giver has much discretion over." He observes that:

> A person with excess food is expected to share it and if this is not done others do not hesitate to ask for some. And it would be virtually impossible for someone to hoard food in the open shelters of a Batek camp without everyone knowing about it. Recipients treat the food they are given as a right; no expression of thanks is expected or forthcoming, presumably because that would imply that the donor had the right to withhold it. (Endicott, 1988:117)

Why do foraging people accord such importance to sharing? A standard anthropological explanation (cf. Sahlins, 1972) is that sharing is a way of redistributing resources which are naturally spread widely and unequally among people in a group in order that everyone benefits and nobody is disadvantaged from the vagaries of the food quest. According to this view, people give food to others at time of plenty with an expectation of being reciprocated at times of need. Several anthropologists (for example, Woodburn, 1980) associate sharing with egalitarianism. The variation in productivity as a result of differences in skill, fortune, and labor capacity and efficiency, as one would expect, can impose some pressure on an egalitarian ethos. It is contended that increased productivity and the provision of greater quantities of food and other products may accord higher status or privilege to the producer. To minimize this or to remove this possibility, individuals are socially obliged through a set of rules, beliefs, and norms which function to encourage, stimulate or subtly coerce people to share. Sharing is hence perceived to be a form of levelling mechanism, which serves to militate against accumulation and in the process, operating to thwart or retard the development of inequalities of wealth, power and prestige.

There is clearly an element of levelling in the case of the distribution of large animals obtained in hunting. Such distribution is procedural. The following is an extract from my field journal relating to the distribution of a wild pig I witnessed in 1976:

> The pig was laid on a mat of leaves at the back of the house of the headman. Several people were present, some squatting, some standing and a few sitting on the ground. One of the men then started cutting up the pig with a machete. He seemed to be butchering the carcass according to a prescribed technique. The meat is separated into heaps made out of similar cuts or from the same part of the animal. The butcher then picks up portions of the

> meat from each heap and places them in a set of separate smaller heaps ar-
> ranged around the large heaps of meat. He ensures that each small heap has
> almost equal portion of meat from all the different parts of the animal. A
> member of each family then collects a heap of meat to take home.

In such sharing the inequalities in production arising from differences in hunting abilities, talents and successes are neutralized by redistribution so much so that everyone in the camp or group, irrespective of gender, age or skill, has equal access to food.

There is however little or no obvious benefit in leveling or redistribution in small-scale and quotidian forms of sharing which hints that such exchange transaction has benefits other than purely economic or materialistic ones. During my field research I have observed people giving food to one another on a regular and daily basis. People do not just share wild foods that they obtain from hunting and gathering but also habitually distribute purchased food such as rice, dried fish, sugar, salt and biscuits as well as other con-sumables such as tobacco and cigarettes. In such distribution, the donor fol-lows an order of priority according to social distance; as Endicott (1988: 116) observes, "they must give shares first to their own children and spouse, then to any parents-in-law or parents present, and finally to all other families in camp." Occasionally, this food giving practice appears to be economically irrational, as people would give each other the same sort of food. I have come across people giving rice they have bought in the market or a shop to their neighbours who would make a return in kind. Endicott (1988: 116) says that "[t]his apparently unnecessary distribution confirms that sharing of food is a dominant value in Batek culture."

When asked why they gave their food to their fellow camp members, Menraq offered reasons such as "we must help each other," "it's *adat men-raq*" (our custom), "we've always done this, it's a custom from our ances-tors," and "it's *punan* (tabooed) not to do so." These reasons touch on the sociality created by sharing in the functionalist sense that it establishes and maintains social relations among members of the band. As Endicott (1988: 112) contends, "[t]he unity of a camp is based not on political organiza-tion...but on a moral obligation incumbent on each family to share food with all other families in the camp." The concept of *punan*, which appears to derive from the Malay *kempunan*, meaning yearning or desire, seems to be central in justifying as well as motivating sharing and gift-giving in general among Menraq and in most, if not all, other Orang Asli communities. Endi-cott (1988: 117) describes *punan*, which he spells as *pohnen*, among the Batek as "a belief that to refuse a reasonable request for something can cause harm to the person refused." My understanding of this concept differs from Endicott's. Rual people's explanation of *punan* appears to be similar to the Semai concept of *pehunan* which Robarchek (1977: 105) explains as the "state of being unfulfilled, unsatisfied, or frustrated in regard to some specific and strongly felt want…" Similarly, as in the case of the Semai, someone who has incurred *punan* among the Menraq is believed to be at risk of attack by supernatural forces and/or wild animals and/or susceptible to accidental injury, illness and even death. Aptly, Van der Sluys (2000: 445) defines the concept (which she spells as *pehunen*) as "accident proneness." *Punan* refers to the experience of unfulfilled desire as well as the sanctions or punishment resulting from it. Since people in a camp are likely to be kin-related and generally socially close to one another, a state of *punan* in one of its members is going to have implications for the whole group. As Van der Sluys (1999: 310) observes, "Affliction falls on the victim, thus reinforcing the ethic of caring for one another." In order to avoid *punan*, a person may drop hints of his or her desire by making statements such as "I haven't eaten rice for a while" or "you have lots of tapioca in your rattan basket." Among the Menraq, people may demand a share of food or tobacco. This is a form of sharing that has been appropriately referred to as "demand sharing" and appears to be a common practice among foragers. As Peterson (1993: 860) points out, "…observation and ethnographic evidence suggest that much giving and sharing [in forager groups] is in response to direct verbal and/or nonverbal demands." Hence, sharing in this way occurs "by taking rather than giving" (Peterson, 1993: 861) and is not governed by unsolicited generosity. Irrespective of whether sharing is guided by purely altruistic values, it serves to draw people into a network of cordial relations and social exchanges that works well in maintaining social cohesion and peace. Gift-giving among the Menraq does not operate in the Maussian sense of a "means of controlling others" (Mauss, 1970: 73) because it is practiced in a normative order centered on egalitarianism and generalized reciprocity. Furthermore, Menraq value cooperation and mutual aid over competition.

While nomadism and social group flexibility are adaptive to a foraging lifestyle, they may also be seen as strategies associated with a dark side of Menraq and other Orang Asli history. This is the history of slave-raiding carried out against them and their fellow Orang Asli by outsiders, especially Indonesian immigrants to the Malay Peninsula in the 1800s and early 1900s. It is a history of physical and structural violence which seems to have left an indelible mark on the people. Skeat and Blagden (1906: 532-33) narrate this sad event in the lives of the Orang Asli:

> Hunted by the Malays, who stole their children, they were forced to leave their dwellings and fly hither and thither, passing the night in caves or in huts ("pondok") which they burnt on their departure. "In those days" they say, "we never walked in the beaten tracks lest the print of our footsteps in the mud should betray us." For wherever the Malay perceived any indication of their presence, he would build himself a small shelter, and never leave it until he had discovered the place of retreat where they generally spent the night. Accompanied by a few accomplices, he would then repair to the spot at nightfall, and the party, concealing themselves until dark, would wait until the "Hill-men" were asleep. The Malays would then fire several rifle shots, spreading terror and confusion in every family, whose breaking up made them an easy prey to their assailants, who would promptly rush to the spot where they heard the shrieks of women and children. The girls were, as a rule, at once knocked on the head, and the boys were carried off and sold as slaves. There is hardly a family that has not its own especial calamity to relate, the result being the profound aversion that they avowedly cherish for the Malay....Any act of vengeance, moreover, would be fatal to them, in view of their insignificant numbers and lack of means of defence. They prefer therefore to sacrifice the part for the whole, and this is certainly the only possible course open to them.

Kirk Endicott (1983) maintains that slave-raiding had enduring effects, of which one was that it planted the seeds of deeply rooted fear of encounter with strangers. Slave-raiding is remembered in oral traditions which serve to "shape and justify a world view in which outsiders, especially Malays, are pictured as dangerous and untrustworthy" (Endicott, 1983: 237). Orang Asli children are often taught to fear and distrust outsiders. Illustrative of the Orang Asli fear of outsiders, in this case Malays, Nagata (1995: 103) relates an incident in a "Semang" resettlement in Kedah:

> One night in November 1991, there was a *kenduri* (feast) and *ceramah* (lecture) in Kampung Memali, about two miles from Legong village, to commemorate the Memali incident of 1985, in which the people of Memali (not Orang Asli) and the police had clashed and some women and children were killed in the skirmish. On the night in question, a lot of people were converging on Memali village by motorcycles and cars, which created a considerable commotion on the streets. Suddenly a group of Orang Asli emerged from the darkness of the night, men carrying babies on their back, wearing *parangs* (machetes) and carrying bamboo blow-

pipes, and women leading older children and carrying sleeping mats and pots and pans. An old man then approached me to go with them to take refuge on the hilltop as the Malays were going to kill them. So saying, he pointed to a stream of headlights heading to Kampung Memali. I pointed out that since a public meeting has to have a police permit, the police would be there to prevent any trouble from breaking out. I was then countered by the son-in-law of the old man who said that they could not feel safe since the police were Malays.

Orang Asli xenophobia could also be a reaction to Malay prejudice and discrimination toward the Orang Asli (cf. Dentan, 1997). Many Menraq have told me that Malays typically treat them condescendingly and sometimes with contempt. Some Malays I have talked to in Jeli have expressed negative stereotypes of Menraq. The common statements I have heard are: "They are unkempt," "They live like animals," "They have *kurap* (skin sores) and lice," "They cannot be trusted." At a coffee shop once, a Malay man enquired with a puzzled look, "How come you are staying with the *Orang Hutan* (Jungle people)?"

To summarise, I contend that the inter-related aspects of Menraq normative order such as egalitarianism, social group flexibility, generalized reciprocity, and the inclination to flee from aggressive and violent others (manifested in their xenophobia) underscore the conditions of their peaceful and nonviolent existence. As I will discuss in the following sections, Menraq entanglement with modernity in the form of resettlement and development has all but undermined and destroyed this order and in turn destabilized and weakened the social and ideological basis of Menraq peacefulness and nonviolence. How have Menraq lives been violated by development? I shall show that development instead of engendering as explicitly intended a better life for the people has led to discontentment and dejection.

The Violence of Modernity

As Stanley Tambiah (1996: 3) observes, "A somber reality and disillusionment of our epoch, which emerged from the ashes of World War II, is that although there have been successes in the push toward development and modernization, eradication of disease, and the spread of literacy, economic and political development programs have generated and stimulated, whether by collusion or in reaction, in good faith and poor anticipation, massive civil war and gruesome inter-racial and interethnic bloodshed." In her book provocatively titled *The Violence of the Green Revolution*, Vandana Shiva has linked the communal violence between the Sikhs and the Hindus in the Punjab, which left about 15,000 people dead between 1986 and 1991, to the adverse effects of agricultural developmental programmes, known as the "Green Revolution," implemented by the Indian government with financial and scientific support from international agencies. Contrary to expectations and the official rhetoric proclaiming the successes of such development programmes, Shiva contends that the social, economic, and ecological changes associated with the Green Revolution have left the Punjab with "diseased soils, pest-infested crops, water-logged deserts, and indebted and discontented farmers" (Shiva, 1991: 12). This legacy, according to her, has led to a high level of frustration, anger and discontentment among the people. Unable to contain or resolve such feelings of despair, people began to direct their anger and frustration toward members of other communities, escalating into communal strife and violence.

Another celebrated case of conflict in rural areas is the Zapatistas' rebellion in the Chiapas region in Mexico. In her ethnography, *Mayan Visions*, Nash (2001) connects the mobilization of Mayan indigenous forces into the Zapatista movement to the impoverishing effects of globalization and free trade. In 1994, peaceful demonstrations turned violent after the Mexican government attempted to crush the movement by force. In the course of armed conflict, hundreds of people have lost their lives and their property and livelihoods. Such ethnographic cases are two of many others which reveal and document the violence of development. We shall now look at the violence of development at Rual.

Economic Violence

Since 1972, the range of development projects implemented at Rual has transformed the Menraq from "traditional" subsistence-oriented foragers to cash-oriented commodity producers. They are by no means unaccustomed to the market economy; they have traded forest products for various commodities with merchants and shops for a very long time. However, resettlement and the various accompanying development programmes implemented in the past three decades or so have pushed the people deeper into the market economy. Consequently, they now engage increasingly in the production of goods to earn cash. This is because their need for money has grown immensely as they now have to buy most of the things they need, including food, from traders and shops. In the process, they have been entrapped in the commodity "exchange" or circuit. They have to work to produce commodities such as rubber and oil palm fruit to earn cash to buy other commodities, which they are increasingly dependent on. This focus on commodity production has engendered many changes in Menraq economy and society. In economic terms, it has, among other things, led to a decline in subsistence-oriented foraging as people devote more time and effort to growing cash crops and participating in other market-oriented activities.

Another major consequence of the resettlement economy has been the increasing dependence of Menraq on the government for their day-to-day survival. The provision of food rations to secure people's involvement in the projects has spurred such dependence. Menraq expectations of rations or gratuities had reached such a level that they would refuse to participate in state-sponsored activities that did not come with handouts. In 1978, when their requests to the JHEOA field officer for food rations appeared to be falling on deaf ears, they threatened to uproot the rubber seedlings they had just planted. Their requests were quickly met. This dependence seems to have conditioned the people to behave differently with outsiders. People frequently demanded food and other things from visitors to Rual.

Writing about a similar situation among the Semai at the Betau Regroupment Scheme, Nicholas (1990: 78) contends that:

> With much of their traditional structure being eroded and their ability to be self-sufficient and self-reliant being drastically impaired, the Semai have been forced to seek government aid in almost every sphere of development. Consequently, in place of traditional self-confidence, the Semai were reduced to a state of 'imitative dependence.' This is a highly degraded state associated not only with an inability to provide themselves adequately with the material means of sustenance but also with the loss of cultural and psychological integrity.

Development for the Menraq has expanded the amount of material goods in the village such as household furniture, stereo sets, televisions, and fancy clothes. It has improved the quality of houses; several are now concrete with separate rooms. It has introduced "modern" conveniences such as electricity and piped water to the homes. Many own motorcycles and one or two individuals have cars. These are some of the visible and obvious material benefits of development in Rual. But the economic costs are high. They have lost their economic independence and they are now more vulnerable and susceptible to economic failures since they no longer have control over the vicissitudes of their economy which is now less diversified than before. Production failure or drop in commodity prices can now spell economic disaster for the people. They are no longer able to fall back on their subsistence pursuits of hunting, fishing and gathering to see them through times of economic hardships. The economic transformation has severe ecological and social costs too, which have plunged the Menraq into a maelstrom of despair and discontentment.

Ecological Violence

Endicott (1974: 29) has observed that

> ...the Batek feel at home in the jungle, especially the primary jungle, but feel out of place in clearings and in villages outside the jungle. This attitude is expressed in their belief that the jungle is healthy because it is cool and clearings unhealthy because they are hot.

Rual Menraq have often expressed to me their preference for the forest, particularly during hot days. They complain about having to endure the very hot conditions at the settlement. The cutting of forests from logging and agriculture has affected the microclimate of the area. In his study of the climatic conditions prevailing at Rual in 1976, Rambo (1985: 54) found that

> Daytime air temperature was always higher in the settlement than in the forest, averaging 29.4° C in the settlement clearing compared to 27.2° C in the forest. There was a daily range of 11.3 degrees between the lowest and highest temperatures (22° to 33.3° C) in the settlement compared to 8.5 degrees (22° to 30.5° C) in the forest.

Rambo's study was conducted in 1976 when there was still substantial forest cover. With the almost complete deforestation at Rual, the current situation would certainly be worse.

It is a common finding in studies of Orang Asli resettlements or re-groupment schemes that the land chosen for settlement is not of good quality for agricultural development. Mohd. Tap (1990: 69) refers to the land provided to Orang Asli as "second class land," that is plots rejected by other people because they have poor soil, located in remote areas, "devoid of any commercially viable resources like timber and minerals" and mostly unsuitable for agriculture, unless they are "well rehabilitated." The soil at Rual is mostly sandy at the settlement and lateritic (subject to leaching) in other parts. It is generally of poor quality.[6] Hence, land around Rual needs

---

[6] Soils in tropical forest areas tend to be poor. The rich nutrients normally found in soil are absorbed by the lush forest vegetation. Hence, the removal of this vegeta-

to be "well rehabilitated" and this involves the heavy use of fertilizers. In the oil palm cultivation at Rual about 10 per cent of the initial cost was for the supply and application of fertilizers. In traditional slash and burn or swidden agriculture in forestlands, the nutrients in the vegetation are released into the soil through burning, which effectively enhances soil quality and enables productive farming (albeit with regular rotation) without the use of artificial fertilizers. The use of chemical fertilizers and pesticides in the various agricultural projects at Rual is bound to have ecological implications for the quality of the land and water in the area, but I do not have data to support this.

Another consequence of resettlement with ecological implications is the depletion of resources due to overexploitation. Higher population density in the area and the accumulative tendencies in commodity production have led Menraq (and their Malay neighbours) to increase harvests in order to redress reduced output from subsistence oriented production and to meet demands for imported commodities. Overexploitation has led to an almost total disappearance of riparian fauna in the Rual area. Fishing by poison has devastated fish stocks while the market demand for frogs and turtles has spurred Menraq hunters to over-harvest these species.

Much of the impact on the environment is, however, exogenously imposed. Commercial logging has greatly affected the Rual environment. Intensive logging began in April 1976, when a logging company was given a concession to extract timber near Rual and in parts of the resettlement area. By 1979, there were six logging companies operating in the area. The environmental impact of logging in tropical forest is well documented. Dentan et al. (1997: 98) provide a summary of the ecological changes resulting from logging:

> The absence of shade raises the temperature of the soil to desert conditions, so that it no longer holds water well and easily blows away....Since there are no roots to hold the thin, dusty topsoil in place, heavy rains then flush the topsoil into the rivers. Mud bars choke the rivers, making them unavailable for transportation and killing the more sensitive fish on which rural people depend for food....Logging roads, even more than loss of trees, cause erosion. Exposed to torrential rains, the soft laterite soil washes away as soon as the loggers move on. Logging roads also interrupt drainage, creating stagnant pools, ideal breeding places for the mosquitoes that carry malaria. Often the land is left too eroded to allow the forest to regenerate. Eventually, the succession is to grassland, typically of useless *lalang* grass.

tion leaves behind nutrient-poor soils. Furthermore, the loss of vegetation also exposes the soils to leaching by rainwater.

During the height of logging in the late 1970s and early 1980s,[7] more than ten timber trucks daily would ply up and down through the Rual settlement to transport logs to the depot at Jeli. Each time a truck went past it left behind a cloud of dust and dirt, which was blown into the dwellings.

Logging has also transformed the Rual landscape and waterways. In 1975, the hills surrounding the Rual settlement were covered with lush green vegetation, making it seem very much like a settlement in the deep forest. The Rual River had clear running water. A few years later, during my 1979 visit, I noticed that the hills were almost barren and that the settlement appeared more like a homestead in an abandoned tin mining area, with obviously dirty streams and pools. But it is not just the aesthetic implication of deforestation that is of concern; it has also had an adverse impact on people's ability to meet their subsistence requirements from foraging in the immediate environment.

In the past thirty years, the Menraq population has almost doubled, largely due to natural increase but this is not as significant in terms of population pressure on resources as the growth of the Malay population in the areas around Rual, primarily as a result of land development schemes benefiting Malays.

Severe ecological degradation is a form of violence. It has undermined and destroyed peoples' livelihoods and lowered their quality of life. As I shall discuss below, ecological violence has adversely affected the health status and morbidity of the Menraq, leading to higher rates of mortality, especially child mortality.

Structural Violence

As Arturo Escobar (2004: 160) argues, "...modernity is essentially about displacement—conquering territories, uprooting peoples from place, restructuring spaces, such as creating plantations and urban sprawl or ghettoes, and so forth..."

---

[7] In the 1970s and 1970s Malaysia was the world's leading producer of tropical hardwoods. Commenting on timber trade in Malaysia, Jomo et al. (2004) indicate:

> ...timber has generally been a major source of export earnings for Malaysia. Indeed, timber has been Malaysia's second largest net export earner, after petroleum, since the early 1980s, greatly exceeding palm oil...and rubber. In 1990, for instance, timber export earnings and timber products amounted to RM8.9 billion, or 11.3 per cent of total export proceeds, compared to RM10.6 billion for petroleum, RM4.4 billion for palm oil and RM3.0 billion for rubber. In 1995, the contribution of timber exports to export earnings from primary commodities still accounted for some 20.4 per cent, although it declined, as expected, to 5.5 per cent by 2000.

Resettlement has removed Menraq from their homeland (*sakaq*), resulting in people losing control and ownership of the land that was once theirs. Land allocated to Orang Asli settlers is invariably less than and different from the land they occupied traditionally. As Nicholas (1990: 71-71) observes, the size of the resettlement areas ranges from 1.1 to 15 percent of the size of their former territories. In one Semai community in the Betau Regroupment Scheme, he notes that the 95.1 hectares of land allocated to the village amounts to a mere 1.4 percent of the approximately 7,000 hectares of their communal land. Every time I have visited Rual, people have complained about their confinement into much smaller areas than they are accustomed to, about the Malay encroachment onto Menraq hereditary territory, and about its destruction by logging. Displacement from their homelands, loss of access to its resources and loss of other rights, as they see it, to their traditional land have been a source of much discontent among the Rual people.

On one of my visits to Rual in the late 1970s, I had an interesting experience that revealed the implications of deterritorialization. Early one hazy morning, I saw several Menraq men talking to two Malay men who were introduced to me as forestry officers. A Menraq man told me that they were rounding up guides to assist the officers to "survey the trees." I asked whether I could join them and hwo long the "survey" would take. They said that I could join the party of six Menraq and the officers to conduct the "survey" which they anticipated would not take long. We walked for several hours up to the crest of the hill and then the guides suggested that we take a rest. While resting, I noticed that the guides were engrossed in an animated discussion. I then learnt that they were unsure which of the paths that radiated from the resting spot they should take. One guide explained to me and the Forestry officers that the paths were leading to different locations far from each other, one to Jeli, another to Rual and yet another to Batu Melintang, and they were not sure which of these paths would take us back to Rual. In other words, they were lost. I was baffled as I pondered: How is it that the guides, renowned as "forest peoples," have become lost in a forest that they should know well? Don't they have mental maps that they have formed through all those years of moving and travelling in the forests or through instructions from their elders? It then occurred to me, after identifying the band affiliations of the guides, that they were all new to the area. They belonged to a band from a different *sakaq*, one which was resettled in Rual only a few years ago. Their knowledge of the territory was therefore limited by the little time they had spent in the place. Their willingness to be recruited as guides is perhaps an indirect expression of their "rights" to their present *sakaq*. Or it could simply be an opportunity to earn some money from the Forestry Department for their service. Whatever the reasons were, this is clearly another ethnographic instance, as in the case of the Meratus Dayaks of Borneo, where Tsing (1993: 153) found that resettlement was turning people into "strangers in their own lands." As "strangers," what are their rights to land? Do they have legal ownership of the land they claim as their own? The Jeli incident discussed earlier would suggest that claims of ownership and control are shaky. Furthermore, the boundaries of the "territory" belonging to the Menraq are at best fuzzy. How then could the Malay farmers who tried to evict the Menraq band claim that they had "bought" the land the people were residing on? It appears that Menraq do not have secure rights to the land that they perceive is "theirs."

Land—or more exactly indigenous conceptions of territory (*sakaq*)—is an important source of history and identity for the Menraq. People tell stories of past events in connection to the place where these events occurred. In other words, for Menraq, their past is inscribed in their land. This is a spatialized historical consciousness, spaces are transformed into places as they are incorporated into people's social and cultural maps. Place is also an important symbolic source and substance for Menraq social identity. Who they are depends largely on where they are from. Displacing them from their *sakaq* then has major implications for their identity and their history.

Resettlement also engenders the considerable spatial re-ordering that Evrard and Goudineau (2004: 938) have referred to as reterritorialization. It is possible to see some of the social implications of such re-ordering in a comparative analysis of the traditional camp and the current settlement. In a camp, the shelters are erected close to one another in a semi-circle with the main hearth in the centre of the camp. They are also open, with almost no privacy. There is an air of intimacy and closeness, and this, along with the open nature of spatial arrangement, facilitates social interaction and communication, sharing of food (as it is impossible to hoard food), and the exchange of knowledge. It also eases the decision-making process. In contrast to the intimacy of the camp, the settlement is structured in a grid form, where the houses are arranged in a row or clusters and the hearths are located inside the dwellings. In the new settlements there is less village intimacy and greater privacy, with the houses having doors that are usually closed and even locked when the residents are away. The closed and private nature of the houses makes possible hoarding or concealment of wealth and possessions. People can avoid sharing by hiding things they do not want to share. If, as discussed earlier, sharing is an adhesive in Menraq social grouping, then the spatial arrangement in the new settlements goes against the grain of the traditional culture of the Menraq. The temporary nature of the shelters in a traditional camp makes the camp more flexible than the new settlement where the houses are permanent with concrete floors and power connections. The flexible and temporary nature of the camp allows people to erect their shelters in accordance to their sharing network and social alliances. They can easily change the location of their shelters according to changing relations or shifting alliances. They can also avoid tension and possible confrontation if problems with other families emerge. People in the settlement do not have the option of moving houses whenever they liked. Moving away is no longer an easy strategy for escaping confrontations or altercations with neighbours (cf. Endicott, 1979: 185). Fixity in settlement and housing not only has implications for social relations among Menraq but, as the incident of killing in 1993 reveals, it has also compelled people to "stand their ground" in face of encroachment from outsiders.

The dire state of affairs at Rual is not solely the outcome of economic and demographic changes. It is also the product of the social and cultural transformations accompanying commoditization and state sponsored development programmes. Processes such as commoditization and monetization have led to growing Menraq dependency on outsiders and loss of personal autonomy. The social fabric traditionally kept intact by the binding forces of sharing and generalized reciprocity has been undermined by the individualistic tendencies and self aggrandizement associated with simple commodity and capitalist-oriented production and consumption. There is evidence of incipient social differentiation. Social inequality will make for radical change in Menraq communities, given that egalitarianism is a salient feature of their traditional way of life.

The most severe aspect of structural violence inflicted through Menraq encounter with modernity is the increase in morbidity and mortality. Most of the deaths in Rual, about 96 percent were brought about by disease. From the death records kept at the Rual administrative centre that I obtained in 1988, it was reported that 12 or 40 percent of the 30 deceased whose deaths were registered with known causes suffered from chronic diarrhoea and blood in the stool, which are symptoms associated with such diseases as acute amoebic dysentery and cholera.[8] Another nine (30 percent) people died of respiratory-related diseases, such as acute bronchitis

---

[8] My data on the cause of deaths is somewhat sketchy and the records I have obtained from the JHEOA death registers do not provide precise information on the cause of deaths.

and tuberculosis. In 1993, there was a cholera outbreak with 18 detected cases, which in fact led to the temporary relocation of many of the Rual people. This outbreak killed eight people in Rual. Pertinent questions that need to be addressed include: Has there been an increase in the incidence of disease in the Rual community over the years? If so, is this increase due to the changing conditions emanating from resettlement and development? In the absence of data on disease occurrence before resettlement, it is not possible to answer the first question with any certainty. Several Menraq have commented that unlike in their past traditional life they and their family members fall sick more frequently these days. They also felt that more people in Rual seem to die from sickness these days than before.

This view is clearly reflected in the mortality statistics. Extrapolating from genealogical records, reproductive histories, and comparative analysis of the population censuses, I counted 178 deaths in the Menraq population from 1978 to 1998. This means that an average of nine people died each year and in a population ranging from 193 to 331, this is a rather high number of deaths in a year. The population grew by 138 individuals during this period. Hence, in absolute terms it is apparent that more people died during this period of twenty years relative to the addition in the population. These deaths have certainly minimized the potential growth of population, as calculations will show that if each woman had 4 to 5 children each (which is the average birth rate) this should result in a population size of anywhere between 392 to 490 in 1998. The population in 1998 totalled 331 and this includes about twenty or so inmigrants.

From a comparison of death records compiled in different survey periods, it appears that more people in Rual are dying annually than before. In my survey of the period between December 1974 and April 1978, I counted 23 deaths, which averages to seven deaths per year, two less than now. Of course one could argue that the absolute number of deaths is bound to increase as the population size expands. There are however several statistical measures that can be used to provide a more accurate and precise estimation of the level of mortality. In the absence of a reliable system of vital information registration, one method of extrapolating the level of mortality is to examine comparatively the survival rates of the offspring of post-reproductive women. In my analysis of these rates I found that the number of children dying before their mothers has gone up from 0.67 in 1978 to a staggering 1.69 in 1988, which means each post-reproductive woman living in 1988 had lost one child more than her counterpart living in 1978, to 2.13 in 1998.

As for the health consequences of resettlement, Chee (1995: 50), among others, contends that "Resettled communities which are at higher population densities...can sustain parasitical infections which could not previously be sustained; and crowding provides ideal conditions for the spread of infectious diseases." As noted earlier, resettlement has brought about the concentration of Menraq into an area much smaller than they are accustomed to, resulting in deplorable sanitary conditions in the Rual resettlement. The rubbish disposal system and toilet facilities in Rual have been poor ever since its establishment in 1972 and this will no doubt increase the susceptibility of people to such communicable diseases as dysentery and cholera. Another factor is the settlement layout which turns out to be conducive to the proliferation of certain diseases like malaria. As Baer (1999b: 303) indicates, the low-built and closely spaced houses, unlike the traditional living arrangements, prevent people from "penning domesticated or wild-caught animals (alternative blood-meal sources for mosquitoes)" or making "smudge fires" under their houses to drive off mosquitoes from the area. Having more people living close to one another, as Baer (1999b) also notes, facilitates the transmission of malaria from an infected person to others.

As Baer (1999a), among others, has indicated, there is a correlation between medical problems and nutrition. Good nutritional status undoubtedly ensures a balanced immunochemical system and therefore good health and better protection against disease. Traditional foraging societies are noted to maintain a reasonably good diet, as they typically have access to an adequate supply of animal protein and carbohydrates in the form of wild tubers, fruit, and vegetables from hunting, fishing and gathering (cf. Dunn, 1968). What happens to their diet when foragers are forced to settle down and/or become increasingly dependent on purchased foods? In a longitudinal study of several Ariaal and Rendille pastoral communities in East Africa, Fratkin et al. (1999) reported a drop in nutritional status as nomads settled due to a change in diet from high protein foods to cheaper and less nutritious staples. Consequently, "childhood morbidity" had not improved despite "sedentary populations' easier access to health care interventions and higher levels of immunization against polio, diphtheria-tetanus-pertussis, and measles" (Fratkin, et al., 1999: 733). There is no reason to doubt that the same situation applies to the Menraq. Combined with the adverse environmental effects of development, it is evident Menraq diet has deteriorated and this has led to poor health and higher mortality rate.

Conclusion

If we return to the question why the Menraq reacted so uncharacteristically in April 1993, the reasons ought to be clear now. The changes in Menraq economy and society have been sweeping and far-reaching. By the late 1990s Rual seemed endowed with all the trappings of modernity. For Rual Menraq, the process of modernization has had unanticipated and unfortunate consequences for the beneficiaries and in fact has created more problems for the Menraq. Their lives have been deeply and drastically affected, so much so that they no longer adhere to the fundamental principles of being nonviolent and communally-minded foraging peoples. Here we have a group of people who have been displaced and consequently detached from their "spatialized history," with an insecure economic future and frequently having to mourn the loss of their children dying of diseases associated with living in crowded and unhealthy conditions and being hungry, and having to retain their identity under attack by Islamization and assimilation. They have been pushed into a small pocket of state-owned land, mainly devoid of forests that they once depended upon for their livelihood. In the process, people have lost control of their own destiny. They are often seen smiling when outsiders visit them but their smiles mask a deep sense of discontentment, disillusionment and desperation. The violence which resulted in the sad loss of the lives of three Malays will need to be comprehended, perhaps not explained, in the context of Menraq dire state of affairs emanating from development. It was an act by a group of people in desperation and experiencing social upheaval who has cast aside their deep sense of nonkilling for just a moment of aberration, an act that will now haunt them for the rest of their lives.

References

Baer, Adela (1999a). *Health, Disease and Survival: A Biomedical and Genetic Analysis of the Orang Asli of Malaysia*. Subang Jaya: Centre of Orang Asli Concerns.

Baer, Adela (1999b). "Rainforest malaria, mosquitoes and people," *Malayan Nature Journal*, 53: 299-305.

Bellwood, Peter (1997). *Prehistory of the Indo-Malaysian Archipelago*, Revised edition. Honolulu: University of Hawai'i Press.

Bellwood, Peter (1999). "Archaeology of Southeast Asian hunters and gatherers," in Lee, Richard B.; Daly, Richard, Eds., *The Cambridge Encyclopedia of Hunters and Gatherers*. Cambridge: Cambridge University Press, pp. 284-288.

Carey, Iskandar (1976). *Orang Asli: The Aboriginal Tribes of Peninsular Malaysia*. Kuala Lumpur: Oxford University Press.

Chee, Heng Leng (1995). "Health and nutrition of the Orang Asli: The need for primary heath care amidst economic transformation," in Rashid, Razha, Ed., *Indigenous Minorities of Peninsular Malaysia: Selected Issues and Ethnographies*, Kuala Lumpur: Intersocietal and Scientific Sdn. Bhd. (INAS), pp. 48-71.

Collier, Paul; Hoeffler, Anke (2002). "Greed and grievance in civil war," *Working Paper Series*, 2002-01, Centre for the Study of African Economies. Available at: <http://www.csae.ox.ac.uk/workingpapers/pdfs/2002-01text.pdf>.

Dallos, Csilla (2003). *Identity and opportunity: Asymmetrical household integration among the Lanoh, newly sedentary hunter-gatherers and forest collectors of Peninsular Malaysia* [Ph.D dissertation]. McGill University.

Dentan, Robert Knox (1992). "The rise, maintenance and destruction of a peace polity: A preliminary essay in poltical ecology," in Silverberg, James; Gray, J. P., Eds., *Aggression and Peacefulness in Humans and Other Primates*. New York: Oxford University Press, pp 214-270.

Dentan, Robert Knox (1997). "The persistence of received truth: How ruling class Malays construct Orang Asli identity," in Winzeler, Robert L., Ed., *Indigenous Peoples and the State: Politics, Land, and Ethnicity in the Malayan Peninsula and Borneo*. New Haven: Yale University Southeast Asia Studies Monograph 46, pp. 98-134.

Dentan, Robert; Endicott, Kirk; Gomes, Alberto; Hooker, Barry (1997). *Malaysia and the Original People: A Case Study of the Impact of Development on Indigenous Peoples*. Needham Heights: Allyn and Bacon.

Dunn, Frederick L. (1968). "Epidemiological factors: health and disease in hunters-gatherers," in Lee, Richard; DeVore, Irven, Eds. *Man the Hunter*. Aldine: Chicago University Press, pp. 221-228.

Endicott, Kirk Michael (1974). *Batek Negrito economy and social organization* [Ph.D. dissertation] Harvard University.

Endicott, Kirk Michael (1979). *Batek Negrito Religion: The World-view and Rituals of a Hunting and Gathering People of Peninsular Malaysia*. Oxford: Clarendon Press.

Endicott, Kirk Michael (1983). "The effects of slave raiding on the aborigines of the Malay Peninsula," in Reid, Anthony, Ed., *Slavery, Bondage, and Dependency in Southeast Asia*. Brisbane: University of Queensland Press, pp. 216-245.

Endicott, Kirk Michael (1988). "Property, power and conflict among the Batek of Malaysia," in Ingold, Tim; Riches, David; Woodburn, James, Eds., *Hunters and Gatherer Vol. 2: Property, Power and Ideology*. Oxford: Berg, pp. 110-127.

Escobar, Arturo (2004). "Development, violence and the new imperial order," *Development*, 47 (1): 15-21.

Evans, Ivor H. N. (1937). *The Negritos of Malaya*. Cambridge: Cambridge University Press.

Evrard, Olivier; Goudineau, Yves (2004). "Planned resettlement, unexpected migrations and cultural trauma in Laos," *Development and Change*, 35: 937-962.

Fratkin, Elliot M.; Roth, Eric Abela; Nathan, Martha A. (1999). "When nomads settle: The effects of commoditization, nutritional change, and formal education on Ariaal and Rendille pastoralists," *Current Anthropology*, 40: 729-735.

Gomes, Alberto G. (2004). *Looking for Money: Capitalism and Modernity in an Orang Asli Village*. Subang Jaya; Melbourne: Center for Orang Asli Concerns; Trans Pacific Press.

Gomes, Alberto G. (2007). *Modernity and Malaysia: Settling the Menraq Forset Nomads*. Milton Park: Routledge.

Gurr, Ted Robert (1993). *Minorities at Risk: A Global View of Ethnopolitical Conflicts*. Washington: United States Institute for Peace.

Jomo, K. S; Chang, Y. T.; Khoo, K. J. (2004). *Deforesting Malaysia: The Political Economy and Social Ecology of Agricuttural Expansion and Commercial Logging*. London: Zed Books; United Nations Research Institute for Social Development.

Koff, Benedikt (2005). "Rethinking the greed-grievance nexus: Property rights and the political economy of war in Sri Lanka," *Journal of Peace Research*, 42 920: 201-217.

Kropotkin, Peter (1972 [1914]). *Mutual Aid: A Factor of Evolution*. London: Penguin.

Lye, Tuck Po (2005). *Changing Pathways: Forest Degradation and the Batek of Pahang, Malaysia*. Petaling Jaya: Strategic Information Research Development.

Mauss, Marcel (1970). *The Gift: Forms and Functions of Exchange in Archaic Societies*. London: Cohen and West.

Mohd Tap Salleh (1990). *An examination of development planning among the rural Orang Asli of West Malaysia* [Ph.D dissertation]. University of Bath.

Murdock, George P. (1934). *Our Primitive Contemporaries*. New York: Macmillan.

Nagata, Shuichi (1995). "Education and socialisation in a Semang resettlement community of Kedah, Malaysia: The case of the Kensiu, the Kintak Bogn and the Kintak Nakil," in Rashid, Razha, Ed. *Indigenous Minorities of Peninsular Malaysia: Selected Issues and Ethnographies*. Kuala Lumpur: Intersocietal and Scientific Sdn. Bhd. (INAS), pp. 86-108.

Nagata, Shuichi (2004). "Leadership in a resettlement village of the Orang Asli in Kedah, Malaysia," *Contributions to Southeast Asian Ethnography*, 12: 95-126.

Nash, June (2001). *Mayan Visions: The Quest for Autonomy in an Age of Globalization*. New York; London: Routledge.

Needham, Rodney (1964). "Blood, thunder, and mockery of animals," *Sociologus*, 14 (2): 136-149.

Nicholas, Colin (1990). "In the name of the Semai? The State and Semai society in Peninsular Malaysia," in Ghee, Lim Teck; Gomes, Alberto G., Eds. *Tribal Peoples and Development in Southeast Asia*, Special issue of the Journal *Manusia dan Masyarakat*. Kuala Lumpur: University of Malaya, pp. 68-88.

Nicholas, Colin (2000). *The Orang Asli and the Contest for Resources: Indigenous Politics, Development and Identity in Peninsular Malaysia*. Copenhagen; Subang Jaya: International Work Group for Indigenous Affairs; Centre for Orang Asli Concerns.

Peterson, Nicholas (1993). "Demand sharing: reciprocity and the pressure for generosity among foragers," *American Anthropologist*, 95 (4): 860-874.

Rambo, A. Terry (1985). *Primitive Polluters: Semang Impact on the Malaysian Tropical Rain Forest Ecosystem*. Ann Arbor: University of Michigan Museum of Anthropology, Anthropological Papers, 76.

Razha, Rashid, Ed. (1995). *Indigenous Minorities of Peninsular Malaysia: Selected Issues and Ethnographies*. Kuala Lumpur: Intersocietal and Scientific Sdn. Bhd. (INAS).

Razha, Rashid; Karim, Wazir Jahan, Eds. (2001). *Minority Cultures of Peninsular Malaysia: Survivals of Indigenous Heritage.* Penang: Academy of Social Sciences.

Robarchek, Clayton (1977). *Semai non-violence: A systems approach to understanding* [Ph.D. dissertation]. University of California at Riverside.

Sahlins, Marshall (1972). *Stone Age Economics.* Chicago: Aldine.

Schebesta, Paul (1973 [1928]). *Among the Forest Dwarfs of Malaya.* London: Oxford University Press.

Schebesta, Paul (1954). *Die Negrito Asiens: Wirtschaft and Soziologie.* Vienna: St. Gabriel-Verlag. Partially trans. by Frieda Schutze, Human Relations Area Files, 1962.

Shiva, Vandana (1991). *The Violence of the Green Revolution: Third World Agriculture, Ecology, and Politics.* Penang: Third World Network.

Skeat, Walter William; Blagden, Charles Otto (1966 [1906]). *Pagan Races of the Malay Peninsula.* London: Frank Cass.

Sponsel, Leslie E. (2009). "Reflections on the possibilities of a nonkilling society," in Evans Pim, Joám, Ed., *Toward a Nonkilling Paradigm.* Honolulu: Center for Global Nonkilling, pp. 35-72.

Tambiah, Stanley (1996). *Leveling Crowds: Ethnonationalist Conflicts and Collective Violence in South Asia.* Berkeley: University of California Press.

Tsing, Anna Lowenhaupt (1993). *In the Realm of the Diamond Queen: Marginality in an Out-of-the-Way Place.* Princeton: Princeton University Press.

Van der Sluys, Cornelia (1999). "The Jahai of northern Peninsular Malaysia," in Lee, Richard B.; Daly Richard, Eds., *The Cambridge Encyclopedia of Hunters and Gatherers.* Cambridge: Cambridge University Press, pp. 307-311.

Van der Sluys, Cornelia (2000). "Gifts from the immortal ancestors: Cosmology and ideology of Jahai Semang," in Schweitzer, Peter P.; Biesele, Megan; Hitchcock, Robert K., Eds., *Hunters and Gatherers in the Modern World: Conflict, Resistance, and Self-Determination.* New York: Berghahn Books, pp. 427-454.

Woodburn, James (1980). "Hunters and gatherers today and reconstruction of the past," in Gellner, Ernest, Ed., *Soviet and Western Anthropology.* London: Duckworth, pp. 95-117.

Woodburn, James (1982). "Egalitarian societies," *Man,* 17: 431-51.

Chapter Eight

James Bay Cree Respect Relations within the Great Community of Persons

Who Should Be Killed and How

Richard "Dick" Preston
McMaster University

Long before the Twentieth Century

The hunting traditions of James Bay (Northern Quebec and Ontario) Crees are of interest to the development of a nonkilling anthropology in part because for thousands of years they made their living by killing food-animals, including large animals, according to a morality of disciplined violence. Their "great community of persons" (Preston, 1997, 2002; Hallowell, 1955) included other humans, other kinds of animal species, and spirit-persons. Their "techne"—strategies and skills for killing—were disciplined by practice, by attending to their success and failures, and by a traditional hunting ethic that is based on maintaining respect relations between persons of all kinds. In turn, the hunting ethic expressed the spirituality of the hunt, and set strict guidelines on the use of violence. Hunting was spiritually and literally the "ground of their being," and hunting was also the basis of their morality of respect and measured violence.

And the traditional, respect-based hunting ethic sustained them for many centuries. Here I present an approximation of the pre-contact and early contact periods, and documentary evidence of the sustainability of this ethic through the 17th, 18th, 19th and 20th centuries, with some concluding thoughts on how this ethic has been transformed and guides the Crees' political negotiations in the globalized world of the present.

It is very important to remember in this discussion that the respect we are considering—arguing for as a central quality—is not an abstract principle or proclaimed ideology. It is rather an attitude—an emotion in the context of readiness for action—that goes with and guides the very pragmatic actions of the hunters.

More than 95% of human history is a history of hunters. The Crees share this ancient human heritage. The Cree world had a personal factor not often found today, that would have substantively influenced their ethic. Relations were built on a small number of persons in a vast region—perhaps averaging as few as ten human persons per 1,000 square kilometers. The old Cree hunters believed that there was some unseen and unnamed power that governed the land (Long, Preston and Oberholzer, 2006) and so provided the animals. The animals, in turn, were believed to provide—to in some mystical sense choose to show their presence in tracks and other traces, and the humans were, in their turn, obligated to respond by the deep play of the hunt, and so to kill their food (Preston, 2002). They were capable and habituated to killing animals. But unless there is a scarcity of resources and intrusive groups of strangers, most of the world's hunting cultures are characterized by avoiding violence against, and specifically killing humans.

The Cree hunter matured by experientially learning the discipline of the bush, including the typical behaviour of the animals, who were viewed as species-specific types of persons. And the hunter's maturation proceeded by developing and practicing the measured violence that was called for in each hunting situation. Killing humans would have been technically relatively easy, but the close dependency of humans on their food-animals included a clear and strong line between what is food for their families, and what simply can-not—must not—be food. In other words, there was a fundamental line be-tween food-persons and human persons. This line was a virtual precipice, for the idea of eating a human was a sign of extreme desperation tantamount to madness, and to give in to this urge meant transformation from a human into a Wiitiko (cannibal) monster (Preston, in press, 2002, 1980).

Failures of the hunt were normally an indication of wrong relations with the animals, or ineptitude, but normally not the fault of somebody else (un-less, in unusual cases, the animals avoided the hunter, by reason of sorcery). Or failures may be caused by the vagaries of an essentially contingent and mysterious world. What this requires of the hunter is fortitude, resoluteness, and hope, with self-control in order to respect for and engage in deep play with the animal he is hunting (Preston, 2002). There is a necessary and mor-ally quite sensible respect for the animals who give their lives so that humans can live. The anthropologist Frank G. Speck claimed that for these hunters, "eating is a holy act" (1935). This may be true in many cultures, and not only hunting cultures, but it tells us something about the context of killing.

So failure was more likely a failure of the web of mutual respect rela-tions between humans and animals, or of hunting techne. Failure is not normally blamed on an "other" person, but on one's own limits or short-comings. In the rare cases of one human killing another, it is usually a response to a person who shows what we would call violent madness—a complete loss of self-control. Being out of control made the insane person too dangerous to have near the family when the men were out hunting. Alternatively, the issue may have been sexual and the perpetrator was a man who was scheming to get rid of a flawed woman; in one case I have recorded she was crippled and unable to walk on snowshoes, in another she was a lesbian in disguise, in two others a woman has sex with a non-human animal, and in a few others a woman kills her infant because she is embarrassed by having become pregnant via the wrong man.

Whether a death by starvation is violent is moot; there may be a sorcerer behind the failure of hunting, or there may be a hunter's failure to maintain respect relations with the animals he is seeking, and so the food persons are not found. But there are many stories of people who, in their extremity, make efforts to show that they died with full self-control, rather than resorting to cannibalism.

Oral Tradition Evidence: Seventeenth Century

Cree stories of raids by the Inuit to the north of them are vivid, often emphasizing the killing of adults as a step for the kidnapping of children – trait used by Inuit against other Inuit groups. It is my impression that the Crees preferred to stay away from areas where they might have a chance encounter with Inuit. Retaliatory raids may have occurred but I have no stories to that effect. The Crees feared the violence and regarded the Inuit conjuring as stronger than their own.

Even more fearful were raids from the Nottoways (Iroquois) to the south of them, where women and children might be taken captive but men were normally killed. The Cree response to a raid, usually in winter and lauched at dawn when the women were just starting to build the fire, was for the men to rapidly put on their moccasins, for escape barefoot was sure to bring death from frozen feet. Retaliatory raids may have occurred but I have no stories to that effect.

Ethnohistoric Evidence: Seventeenth Century

Thomas Gorst is the first to keep a detailed account of the characteristics of the Indians. He speaks from his residence from 1670-1675 at the mouth of the Ruperts River (and mentions exploratory travels along the south and west coasts, including the regions around the Moose Cebee, Shechittawan and Ekwan rivers). His journal has not been found, but we have some interesting passages published in John Oldmixon's *The British Empire in America* (1708) and an undated, handwritten excerpt now located at Guildhall Library, London (Ms. 1757[19]). Portions of this excerpt are published on pages 134-139 of the text and the whole is in an appendix, in *Caesars of the Wilderness*, by Grace Lee Nute (1943). Since the Nute's purposes were to relate the history of European exploration, most of the ethnographic content was edited out in the main text. The appendix, although disappointingly brief, is complete and correct, however, as I have obtained a copy of the original Guildhall document, and checked it against Nute's appendix. I will present some of the ethnographic passages here (with explanatory notes and spelling slightly modified without any loss of informational content), since they are our earliest descriptive material (save for Henry Hudson, which is very brief).

> [August 31, 1670] We anchored there [Point Comfort, about 14 leagues short of Rupert's River]. The Capt., Mr. Foster, Mr. Gooseberry and I went ashore, killed some fowl, and stayed all night. In the morning two of the natives of the Captain's old acquaintance came to us, called Noah and his Brother.
> [September 1] Six canoes more with men, women, and children.

Note: The Captain's "old acquaintance" probably refers to a meeting of the two men as a result of the first (1668-69) Hudson's Bay Company exploratory voyage, two years earlier. It is interesting that at this point in early September, we have the probability of eight families in the vicinity of Point Comfort, about 42 miles north of the mouth of the Rupert's River. It is possible that they were expecting a ship, but it may also be that they were there for their own, ordinary harvesting purposes.

> [September 8] ...anchored before Charles Fort... An Indian called Damaris came to us and quickly went to call his companions from the woods where they were hunting.
> [September 12] ...The Indians come to us a pace and are willing to trade.
> [September 27] The Indians set up their wigwams, or huts, which is almost in the manner of a tent, covered with moose and deer skins dressed, close of all sides and a hole at the top for the smoke to vent itself at. Their Bedds are bows of pine and spruce, which are much like the English Ferne and their beaver coats serve them for sheets, blankets, and rugs. These tents they make bigger or lesser at pleasure. Sometimes I have known 16 or 18 men, women, and children pigg all together, much like the Irish, but only that there are no cows nor hogs to keep them company, although indeed those poor wretches are scarce fit for any better society.

Note again there already were several families in the vicinity of the mouth of the Rupert's River when the ship arrived. The multiple family tipi layout is a familiar arrangement to 20th century ethnographers as well as to archaeologists. English fernes probably refers to balsam fir. The pejorative references to the Irish inclusion of livestock in the household, and to the Indians' lack of fitness for better society, are not so familiar or comfortable to 20th century ethnographers.

> [September 29] Some of the Natives brought store of fresh fish as Pikes which are very large. Some I have seen 6 foot long; with attickemeck or scaly fish of the bigness of a perch. There is also fresh Sturgeon very good & Salmon trout plenty enough. They themselves feast chiefly on dried moose and Beaver, bread they have none nor anything in stead of it. The bones of those beasts they use to bruise and boil, and the fat arising thence they skim off and keep like butter, which they call cockamo and serves for sauce to all their delicate dishes—heretofore they used to boil their victuals in some of the skins of those beasts they feed on, but now they find the better convenience of our English kettles. Their dishes are made of the outmost rind of Birch which they work so close together that they will hold water as well as our wooden platters. When they eat they sit upon the ground which serves them for Tables, stools & Table cloth; Trenchers they use none & their own tawny bodies serve for napkins, which are so much more beautiful by how much they are the more greasy.

Note: Six foot fish are much more likely to be sturgeon than pike (for which the current record in North America is less than four feet). Or perhaps Gorst stretches the truth. With regard to cooking, before the English kettles were available, they probably put water into the stomach of caribou or moose, with heated rocks added from time to time to the heat the water and thus cook the food. The seams of birchbark containers may have been made watertight using a strip of fish gut and/or a glue made from the air sac of sturgeon.

> [undated] When the weather grew colder they removed their Wigwams from us some leagues into the woods for the better convenience of killing Deer and wild fowl with which they often came and supplied us, as also with some of hares in winter as white as Snow.
> The men are much about our stature and born in a manner as white as the English but with grease and paint they spoil their skins and make themselves look very deformed. The women differ not from them in habit, only that the Cape of their coats hang down behind Somewhat like a monk's hood

> whereas the men wear theirs close to their necks. Also the mens' hair hang long and for the most part downright, but the womens' are generally plaited. [November 23] The Indians brought us a young deer which they had killed in the woods and they used daily afterwards to bring us fresh venson and truck [= trade] it for our peas which they love extremely but hate beef and pork and every thing which tastes of salt.
> [March 14] He [Radisson] returned from thence [Moose Cebee] ... and that was the place where afterwards the Governor went along with him and traded with the people of that place...

Oldmixon is more ethnographically forthcoming in his (apparently verbatim) use of Gorst's journal. Here we learn something of one observer's opinions of native leadership with regard to traditional pursuits.

> The Indians about Rupert's River and other Places in the Bay, are more simple than the Canadans, who have had longer Commerce with the Europeans. They are generally peaceable, and not given to quarrel either with themselves or others, except the Nodways, a wild and barbarous People on the Borders of Hudson's Streights; who sometimes in slight Parties make Incursions on the other Indians, and, having knock'd 8 or 10 on the Head, return in Triumph.

Note that the Nodways (a term meaning strange people) are violent, but there is no mention of retaliatory violence. Canadans probably refers to any of the more southerly groups.

> The Indians of certain Districhs [sic], which are bounded by such and such Rivers, have each an Okimah, as they call him, or Captain over them, who is an Old Man, consider'd only for his Prudence and Experience. He has no Authority but what they think to give him upon certain Occasions. He is their Speech-maker to the English; as also in their own grave Debates, when they meet every Spring and Fall, to settle the Disposition of their Quarters for Hunting, Fowling, and Fishing. Every Family have their Boundaries adjusted, which they seldom quit, unless they have not Success there in their Hunting, and then they join in with some Family who have succeeded. (Oldmixon 1708, reprinted in Tyrrell 1931:381-382)

Here we have a very early statement by a respected leader (Okima), of the assignment to and extent of recognized hunting areas. The exact nature of the districts is uncertain, but certainly debatable (Bishop, 1984: 29). If Gorst had it right, and if Oldmixon has not altered it, rivers served as district boundaries. But it is not so clear as to whether the district is that area

designated to each family, and the boundary rivers would then be two tri-
butaries to a larger river, or whether the district is that area designated to
the group of families headed by an Okimah, and boundary rivers would be a
large portion of the drainage, and the groups would be regional bands com-
posed of several hunting groups. Fortunately, as far as the *principles of organization* are concerned, it probably doesn't matter, since if the family unit
was what Gorst intended, tributary rivers would boundary smaller seg-
ments of drainage, and the larger group of families would, in all likelihood,
have comprised the latter, larger drainage area, alternative.

For the James Bay region, at least, major river drainages apparently defined districts within which regional bands dispersed and aggregated according to seasonal shifts in hunting strategies and probably also for event specific gatherings for feasts after a very successful hunt by one hunting group.

It is probably only within these larger districts that people may say "I can
hunt wherever I want to." We can take this as a claim to a high level of mutual
respect—that is, as a social comment, not a willful ignoring of others' rights
(Preston 1986:14). I believe that it is saying, in effect, "I am known and respected by others as a desirable and dependable co-hunter." The statement
of apparent individual freedom of movement and hunting locale is surely
moderated by the traditional hunting ethics, as communicated in the "grave
Debates," and any specific claim might have been given a consenting re-
statement by the Okimah (see also Honigmann, 1956: 64). However, if the
"wherever I want to" statement is made with reference to another of these
large districts, it is possible that the speaker may have been rationalizing his
desire to trespass on people less closely related to him.

In times of famine, boundaries are suspended for the sake of survival, and
people would be expected to move constantly and for as great a distance as
necessary to find food, and with the expectation that no one would oppose
them in this search, and the more successful families would take in the needy.

Ethnohistoric Evidence: Eighteenth Century

The persuasive influence of the Okimah was adapted fairly quickly to
the fur trade, in organizing numbers of familes to proceed as a group to the
post, and in negotiating the terms of the trade. The respect due to these
leaders was given tangible form in gifts by the trader, which the leader
might then redistribute to the men of his group. From Glyndwr Williams
(1983: 30) we read, "At Albany in 1706 the Indian captain [presumably Oki-

mah] Whatting, who brought down twenty canoes, received one coat, six pounds of tobacco, six knives and a hatchet."

But we must already be cautious as to whether the natives being described are Crees. Bishop found reference to Ottawa Indians trading at Fort Albany as early as 1703 and Ojibwa moving into the area from the 1760s (1972) and perhaps much earlier (1984: 33-36). Albany and Moose have rich and complex native histories, most of it still not written.

Sometime between 1726 and 1737 the traders at Moose and Albany began extending credit for outfitting equipment, for the humane purpose of aiding families with supplies to survive through the winter, and in a more political sense, for the setting up a reciprocal obligation for the Indians to continue to take their future furs to the trader who had offered the goods in trust of later payment (Williams, 1983: 32).

I would like to propose that there was more at stake than we have realized in this credit relationship. The ability and willingness to provide these outfitting goods was also a political act in the sense of establishing, from the Cree point of view, a significant new leadership role. I believe that the trader was, consciously or otherwise, competing with the Okimah. Both were in a position of power in the sense of acting as a good steward, the trader allocating his technological resources, and the Okimah allocating the animal resources of hunting areas, for the success of the families in the coming winter.

Giving credit set up a reciprocal and long-term relationship of inequality. The first gesture is from the trader, and in exchange for his goods he would be given respect and prestige for his willingness to give "on trust." That this was viewed by the natives as a personal leadership relationship and not an impersonal business deal is suggested by the report of a credit default.

> When Henry Pollexfen took over at Moose in 1757 he found there debts of more than 800 Made Beaver which the Indians concerned seemed to have little intention of settling on the grounds that they were presumed to have lapsed with the departure of the factor who had granted them (Williams, 1983: 32).

If we can accept the concept that credit giving was reciprocated by recognition of this act as one of leadership, and add to that the implication in the Okimah's new role in bringing his group to this same person, a trade goods Okimah, at the post, the displacement of leadership seems to be increased. By the act of leading his families to the trader, the traditional Okimah is placing himself in an intermediary and potentially secondary prestige position. The "potentially secondary" implies a hierarchy of rank, regarded by most traders as the proper order of their social world but regarded by most Crees as contrary to their egalitarian ethic. The trader should therefore show equitable respect for this Cree ethic, giving gifts to the Okimah as tangibe symbols of reciprocation between equals for these cooperative efforts. If the trader instead acts toward the Cree Okimah as if he has secondary rank, the potential of competitive conflict becomes clearer.

Charles Bishop's account of the Henley House "massacre" in 1743 provides a likely case of the consequences of this competitive conflict. These were not James Bay Cree, but Ojibwa to the west of James Bay. Bishop describes the situation of a trader who, finding the expectations of reciprocity more than he is willing to sustain, makes a rash effort at "pulling rank" on an Okimah, and precipitates an extreme reaction.

Ethnohistoric Evidence: Nineteenth Century

There is an exception to the rule of nonkilling of humans, and yes, I believe that it proves the rule. It is crucial enough to deserve some detailed telling. By the nineteenth century the fur trade relations between the Crees and the Europeans had become a tradition of its own. In times of hardship, the Crees expected that people who had enough food would share with those who had very little or none. And the Crees might resort to the trading posts in times of great scarcity, for relief. Normally it was provided at the post, even when the provisions were running low. The Crees had been paid to bring in food in the fall and during the winter, and might expect to have some claim to enough to tide them in a desperate situation. To refuse such a request when food was in storage was harsh.

In the winter of 1832 the region around the bottom of James Bay had few food-animals, and people were enduring starvation. Then there was a sudden thaw and refreezing, making a coating of glaze ice, and making movement on the land, and therefore hunting, very difficult for everyone (including other animals). In very poor and starving condition, the hunting group headed by old Quappekay managed to reach the Hudsons Bay Company outpost at Hannah Bay. The manager, old Corrigal, was finishing his undistinguished career as a trader in an outpost. The two old men faced off and Corrigal refused to give relief to Quappekay for his group. The group then left to go back into the bush.

Since the hunting group leader is responsible for successfully guiding their food getting activities, and since he felt that one or more deaths from starvation was very likely, he made a profoundly radical decision. In his extremity he conjured for guidance and was told by the spirit-person to go back to the outpost, overpower Corrigal and seize what they needed.

We will probably never know how violent they anticipated becoming. It is possible that their initial intentions were not murderous—were determined but controlled. Perhaps, in the heat of the moment, their measured violence "got out of hand" (Cecil Chabot, p.c.). In any event, they killed Corrigal, his Cree wife, their children, and the others except for two that they could not catch.

There was a rumour that they expected that their boldness would stir up a revolt against the Hudson's Bay Company. It did not happen. Instead most were found and the men and boys summarily executed by a punitive expedition. Other men were given up by Cree relatives to whom they had fled.

The main point to this narrative is that the Hudson's Bay Company mens' violence in killing the perpetrators was not reciprocated by the Crees, although we have evidence that strong feelings existed among the relatives of the dead men. The Crees could have revolted against the Company, but instead they were offended by the killings and rejected the option.

The "Hannah Bay Massacre" was recalled by old John Blackned as an example of where the Crees went off the edge of Cree morality, and were given wrong advice by the conjurer's spirit. The ghost of Thomas Hobbes rises unexpectedly from the muskeg of the eastern Subarctic of Canada, and finds… that thousands of years of hunting and gathering in small scattered groups has given serious real world challenge to Hobbes' vision (for that is what it was) of life in a state of nature as solitary, poor, nasty, brutish, and short.

Major river drainage districts, as defined by the Crees, have by now also been identified as appropriate to the regional divisions of the fur trade, and posts or outposts are typically located at the mouths of some of these rivers.

During the 1860s, trespass (constituting disrespect) was reported in terms of these "large river" districts, for which we have documentary evidence for two specific examples from the Albany River district on the west side of James Bay. Note that there has already been a change in designation, from the Cree *Okimah* district leader to the HBCo factor as the person who is appealed to as the Okimah—translated for me as meaning "governor of the land" (Greg Spence's translation, pers. comm., Feb 1990). This does not necessarily mean a complete displacement of the traditional district leader by the HBCo factor, but it does mean at the very least, that the factor is now regarded not only as the person responsible for outfitting supplies, but also as the person responsible for resolving grievances regarding trespass by persons from other post-districts.

Issac Hardisty complains Apischa[pi?]ish & companions broke into his beaver lodges he had been preserving; they should return the skins to Hardisty. (HBCA B.3/b/94, Alexander Macdonald to James Anderson (of Moose Factory), 14 March 1864, fo. 44)

Ootappe or one of his party took a Bl[ac]k Bear, or rather stole it out of a snare set by one of our Indians, please make him give it up. (HBCA B.3/b/95, Macdonald to Anderson, 27 September 1864, fo. 11)

It would appear that these two men chose to disregard the ethical restraints on hunting anywhere they pleased; in the latter case even to the point of deciding to let another man's hunt satisfy his needs. Whether these trespassers took particular actions against particular other hunters, for specific reasons, or whether they are examples of individuals who had little regard for the ethical norms, we do not know.

When missionaries come on the scene, they give moral and ethical power to help the native people live free from sorcery and with the power of hymns that compare closely, as songs sung *to* spirit persons, to the power of hunting songs (Preston, 1985). Unlike the hunters, for whom songs are privately created, owned, and bequeathed, the missionaries generously give their songs to all who will care to learn and sing them, and in return are given respect and prestige. Here the ethical leadership of the Cree Okimah is faced with competition by a new religious Okimah. It is at about this time, Ellis believes, that the term Okimahkan, with its suffix implying "chief-like" (1960; Rogers, 1965) or diminished chief, is used for native leaders, and Okimah is given to traders, missionaries, and later, to government authorities.

It is also in the 19th century that traders more actively intervene in the old order, by trying to allocate the hunter's harvesting locations and protect them from trespass. Besides trying to get hunters to spread themselves efficiently into fur bearing ranges rather than efficiently into food providing ranges, there is greater emphasis on "Homeguard" families who stay close to the post and make their labor available as required.

Leading up to 20th Century Transformations

Chief Reg Loutit, Attawapiskat, Ontario, speaking at The James Bay Trappers Council's Third Annual Assembly, August 24, 1990, observed that his grandfather signed the treaty, but that the freedom to continue traditional economic harvesting pursuits has not been respected since the treaty.

James Wesley, an elder of Attawapiskat, spoke eloquently of the diminishment of trapping and especially of the ethical principles that guided their actions. He said that, with setting up the schools, it was like cutting the life-line of trapping as a way of life of the Cree people. "We remember how hard people tried to keep this going...—the people who starved and even died, when the government was not looking after them. I do not want to see the end of trapping. Limiting people to territories caused great hard-ship. *Before the trapline designation came into being, they did much better and respected each others' rights*" (emphasis mine).

These concerns for the continuance of freedom in traditional pursuits and the respect for each others' rights that existed long before government inter-vention, demands our understanding and support. What follows is an ethno-historic and ethnographic reconstruction of the culture-historical basis of this individual and concensual respect for rights for land use and harvesting.

During the 20th century we anthropologists developed a prolonged de-bate on the various definitions of "hunting and trapping territory" and then used one or more of these definitions as a reference point to compare con-temporary practices to their pre-contact antecedents.

Put simply, and focussing on the James Bay region in particular, there is a process of change to be traced back from the present regime of provincially regulated, individually held, boundaried trapline areas, to some distinctly dif-ferent, antecedent, indigenous "cultural system" for coordinating the actions of native harvesters. The main contrast that is to be made is between:

1. a Euro-Canadian cultural conception of the designation of uniform and specified rights to a specified material good, that is, allocation of a piece of land—essentially the rental of some real estate—for trapping and hunting purposes, and
2. an indigenous cultural system best conceived of in terms of the Cree personalized and fluidly adaptive hunting ethics that normally guided and constrained the respectful activities and locations of harvesters.

Hunting *ethics* focuses on the right conduct of relationships between people, and between people and animals. This refers to a great deal more than a material good. It includes a culturally patterned and individually un-derstood mental "map" of relationships to places, people, and animals:

1. places: where people would typically have been active in harvest-ing, through the annual cycle,
2. people: how they would have respected others in their decisions on where and what to harvest, and

3. animals: how these decisions and actions would have been accommodated to the different behavioural characteristics, including expectations of respect, of various species of animals and to their fluctuating populations.

20th Century Evidence: Ethnographic History

In the later 1920s and early 1930s, John M. Cooper obtained detailed accounts from capable informants, for land use patterns extending back in time for three or more generations. His 1932 mapping has been revised recently in the light of data that he obtained in 1933 and 1934, by Flannery and Chambers (1986) who add some very useful ethnographic details and critical discussion. In short, we find that the principles for allocating land areas is very similar to that reported two centuries before by Gorst-Oldmixon. Rivers and their tributary small rivers define the areas. The scale of the areas and the density of the population in the 1870s may or may not be quite different from the situation of the 1670s, but the principles sound very familiar indeed.

> Territories centered on a drainage system, often tributaries of the major river systems which were the primary routes of travel. The inland lands were always described by reference to natural features of the terrain, such as river banks, confluences or forks of streams, sides of lakes, rocky points, rapids, and sometimes the distance from a post. The territories of families related by marriage were often contiguous, as in the example of two sets of half-brothers having a common father. To the extent that "edges" of holdings were referred to (although the term "boundaries" was seldom used by Cree respondents), the boundaries of contiguous holdings were reckoned within several miles, by reference almost always to landscape features, and sometimes to the grounds recognized as belonging to someone else. (1986: 127-128)

With regard to trespass, Flannery and Chambers summarize the norms and indicate where there was strong agreement, and where unanimity was lacking. They also illustrate with one extreme case of a shooting of a man and his older son (but not the wife and two younger children) of a Moose family, by a more southerly Abitibi Ojibwa Indian man whose territory it was. More normal circumstances included appeals to the trader, who could refuse credit for the stolen furs (1986: 129).

What we lack in the Cooper-Flannery-Chambers data is an analysis of the effect of the traders on the allocation of harvesting land. I think it very plausible that the effects would include some individuation in the sense of smaller hunting groups on smaller family territories. Yet this remains to be demonstrated.

We have a dramatic comparison case in the coastal territories for Fort George, as a map in Flannery and Chambers (1986: Fig. 5) shows, and as Cree elder Geordie Georgekish explained. In the 1970s he told me that, years ago, the HBCo manager had divided these lands, "just like a checker board" into a string of ten miles square territories (Preston, 1981: 198).

Interventions on the south and west coasts of James Bay were apparently more subtle, probably more typically a matter of recruiting hunters away from their lands to serve as homeguard Indians, or settling disputes over trespass and perhaps over inheritance. And when some people did appear to just go anywhere, the post managers might try to restore the old order, as they understood it. Whether, in any specific instance, they misidentified the adaptive flexibility of Cree ethics, or more correctly responded to times when one or many families "gave up" on the traditional ethics, to the distress of their neighbours, has yet to be described.

The extent of family-hunting groups and the extent and locations of their hunting areas in the 1670s can only be guessed at. Recall that Gorst says he has seen 16 or 18 persons as a co-residential unit. So it is significant that Flannery found evidence for rather large hunting groups, larger than Gorst's 16 or 18 (Nute, 1943: 287), at a time of plenty. She recorded a maximum of seven commensal groups or "families" as a co-residential group during a winter when there were lots of caribou, about 1885 (1986: 125-126). Olaus J. Murie recorded in his journal (but left out of his book) a similarly large group in a large 3-fire wigwam, on the east coast (Swallow's group, north of Eastmain) in the first decade of this century (Murie, n.d.).

The size of the group may be very easily adjusted, not only during changing conditions of the seasonal cycle of aggregation and dispersal, but on the longer terms of named hunting groups as well. It may be that the ratio of human to animal populations is the most effective factor, and the extent of concensus in ethical actions during the immediately preceding seasons may be the second most effective factor in determining whether there will be large co-residential groups on large hunting areas with few concerns over exclusive access. The extent of respect for the leader would be one aspect of this second factor.

Comparative Ethnographic Evidence

To develop some comparative evidence and hypotheses regarding historical changes in the James Bay concept of hunting ethics, I am also using and supplementing from my own ethnographic data the insights contained in *Who Owns the Beaver? Northern Algonquian Land Tenure Reconsidered*

(Bishop and Marantz, 1986), especially regarding two main topics: 1) the adequacy of our concepts, and 2) the more precise uses of ethical rules.

In terms of Cree harvesting ethics, the statement, "I Can Trap Anywhere" matches the more general ethical statement, "It's up to the individual." Yet each autonomous individual is expected to be respectful of the autonomy of other individuals. This "ethic of non-interference" is, ideally and normally, the moderating principle of the free exercise of individual will. "I can go anywhere" is a social (and now, a political) proclamation of one's autonomy. But the social and ecological situation is not random; people do not really just go anywhere, any time they please. To go where one is not welcome is always possible, but is not done often or, even more rarely, without some reason. Others may not take this unwanted presence lightly. And this ethical standard was embodied and taught by the most competent, senior people, the "person who makes decisions well," at the level of each beykodeno (commensal group), and for each cluster of these groups, the headman of the hunting group, and for the summer gathering of the hunting groups of a region, the man who was the traditional Okimah.

There is another variable to add to this, which is the individual differences between individual traders and between traders and other authorities, in their responses to issues regarding land allocation and use. While some traders are on record as trying to salvage the old system of land allocation, which seems to have broken down in the early 20th century, we also have Willy Allen telling Cooper that, after the treaty, when Indians complained to the (treaty party) White authorities about other Indians' trespass, the White said they could hunt "where they pleased."

This report suggests that the Treaty was intended by the Indians to give authority over ethical land allocation and resource allocation to the government, but the authority was not soon accepted, so that territory allocation and respect nearly broke down. This near breakdown occurred before the Treaty and was a reason for asking for a Treaty. The problem was that it then nearly broke down again, after the Treaty. The Crees intended the Treaty to give the government authority to respond effectively to hardships and threats to environmental and cultural integrity, and when these hardships and threats continued after the Treaty, it appeared to the Crees that the Government was not aware of the responsibility it had taken on. Thus the statement that "the treaty almost broke down."

Briefly, I want to return to some comments at the James Bay Trapper's Council meeting last August.

> We had the will and the path in 1905 [the time of the treaty], and we have it today.
> Then [after the trapline system was drawn up and enforced] some land in some areas became overtrapped, and they were frustrated to have to stay in that one spot and not move inland. I hear these complaints all over Ontario.
> It is important to teach trapping and land skills, and the deep understanding that their ancestors' very lives depended on this. In those days there was nobody to tell us what to do, or where to go, and we did very well.
> We should take the road that John Turner has outlined today [for a cooperative corporation to be named the Omushkegowuck Harvesters Association].

Cree management of trapping and other harvesting activities is seen as a contemporary form of self-governance that may be the best possible route to return to a traditional Cree ethical system. The old way may be retrieved to the extent that there can be a return to guidelines for individual autonomy and social responsibility. These guidelines may be formulated on the old model, a model that made good sense and worked more successfully than the colonial, federal and provincial systems that replaced it.

In the wisdom of hindsight, it seems that, when the HBC trader became the fur trade okimah, and the missionary became the moral okimah, the Crees had over-accommodated to the eagerness for authority that these European agents expected and demonstrated. Cree leadership was weakened, and with the diminishment of Cree okimah roles, we have the diminishment of the exemplars, the teachers, of the Cree system of hunting ethics. Now, the strengthening of Cree leadership and ethics is wanted. And it appears in an unexpected place.

Twenty-first Century Politics of Respect

For many Crees, their life cycle has now mostly lost the basic lessons of the discipline of the bush, where much of the learning came from the animals and from others' stories. This learning context is largely replaced by learning from Cree townspeople's statements and interactional strategies, from global media, and from school. These several replacements have been radical. What kind of Cree autonomy emerges from these encounters? Not an individualistic autonomy, but an autonomy that is performed, shared and respected in local groups or personal communities within larger groups, and sometimes with non-Cree groups. In my opinion, this is not an imposition of modernity, and may prove to be part of a larger, globalizing process of Indigenous spirituality.

Political autonomy is typically the secular opposite of personal community spiritual autonomy. Secular political autonomy makes sense as a goal for the negotiation of collective distinctness when a group is encapsulated within a nation-state. Negotiation and credible identity are unlikely to be achieved without speaking the recognizable and approved language of those in political power, as the Crees discovered in the early 1970s. But since political autonomy carries the sense of legitimizing and maintaining a boundaried separateness, there is a radical attitudinal problem if this political and externally directed sense of autonomy is allowed to leak over into the internal formation and nurturing of community. We saw this in the exclusionary competition between the denominations represented by missionaries. It was their ambition not only to win converts, but to define and maintain boundaries that would exclude people of other denominations.

The type of autonomy that is congenial to personal communities is based on inclusion rather than exclusion. In families, or in marriages, or in larger personal communities, autonomy of the type that evidences a shared ethos based on sustained responsible, respectful decisions and actions is successful, where exclusionary and power seeking autonomy is destructive. As we will see below, there is a strong component of personal autonomy brought into the political arena by the Cree leaders.

Politically, the future of the Eastern Cree is much less tenuous than is the case for the future of hunting spirituality. But perhaps there is an unexpected element of carry-over from hunting to politics. I find an underlying element of spirituality in some statements made by political leaders. The nature and scope of the vision portrayed is often essentially spiritual, and we might usefully look for the roots of this vision in traditional hunting spirituality. In the statement that follows, the theme of hope is given central, spiritual prominence.

People talk about surviving, even thriving, because they didn't give up, because they had hope—not because everything turned out the way they wanted. Hope is ... interpret[ed] ... very personally, not as some depersonalized reference to goals or expectations. Hope is *not* about naïve or excessive optimism. It is *not* solely about achievement. It *is* about not losing sight of the goodness of life even when it is not visible (Jevne, 2004: 2:6-1).

I find that the political stance of Cree leaders has sometimes very effectively emphasized the morality of personal autonomy, placing hope at the front and trying to expand public awareness, in preference to protesting the politics of minority group identity in opposition to hegemonic national identities. The goal is to maintain respect relations, even when they are not reciprocated. In a fashion reminiscent of Gandhi, the hope is that respect will eventually be reciprocated. Some professionals in the area of Indigenous politics say that the Crees are the leading edge of developments of this sort. It appears to me that the respect and hope aspects of hunting spirituality have been transformed into political ideology. In negotiation of the 2002 *Paix des breves* this has succeeded to the point of the Quebec Crees being formally recognized as a nation, and where the economic benefits of a very large hydroelectric development includes, for the Quebec Crees, a percentage of the profits, over the years. From the outside, it looked like a very unequal contest, but the neoliberal ideology of the developing corporations and the Quebec government posed no insurmountable obstacle to negotiation with the Cree leadership.

References

Bishop, Charles A. (1972). "Demography, Ecology and Trade among the Northern Ojibwa and Swampy Cree," *Western Canadian Journal of Anthropology*, 3(1):58-71.

Bishop, Charles A. (1984). "The First Century: Adaptive Changes among the Western James Bay Cree between the Seventeenth and Early Eighteenth Centuries," in Krech, Shepard, Ed., *The Subarctic Fur Trade: Native Social and Economic Adaptions*. Vancouver: University of British Columbia Press, pp. 21-54.

Bishop, Charles A.; Morantz, Toby, Eds. (1986). "Who Owns the Beaver? A Reexamination of Northern Algonquian Land Tenure Systems Then and Now," *Anthropologica*, 18(1-2): 11-18.

Cooper, John M. (1938). *Snares, Deadfalls, and Other Traps of the Northern Algonquians and Northern Athapaskans*. Washington: Catholic University of America.

Cooper, John M. (1939). "Is the Algonquian Family Hunting Ground System Pre-Columbian?" *American Anthropologist*, 41(1):66-90.

Ellis, C. Douglas (1960). "A Note on Okima.hka.n," *Anthropological Linguistics*, 2(3):1.

Flannery, Regina; Chambers, Mary Elizabeth (1985). "Each Man Has His Own 'Friends': the Role of Dream Visitors in Traditional East Cree Belief and Practice," *Arctic Anthropology*, 22:1-22.

Flannery, Regina; Chambers, Mary Elizabeth (1986). "John. M. Cooper's Investigation of James Bay Hunting Grounds, 1927-1934," *Anthropologica*, 218(2):108-44.

Gorst, Thomas (1943 [1670]). Extract from his Journal. Appendix 2 in Nute, Grace Lee, *Caesars of the Wilderness*. New York: Appleton

Gorst, Thomas (1931 [1670-1675]). In Oldmixon, John, *The British Empire in America*, 1708, 1741; In Tyrrell, J. B., Ed., *Documents Relating to the Early History of Hudson Bay*. Toronto: The Champlain Society.

Hallowell, A. Irving. (1967 [1955]). *Culture and Experience*. New York: Schocken Books [Philadelphia: University of Pennsylvania Press].

Honigmann, John J. (1949). Foodways in a Muskeg Community. Ottawa: Northern Co-ordination and Research Centre.

Honigmann, John J. (1956) "The Attawapiskat Swampy Cree: an ethnographic reconstruction," *Anthropological Papers, University of Alaska*, 5(1): 23-82.

Jevne, Rona (2004). Cited in GCCQ (Grand Council of the Crees (of Quebec), et al., "Towards a U. N. Declaration on the Rights of Indigenous Peoples: Injustices and Contradictions in the Positions of the United Kingdom," September 10.

Long, John S.; Preston, Richard J.; Oberholzer, Cath (2006). "Manitu Concepts of the Eastern James Bay Cree," in Papers of the 37thAlgonquian Conference.

Morantz, Toby (1978). "The Probability of Family Hunting Territories in Eighteenth Century James Bay: Old Evidence Newly Presented," in Cowan William, Ed., *Papers of the Ninth Algonquian Conference*. Ottawa: Carleton University.

Murie, Olaus J. (n.d.). Fieldnotes in the National Archives of Canada. Ottawa.

Preston, Richard J. (1980). "The Witigo: Algonquian Knowledge and Whiteman Knowledge," in Halpin, M.; Ames M., Eds., *Manlike Monsters on Trial: Early Records and Modern Evidence.* Vancouver: University of British Columbia Press, pp. 111-131.

Preston, Richard J. (1981). "East Main Cree," in Helm, J., Ed., *The Subarctic,* Vol. 6, *Handbook of North American Indians.* Washington: Smithsonian Institution, pp. 196-207.

Preston, Richard J. (1985). "Recent Developments in Eastern Cree Leadership," *McMaster University, TASO Report,* 20.

Preston, Richard J. (1986). "Twentieth Century Transformations of the West Coast Cree," Cowan, W., Ed., *Actes du 17eme Congres des Algonquinistes.* Ottawa: Carleton University, pp. 239-251.

Preston, Richard J. (1997). "Getting to know the great community of persons," in Pentland, D., Ed., *Papers of the 28th Conference on Algonquian Studies.* Winnipeg: University of Manitoba.

Preston, Richard J. (2002). *Cree Narrative: Expressing the Personal Meanings of Events.* Second edition. Montreal: McGill-Queen's University Press.

Preston, Richard J. (2010). "A life in translation," in Swann, Brian, Ed., *Born in the Blood: Translation of Native American literature/oral tradition.* Lincoln: University of Nebraska Press.

Rogers, Edward S. (1965). "Leadership among the Indians of Eastern Subarctic Canada," *Anthropologica*, 7(2):263-284.

Speck, Frank G. (1935). *Naskapi: the Savage Hunters of the Labrador Peninsula.* Norman: University of Oklahoma Press.

Williams, Glyndwr (1975). *Hudson's Bay Miscellany, 1670-1870.* Winnipeg: Hudson's Bay Record Societ.

Chapter Nine

Ending Violence, Changing Lives
Identity, Domestic Violence and Culture Change in Southern Belize

Laura J. McClusky
Wells College

Introduction

The Maya I know in southern Belize do not live in a peaceable society. For 10 months in 1995 I lived and conducted research on wife abuse in one of the larger Mayan villages in the Toledo District of southern Belize. I collected stories about and witnessed the results of domestic violence, specifically husbands beating wives. I watched as interactions between family members, as well as other community members, worked to legitimize or delegitimize specific acts of violence. My purpose then was to examine a behavior that social scientists treated as a monolithic phenomenon. That is, few social scientists examined domestic violence as a complex variable in itself, but instead treated it as one of many symptoms of patriarchy. It was my goal to suggest that "men hitting women" is not the same everywhere. It's not even the same in a single place (McClusky, 1999, 2001).

Since my original research, I have returned several times to visit friends and to keep in touch with a community of people facing great change while practicing a persistent way of life. Over the past 12 years, I have watched that community, and many of my friends, change. This chapter explores one cause of that change, the purposeful movement to diminish domestic violence. This chapter is therefore not about a peaceable community, nor does it contribute to the discussion of whether violence is inherent or learned, as many of the chapters in this book do. Instead, it contributes to a discussion about the intended and unintended changes that take place when a community takes steps to diminish one aspect of normalized violence. It further contributes to a discussion about what violence means among one specific peasant group, and how that group uses violence to build community.

Violence and Maya Stereotypes

Global stereotypes of Maya tend to depict Maya as downtrodden peasants who have suffered for generations under colonial and neo-colonial conditions in Mexico and Guatemala. This stereotype suggests Maya have finally had enough. So they joined others who had already taken up arms and contributed to the revolution. Ya Basta! Postcards and posters of Maya women or men holding a gun, hiding their face and looking down to avoid the eye of the camera symbolize a people shy and quiet, but finally fighting for their rights. Provoked, anyone might take up arms. Rigoberta Menchu contributed to this stereotype with her depiction of Maya as participants in a civil war in Guatemala (Burgos-DeBray, 1984). David Stoll (1993, 2007) called her on it, pointing out that Menchu's story was not the only story of "all poor Guatemalans," and that most Maya did not side with the guerillas. Instead, he suggested another scenario where Maya were stuck in the middle between the genocidal army and the trouble-making guerillas (1993).

Neither of these stereotypes, the provoked peasants reluctant to fight, but willing to fight for their rights, nor the peaceable people living between two warring parties, allow for Maya to be *originators* of violence. At best, Ladinos or other outsiders politicized them and then offered violence as a solution to end Maya oppression. Their reluctant violence, the first stereotype suggests, will save them.

Thinking of Maya in these stereotypical ways is long standing. J. Eric Thompson's (1930, 1990) early works on Maya archaeology suggested Maya were a peaceful people, focused on astronomy, mathematics, a complex calendar and hieroglyphics. It took Linda Schele (1972) to point out, in the 1970s, that Maya were warlike and participated in blood ritual.

These global long standing stereotypes differ somewhat from the stereotypes that tend to be in place locally, although local stereotypes certainly influenced Thompson's depiction of Maya. Whether in Mexico, Belize or Guatemala, non-Maya tend to see Maya as simple, submissive peasants, easily swindled and pathetically naïve. Seeing Maya as violent is far from a Belizean's mind when s/he sees a short slight Maya man occupying a seat on a packed bus and convinces him that that seat is hers/his, s/he has a ticket to prove it, and that he must vacate the seat so s/he can sit down. The Belizean knows that the Mayan man will typically slink out of the seat and never even ask to see the ticket. Maya are not known for standing up for themselves, and certainly not for their violence. Bellicosity is not the first character trait that comes to mind when describing most Maya.

But Maya do live in a violent world. This is true even for Maya who live in Belize, far away from the dramatic state violence of war-torn Mexico or Guatemala. Belizean Maya, except for refugees and transplants from Mexico or Guatemala, have never suffered state violence on that physical level, although they have, and still do suffer the "structural violence" of racism, poverty and legal land theft. Indeed, most Belizean Maya see physical violence as an acceptable, albeit unfortunate, means to enforce social roles and to resolve conflict. In a sense, most see violence as a way to build community, although it is not usually their preferred way to do so.

Maya Violence in Southern Belize

Examining and contextualizing the forms of sanctioned violence among Maya in southern Belize is a prerequisite to understanding how violence might be thought of as a way to create community, and to understand the changes that are taking place due to women's efforts to curb domestic violence. Understanding why violence occurs in a specific cultural context helps to make sense of *how* efforts to curb violence might work, *why* certain efforts *do* work, and to what degree they work. As I've argued elsewhere regarding domestic violence, (McClusky, 1999, 2001) violence is not the same everywhere.

Few Maya seem to enjoy violence. They do not seek out violence against fellow human beings, nor do they discuss it with relish. Maya do not gather after committing or seeing violence against fellow human beings and retell the tale with excited animation in efforts to justify the act, nor do they produce violent media for entertainment as we do in the U.S. Happy violence (Gerbner, 1994), in which people gleefully celebrate representations or tales of violence against wrong doers, is not a part of Maya ways of being, even though some of the violence I discuss below is indeed against wrong doers and is meant to correct behavior. Instead, such violence is seen as necessary, but regrettable.

For this reason, those who must commit such violence sometimes drink alcohol before they do so (Eber, 1995; McClusky, 2001). Alcohol, among Maya, tends to relieve inhibitions and make drinkers feel braver than they might be while sober. It also allows the drinker to obsess about the damage the victim has done to him, making the violence seem more justified, appropriate and sometimes necessary.

I should point out that while Maya do engage in violence, few actually kill. There were no murders in the village during my stay, nor, to my knowledge were there any murders committed in any Mayan village in southern Belize. Most murders in Belize are in Belize City, where an illicit drug trade exists. Maya violence is primarily a kind of punishment not meant to end someone's life, but to "correct" a person's actions and attitude.

Below I outline the types of violence which Maya in southern Belize experience and see, and in which way they may participate. The next section will present a Mayan theory of violence. Such a theory might help to explain why violence is a part of Mayan lives.

Pig Killing and Cargo

While there were no murders in the village during my stay, there was a lot of pig killing. I can attest to the calm acceptance of this bloody violence, and to its value. Pig killing is the only form of violence that takes place in a jovial, albeit pensive, atmosphere, as nervous looks, lip biting and tense muscles give way to laughter, jokes and a little bit of horseplay. Pig killing is dangerous; an angry frightened pig can cause considerable damage to a human. The jovial atmosphere, I think, alleviates fear rather than to celebrate the violence. Killing a pig also signals a celebration, a time of joy since pig meat is usually the main food of a large feast. Being jovial is part of that celebration. However, killing and preparing a pig for consumption is serious and is important in creating and re-establishing social roles, responsibilities and commitments. It plays a large part in the most visible remnant of the cargo system in Belize, feasting.

The cargo system, common among peasant populations throughout Latin America, is an economic leveling mechanism that transforms resources into social status via service to the saints and to the community (Cancian, 1965). For the most part, this civic-religious system has faded away in Belize. James Gregory suggests the collapse of the cargo system among Maya in Belize is due to what he calls "the Young Men's Revolt" of the 1970s (Gregory, 1987, 1984). Before this "revolt," men, and their nuclear families, would host community-wide feasts to honor saints. These feasts would require spending the bulk of their economic resources and required borrowing cash and labor from relatives and other community members that would later be repaid. The hosts, both the male and female heads of the household, gained status within the community by organizing these large parties. The feast could not happen without debt. Status was based on a system of indebtedness and repayment of debt (Cancian, 1965).

The "revolt" was a shift in the way men gained status and political power in the village. In the 1970s, young men could obtain relatively large sums of cash by raising or transporting pigs to the district capitol where they might be bought by someone living far from Toledo. Accumulating cash and becoming familiar with non-Maya ways constituted a new source of status and to some extent displaced the traditional civic power of the *pasados* (older men who gained status via cargo).

Today, there is still a tension between monied and non-monied Maya. The values of the old cargo system emphasizing social and spiritual connectedness over the accumulation of resources have not completely evaporated. Attitudes toward accumulating cash still remain ambivalent. Maya still, for the most part, value serving the community and maintaining ties with family and other community members through the indebtedness of labor. Celebrations that are part of the rites of passage of baptism, marriage and now high school and grammar school graduations, rather than feasts for saints, still express, embody and re-enforce such service and such ties. For this reason, male and female heads of households maintain the tradition of calling upon certain, and sometimes specific, extended family members and friends to perform key roles in the killing, butchering, cooking and serving pigs, as well as grinding corn and preparing the tortillas or *pox* (meatless tamales) that will accompany that meat.

These celebrations also embody, re-enforce and visually illustrate traditional gender roles as men and women perform traditional gender specific duties. Eber (1995) and Rosebaum (1993) have both argued that such feasts, as part of the cargo system, symbolize and reify the Mayan concept that male and female marriage partners are equally important, and that Maya marriage ideals emphasize a couple's working partnership as the foundation of Maya society. Maya marriages are economic dyads. Males cannot survive without women's work and women cannot survive without male labor. Both are important for survival.

Indeed, the ability to successfully organize a celebration, the killing and preparing of a large animal, usually a pig, but sometimes a cow, and producing enough tortillas or *pox* to feed a party, can indicate that both the male and the female heads of the household have reached a certain place in a status hierarchy. They have embedded themselves into the community, served the community, and have indebted enough people to themselves to successfully host a large party.

Killing a pig is essential for a large celebration, and a large celebration is essential to express service to the community and the accumulation of resources, both in cash and the repayment of debt (both cash debt and labor debt) via labor. Celebrating with a smaller feast by killing a chicken or two might indicate that the family has little social and economic capital to hold a larger feast. This might be a family comprised of a young couple or a family that does not have enough *tsik*, or respect, from their extended family or the rest of the community. They have few connections throughout the community and are not making any by hosting a small party.

Revenge - Choppings and Arson

Revenge involves violence against humans. Men may form a posse to burn the house or business of someone who has consistently acted against the community. For example, the posse might burn down the house of someone who repeatedly swindles others in business deals or fails to control their roaming pigs, allowing them to root in others' fields and destroy crops. I have never heard of any sanctions against men who burnt other people's property. Maya seem to accept such violence. When I was last in the village there was a burned out bus along the road that winds its way through the village. While doing my fieldwork in the 1990s, I heard several whispered tales of house burnings, usually told to warn me not to trust the person whose house was burnt.

Individually, an angry community member might alternatively seek revenge with a machete, "chopping" the offender. Sometimes the blows are fatal, but usually are not. I witnessed a near beheading of a man as he knelt before an acquaintance of mine on the front veranda of a local shop. My acquaintance, Benificio, held the man's head down with one hand as he raised his machete high. Watching from a distance, a group of my women friends and I gasped and held our hands to our mouths or turned our heads away, anticipating the fatal chop. But Beneficio stopped short and did not land the machete on the man's neck. Hours later I entered that shop to ask the shopkeeper what had happened. There I found Beneficio drinking rum and crying, "I nearly killed my brother. One Ma, one Pa." He looked up at me, eyes red, speech slurred, and said, "Miss Laura, I nearly killed my brother." The shopkeeper told me in that Beneficio's brother slept with Beneficio's wife while Beneficio was away in Belize City. Although the shopkeeper said he was glad Beneficio did not follow through with the chopping, he expressed no condemnation of the act. Indeed, I never learned of any sanctions against Beneficio either formal or informal. At my most recent visit to the village, the community still respected Beneficio.

Another friend of mine, Orlando, a government worker, was chopped. One night, his mother found him on the steps of their house bleeding and close to death with gaping wounds in his face and shoulder, the victim of another jealous husband. Orlando bears deep scars to remind him of his infidelity. His wife, also a dear friend, and his mother separately told me that Orlando has been a devoted father and husband since then. When I asked if he has pressed, or will ever press charges, against the man who chopped him, Orlando told me that he wouldn't. He sees his wounds as more of a shame than a cause for retribution. Again, I know of no sanctions either formal or informal against the attacker.

Neither burnings nor choppings are common, but they do happen. When they happen the general attitude among people to whom I've spoken to is that the victims got what they deserve and that the threat of more violence reminds the victim that he needs to act in ways consonant with community values.

Violence Against Wives

Domestic violence is common in the Belizean village where I did my fieldwork. In fact, women in the village often suggested that to be Mayan and a woman is to be beaten (McClusky, 1999, 2001). It is also common in other Maya communities both in recent years and in the past (Hahn, 2006; Danziger, 1991; Eber, 1995; Rosenbaum, 1993; Wisdom, 1940). As with choppings and arson, Maya see domestic violence as a corrective that encourages adherence to social roles they feel are necessary for the survival of the family and the community as a whole. Young wives and children are especially subject to such corrections and encouragements and therefore suffer the majority of violent attacks between family members. This is not to say other family members never suffer abuse. Parents, husbands, and grandparents do sometimes suffer the blows of kin. However, few people accept such violence as legitimate. Violence against wives, by contrast, is sometimes legitimate.

For young wives two main infractions for which family and community members might legitimize beatings are: infidelity and laziness. Legitimizing beatings for these infractions takes a lot more than just believing what the abuser has to say about his wife's actions. Both family members and gossiping community members will determine whether the beating was deserved or not, by weighing whether the husband was drunk or not, the wife's age and relative position within the community (young wives have less ability to garner support), the severity of the beating, and whether the husband's mother nags her son to see his wife's laziness. Gossiping community members' informal individual decisions affect their willingness to engage either the husband or the wife in services, such as helping cook at a baptism party, planting corn, or honoring them by asking them to serve as *comadre* or *compadre*. As noted, these activities form the system of indebtedness and repayment that remains of the cargo system, and are the means by which someone obtains *tsik*, respect.

The family members' decision normally emerges from a series of meetings between the husband and wife's parents and the fictive kin (*comadre* or *compadre*) that their parents chose just before the marriage. These fictive kin are people the parents respect and have asked to serve as moral models of a good marriage. *Comadres* and *compadres* for marriages may offer advice but most often just serve by example. (Those chosen for baptism act as godparents, supporting the children if they need economic or spiritual help while growing up.) At the meetings they will determine whether or not the beating is legitimate or not and which partner, the abuser or the abused, was acting without *tsik*, respect. Each person at the meeting will remind the one whom they have determined to be acting improperly that the core of Maya society is the married couple and that working together is important for success. Life will be hard on both if the marriage ends and both are left without a spouse. There will be no way to find success and survival will be difficult. If illegitimate beatings persist, the family may determine that the wife should return to her parents temporarily until the husband learns respect for his wife.

Women from poor families, however, have little chance of returning home to their parents, especially if they have already had children. Marrying off their daughters and sisters means poor families have fewer mouths to feed. When divorced or separated women with children return to their families of origin, the family has more mouths to feed. Leaving an abusive husband therefore might mean setting up a home without a male to do the men's work of planting and harvesting corn. It's a sure path to life-long poverty (McClusky, 2001).

Older wives do not have the benefit of a family decision. They must garner their own support. Having provided service at celebrations or acting as a *comadre* will help her prove that she has *tsik* and that the beatings are unjustified. She is clearly not lazy or undermining family solidarity.

In general, Maya determine the legitimacy of violence against wives and children according to the degree that the targets shirk hard work or undermine family solidarity. Both infractions hinder the family's ability to gain *tsik* or status within the community. Legitimate violence against kin is therefore related to the family's ability to work together as an economic unit, support themselves and use surplus resources and energy (labor) to serve the community. Actual laziness or infidelity is not at issue. What is at issue is whether community members or family think you are lazy or undermining family solidarity (McClusky, 1999, 2001).

Spiritual Violence

Besides physical beatings, choppings and house burnings there is another form of violence that people might suffer among Maya: soul loss, or *susto*. Young children most commonly suffer this *susto* when they fall down. However, their souls might loosen and float away because of someone's disruptive startling actions. Outsiders might not consider this violence since there is no intended harm, but Maya see disruptive behavior as violent in the sense that a thunder squall is violent. It doesn't intend harm, but it might do so anyway.

Adults often monitor children's play to prevent actions that are jarring or unexpected. For example, my child friends gladly and excited accepted my gifts of large brightly colored inflatable punching balls. Within moments, however, parents commandeered these gifts and convinced the children that they would make better decorations than toys. Parents were afraid that playing with these toys as intended would be too disruptive and jarring.

Adults, including anthropologists, can also suffer such soul loss. Both Missy Garber (1999) and Hilary Kahn (2006) suffered soul loss during their fieldwork; Kahn after being bitten by a dog, Garber after a drunken man accosted her. Maya healers diagnosed and treated both anthropologists for this illness with prayer, bathing them in copal smoke and by burning some of the hair of the person or animal that frightened them.

Soul loss is serious. Children can die, adults can become extremely ill. This violence, however, is unintentional and never legitimate. It is one of the major illnesses that traditional healers cure on a regular basis (Garber, 1999). The other illness traditional healers treat regularly is another kind of soul loss. This soul loss is the result of the spirit of a recently deceased person cajoling the soul out of a child so it can keep that spirit company (McClusky, 2001).

A Mayan Theory of Violence

Neither my Maya friends nor Mayanist anthropologists have articulated the following theory of Mayan violence. I've pieced it together from discussions, readings and from events I witnessed or was told about. In this sense, it is a working theory of Maya violence that needs to be tested. The theory ties together concepts of *tsik* (respect) and ownership, and is informed by discussions of soul loss. Once we have a theory of Mayan violence, we can better understand why some efforts to end a specific form of violence, the beating of wives, might work, while others do not.

Tsik

I have glossed the word *tsik* in several different ways so far. It is a difficult term to explain. Most anthropologists gloss it as respect, but it is much more complicated than the English term "respect" (Danziger, 1991). *Tsik* refers to a spiritual and social connection between people, both between individuals and between all members of the community. It is not a characteristic as much as it is a fluid state that must be re-enforced and re-gained (Danziger, 1991; McClusky, 1999, 2001). It makes people human beings rather than animals, and in Belize, it makes Mopan Mopan rather than members of any other group. Mam have a similar concept in *naab'l* (Watanabe, 1992).

Cargo was an important means by which people visibly gained *tsik*. The collapse of the cargo system that Gregory (1987) describes does not mean that people no longer serve the community to gain status. They still do. However, that status system has changed somewhat with *compadrazgo*, serving as *comadre* or *compadre* (godparents) (Foster, 1953), as the major means to gain *tsik*. Today both *compadrazgo* and feasting provide set roles, e.g., *comadre*, *compadre*, cook, pig-killer, that people ask each other to play. The less salient roles in making a feast, such as pig-killing and cooking, also provide *tsik*, they are just less formal. Accepting the offer to play this role both creates and expresses a connection of indebtedness through service. This kind of service creates and expresses *tsik* both through the act of being asked and through fulfilling that role as best as you can.

Once you have the role of *comadre* or *compadre* the people you served will make *tsik* greetings (a set, deferential, formal greeting) each time they see you (Danziger, 1991). This greeting creates and expresses *tsik*, the connectedness between the greeter and the greeted. People make such greetings to most elders, since most have served the community in some way. The webs of connectedness stretch far and wide within a small community and foster mutual aid among certain members of that community.

I include the roles people ask family members and others to play when organizing a big party in this discussion of *tsik*. I do this even though *tsik* greetings are not for family members, unless they are very old. Nor are they for close friends, even though the friend may serve in the role of your *comadre* or *compadre*. There are few instances in which people verbally express the *tsik* of those that close. It is simply understood. Similarly, husbands and wives do not express *tsik* each time they see each other. It is expressed and maintained instead through silent devotion to one another, dutifully serving in the roles of husband and wife. Some things just don't need to be said, but sometimes you can "own" another's work. "Owning" and relying on the fruits of an established relationship may not be mutually exclusive for Maya. There is a fine line between relying on someone and taking them for granted.

Ownership

In Livingston Guatemala, the Q'eqchi Maya word *loq'inkin* is similar to *tsik* (Kahn, 2006: 63). This word refers to that interconnectedness and mutual aid that Kahn thinks of as interpersonal respect, the kind that comes from intimate relationships forged in a "living community," by acting with respect. It is related to the verb "to buy," and from the term that refers to "highly regarded." Kahn sees this as suggesting that Q'eqchi can buy prestige through the types of actions that I have described as giving Mopan *tsik* (McClusky, 2001).

Q'eqchi Maya, however, have another term that Kahn glosses as "respect," *kehok sa snaq xpaab'ankilal* (Kahn, 2006: 63). While both types of respect are similar in that they both, like *tsik*, require action to be created and maintained. The second term refers to the kind of respect that people reserve for outsiders, *finceros* (plantation owners), and deities. It can be glossed as "obey" or to "serve in one's religion" (Kahn, 2006: 63).

Kahn (2006) has an eloquent discussion regarding ownership and foreignness among Q'eqchi Maya in Livingston that weaves Maya concepts of time with historical events. Since ancient time, Maya have made a connection between invisible deities and civic leaders. Historical events, such as the arrival of missionaries, the rise of the coffee trade, and colonialism put these foreigners in positions of power. Deities and civic leaders are in similar positions of power. Q'eqchi also think of them as outsiders. These powerful outsiders, because of the Maya sense of time being both cyclical and cumulative (Tedlock, 1992; Kahn, 2006), have all become part of a single category of people who must be obeyed, served and respected (Kahn, 2006). These powerful foreigners, in this way, came to "own" Maya. This ownership relationship was, and still is, oppressive. However, oppression is not the only characteristic of this relationship.

Owners, whether they are deities or *finceros*, provide food, shelter and assistance to those who are needy. Kahn (2006) says Maya reminisce about how German *finca* owners for example, were kind and caring of their workers, despite the fact they paid them little and worked them hard.

I raise this because Kahn says Q'eqchi men "own" their wives and children (Kahn, 2006). I've never heard Mopan say this, nor have I heard a similar term referring to the respect people must pay those who own them. However, Mopan actions around domestic violence seem in line with this way of thinking. The paternalism of Maya marriages that anthropologists discuss as "responsible patriarchy" (Eber, 1995; Maynard, 1963) is also similar to this concept of "ownership." In this form of ownership, the owner should not abuse those people and things that he owns, and can rely on, but should care for and respect them, as they would someone less obligated to them, but bound to them through *tsik* ties.

Ownership in marriage, I would argue, resembles ownership characteristic of *finceros* and other foreigners. Like *tsik*, it involves connectedness that obligates two parties. The link, however, does not reflect a long moral history of mutual aid, but a contract that begins such agreed upon aid. The long speeches

that are part of the engagement ritual create the agreement between two distant unrelated parties entering into a high level of interdependence (Danziger,
1991), just as the distance between worker and *fincero* is bridged by the agreement to work for someone else's benefit by the agreement to act as patron.

Soul Loss and Capriciousness

Parents encourage and express fear of soul loss through frequent warnings to children to mind their step, take their time in walking, and avoid
drunks (Garber, 1999). Despite these warning children undergo cures for
soul loss quite often. Garber (1999) suggests such warnings and healings so-
cialize Maya to avoid capriciousness in themselves and others. In this way,
children grow to be thoughtful and deliberate when following prescribed
social roles. Indeed, for Maya, life should go along as planned and as expected. Jarring disruptions like infidelity should be avoided. Garber also attributes a Maya tendency to be suspicious of new things and new ways of
solving old problems to this avoidance of the unexpected.

People who act capriciously, against *tsik* or their "owners," make themselves vulnerable to violence, either spiritual or physical. People rely on
spouses, children and business partners to be straightforward and predictable, in other words they rely on them to act according to their appropriate
social roles. Being able to rely on predictable behavior allows family and
community members to engage in the kind of cooperation and respect that
is traditionally necessary for prosperity, *tsik* and indeed survival.

Owning Dependable Mutual Aid

Many of the chapters in this book discuss nonkilling among what Dentan
(this volume) refers to as anarchs, small non-hierarchical primary groups
engaged in mutual aid for the purpose, whether intended or not, of raising
children to be adults. Anarchs engage in mutual aid and nonkilling of humans
because of the intimate daily interactions they have with a small group of
people in a small local region (Dentan, this volume).

Peasant groups are not anarchs. They are hierarchical and have more interactions with people who are not in their primary groups than do anarchs.
Yet, for Maya, mutual aid is a characteristic of their daily interactions and is
at the foundation of the hierarchy that was once established through the
cargo system (Cancian, 1965). Formalizing *tsik* relationships helps to continually demonstrate, renew and perform relationships based on mutual aid,
and accumulating people you can rely on provides status. This formalizing
and accumulating makes intentional what anarchs do without thought.

But not everyone in the village is part of your artificially created primary groups, yet you might need these people. Further, not everyone you have made these relationships with always acts in ways appropriate to this relationship. Mutual aid works best if you can predict the ways others might act. Childhood experiences with soul loss, and the rituals of healing in response to that spiritual violence help to instill value to being predictable, stable and reliable both to those you are close to and those you are not.

For Maya then, violence is acceptable when it is a means to keep people in line with their moral obligation to act predictably and appropriately, and in a way that promotes mutual aid. In this way, we can see that all of the forms of violence in the above section are the result of creating community (pig killing and cargo), punishing infractions of those you "own" that work against survival (wife beatings for laziness and infidelity), and punishing infractions that work against creating predictable social roles (chopping, house burnings). It's a lot like Cree in this volume, or Dentan's "patriarchal democrats" also in this volume.

Ending Violence Against Women

As I mentioned above, few acts of violence in the Maya world, outside of the wars against Maya in Guatemala and the Zapatista uprising, result in killing. Maya eschew violence, but sometimes use it as a means to "set things right." That is, they use it to ensure predictable relationships of mutual aid. Domestic violence among Maya can be legitimate or illegitimate (McClusky, 1999; 2001). Family and fictive kin can frame acts of violence as legitimate if they can see the wife acting against traditional patterns of mutual aid. That is, if a husband cannot rely on her work to benefit their family, he may have a legitimate justification to beat her. No other reason for violence is legitimate.

However, while in Belize during the mid-1990s I watched as several middle-aged married women with daughters reaching maturity began to orchestrate a subtle campaign against spousal abuse of any kind. Too often had the conditions of violence been too blurry to determine legitimacy. Further, too often had husbands abandoned their need to be seen as having *tsik* to care about anyone's judgment. These women, some of whom had suffered abuse as young wives, wanted to protect their daughters from similar experiences, and so they developed several tactics and enlisted various means of support.

The first tactic was to be more vocal and to adhere more closely to a traditional way of making your abusive spouse change his ways: stop working for him. In the past when a man was mistreating his wife, she would refuse to cook for him. This withdrawal from the duties that traditional marriage agreements required, the agreement to work for each other along traditional gender roles, made it clear that abuse undermines survival. Few Maya men know how to prepare food. This is especially true of corn, which Maya feel is required to make a meal more than a snack. Making corn is a long and fairly complicated process requiring knowledge about tending fires, liming corn, grinding it to the right consistency, patting it into tortillas and patting the tortillas on the hot grill until they rise and fall just right. Women not cooking for their husbands have ample opportunity to tell others about their abuse: at the grinding cooperative, at the craft group meetings, at the river while washing clothes, at the literacy classes, and while visiting family. Women made a point of telling people that they were being abused and that they were taking action against it.

This tactic made illegitimate abuse visible. It was limited to women who clearly had support from others to frame the abuse as illegitimate. Otherwise, not working for your husband could be interpreted as laziness and it could be cause, in itself, for justifying the abuse.

Another tactic was to refuse permission for daughters to marry young and to reject arranged marriages. Sometimes women strengthened this tactic by gossiping with daughters about how miserable life was for currently abused women, or repeating stories from the past of wife abuse that made marriage undesirable for young women. These stories frequently stress the fact that marriage is hard to end in the village, and that divorced women have little to no means to support their children.

In the mid-1990s, traditional arranged marriages of children in their early teens were rare. Delaying marriage was a successful tactic to a point. Women might be older upon marriage, but they still had few economic opportunities outside marriage that allowed them to reach adulthood. Maya do not consider women adult until they have borne children and help support themselves and their families. Most women would marry. Those who did not were usually sexually active and therefore undesirable, even to those with whom they were sexually active. Pre-marital sex indicates to Maya a strong likelihood that the woman will seek adulterous relations after marriage and therefore be an unreliable partner.

These tactics of gossip and delaying marriage would have had little impact if not for a few government initiatives. A few years before my field stay, Belizean government workers from the Department of Women and Development began an effort to "raise women up." While this government office provided services and assistance for all Belizeans, they saw Maya as especially needing help.

Small development projects meant to help women become less economically dependent sprung up everywhere in the Toledo District. Indeed, most crafts for sale today in Belize stem from this effort. These projects did help women make some money, but not much. They certainly don't provide enough money for a young woman to subsist on if she had to buy the corn necessary to survive, or to buy the labor her husband and those indebted to him would provide.

Money from development projects might, however, be enough for her mother to buy books and a uniform which would help her attend high school. At the time of my first visit to the village, few young women went to the high school, which was in Punta Gorda, the district capital two hours away on bus (the time was more due to bad roads than distance). Since there was no regular bus running at the time that would get students to school on time families had to arrange room and board for their young scholars. Parents with kin or fictive kin in Punta Gorda could call on them much as they would call on them in the village to help harvest or cook for a celebration.

This arrangement was a simple variation on the traditional *compadrazgo* system that formed the basis of community respect and insured the cooperation and devotion needed to become prosperous, and in some ways survive. Asking urban Maya or even non-Maya to act as *comadre* or *compadre* developed decades before I reached the village, when Maya began selling pigs on the national market (discussed later in this chapter). The arrangement primarily helped young men go to high school (Gregory, 1984, 1987).

But as late as Crooks' time in the village (1992, 1997) parents were still reluctant to send girls to high school. People told me they feared that without parental supervision their daughter might become pregnant and therefore could no longer focus on her education. Without a means to make money to buy goods, or a husband to help perform the duties necessary for survival, or the social ties created though community service, such young women would have hard lives in abject poverty, unless their parents were especially wealthy. There were few wealthy Maya at that time.

When I left my field work, a daily bus went from the village to the high school in Punta Gorda so that more young women could attend high school. However, it was still expensive to send a child to school, and few boys or girls could go. The loss of labor a family would sustain was a key to determining which child went to high school. Besides the child's aptitude and the family's economic resources, birth order and gender of the siblings are as important. Few mothers would allow an eldest daughter to go to school, since they needed that daughter's labor to run the household and care for her younger siblings. Children whose labor was expendable most often got to go to school.

Therefore, older children most typically followed traditional gender roles, with parents encouraging and giving permission for their daughters to marry men from prominent families who they felt would be most likely to be nonabusive, thus insuring that traditional patterns of debt and repayment would care for the parents in their older years. Sending kids to school was still a high risk return.

What Doesn't Work

When I left the village after my initial extended field work, some tactics were not working against domestic violence. Others had potential. Those that didn't work were those that interfered with Maya traditional gender roles in ways that confused women's ways of serving her family. Such tactics, primarily government development projects, provided women with economic resources separate from her husband.

Similarly, participating in craft co-operatives in Chiapas provides Maya women with economic resources. They needed, and still need, to work hard to frame their leadership roles as necessary and an important way to serve their community, not just themselves (Eber, 1995). Otherwise they find themselves marginalized and subject to legitimatized beatings by their spouses (Eber, 1995).

Therefore, the tendency in Belize was for older widowed women to get involved in these projects. They often told me they could not participate if they were married. Their husbands would not see their work as beneficial to the household or the community and often would become abusive. Community members would see this abuse as legitimate, since the victim had ignored the mutual economic bond of marriage.

Indeed, one young Mayan woman in southern Belize was raped because of her involvement in a government development program. She agreed to serve as a chairlady of a group, which put her in a vulnerable position having to travel alone with a male government official. This violence generated extensive discussion about whether she deserved the punishment. That is, people argued as to whether that rape was legitimate. In essence, people were not just debating the legitimacy of the rape, but also whether the path she took was an acceptable means to gain *tsik*.

Development projects failed as a means to prevent domestic violence because they create roles for women that are less clearly understood as a means to create *tsik*, community connectedness. This chapter's theory of Maya violence would predict the failure. Attempts to end violence need to assure that women can serve their community in predictable understandable ways. During the mid 1990s there were few such avenues available. It took several years before one way, education, seemed to be acceptable.

The Late 2000s - Education and Identity

While there are no statistics to tell whether education helps end domestic violence, during my return to the village in 2010, it seems to do so. Few people volunteered during my two visits to the village this time to talk about the abuse they suffer. In the mid-1990s when I began my relationship with the village, women talked to me about such things openly, and thought of the violence they suffered as part of their identity as Mayan women. White women from the U.S., like myself, they insisted, know nothing of such abuse (McClusky, 2001). No one expressed such sentiments during my more recent visits.

Likewise, in every household I visited, parents with children soon to graduate from the local grammar school that I visited were worried about their daughter's passing the entrance exams for high school when the time came. Young women who had graduated from grammar school, but did not get into high school, all made a point to tell that they were not going to get married until they were "older" (i.e., in their late teens or early twenties). In contrast, during my first visit to the village when I was 23, young women discovering I was not yet married, asserted I was already too old to get married. One said my womb had probably dried up already and wouldn't be able to bear children. Times have changed.

While I cannot say for sure that the strategies of delaying marriage and stressing education have reduced the rate of domestic violence, I can say that those strategies integral to the women's subtle campaign to reduce such violence had taken hold and were affecting many people's lives in significant ways, especially in terms of ethnic and gender identity. Women who were mothers when I first met them are now grandmothers, and most of their daughters are now mothers. All these women were still hopeful and still supporting these tactics to reduce women's chances of being in an abusive marriage.

Since young women have been attending high school they have been redefining gender roles. The most obvious change was greater interaction with males who were not relatives, either fictive or biological. Non-Maya teachers did not understand or tolerate the sex segregation traditional to Mayan society. Traditionally, family community members encourage Maya women to avoid interacting with men and boys either directly or via gossip (Kray, 2007; Eber, 1995; Danziger, 1991). Such interactions might lead to sex, the promise of sex, or other people's perceptions that the two might be sexually active. Any of these actions might diminish the young woman's ability to marry. Since marriage was the only way a woman might find economic security, such missteps could impoverish her for life. One of the only ways to avoid this consequent poverty was to be the mistress of a married man, a shaky means to security at best, since the first wife might have the support to stop her husband from continuing with infidelity.

In school, especially in high school far away from the village, teachers required boys and girls to sit next to each other, collaborate on class projects and study together for exams. Teachers also required young girls to speak up in class, state their ideas and participate in in-class memorization drills, alone, without the watchful eye of a family member, or even a community member who would prevent her from endangering her chances for marriage. Parents and community members had to accept these activities as part of ascribed gender roles if their daughters were to succeed in school. In this way, young Maya women have become more outspoken and self-assured than ever before (McClusky, 2001).

Furthermore, the experience of being outside the village made students realize the power of the negative stereotypes that both Maya and non-Maya held about Maya being submissive, dirty, naïve—nothing more than stupid Indians. This realization and other pressures that classmates, teachers and principals placed on young Maya women led many attending high school to deny symbols of Maya-ness. Most refused to wear the traditional Maya dress on weekends and when school was not in session. Instead, they would wear the shorts and t-shirts common to Creole and urban dwellers. Some refused to eat tortilla or *pox* (meatless tamale), the most important symbol of Maya heritage. One young woman I know even claimed to forget all of the knowledge her grandmother, a respected healer, had taught her about herbs and ceremonies for curing a wide range of illnesses.

Therefore many but not all embrace a more national identity, as "Belizean." Some maintain pride in being Maya. These young women concerted efforts to gain *tsik* and become or remain interconnected by acting as *co-madres*. However, someone must ask them to serve in this way, and in order to be asked, they must have some level of *tsik*. Someone must see them as competent in some way. Others are sure to serve the community, and gain *tsik*, by cooking for celebrations or offering money donations to make the hiring of musicians or the purchase of alcohol or some other ingredient necessary to party. Most make a point of helping their mothers cook and take care of young siblings while school is not in session. Some help their mothers financially, allowing them to set up new households and escape abusive partners. Those who take a more pan-Belizean identity may not return to the village, except for short infrequent visits.

Giving or lending money and resources and providing labor for celebrations help young Maya women maintain their connection to the community. Serving in these ways keeps them tied in to the systems of formalized mutual aid that marks their continued acceptance of a Maya identity by gaining respect, *tsik*, in a traditional way. In this way, they can act according to prescribed social roles, abandon some expected social roles, and re-define themselves.

So why does this work while development projects don't? If Maya eschew capriciousness, and are legitimately punished if they go against the roles in place that formalize patterns of mutual aid, why do people tolerate young women talking to young men and questioning their Mayan-ness? The answer is that parents tolerate these actions because they hope these daughters will support their family of origin, and hope for the future financial help outweighs maintaining the traditional system of gaining *tsik* in the village, or maintaining traditional Maya identities. Young educated women seem to have little interest in marriage. Therefore, any economic, social or cultural capital that they accumulate through education returns directly to the family of origin. Like the families of origin in Mexico and China that send daughters to urban areas to work in factories, Maya parents see the hope of success not just for that daughter, but for themselves and their other children.

The route to economic success is now possible because of better transportation. The daily high school bus brings students home directly after school where, although they are allowed more freedom than their sisters who do not go to school, they still remain under the watchful eyes of the community. Furthermore, others have been successful students who did not "waste the investment" by getting pregnant.

The Graduating Class - Growing Structural Violence

Maya have been hierarchical since ancient times. After the collapse of the Mayan civilization, however, stratification has been minimized through the redistributive cargo system, where economic capital was replaced with a kind of social capital (Cancian, 1965; Bourdieu, 1986). That is, economic resources were transformed into relationships of mutual aid and respect. For many farmers in the village, this transformation is still possible to the degree that *compadrazgo* and feasting, remnants of the cargo system, remain in place. Professionals, however, have been able to accumulate economic capital, as well as a kind of social capital that differs from the social

capital that the cargo system provides. Education has allowed them to accumulate cultural capital that distinguishes them from nonprofessional Maya. I will use the problematic word "class" as a short cut to describe people's relationship to these forms of capital, and to suggest that there is a
growing divide in access to these forms of capital within the village.

Gregory (1984, 1987) described the beginnings of a class divide in the village due to increased access to cash for some through the raising, transporting
and selling of pigs in Punta Gorda. He argues that this divide helped to divorce
the cargo system in southern Belize from its religious significance. The results
of this early divide can be seen today. Indeed, since many of those who made
money and gained status in the community through the pig market sent some
of their children, mostly young men but some young women, to school in
Punta Gorda, that early divide is at the foundation of the growing divide today.

Partying was integral to *tsik*. Partying was an economic leveling device
for as long as anthropologists have been studying Maya lifeways. However,
today because of entrance into the national economy and because some
Maya can achieve higher levels of education, the remnants of the cargo system are weak and no longer act as much of a leveling mechanism. True,
parties are still expensive to throw and are labor intensive, necessitating
some level of debt and repayment. But families now can accumulate large
amounts of money. Parties are less of an economic burden for the new rich.
Their money can be transformed into education for their children.

This education obviously provides sons and daughters with greater opportunities for employment. However, it also later provides the children of those
sons and daughters with savvy parents familiar with how the education system works, able to help with homework and to focus on what is important
for academic success. All educated people have the choice as to whether to
participate in the traditional status hierarchy based on mutual aid or the pan-
Belizean status hierarchy based on urban lifestyle, ethnicity and the accumulation of goods; or to try to do both. Gaining *tsik* is not optional if you want to
maintain a position within the village, and to secure a Maya identity in that
context. However, *tsik* is irrelevant to a pan-Belizean identity. Those who
chose to build that identity typically move out of the village and follow employment opportunities. Moving away does not mean however, that they are
not sending money back home. Parents sometimes use this money to send
another child to school. Social connections sometimes provide a brother or
sister with work opportunities—more money sent home.

It is too soon to determine the full effects of increased academic education on class divisions. In the 1990s several families had children who left

the village for employment, mostly for occupations that required little or no formal education, such as housekeeper, nanny, police officer or as military personnel. Most returned to the village often and gave their mothers money specifically to help for their younger siblings' education. So normally even those living outside the village supplement their parent's income. These funds don't help extended family or other community members the way the labor provided through the cargo system did.

Moreover, education and success beyond high school are not available to everyone; Cash resources make the difference. If education is a means to escape domestic violence, and if education provides people with access to cash resources, then those who have money and education might leave the others behind with only the old system of status and old gender roles available. Traditional Mayan women's tendency to see themselves stereotypically suffering abuse might be accurate.

Forging New Identities - Graduation Parties as Sites of Performing Identity

Earlier I discussed the ways *tsik* greetings enact and re-enforce *tsik*. This "living" aspect of *tsik* lends itself to analysis based in performative theory (Austin, 1975; Butler, 1990). The performance of certain actions both provides and embodies *tsik*. Graduation parties illustrate how young Maya women and their families enact and re-enforce traditional gender roles and how Maya are forging new identities, negotiating new meanings to ethnic identity and gender through action and symbol. In this way, graduation parties are sites of performing identity and systems of mutual respect, both old and new.

My last visit to the village in June 2009 was to attend two high school graduation parties. Both graduates were young women. One, Karema, was her parent's eldest daughter; the other, Cecelia, was her parent's second child and their second eldest daughter. Her older sister Lisa would be graduating from a two-year college next year. What follows is a description of Karema and Cecelia's graduation parties. The two parties were on consecutive nights; I could attend both from their beginnings. Due to an oncoming flu, I left Karema's party fairly early. However, I was able to stay for Cecelia's entire party.

The Parties

Cecelia's father, Felicio, is a police officer; her mother, Rosana, is a housewife who does not participate in any of the women's projects. Cecelia has not yet been accepted into a college, although that is her goal. Karema's father, Maricio, is the principal of one of the two high school in the area.

Her mother, Juana, runs the village pre-school which she helped found. Karema is now attending college.

Both parties began with pig killing. Felicio bought two pigs from a farmer who lived just outside the village. Four of his brothers-in-law worked together to kill the pigs and carry them to the road where a hired truck bought them to the house. Here Felicio butchered the pigs himself, while his brothers-in-law rested and began to drink rum. Two other distant male relatives began making chicarone, fried pig skin, while the mother of the graduate and several women related through *compadrazgo* began making caldo, pig soup, stew pork, rice and beans and tortillas for the chicarone. Felicio made barbeque, using a small grill next to their modest cement house. Guests stopped by the kitchen as they arrived to greet Rosana, before they made their way to the area cleared for a dance floor. Felicio hired local musicians to play marimba and asked his brother to act as DJ.

Maricio, the school principal, had several of his brothers kill three pigs he raised just for this occasion. At least seven other men butchered the pigs, cooked chicarone and made barbeque. Maricio, recently recovered from an illness, greeted guests, and the DJ set up his equipment. Juana, the graduate's mother, did not oversee or join the women she had asked to help cook stew pork, rice and beans and the tortillas for the chicarone. Instead, she greeted guests and helped prepare alcoholic punch. When most of the guests had arrived the graduate's father and male relatives offered drinks. Maricio officially opened Karema's party by turning on a microphone and beginning a "short program" to honor the graduate. He then turned the microphone over to his brother-in-law, also a school teacher, to serve as master of ceremonies. After a few preliminary words of appreciation and welcoming the guests, the MC introduced the graduate. Karema then came down the stairs of the house to the party below, to applause. Her parents then both made speeches stressing the importance of education and how proud they were of their daughter. Maricio also pointed out and thanked several prominent guests for coming, like the principal of the other high school and myself. Maricio and the MC invited guests to come to the microphone and say something. Those who spoke in Belizean Creole, including the father's father, a prominent man in the village, provided opportunity for the MC to discuss the importance of learning Creole, and those who spoke in Maya used the opportunity to express appreciation for their native tongue. After the ceremony, female relatives and other women Juana had asked to help cook distributed plates of food.

At Felicio's house, Lisa, his oldest daughter, and some women who had been working in the kitchen distributed the food when it looked as though most of the guests had arrived. There was no formal program, no announcing the graduate, no speeches on the importance of education.

At both parties, after the guests had eaten, there was music and dancing for the party-goer's entertainment. At this time, some of the women guests, at both parties, began to accept a bottle or two of stout. The music at Cecelia's party was both traditional live marimba and a mix of recorded punta, reggae, soca and ranchero. The music reflected the ethnic diversity of Belize, and of the guests. The marimba band came from a nearby village: they used the marimba normally stored at the church. The church was unable to afford to hire marimba players to use it for the recent celebration of the feast of the village's patron saint. Between the marimba and the DJ's picks there was music to get most everyone to move their feet. Those who didn't dance were mostly children and women of various ages, mostly older women, too shy to dance.

Maricio's son, Karema's brother, DJed Karema's party until the hired DJ from the district capitol arrived. Both played only pan-Caribbean dancehall music, nothing specific to Belize or to Maya. One most disturbing song was about the ills of father/daughter pedophilia, a social problem many non-Maya believe is endemic in Maya communities. While I was at the party, few people danced. Most guests stayed on the outskirts of the dance floor, older people in the inner ring, younger people and non-Maya on the far perimeter. Tired and beginning to feel the effects of an oncoming flu, I left the party having only seen the official father/graduate and the mother/graduate dance. These dances were much like father/daughter dances performed at weddings in the U.S. The MC was urging guests to join in.

Differing Access to Capital

Besides the growing class divide between professional and nonprofessionals in the village, a split is emerging between types of professionals. Professional men serving in the roles of father or husband head both of the families celebrating graduations, one a school principal, the other a police officer.

The performance of differing access to wealth begins with the stag: the type of house each family lives in, where the celebration takes place. Cecelia's family, five children including Cecelia and her two parents, lives in a small cement house. It's a cramped space, but much more extravagant than the wattle and daub houses that make up the majority of the village residences headed by nonprofessionals. But unlike the wattle and daub constructions, it symbolizes access to money and the possible future accumulation of wealth since the owners can sell or rent out the building to various non-Maya (anthropologists, school teachers, Peace Corps volunteers, etc.) who stay temporarily in the village.

Karema's family, headed by the school principal, lives in a large cement house raised on cement pillars providing additional living space, a garage and storage underneath. It sits on a high hill overlooking the village on a fairly large lot with pig stalls, an additional cook house, several fruit and avocado trees. The style is like the houses of the rich in Punta Gorda, or Belize City. It's the best of both worlds, comfortable and serene, with enough land to grow a little food. This property entailed a greater investment than the police officer's house. As the principal once said, he built his house here so here could "watch the village get big," meaning that he was well positioned to usher in a more prosperous time for himself and the entire village.

Other performances of class difference are within the celebrations themselves. Some of the performance is traditional, signaling older forms of prestige, others are "modern," signaling greater access to different kinds of resources. For example, large numbers of people helping to prepare food or butcher the pigs, and large numbers of guests attending and enjoying the food and drink, remain an ancient performance of *tsik*, social capital in the form of respect of local villagers and family. However, for both parties there was also a display of "honored guests," social capital from outside the village, or from within the village but outside the Maya world, such as school teachers of various ethnicities and the Garifuna community health nurse and her family. The principal made a point to introduce his most honored guests, the police officer did not. Both however, gain prestige and express the types of connections to which successful Maya should have access.

The performance of a graduation party displays class differences while at the same time illustrates how traditional and modern systems of prestige coexist. The tradition of giving back to the community via a large party with plenty of food, drink and entertainment is required for others to tolerate differing access to resources. Sometimes this is not enough, as the rich still remain somewhat questionable in character.

Performing With Food

Both families killed in order to celebrate. This violence remains a way to express and embody, to perform, the relationship between the family hosting the party, especially the male head of the household, and those, especially male relatives, to whom they are indebted to for making the celebration happen. Killing pigs to express and embody social connectedness remains despite the fact that neither Maricio nor Felicio are traditional farmers and do not have time to tend to fields.

Farmers express and embody this type of relationship several times throughout the corn or cacao growing seasons. Whenever fields need clearing, corn needs planting, corn and cacao need harvesting, and corn needs planting again, nonprofessional males perform *tsik*. For professional men without corn fields or cacao trees, graduation celebrations, along with baptisms and weddings, and more and more commonly quinceanos celebrations, create and reinforce such bonds between men and families.

Killing pigs, or larger domesticated animals like cows, makes this bonding happen. Other animals are not associated with large feasts that require the help of many people. Women kill chickens on their own and use them for daily meals. Men kill game animals like gibnut (paca), deer and cussarrow. But again game is for daily meals and does not require help in preparation. Moreover, the method of killing chickens and game meat is not nearly as violent as the killing of pigs, which is loud, bloody and often requires someone to put his hand into the stab wound in the pig's neck and reach down to cut the heart. Killing large domestic animals is unique to celebrations and is unique in creating bonds between male relatives and community members. Women make similar bonds through cooking rice and beans, tortilla and *pox*. These bonds don't require violence.

Educating daughters requires flirtation with and the acceptance of non-Mayan ways of being. Just as allowing daughters in high school the freedom to interact with males who are not part of the family is required, so is incorporating non-Mayan foods such as rice and beans, stew pork and barbeque into celebrations. Rice and beans, with stew pork (or chicken) is not a Mayan dish, but is common to Creole and pan-Belizean. It is the national dish of Belize (Wilk, 2006). Serving rice and beans and stew meat has come to symbolize, for Maya, familiarity, comfort and acceptance of non-Maya values and identities. It symbolizes entrance into the Belizean national landscape not simply as an "indigenous problem," or as a means for cultural tourism, but as equal citizens. Serving these foods enacts and reinforces a family's identity as not just Mayan, but as Belizean as well.

Performing With Music and Microphone

Like food, the entertainment provided for each party performs and creates an ethnic and a class identity. As mentioned previously, the two DJs at Karema's party both spun pan—Caribbean dancehall music, nothing specific to Belize or Maya. This entertainment and the "short program" of lip-service to Mopan Maya language and speeches paying homage to elders' efforts to speak English both enforce and illustrate a particular way of being Maya in a national and Caribbean context. Holding onto Maya roots means serving traditional food like chicarone and tortillas. The social capital displayed and reinforced at this party was not just the traditional connections of mutual aid of family and fictive kin, but also of important outsiders.

At the other party, even though Cecelia's father the police officer is more vocal in his complaints about how Maya ways and identity are not beneficial in the outside world, they has music to suit everyone, including a live Maya marimba band and recordings of Maya harp music. Here there was no official short program. The graduate was not even introduced, let alone "important guests." Systems of mutual aid were on display, but not obvious. Family from Guatemala attended the party, as well as family and fictive kin who worked to make the party happen. The police officer had less of a need to emphasize connections outside the Maya world, because he had fewer than did his more economically successful counterpart.

Performing New Gender Roles

Young women who go to high school perform and forge new gender roles daily as they wear shorts and t-shirts instead of traditional Maya women's wear. They also perform and forge new gender roles as they interact with boys in and out of school. At the parties they took a place of honor: Karema officially presented to the party goers, Cecelia more subtle but still overtly divergent from traditional female gender roles of dancing with guests and clearly showing that she was having a good time. Neither were acting tranquil, subdued or noncapricious, as Maya women are traditionally supposed to behave (Kray, 2007). Traditionally, their behaviors might spark suspicions of having or desiring pre-marital sexual relations.

Older women also performed gender roles, some new, some old. Women connected by systems of mutual aid helped cook and serve food. Guests, women a step further outside the circle of those honored by titles as fictive kin, acted in various ways. Some sat quietly and watched, as they had done many years ago when I had lived in the village. Others drank stout, still others danced. Some accepted stout with a tiny shy smile, as if they were about to do something quite daring. Drinking and dancing are things women would never do openly before without fear of gossip about their moral character.

Young men also performed gender roles. Most male behavior was not that different from previous years. Some danced, drank and were clearly inebriated; others just sat and watched, just as they would have done years ago.

Still others closely connected to the system of mutual aid for this family having finished the bulk of their work for this party, such as killing and cooking pig, now helped serve alcohol and soft drinks. At Karema's party, educated men took the microphone and took part in the official program. Old men sat and watched, and young men took to the dark periphery surrounding the party.

A tiny group of young men who attended Cecelia's party might not have been invited a few years ago: the "Rasta boys," Maya who identify with what they understand as Rastafarian culture; wearing red, gold, black and green, heads laden with dreadlocks and encased in a constant cloud of the sharp strong smell of marijuana, they drank and danced and ate a lot of pork. While Jamaicans might not recognize these boys as Rasta, these young men are Rasta in the village, appropriating a cultural tradition not their own, but defining a new way to be Maya. As Maya Rasta they eschew violence and espouse peace. Their presence at the party is complicated, since in the past they would be feared and excluded from such celebrations. However, these young men are among the pig killers for Cecelia's party. They are family and well tied to the system of mutual aid that made this party possible.

The performance of new gender roles, old systems of mutual aid, new ties to the outside, ways to blend Belizean identity with being Maya, these are all part of a process in which Maya are enacting and creating ways of being. Blending the old and new, abandoning old meanings in favor of new ones is the stuff of culture, a fluid repertoire of actions and meanings. It is difficult to say exactly what the relationship will be between these newly forged ways of being and violence in Mayan village in southern Belize. What I can say, however, is that people's relationship to violence, the Maya theory of violence must be changing as well.

Conclusions

Maya are not a particularly violent people, yet like Cree (this volume), they engage in violence that is justified if members of the community frame the violence as a means to punish those who are working against the systems of mutual aid developed long ago. Still Maya violence rarely ends in killing. The exception is killing large animals for the purpose of hosting feasts. Organizing large feasts continues to be a source of prestige and demonstration of commitment to community, even with the collapse of cargo system in southern Belize.

Since the mid-1990s women have been engaged in tactics they feel will help end spousal violence that men commit on their wives. Wife beating among Maya has been legitimized if the husband and wife's family and fictive kin frame the reason of the beating to be a man's attempt to make their wife engage in the mutual aid agreement of marriage. For Maya, marriage is a contract between two outside parties that may signal a kind of ownership of husband over wife that later becomes a relationship of mutual aid solidified by close intimate relationships between two people who have come to rely on one another in predictable ways.

These tactics to end violence against wives are not isolated, but are part of a larger attempt for Maya to take their place in the nation of Belize as equal actors. Promoting education among young women is one of these tactics. Participation among young Maya men and women in the national systems of education works to change their identity and their relationship to their parents, their village and the nation. Young women forge new gender roles, and enact them in a way that contributes to the systems of mutual aid integral to Maya village identity. There is a cognate need to forge new meanings to what it is to be Maya, and what one's relationship to the larger Belizean identity might be.

Women's greater access to education contributes to a growing differential distribution of resources that are available to some Maya and not others. While this "class" division began in the 1970s Young Man's Revolt, the effects of the growing access to education are significant. The Young Man's Revolt saw the collapse in southern Belize of the cargo system, a system found throughout Latin America that acts as a leveling mechanism to transform economic capital into social capital, re-enforcing relationships of mutual aid. It is possible, although we have no statistics or oral history to support it, that the collapse of this system has led to greater rates of violence against wives. The value of collecting and enacting *tsik* may have been lessened as men had other means of gaining status in the village, by accumulating economic capital.

To this day Maya find being rich uncomfortable. Individuals need to give to the community. Their discomfort, however, doesn't halt people's accumulation of economic, social and cultural capital that facilitates economic success for oneself and one's family. The ways one gives back to the community doesn't transform one's assets into social capital within the village. Instead, social and cultural capital, for those better off, tends to be focused outside the village into the larger Belizean context. Education increases families' social and cultural capital; it also lets Maya challenge regional stereotypes by demonstrating that Maya can be forceful, intelligent, and harder to manipulate than once thought.

Graduation parties are sites for performing, displaying, enforcing and forging new identities and new commitments to community. Young women take the center stage surrounded by ethnically symbolic food and entertainment, in a way appropriate for their position in the "class divide," as older people,

people less educated and people with less access to resources enact traditional systems of mutual aid, sometimes shyly practice new gender roles and
negotiate a Mayan ethnicity. As some Maya organize parties and work to educate their daughters, others do not, or cannot because the economic cost of
education remains high. Those without access to resources serve as an audience as the rich perform how such resources allow them to blend traditional
and modern forms of mutual aid, and re-define what it means to be Maya.

People without economic resources to educate at least one son or
daughter, and their children, maintain tradition, living in wattle and daub
houses, eating primarily tortilla, and creating systems of mutual aid that
might tie them to richer people. Richer people, however, although they see
importance to gain *tsik* also see the need to gain status in ways more familiar to non-Maya outside of the village. They may or may not provide significant aid to their poorer kin, fictive or biological. Thus the daughters of the
poor remain vulnerable to "legitimate discipline."

In this way, education as a catalyst for class difference can prevent some
women from suffering domestic violence, but might also contribute to a
kind of structural violence that leaves some behind to perform the regional
stereotype of naïve, poor, submissive, passive "Indian" that suffers numerous social ills, especially domestic violence.

References

Austin, J. L. (1975). *How to Do Things with Words*. Cambridge: Harvard University Press.
Bourdieu, Pierre (1986). "The Forms of Capital," in Richardson, J., Ed., *Handbook of Theory and Research for the Sociology of Education*. New York: Greenwood, pp. 241-258.
Butler, Judith (1990). *Gender Trouble: Feminism and the Subversion of Identity*. New York: Routledge.
Burgos-Debray, Elisabeth (1984). *I, Rigoberta Menchu: An Indian Women in Gua-temala*. London: Verso.
Cancian, Frank (1965). *Economics and Prestige in a Maya Community: The Religious Cargo System in Zinacantan*. Stanford: Stanford University Press.
Crooks, Deborah (1997). Biocultural Factors in School Achievement for Mopan Children in Belize. *American Anthropologist*, 99(3): 586-601.
Crooks, Deborah (1992). *"Make They Find it Easier": A Biocultural Study of Growth and School Achievement for Mayan Children in Belize* [Ph.D. dissertation]. State University of New York at Buffalo.
Danziger, Eve (1991). *Semantics on the Edge: Language as Cultural Experience in the Acquisition of Social Identity Among Mopan Maya* [Ph.D. dissertation]. University of Pennsylvania.

Eber, Christine (1995). *Women and Alcohol in a Highland Maya Town: Water of Hope, Water of Sorrow.* Austin: University of Texas Press.

Foster, George (1953). "Cofradia and Compadrazgo in Spain and Spanish America," *Southwestern Journal of Anthropology,* 9:1-28.

Garber, Mary Elizabeth (1999). *Na'chiin: Reproduction, Illness, and Ambivalence in A Mopan Community in Southern Belize* [Ph.D. dissertation]. State University of New York at Buffalo.

Gerbner, George (1994). "Reclaiming Our Cultural Mythology," *The Ecology of Justice,* 38:40-43.

Gregory, James (1987). "Men, Women and Modernization in a Maya Community," *Belizean Studies,* 15(3):3-13.

Gregory, James (1984). *The Mopan: Culture and Ethnicity in a Changing Belizean Community.* Columbia: Museum of Anthropology, Missouri University.

Kahn, Hillary E. (2006). *Seeing and Being Seen: The Q'eqchi' Maya of Livingston, Guatemala and Beyond.* Austin: University of Texas Press.

Kray, Christine A. (2007). "Women as Border in the Shadow of Cancun," *Anthropology Today,* 23(4): 17-21.

Maynard, Eileen (1963). "Guatemalan Women: Life under Two Types of Patriarchy," in Matthiason, C., Ed., *Many Sisters.* New York: Free Press.

McClusky, Laura (2001) *"Here, Our Culture Is Hard": Stories of Domestic Violence form A Mayan Community in Belize.* Austin: University of Texas Press.

McClusky, Laura (1999). "Domestic Violence among Belizean Maya," *Humanity and Society,* 23(4): 319-338

Rosenbaum, Brenda (1993). *With Our Heads Bowed: The Dynamics of Gender in a Maya Community.* Albany: State University of New York at Albany.

Schele, Linda (1992). *The Blood of Kings: Dynasty and Ritual in Maya Art.* New York: George Braziller, Inc.

Stoll, David (2007). *Rigoberta Menchu and the Story of All Poor Guatemalans.* Boulder: Westview Press.

Stoll, David (1993). *Between Two Armies in the Ixil Towns of Guatemala.* New York: Columbia University Press.

Tedlock, Barbara (1992). *Time and the Highland Maya.* Albequerque: University of New Mexico Press.

Thompson, J. Eric (1990). *Maya History and Religion.* Norman: University of Oklahoma Press.

Thompson, J. Eric (1930). *Ethnology of the Maya of Southern and Central British Honduras.* Chicago: Field Museum Press.

Watanabe, John M. (1992). *Maya Saints and Souls in a Changing World.* Austin: Texas University Press.

Wilk, Richard (2006). *Home Cooking in the Global Village: Caribbean Food from Buccaneers to Ecotourists.* Oxford: Berg Publishers.

Wisdom, Charles (1940). *The Chorti Indians of Guatemala.* Chicago: University of Chicago Press.

Chapter Ten

You Can't Be Nonviolent Without Violence

The Rainbow Family's Nonkilling Nomadic Utopia and its Survival of Persistent State Violence

Michael I. Niman
Buffalo State College

Since 1972, the Rainbow Family has been holding large noncommercial Gatherings forming spontaneous temporary cities of up to 30,000 people in remote public forests. Originally an American phenomenon, Rainbow Gatherings are now globally dispersed, regularly occurring across Eastern and Western Europe, Australia, New Zealand, Asia, Africa, Latin America and the Middle East. Despite this growth, the Family, wherever on earth it gestates, adheres to its founding values: it's an acephalous group committed to nonviolence; members make policy decisions by consensus with all Gathering attendees welcome to participate in consensus councils; everyone is welcome at Gatherings and anyone who attends a Gathering is a Rainbow Family member, and hence, can participate in these councils; Gatherings are noncommercial—members share all necessities and there is no admission or participation charge. In short, Gatherings are nonviolent, nonhierarchical and noncommercial. These are the Family's three core defining principles— remove any one of them and an event is not a Rainbow Gathering. Include them all, and you have a gateway into the world of nonkilling.

Gathering participants form an "intentional group," purposefully coming together to actualize a supposedly shared ideology (Erasmus, 1981) demonstrating the viability of a cooperative utopian community whose participants live, albeit temporarily, in harmony both with each other and with the environment. Hence, from the onset, Gatherings modeled environmental sustainability (e.g., initiating source separation recycling in 1972), nonviolent conflict resolution, and an all-inclusive egalitarianism that extended beyond social class to embrace divergent gender, religious and ethnic identities. Gatherings also welcome people recovering, or wanting to recover, from a plethora of illnesses, both mental and physical. Hence,

Rainbows describe the Gatherings as "healing" spaces—places to heal both individuals and societies. In constructing and maintaining both a utopian model and a healing space, the Family has established itself as a "revitalization movement," a "deliberate organized, conscious effort by members of society to establish a more satisfying culture" (Wallace, 1956: 265, 279). Ultimately, Rainbows seek to reform the mainstream societies that birthed them—what they term "Babylon," a phrase from the Book of Revelation. The Rainbows gleaned this phrase from Rastafarianism.

Rainbows maintain their separation from Babylon by retreating deep into the woods and liberating an autonomous zone of existence. What Rainbows liberate is not so much physical terrain, since they always dissolve within a few weeks and volunteers strive to remove their trace footprints from the environment, but time. And they liberate the imagination, so for a week or a month, Rainbows imagine utopia, and they live in it, ultimately liberating what anarchist theorist Hakim Bey terms a Temporary Autonomous Zone, or TAZ (Bey, 1991: 100-101). When the Gathering is over, Rainbows dissolve their TAZ and disperse into Babylon, only to reappear in another place and time, essentially unchanged and continuing where they left off. Demographers refer to this practice as a "fission-fusion" (cf. Dentan, 1992, 1994, 2008: 116; Fix, 1975; Neel et al., 1964). Unlike conventional revolutionaries or land-based utopian communities, the Rainbow Family purposefully avoids the threats and strains associated with controlling territory, hence avoiding prolonged external conflict with the state and internal conflict with each other—things that can lead to violent clashes. Ultimately the Rainbow Family's longevity is tied to its strategy of regularly moving "the entire tribe" (Bey, 1991: 102).

The Rainbow Family is a nonkilling society (Paige, 2009 [2002]). The Family is committed to both practicing nonviolence at its own Gatherings, and to proactively advance the practice in Babylon. Hence, Gatherings serve as models and refuges of peaceful coexistence, and as laboratories for testing and advancing nonviolent conflict resolution strategies. While Councils regularly reaffirm the Family's commitment to nonviolence against humans, the Family is split, however, on the subject of violence against animals perpetrated though an omnivorous diet. Most Rainbows are either vegetarian or vegan, and Councils almost always prohibit the use of common ("Magic Hat") funds for the purchase of meat; however, Rainbow libertarianism toward humans prohibits the Family from banning meat entirely from the Gatherings. Hence Rainbows often have the individual option of eating at meat, vegetarian or vegan kitchens, with meat usually eschewed from larger communal meals served at central circles. While some Rainbows voraciously argue that such meat-eating constitutes violence, the persistence of the argument and the careful consideration both sides pay to it is indicative of the central role nonviolence plays in Rainbow identity. Today's international Rainbow Family has a four-decade long history as a "peaceable people" (cf. Niman, 1991, 1997, 2011, in press; Dentan, 1992, 1994; Amster, 2003: 17; Solnit, 2009: 295-299).

Being a peaceable people, however, doesn't mean that Rainbow Gatherings are always peaceful. Violence, usually in the form of state sanctioned police violence, or violence among bickering drunks segregated away from the general Gatherings in Alcohol Camp (A-Camp) often mar Rainbow Gatherings. Such violence distinguishes the Rainbow Family from other contemporary and historic "nonviolent" utopian communities who achieve or have achieved their tranquility through restrictive membership policies that excluded people who the groups thought might have a proclivity toward violence. Rainbows, by contrast, not only accept violent individuals in accordance with their open membership policies, but sometimes seek such individuals out, recognizing that they need the healing environment that the Gatherings offer. Rainbows feel that banishing such individuals would be an admission that violence can't be overcome, and that "pacifist ideals that appeal only to those already safe from violence are not going to transform society" (Dentan, 1994: 95).

In this respect, the Rainbow Family is akin to the "family" that Anarchist theorist Peter Kropotkin envisioned when he argued in 1877 that anti-social behavior could best be treated with immersion into a loving supporting community or "family." He proposed "a new family, based on community of aspirations":

> In this family people will be obliged to know one another, to aid one another and lean on one another for moral support on every occasion. And this mutual prop will prevent the great number of anti-social acts which we see today (Kropotkin, 2002[1877]: 233-234).

The Rainbow Gatherings, intentionally or otherwise, have served as a laboratory where, over the course of four decades, and with hundreds of thousands of participants, Kropotkin's theories have withstood testing.

Violent or potentially violent members provide the opportunity for the Rainbows to transcend simple tranquility and, with the successful engagement and pacification of violence, put their nonviolent principles and strategies into practice. Such practice both field-tests nonviolent conflict resolution tactics for efficacy while, in the best cases, demonstrating their effectiveness. Rainbows argue for both the efficacy of nonviolent strategies in mitigating both immediate and long-term violent threats, and the moral imperative associated with the preference of violence over nonviolence. It's a double-edged argument that nonviolence not only works better, but that it's the right thing to do. The former line of reasoning might appeal to government bean counters fretting over the monetized costs associated with violent compliance regimes, while the latter argument would appeal to human cultural and hard-wired aversions to violence (cf. Dentan, this volume)—what we often call human decency.

The Family's nonkilling ethos sometimes mandates noncooperation with Babylonian authorities whom they see as inherently violent, either directly engaging in on-the-spot violence, threatening the use of such violence, or threatening delayed violence, usually in the form of incarceration. Contracting out violence to such a force stands in conflict to nonviolent principles, hence Rainbows avoid asking for support from traditional armed police agencies, instead preferring to confront violence and violent provocations themselves—usually with success.

Conflict between the Rainbow Family and government authorities began with the first Gathering in 1972. That year, over 20,000 would-be Rainbows converged on the Roosevelt National Forest in Colorado, all responding to a well spread rumor of a sort of wilderness Woodstock festival without bands or promoters. Colorado's ironically named governor, John Love, responded by declaring the Gathering illegal and ordering up police roadblocks to bar participants from attending. Rainbows, probably inspired by Gandhi's historic march on India's salt mines and the then-recent nonviolent civil rights actions in the southern United States, nonviolently marched on the barriers. The police arrested them by the hundreds. Finally, when four thousand people advanced toward the roadblock prepared to be arrested, the authorities backed off, removed the barriers, and let the Gathering, now gestated in an act of civil disobedience, proceed (Niman, 1997: 32).

This commitment to nonviolent civil disobedience, buoyed by thousands of participants who showed up each year prepared either to gather in the woods, or gather in jail, allowed the Gatherings to develop and grow relatively unhindered well into the era of the Reagan presidency. With U.S. Rainbow Gatherings occurring exclusively on National Forest Service land, the Forest Service became the lead government agency responsible for interfacing with the Rainbows. Early on in this relationship, it seems, these officials also bought into their own sort of nonviolence, essentially leaving well enough alone, knowing that eventually the Rainbow TAZ, like the weather, would pass. The challenge for the bureaucrats was to see the Gathering pass with as little damage as possible to any law enforcement official's career. Their own relative nonviolence provided them with the best strategy to effectuate that result, also in the process proving the Rainbow nonviolence to be contagious.

By 1983, the Forest Service institutionalized their own nonviolence as a strategy, developing what one official called a "Hands-Off" approach to the Gathering. That year, officials in Michigan's Ottawa National Forest spent a relatively scant eight thousand dollars to monitor the event and provide interpretation rangers to answer questions about the logistics and the unique attributes of their forest. The Hands-Off approach proved to be a watershed event in Rainbow-U.S. relations, resulting in a smooth running Gathering unmarred by police violence—followed up by an effective Rainbow land restoration effort. It also, unfortunately, proved to be an anomaly.

During the years following the 1983 Gathering, the Forest Service ignored its own success and reversed course, not only using its own law enforcement personnel to harass the Rainbow Family, but also to encourage, and finally, pay local law enforcement agencies to do the same. The budget for the 1986 Gathering in Pennsylvania, for example, contained a thirteen thousand dollar line item paying the Pennsylvania State Police for services rendered setting up roadblocks to search Rainbow vehicles en route to the Gathering in a constitutionally shaky exercise of selective enforcement and profiling. The Forest Service justified these stop and search operations as a sort of War on Drugs battlefield despite the fact that after decades of such searches, the quantity of drugs confiscated at and near Rainbow Gatherings appears statistically normal for the number of vehicles searched (Niman, 1997: 189, 190). Notwithstanding the roadblocks, many local Forest Service officials all but went native at the 1986 Gathering, with one ranger seeking massage treatment at the Family's medical unit and with others bringing their families to the event on their days off.

This amity, and the persistently contagious nonviolence that it evidenced, might have struck fear into the hearts of the Forest Service leadership. The following year, at the 1987 Gathering in North Carolina, the Forest Service went to war against the family, spending $270,156, mostly on harassing the Family and disrupting the Gathering, adding an Orwellian twist by calling the new strategy "The Good Host Approach." The Good Hosts blocked deliveries of water pipes and barrels, latrine covers and potable water, leading to a diarrhea outbreak that affected, according to the Centers for Disease Control, 61.7 percent of Gathering participants (ibid, 185, 186). Forest Service officials subsequently petitioned a Federal Court in Texas the following year to grant them a legal right to finally move in and use overwhelming force (violence) to stop the next year's Gathering on the grounds that it posed a health threat. An aptly named Chief Federal Judge William Wayne Justice ruled:

"Indeed, the evidence record developed at the three sets of hearings lends substantial credence to one of the arguments advanced by the defendants [Rainbows], that the health and other problems seen at the 1987 Summer Gathering in North Carolina were exceptional and traceable—at least in part—to a hostile and adversarial relationship between the government and the Rainbow Family ... Indeed, the government did not offer any evidence of major health, safety, or environmental problems from other past Rainbow Family gatherings, except for the 1987 gathering in North Carolina" (ibid, 186, 187).

The Forest Service also based their legal argument on the National Environmental Protection Act (NEPA), arguing that the Family failed to complete site restoration in the wake of the 1987 Gathering—after federal agents arrested the site restoration crew. Justice ruled:

> While it is commendable that the F.S. is concerned about possible adverse environmental effects, there is reason to question the government's good faith in raising this argument at this time ...
> Although NEPA is unquestionably constitutional, even an otherwise valid statute cannot be applied in a manner designed to suppress First Amendment activity, or out of hostility to a particular group" (ibid, 187).

By all appearances, as the Reagan presidency morphed the national Zeitgeist, the Forest Service changed course from a cost-effective nonviolent policy in 1983, to a costly violent strategy in 1987, or put more succinctly in the terms of primitive nonkilling societies, from smart to stupid. The Rainbows prevailed, and in surviving, essentially gained victory over their adversary by strictly adhering to their core nonkilling ethos. Longtime Rainbow Oral Hipstorian Garrick Beck wrote later that year:

> Of all the lessons of the 1987 Gathering, the one that tells me the most is that despite all the harassment and provocation on the part of the agents of government, 16,000 Rainbows kept the peace.
> When they (U.S. Forest Service) ticketed without notice or warning our early on-site vehicles—and demanded immediate payment of fines—no one lost their cool heads.

When they (N.C. State Troopers) prevented a disabled live-in vehicle from being towed up the hill to where we could fix it, no one boiled over,

When they shut our main gate and forced everyone into a hi-pressured and foolish walk across the bridge, no one cursed them out.

When live-in vehicles were arbitrarily detained and forced to encamp on the U.S. highway, no one went home anyway.

When they (state of N.C.) reached an agreement with us, and began a "pass" system for our service vehicles, and when the very next morning they (U.S.F.S.) refused access to vehicles bearing "passes," no one blew up.

When a trailer load of watermelons had to be unloaded, carried across the bridge, and reloaded, no one threw a watermelon through a government windshield.

When a 9-car brigade of officers (U.S.F.S., state troopers, S.B.I., etc.) rode up the hill military-style, stopping to load shotguns in full daylight in front of children, no one reacted violently.

When our medical vehicles (with so-called "passes") were detained at the bridge, no one called for an armed revolution.

When a vehicle with 200 gallons of distilled water for Kid Village was denied access, not one of us overreacted.

When people were indiscriminately I.D. checked on the highway in a threatening and abrasive manner, no one panicked.

When people and vehicles were searched without cause or warrant, no one slugged the illegal searchers.

When people were photoed [*sic*] and videoed (by law enforcement agents) after requesting not to be, no one busted their camera.

When people's license plate #s were recorded by government surveillance agents, no one attacked them.

When a brother who requested the license #s not be recorded was brutally seized on-site, without warrant, and driven out, no one blockaded or stormed the arresting officers or vehicles.

When flashlights were shone repeatedly into people's eyes while loading and unloading at the bridge, no one grabbed and smashed the flashlights.

When officers made obnoxious comments about women's bodies and our children, no one fired a shot.

When our cleanup crew was likewise harassed, no one ignited the ranger station.

The truth is we were provoked, goaded, button-pushed, aggravated purposely. They were waiting for us—any one of us—to take a swing—then let the violence really begin. But we didn't give it to them. 16,000 Rainbows, all 16,000 Rainbows, kept the peace. After all, that's what we're supposed to do, that's what—really—we possess, that's what we can share, and that's what, of course, those who are ruled by violence are so very afraid of (Beck, 1987).

Despite proving to be a massive failure in 1987, resulting in a diarrheal epidemic that seeded micro-epidemics in at least three cities, the Forest Service pushed ahead with the Good Host Approach at the 1988 Rainbow Gathering in Texas. Toward that end, they reassigned the agent in charge of their 1987 anti-Rainbow campaign, a former Dallas narcotics agent, Billy Ball, who served with the Armed Forces Police during their 1965 occupation of Watts, California, to be Incident Commander in charge of the 1988 Gathering. The Forest Service also armed Ball with a fresh new regulation outlawing Rainbow Gatherings—which Justice Justice subsequently termed "constitutionally repugnant," citing the Forest Service's "hostility to the Rainbow Family" (Niman, 1997: 189).

The Rainbows held firm to their commitment to nonviolence through another season of provocations. This time, Forest Service LEOs, under Ball's command, both blocked one open supply road, prohibiting Rainbows from driving on it, while forcing open a closed Jeep trail to general traffic, allowing a drunk to drive into the middle of the Gathering, hitting and nearly killing a Rainbow woman named Noguns. Though incapacitated for almost a year, Noguns, in sticking to the Family's stated nonviolence, chose not to press charges against the driver, but to instead forgive the man. As the days wore on, with Rainbows responding nonviolently to daily provocations, the dignity of their response began to draw sympathy from the local, mostly conservative gun-owning East Texas population, much as nonviolent civil rights protesters won the respect of the nation two decades earlier. When Ball made his "checkmate" move, blocking the only road leading into the Gathering area just as crowds began to arrive, locals converged on the Forest with a flotilla of small fishing boats, ferrying Rainbows and their supplies across Sam Houston Lake to the Gathering site.

In 1989 the "Good Host" approach at that year's Gathering in Nevada involved setting up "informational checkpoints" equipped with drug-sniffing dogs. When Rainbows stopped to get directions, according to law enforcement documents, "general information was provided to those individuals interested in the Gathering. Also at this time, if probably [sic] cause developed, individuals were arrested," presumably for possession of illegal drugs. Despite stopping and searching a large number of vehicles, few Rainbows were actually arrested, however. This should have come as no surprise to the Forest Service since their own reports that year conceded that "the Family does not advocate the use of hard core drugs or alcohol and supports the rehabilitation of anyone addicted" (ibid, 190).

Rather than admit that the rationale for violent repression of the Rainbows was flawed, officials instead spun their failure to find any significant quantity of drugs as proof of what sly and professional drug traffickers the Rainbows must actually be. Agents theorized that Rainbows must have set up [invisible] "information stations" up the road to warn travelers about the Forest Service's own ersatz information stations. Policing efforts at the 1989 Gathering grew to encompass the Nevada Division of Forestry, the U.S. Border Patrol, the U.S. Fish and Wildlife Service, the U.S. Bureau of Land Management, the Department of Defense, the Nevada Brand Inspector, the office of the Governor of Nevada, the Department of Human Resources Health Division, the Nevada Department of Emergency Services, the Nevada Highway Patrol, the Idaho Highway Patrol, the Nevada Department of Wildlife and an undetermined number of local Sheriffs' agencies and police departments from Nevada and Idaho (ibid, 190, 191). Despite this heavily armed presence, Rainbows again kept their cool.

Over the next two decades, the Forest Service continued with a bi-polar approach to the Rainbow Family, ranging from nonviolent and cooperative strategies usually implemented on the local level, to violent and confrontational strategies, usually dictated by the agency's Washington DC administration. There are now clear and enduring patterns of a struggling nonviolent subculture within the Forest Service, buoyed by the Rainbow Family's contagious nonviolence—feds gone native. These nonviolent tendencies are often overwhelmed by a larger violence-prone Forest Service bureaucracy, however.

It appears that the very existence of Rainbow anarchs who mitigate violence without the assistance of a traditional (violent) police force, constitutes a threat. Ultimately, by maintaining the tranquility of city-sized Gatherings without such assistance, Rainbows force such agencies to confront their own obsolescence, or at least the obsolesce of their tactics, whose efficacy is bested by the nonviolent model. Bureaucrats are also threatened by the absence of bureaucracy in such a nonhierarchical society. Ultimately, governments, in a cross-culturally common pattern, construe nonviolent anarchist communities as so severe a challenge to the legitimacy of rule by force as to require violent repression (cf. Edo; Williams-Hunt; Dentan, 2009). Hence, just the existence of the Rainbow TAZ, in the eyes of Forest Service bureaucrats, requires repression even before any regulation is violated. Such repression, based on either direct violence or the threat of violence, however, has proven historically ineffectual in gaining compliance from Rainbows to whatever demands the bureaucrats may have. Ultimately, the pattern that has developed over the four decade existence of the

Rainbow Family shows that the Forest Service usually rudders toward violence, but later abandons such violence because if its lack of efficacy in contrast to their own more successful experiments with nonviolence.

Forest Service proponents of using force to overwhelm and control the Rainbow anarchs appear to have effected their strategy through law enforcement training protocols that focus on violence while fostering fear among law enforcement officers, ultimately increasing the likelihood of them initiating violence. In 2008, for example, the Forest Service spent roughly one million dollars "to patrol" the Rainbow Gathering in Wyoming. Federal law enforcement officers working at the Gathering received training in the use of pepper-ball buns, Taser guns, police dogs and crowd control techniques (Niman, 2011, in press). The curriculum covered "Striking and Close Quarter Defensive Tactics, Pressure Points, Weapon Retention, Takedowns, Ground Defense, Arrest Techniques, Baton Control Techniques, Edged Weapon Awareness, Oleoresin Capsicum Spray [and] Use of Force" (FLETC, 2009).

Absent from this training regimen was any documented mention of the nonviolent compliance techniques that Rainbows and government officers historically implemented with success at Gatherings. It also appears that many officers patrolling the 2008 Gathering were unaware that the Rainbows were a peaceable people. To the contrary, the government admonished law enforcement officers to "keep alert and tactically be prepared for potential threats," and "look out for each other and dangerous situations," while making baseless claims that "family members carried hunting knives and have assaulted Law Enforcement Officials," and "...reports of large numbers of firearms [at previous Gatherings] were received and firearms have been seen and confiscated at past [G]atherings" (Niman, 2011, in press).

That year, at the Gathering in Wyoming, Forest Service law enforcement officers rioted in the Rainbow daycare camp, Kiddie Village. Witness statements, an American Civil Liberties investigation (ACLU, 2009), a Department of Agriculture Office of Inspector General investigation (OIG, 2009) and photographic evidence included in the documentary film, "We Love You"(Kalafer, 2009), document that officers entered Kiddie Village in a "5-10 minute fast walking pursuit" of a man they suspected of sharing marijuana. They entered the camp with weapons drawn, at which time a woman approached the officers and spoke to them—witnesses say she asked them to holster their weapons. Officers immediately threw her to the ground, according to the government's report, after she "moved quickly past [an officer's] security position." Rainbow peacekeepers moved into position placing themselves between the aggressive officers and the Rainbow Family members in Kiddie Village—then joined hands, with their backs to the officers, some chanting the harmonizing syllable "Om." Officers, apparently lacking the training to recognize this traditional peacekeeping technique, opened fire and began shooting people at random with "non lethal" pepper-balls, while pointing Taser guns at other's chests and faces. A government informant reported that the officers acted as if they were in Vietnam or Iraq, rather than a peaceful Gathering of Americans (ibid).

Video documentation (Kalafer, 2009) of the event shows obviously frightened and confused officers shooting at peacekeepers and random Rainbow Family members whom they encountered on the trail during their 30 minute hike out of the Gathering. The official story, dutifully reported verbatim by the Associated Press (Neary, 2008) and thoroughly debunked by the ACLU investigation (ACLU, 2008), claims that officers were violently attacked by a riotous mob of 400 rock-and-stick-wielding Rainbows. Forest Service records document that no law enforcement officers were injured during this supposed 30 minute attack (Niman, 2011, in press).

This last fact is a tribute to the effectiveness of the nonviolent conflict resolution strategies that Rainbow peacekeepers—who tasked themselves with the job of keeping their fellow Rainbows nonviolent, even when confronted with the provocation of watching their children's camp come under attack—had employed. The Forest Service subsequently released documents that the Forest Service law enforcement officers involved in the Kiddie Village incident were outfitted for, and prepared to use, "deadly force." Their training-based proclivity toward violence almost, we now know, turned a routine marijuana arrest into a massacre.

The Forest Service Law Enforcement and Investigations Division mission reads in its entirety: "To serve people, protect natural resources and property within the authority and jurisdiction of the Forest Service" (USDA, 2010). Their violent conflict resolution strategy failed this mission, ultimately endangering both the public and their own employees. The nonkilling Rainbow Family's commitment to nonviolence and its implementation of a nonviolent conflict resolution strategy in the face of violent provocation, in retrospect, proved more effective in attaining the Forest Service's own mission, in the process modeling a more viable alternative to the government's violent policies.

While the ACLU investigation condemned the Forest Service and called for a congressional investigation into their pattern of mistreating the Rainbow Family, the government's own investigation exonerates the officers involved since, the report reads, the "Investigation determined that actions taken by the FS LEOs, including their use of nonlethal force against the crowd, followed FS procedures, and were consistent with their training and FS policy" (OIG, 2009: 4). A letter sent by John Twiss, the Director of the Forest Service's Law Enforcement and Investigations Division, to the officers involved in the incident commends them for "backing each other up and implementing the crowd control training you had been given" (Twiss, 2008). These statements get to the root of the problem. The Rainbow Gathering participants weren't the only victims. The law enforcement officers assigned to the Gathering were also victims of their own training, which positioned violence as their default behavior and fear as their blinding mindset. The end result was that Forest Service law enforcement administrators successfully effected a policy of violence against the Rainbow anarchs without actually stating such an indefensible policy.

This becomes increasingly clear when contrasting the behavior of federal government trained officers with local law enforcement officers who also come in contact with the Rainbow Family. At the 2008 Gathering, local Wyoming Sheriff's deputies also patrolled the Gathering area, separately from the Forest Service officers. Without suffering the heightened fear level that federal law enforcement leaders instilled in their troops, the locals were much better equipped, emotionally, to interface with the Rainbows on a rational level. Hence, for example, the day before terrified federal officers shot up Kiddie Village, local Sheriff's deputies joined hands with Rainbows in a Kiddie Village prayer circle. The local officers engaged in normal human to human interactions with the Rainbows, and when the need arose, successfully enrolled the assistance of Rainbow Family members in a search for a missing person. Stereotypically, many Americans tend not to expect Sheriff's deputies in one of the most remote and conservative regions of one of the most sparsely populated and conservative states to demonstrate more liberal and open-minded behavior than their better paid and presumably better educated and more professional federal compatriots. In practice, however, that was the case at the Gathering in Wyoming. It appears that the lack of training that the local sheriff's deputies received, better positioned them to effectively carry out their duties than the actual training that the federal officers received. Using the local law enforcement officers as a control group illuminates the negative impact of training on the federal officers.

While the Forest Service, with the cooperation of collaborators at the Associated Press, was successful in controlling the initial spin after the July 2008 Wyoming melee, they lost control of the story after the ACLU released their report in October condemning Forest Service actions. Around the same time, various streams of raw footage of the Forest Service LEOs shooting up Kiddie Village were going viral on the Internet. A month later, the Forest Service's Law Enforcement Director, John Twiss, who was on the ground in Wyoming personally overseeing law enforcement operations at the 2008 Rainbow Gathering, unexpectedly and unceremoniously resigned from the Forest Service, making no statement as to why he was leaving. His successor, David Ferrell, issued a legally questionable policy declaring that information pertaining to his agency's "type and frequency of training of law enforcement personnel," such as the information documenting his predecessor's training policies for officers serving at Rainbow Gatherings, should no longer be released to scholars or journalists in compliance with the federal Freedom of Information Act (FOIA) since release of such information "would interfere with the agency's accomplishment of mission" (Niman, 2011, in press). Or put another way, research like that presented in this chapter seem to be interfering with the agency's mission—at least with regard to the Rainbow Family.

The Forest Service's 38 year history with the Rainbow Family is essentially the repetition of the same experiment repeated with the same results proving the superior efficacy of nonviolent conflict resolution strategies over violent ones. In each cycle, the Forest Service escalates its violence until it finally results in some sort of humiliating episode where the agency fails to attain its compliance goals, creates some degree of chaos, and is ultimately exposed for systematically abusing a public it is chartered to serve. This failure is often followed by personnel reassignments and new less abusive, less violent and more effective strategies, which eventually devolve back into abusive, violent ineffective strategies as the cycle repeats itself yet again.

While academics schooled in a culture of experimentation might see these cycles as repetitive experiments, I suspect the actual bureaucrats repeatedly implementing these strategies don't see them as experiments at all. They, I argue, are simply acting out what they consciously or unconsciously see as the mandates of the civilized state model. The Rainbows, by contrast, are consciously replicating an egalitarian primitive nonkilling band society. The clash between these two cultures is inevitable, with the "civilized" society arrogantly seeing itself as the natural evolution of the "inferior" pre-pastoral society, which, as a state, they must control with their force/violence-backed laws. Hence, no matter how many times experimentation proves their violent tactics ineffective in gaining their officially stated goals, they persist with the same tactics. This, I believe, is because as I mention earlier, the very presence of the Rainbows constitutes a threat to the bureaucrats' very understanding of society, which they equate with the state model of civilization. And states have historically, since their creation, maintained their existence through the force of violence. This history predicts that the state will continue its cycles of violent repression against the Rainbows. The Family's TAZ strategy, coupled with their commitment to nonkilling, allow the Family to persist in the face of these attacks. This cycle is likely to replicate itself until the state eventually collapses, as states have historically always done. The reason for this collapse will likely have no direct connection with the Rainbow Family. The Rainbows, in the end, will be left standing simply because their model of organization is more durable than the state model. If we accept the Rainbow Family's claim to have inherited the heritage of a long lineage of previous band societies, then these nonkilling anarchs may have already outlived the violent state.

References

ACLU [American Civil Liberties Union] (2008) "Rainbow Family Gathering in Wyoming," *ACLU Wyoming Chapter*, Available at (consulted January 18, 2010): <http://www.aclu-wy.org/NewsEvents/PressReleases/10_8_08.pdf>.

Amster, Randall (2003). "Restoring (Dis)Order: Sanctions, Resolutions, and 'Social Control' in Anarchist Communities," *Contemporary Justice Review*, 6(1): 9-24

Beck,Garrick (1987). "Keeping the Peace," *All Most Broke*. Chicago: All Ways Free.

Bey, Hakim (1991). *T.A.Z.: The Temporary Autonomous Zone, Ontological Anarchy, Poetic Terrorism*. Brooklyn: Autonomedia.

Dentan, Robert Knox (1992). "The Rise, Maintenance and Destruction of Peaceable Polity; A Preliminary Essay in Political Ecology," in Silverberg, James; Gray, J. Patrick, Ed., *Aggression and Peacefulness in Humans and Other Primates*. New York: Oxford University Press, pp. 214-270.

Dentan, Robert Knox (1994). "'Surrendered Men': Peaceable Enclaves in the Post-Enlightenment West," in Sponsel, Leslie; Gregor, Thomas, Ed., *The Anthropology of Peace and Nonviolence*. Boulder: Lynne Rienner, pp. 69-108.

Dentan, Robert Knox (2008). *Overwhelming Terror: Love, Fear, Peace, And Violence Among Semai of Malaysia*. Lanham: Rowman & Littlefield.

Edo, Juli; Williams-Hunt, Anthony; Dentan, Robert Knox (2009). "'Surrender,' Peacekeeping, and Internal Colonialism: A Neglected Episode in Malaysian History," *Bijdragen tot de Taal, Land en Volkenkunde*, 165 (2-3): 216-240.

Fix, Alan G. (1975). "Fission-Fusion and Lineal Effect: Aspects of the Population Structure of the Semai Senoi of Malaysia," *American Journal of Physical Anthropology*, 43: 295-302.

FLETC [Federal Law Enforcement Training Center] (2009). "Law Enforcement Control Tactics Refresher Training Program," Available at (consulted January 9, 2010): <http://www.fletc.gov/training/programs>.

Erasmus, Charles J. (1981). "Anarchy, Enslavement, and Syntropy in International and Traditional Communities," in Castile, George Pierre; Kushner, Gilbert, Eds., *Persistent Peoples: Cultural Enclaves in Perspective.* Tucson: University of Arizona Press, pp. 192-211.

Kalafer, Jonathan (2009). *We Love You* [DVD]. Mendham: New Jersey Pictures.

Kropotkin, Peter (2002 [1877]). "Prisons and Their Moral Influence on Prisoners," in Baldwin, Roger N., Ed., *Anarchism: A Collection of Revolutionary Writings.* Mineola: Dover, pp. 230-235.

Neary, Ben. (2008). "Five Arrested in Rainbow Family Clash With Feds," *Associated Press* (Lexis-Nexis Universe), July 4.

Neel, J. V.; Salzano, F. M.; Junquerira, P. C.; Keiter, F.; Maybury, Lewis D. (1964). "Studies on the Xavante Indians of the Brazilian Mato Grosso," *American Journal of Human Genetics,* 16: 52-140.

Niman, Michael I. (1991). *The Rainbow Family: An Ethnography From Within* [PhD dissertation]. University at Buffalo.

Niman, Michael I. (1997). *People of the Rainbow: A Nomadic Utopia.* Knoxville: University of Tennessee Press.

Niman, Michael I. (2011, in press). *People of the Rainbow: A Nomadic Utopia,* Volume 2. Knoxville: University of Tennessee Press.

OIG [U.S. Department of Agriculture Office of Inspector General] (2009). *Use of Force Report.* February 27. Available at (consulted January 20, 2010): <http://www.buffalostate.edu/peopleoftherainbow/x520.xml>.

Paige, Glenn D. (2009 [2002]). *Nonkilling Global Political Science.* Honolulu: Center for Global Nonkilling.

Solnit, Rebecca (2009). *A Paradise Built in Hell: The Extraordinary Communities That Arise in Disaster.* New York: Viking.

Twiss, John C. (2008). "Letter," July 21. Available at (consulted January 20, 2010): <http://www.buffalostate.edu/peopleoftherainbow/x520.xml>.

USDA [United States Department of Agriculture Law Enforcement and Investigations] (2010). "Our Mission," Available at (April 17, 2010): <http://www.fs.fed.us/lei/>.

Wallace, Anthony (1956). *Revitalization Movements.* Indianapolis: Bobbs-Merrill. .

Chapter Eleven

Peaceful Islands
Insular Communities as Nonkilling Societies

Joám Evans Pim
Center for Global Nonkilling

Introduction

This essay explores the idea of insular peacefulness that is indicated based on the measurable premise of island communities in which killing is absent or statistically low. Insular peacefulness is explored in three sections. The first section presents the notion of a deep-rooted archetype of islands as places of freedom, wealth and peace which can be traced to mythological and historical constructions scattered through time and space. Ancient descriptions are followed by the late medieval and modern quest for lost insular paradises which are also depicted in fictional literary utopian accounts and contemporary libertarian seasteading projections and experiments. The concept of "Peace Island," following Ko, is also introduced to contextualize the case study sections.

Beyond utopian archetypes and realizations, the next section lays out three real insular communities that have been described as "peaceful" or "nonviolent" and that follow our criteria of being essentially killing-free islands. The three featured societies are Tristan da Cunha (British South Atlantic), Ifaluk (Micronesia) and Tahiti (Polynesia). Even if the strategies and structures of these remote and small communities are not necessarily applicable to larger insular populations,[1] they certainly support the idea of the possibilities for realizing nonkilling societies through revised socio-cultural heuristic models.

---

[1] As Younger (2008) indicates, size is a key factor to correlate peaceful societies: whereas isolated small communities (under 1,000), characterized by the relevance of face-to-face contact and ties, tend toward peacefulness, larger population groups tend to split and compete generating larger social and interpersonal conflicts. Kirch (1996 [1984]) draws similar conclusions based on comparative historical studies of Polynesian islands. (See Ch. 8, pp. 195-216) It is also important to note how foreign interference—or outright colonization—can have a disruptive impact, sometimes initiating or intensifying violence among native population and, otherwise, in the long term, halting it to foster State control. (See Ferguson and Whitehead, 1992)

The final section offers another four examples of larger islands that have defined themselves—through collective social imagination and/or intentional constructions—as "islands of peace," seeking to develop, position, and export their identity in the framework of insular cultures of peace, upon distinct bases within their historical, political, economic and cultural roots. The Åland Islands in Finland (one of the first demilitarized and neutralized territories in the world); the Islands of Hawai'i (with a fragile "equilibrium" of heavy militarization and a deep-seated traditional culture of peace and *aloha*); Jeju Island in Korea (with one of the most active programs for Peace Island development, even if located in a country still technically at war for the past sixty years) and the Canary Island of Lanzarote in Spain (a new international initiative for the diffusion of human rights and a culture of peace). All four examples illustrate through their commonalities the modern attempts for the realization of peaceful and peace-making cultures, programs and experiments from the standpoint of insular societies.

The Peaceful Islands Archetype

> The exemplary image of the whole creation is the Island that suddenly "manifests" itself amidst the waves. (Eliade, 1991: 151)

Insular constructions as places of abundance, freedom and peace are what Professor Mircea Eliade, the eminent historian of religion, described as "myths of eternal return," in which a distinct reality that portrays the celestial archetype is constantly sought. Following Mieiro, the mythical representations of Eden—in its diversity of cultural variations—have many times been transfigured into some lost island(s) in which the original affluence and happiness persists and are maintained intact (2001: 22). This "archetypical tradition of universal mythemes that survive in culture and religion" share the common feeling of "nostalgia over the loss of the primordial paradise" (Mieiro, 2001: 12). The continuation of this tradition through various forms of social and political utopianism persists to our day and is closely linked to the peaceful island archetype. In this section, the quest for insular utopias and their characterization as peaceful societies is explored.

Utopian archetypes generally represent simple forms of society that live in harmony with nature and provide all of their members with abundant resources while avoiding forms of suffering derived from hunger, war, disease, painful labour, oppression and injustice. In contrast with the Hobbesian view of human nature which is still dominant in Western thought, insular utopias are more in tune with Rousseau's idea of the peaceful "noble savage." Considering humans lived exclusively as hunter-gatherers for roughly 99% of their existence (Hart and Sussman, 2009), a form of society that not only tends to have relatively nonhierarchical and egalitarian structures but that is also "grounded in an ethos of routine cooperation, reciprocity, and nonviolent conflict resolution" (Sponsel, 2009: 38), it is tempting to infer the possible origin of these persistent archetypes is based on the biocultural history of our species—although this is not to say that all egalitarian societies are necessarily peaceful. As Sponsel (2009) points out, hunter-gatherer culture epitomizes the attributes of nonkilling societies supporting the basis for nonkilling human capabilities through revised socio-cultural heuristic models. Utopian thinking offers a door toward creative renovation of mental structures through new and innovative political, economic and moral structures that support peaceful, equitable and just societies (Mieiro, 2001: 47).

The idea of insular utopias has certainly been present since antiquity. Timaeus' (ca. 345-ca. 250 BCE) descriptions of the Island of Atlantis (recollected in one of Plato's dialogues) and the diverse accounts of the Fortunate Isles (or Isles of the Blessed) by authors such as Flavius Philostratus, Plutarch, Strabo, Pliny or Ptolemy, all point to the vision of earthly paradises of happiness and abundance (thus their linkages with the Elysium). In Celtic, Germanic and Nordic mythologies the islands of Annwn/Annwfn and Avalon (Wales), Tír na nÓg and St. Brendan (Ireland), Brittia (Low Countries), Buyan (Slavic), etc., are all portrayed as mysterious places of abundance somewhere in between the realm of the living and the otherworld. Other civilizations also featured similar mythological constructions as the Chinese "Tao Hua Yuan" (桃花源) or Turtle Island Iroquois Creation Myth, for example (Mohawk, 2005). As Ferreira (1999: 13) explains, Christianity was unable to erase these deeply-held beliefs in Europe and chose to assimilate them as Edenic vestiges. The late medieval and early modern surge of oceanic explorations brought new attention to these rogue islands, now framed somewhat vaguely as the Antillia, the Isle of Seven Cities, St. Brandan, the Isle of Brazil (from the Gaelic *Uí Breasail*, see Donnard, 2009; Westropp, 1912), Satanazes or Saya, sometimes represented as one single island but mostly as a constellation of isles scattered along the great and still unknown Atlantic. Many contemporary geographers of that era describe these islands as utopian commonwealths based on the exuberant abundance of wealth and the absence of evils and disease. (See Fererreira, 1999: 19-20)

These insular archetypes were eventually translated into fictional representations that had a strong impact on literary history. To mention a few early examples (16ᵗʰ and 17ᵗʰ cc.) a necessary point of departure is Thomas More's *Utopia* (*Libellus vere aureus, nec minus salutaris quam festivus, de optimo rei publicae statu deque nova insula Utopia*), published in 1516. *Utopia* is a fictional description of an ideal insular society characterized through its social and political customs and institutions. This is not a form of primitive society but rather an advanced industrial civilization that incorporates innovations such as the welfare state in which unemployment, private property and hunger have been eradicated. More indicates that *Utopia* does not represent his personal view of a "perfect society" but offers a point of departure for an in-depth debate on the social and political problems of his time. Indeed, in spite of the lack of theft and physical punishment, ideas such as a death penalty, slavery and euthanasia are contemplated in Utopia, and so is the hiring of mercenaries for defence.

Luís Vaz de Camões also includes a utopian island (the "*Ilha dos Amores*", or "Isle of Love") in his epic *Os Lusíadas* (*The Lusiads*), published in 1572 and bringing a fantasized Homeric description of the 15ᵗʰ and 16ᵗʰ cc. Portuguese oceanic explorations (*Canto* IX). The island offers a "model society in which war, suffering, pain and daily fatigue are absent" (Ferreira, 1999: 65), clearly inspired by his country's veiled seafaring quest for the Fortunate Isles, Antillia and the Isle of Seven Cities. (See Mieiro, 2001: 53-60; Ferreira, 1999: 62-66.) Similarly, Cervates features in the second part (ch. XLV) of his *Don Quixote* (1615) the "Ínsula Barataria," awarded to Sancho Panza, who rules the island in and utopian and peaceful fashion. (See Avalle Arce, 1988.) Tommaso Campanella's *The City of the Sun* (*Civitas Solis*) is another early utopian work (written in 1602), also inspired by Plato's *Republic*, as was More's *Utopia*. Following Timaeus' vision of the Island of Atlantis, Campanella idealizes a theocratic insular commonwealth in which goods are shared and war is unlikely, in spite of the heavy militaristic social organization. Francis Bacon's 1627 *New Atlantis* (*Nova Atlantis*) takes place in Bensalem Island, surrounded by the waters of the Pacific. This utopian society could be described as a "scientocracy" characterized by the generosity, enlightenment, dignity and piety of its members.

The search for alternative societies in the oceans has taken new directions in the 21ˢᵗ century, with innovative and sometimes controversial proposals such as seasteading, which incorporate much of the utopian insular tradition. The idea of developing permanent homesteading in the oceans, beyond the Exclusive Economic Zone of any country, has been pushed forward by The Seasteading Institute (<http://seasteading.org>), founded in 2008 by Wayne Gramlich and Patri Friedman with the mission of furthering

"the establishment and growth of permanent, autonomous ocean communities, enabling innovation with new political and social systems" (Friedman and
Gramlich, 2009). Social and political experimentation outside the sovereign
boundaries of any existing country would lead to new forms of seasteading
nations based on libertarian values, even though not all proposed "freedoms"
would necessarily be considered peaceful. Some commentators raise concerns about the challenges of class structures in these proposals.

Happiness, generosity and peacefulness are a shared discourse in insular
utopias and archetypes. The vision of islands as a place for peace is also
widely spread. A leading example is the contemporary formulation of the
"Peace Island" concept which is the result of Dr. Chang Hoon Ko works,
initiated in 1999 and specially focused on Jeju Island and its Peace Island Forum that has been active since 2001. (See Ko et al., 2004.) Ko argues that
islands are a "healthy unit" for the creation of cultures of peace within the
oceans, in contrast with peninsular and continental nations that encounter a
number of setbacks. Island values, attitudes, lifestyles and worldviews contribute toward a unique insular culture of peace philosophy that needs to be
shared with others around the globe (Ko, 2010, personal communication).
The two following sections are relevant to this argument.

Nonkilling Insular Communities

This section presents three cases of insular communities that have been
characterized as "peaceful" or "nonviolent" by the academic literature in
the social sciences, all featured in the online *Encyclopedia of Selected
Peaceful Societies*[2] and that have the commonality of having an absence of
or very rare occurrence of killing within their societies. As the title of the
Encyclopedia indicates, this is just a selection of societies and certainly other
cases could be included. (For a wider set of peaceful insular communities
see Younger, 2008.[3]) Still, the three examples sketched below (Tristan da
Cunha, Ifaluk and Tahiti) provide an interesting chart of real and consistent
examples of the peaceful island "utopia" with various geographic and demographic backgrounds: from the cold seas of the South Atlantic to the tropical
Pacific waters of Micronesia and Polynesia; from the few hundred inhabitants

---

[2] See <http://www.peacefulsocieties.org>.
[3] Among Polynesian islands that could be considered peaceful due to absence of internal violence and war (both aspects quantified as zero) Younger features Nu-
kuoro, Sikaiana, Nukufetau, Funafuti, Nanumaga, Nui, Nukulaelae, Vaitupu, Kapin-
gamarangi and Manihiki/Rakahanga (2008: 928).

of Tristan and Ifaluk to the several thousands of Tahiti. Either way, these examples illustrate the possibilities for the realization of nonkilling insular societies through a variety of social, cultural and psychological mechanisms that tend to nurture conflict prevention, dispute resolution and overarching peacefulness among integrated communities.

Tristan da Cunha

Tristan da Cunha is a remote volcanic island located in the South Atlantic and integrated in the British overseas territory of Saint Helena, Ascension and Tristan da Cunha. Its 275 inhabitants (2009[4]) are descendants of the first European settlers that founded the community in 1817, 300 years after the discovery of the island by Portuguese explorer Tristão da Cunha. The first permanent inhabitants sought "an utopian community based on the principles of communal ownership, absolute equality, and freedom from governmental control" (Munch, 1964: 369).

The main economic activities are still subsistence farming and fishing. Land is communally owned while joint ownership applies to longboats, cattle, apple orchards and huts, setting a firm basis for individually selective and reciprocal cooperative and mutual aid practices (Munch and Marske, 1981: 166-167). Income is complemented with local labour at a lobster packing factory set up in 1950 (Munch, 1964: 371) and administrative functions. Even though currency (and electricity) was introduced in World War II, traditional reciprocity is still highly valued for insular social and economic relations. (See Munch, 1970.)

Although an appointed Administrator acts as head of government and a partially elected Council also performs advisory functions, society is still supported by "largely independent family units tied together by bilateral kinship and mutual recognition, but without any formal authority or control" (Munch, 1964: 370). Munch and Marske (1981) referred to this societal model as an "atomistic community" where cooperation extends to all aspects of life "creating a continuous network of overlapping and interlocking interpersonal obligations, and tying the community together in what we describe as "atomistic social integration"" (1981: 163).

This "aggregate of independent households" (Munch and Marske, 1981: 165) has nevertheless developed into a community characterized by "[k]indness, considerateness, and respect for another person's individual integrity" (id.), where deviance from these principles implies a severe loss of social prestige. Not only are there no records of killings ever taking place

---

[4] See <http://news.bbc.co.uk/2/hi/africa/country_profiles/6748187.stm>.

but there also haven't been fights in living memory (Bonta, n/d): "The person who lost his temper in a quarrel would have that scar on his reputation for life, while someone who diffused a tense situation with a joke would gain general respect." Freedom, personal integrity, equality, peacefulness and anarchy are other values the community takes pride of, also celebrating its "lack of crime, strife, or status distinctions" (id.).

Ifaluk

Ifaluk (or Ifalik) is a small coral atoll in the State of Yap, Federated States of Micronesia. In 2002 it had a population of just over 500, whose primary economic activities were fishing and taro crops, articulated mainly through sharing and cooperative work (Lutz, 1990: 210). The introduction of US currency has been extremely disruptive, as it tends not be shared as all other goods, leading to "emotional ambiguity and conflict" (Lutz, 1990: 212).

Ifaluk society is articulated through a "strong taboo on interpersonal violence or disrespect" (Lutz, 1990: 205). Conflicts are usually dealt with within the immediate family or lineage even though a council of traditional leaders representing the Island's clans arbiters an "informal code of law" (id.) and deliberates in island-wide meetings (*toi*). The response of these leaders is taken as guidance on moral attitudes and emotions toward conflicts and disruptions (Lutz, 1990: 208-209).

The taboo over violence is expressed through the concept *song*, that could be roughly translated as "justifiable anger." *Song* operates as a pro-social concept that regulates behaviour identifying those attitudes that transgress societal values, especially those related to sharing and cooperation. *Song* not only anticipates and prevents violent outbursts—interpersonal violence is "virtually non-existent on the island," (Lutz, 1990: 224)—but serves as an anticipatory system for conflict prevention as behaviour is modelled seeking the avoidance of *song*. As Lutz explains "to become 'justifiably angry' is to advance the possibilities for peace and wellbeing on the island, for it is to identify instances of behaviour that threaten the moral order" (1990: 206). Mallon and Stich (1999) actually argued that anger itself does not exist in Ifaluk, and Marshall (1994) interestingly points out that "[p]ersonal competence in these societies [small face-to-face communities] is contingent upon a continually demonstrated ability to respond to others." Nevertheless, historical studies have also pointed out that Ifaluk has not always sustained peaceful relations with its neighbouring islands, something that must be considered. (For violence in the pre-contact Caroline Islands see Younger, 2009.)

Tahiti

Tahiti is one of the main islands of the so-called French Polynesia, officially an "Overseas Country Inside the [French] Republic" (*Pays d'outre-mer au sein de la République*), holding the seat of the autonomous government (in Papeete) and most of the territory's population. The Kingdom of Tahiti survived as a French protectorate until the forced abdication of King Pomare V in 1880, and has since been an integral part of France. In 2007 the island had 178,133 inhabitants,[5] most of which remain ethnically unmixed in spite the notable presence of inhabitants with European and Asian ancestry. In this paper, we will focus on traditional Tahitian society as studied by Levy (1969, 1973, 1978). For more recent social developments see Lockwood (1993).

As in other Polynesian societies, Tahitian traditional economic activities consisted of fishing, livestock and horticulture, where sharing and cooperation had great relevance. Aggression and open hostility are rare within this society and the display of anger is very uncommon as "Tahitians believe that hostile feelings should be brought quickly out into the open verbally; if not, resulting explosions of open anger could provoke the spirits of the ancestors to retaliate and perhaps even kill the angry individual" (Bonta, n/d). Violence is prevented through a number of social mechanisms including controlled dramatic events in which conflict is expressed symbolically, even though usually avoidance strategies prevail. Nevertheless, this had certainly not always been the case as historical accounts of warfare in the past show (see Wrangham and Peterson, 1997, ch. 5).

In spite of the presence of a large military contingent and increasing numbers of Europeans and Asians through much of the 20th century, official records show that between 1900 and 1962 serious crimes were reduced to two murders, one taking place in 1928 and the other in 1953 (Levy, 1973: 277). Not only is crime low but also interpersonal violence in all forms: "The fear of the consequences of anger, of hostility, of violence—with little apparent experience of such consequences—is noteworthy" (Levy, 1973: 284). In fact, Levy correlates low crime rates with the "pervasive lack of violence in everyday life" (p. 279) that characterizes Tahitian "gentleness."

Insular Cultures of Peace

In this section four cases in which insular cultures of peace have been or are being developed are presented: Åland, Jeju, Hawai'i and Lanzarote.

---

[5] See Institut de la statistique de la Polynésie française <http://www.ispf.pf>.

Even though all four cases have significant commonalities, including past traumatic experiences and multicultural backgrounds, significant differences arise. While Åland has been privileged with a demilitarized and neutralized status for over a century, Hawai'i has suffered an increasing militarization for the same period, transforming the Islands into a target (both in the past—Pearl Harbor in WWII—and in the present). Jeju, on the other hand, seeks to build itself as an island of peace within a country that is still technically at war. Finally, Lanzarote—that, as Hawai'i, saw its indigenous population reduced close to complete extinction—is strategically and symbolically located in the North-South divide, seeking to provide a bridge between the two based on peace and conflict resolution.

Other insular peace initiatives could certainly be mentioned, such as the Alcatraz Conversion Project and its associated Global Peace Center (initiated in 1978 with a focus on indigenous sacred spaces), San Simão (or Simón) Island in Galiza, a Spanish Civil War concentration camp that was to be converted into a Center for the Preservation of Historical Memory (of war victims), the Bermudas and its Society for Nonviolence and Peace; or Spitsbergen Island in the Norwegian Arctic, an effectively neutralized territory that also hosts the so-called "Svalbard Global Seed Vault" (the proposal of converting it into an Arctic Peace Island is credited to Professor Magnus Haavelsrud). Nevertheless, only four cases mentioned above were brought forward considering their significance, diversity and scope.

Åland Islands

The Åland Islands are a Baltic archipelago with political autonomy within Finland and a majority of monolingual Swedish-speaking population. Its demilitarization in 1856 after the Crimean War (Article 33 of the Treaty of Paris), made it one of the first areas of this kind in the world, also being a neutralised territory that necessarily must be kept out of the theater of operations in the event of war. This condition has significantly shaped Ålandic culture, especially since the prohibition of all military activity and conscription in the islands was confirmed in 1921 by the League of Nations and political autonomy granted by Finland (Kainen and Horn, 1997; Eriksson, 2006). In fact, Ålanders frequently refer to their archipelago as the "Islands of Peace," symbolically reaffirmed in the insular motto and even a blended nationalities flag.

The Åland example of neutrality, autonomy and demilitarization as a model for the resolution of territorial disputes has been suggested as an alternative to stagnated conflicts such as those of Kashmir (Bano, 2007: 90-91), Nagorno-Karabakh (Ziyadov, 2007), Kosovo (Republic of Serbia, 2007), Zanzibar,

Kalingrad (Vesa, 2009), etc. As Vesa (2009: 56) explains, the "full protection of minority rights and sufficient autonomy taking into account the historical, local and cultural conditions" jointly with the "positive role of third parties as mediators and the responsiveness toward each others' interests and values" are essential components—together with the already mentioned neutrality, autonomy and demilitarization—of the Ålandic peacemaking approach.

The Government of Åland has been an active promoter of the Ålandic example as a working model for minority issues and crisis management, seeking to influence international organizations and actors (Granlund, 2010; Bailes et al., 2007). This effort is especially visible through the Åland Islands Peace Institute (*Ålands fredsinstitut*) founded in 1992 as an independent charitable foundation. The "Åland Example" is the overarching focus that reaches out through the Institute's research areas: minority-related issues, autonomy and self-government, and security through demilitarisation, conflict management and nonviolence. (See <http://www.peace.ax>.)

The Institute serves on the one hand as an interdisciplinary meeting place for Åland, the Nordic countries and the Baltic Sea region and focal point for the promotion of culture of peace within the Islands, bringing peace education to schools, authorities and the general public. The Finnish Ministry of Foreign affairs, in its peacemaking efforts, has also organized institutional visits to Åland for representatives of regions affected by conflict that could seek inspiration in the Islands history and approach.

Jeju Island

Jeju Island is located in the Korea Strait between the Korean mainland and Japan and is the only special autonomous province of the Republic of Korea. From the late 1940s to the mid 1950s the island witnessed extreme violence linked to the April 3rd Rebellion in which some 30,000 people were killed. By the end of the 1990s local scholar Dr. Chang Hoon Ko introduced the concept of "Peace Island" and in 2001 the Peace Island Forum was initiated in Jeju, as part of the efforts of the World Association for Island Studies. As a result, in 2005 Jeju was declared a "World Peace Island" by the Korean Government and a privileged setting for experiences of rapprochement between the two Koreas and human rights promotion with special focus on minorities and the environment (Jeju Development Institute, 2006: 5).

Since, Jeju has been a focal point for the development of the "Peace Island" idea. It has hosted the "Peace Island *Bulteok* Forum" on an annual basis (this year [2010] the 10th edition will take place), the Peace Island Tribunal, the Peace Island Culture Olympics, the Peace Island Film Festival, regional peace education trainings and a four-week "World Environment and Peace Summer School" featuring courses on human rights, international relations, governance, environmental leadership, marine tourism economy, climate change studies, cultural heritage and tourism, peace education and media, among other subjects (Ko et al., 2004; Ko, 2010, personal communication).

In 2010 (November 1-3) Jeju will also be hosting the Islands 20 (I-20) Summit focused on peace, the environment and oceanic tourism. The Summit seeks to establish a new alliance (United Islands and Cities for World Environment and Peace) bringing together a number of islands and low-lying coastal cities, that are symbolically linked to environmental and peace values. Proposed insular membership includes Jeju, Hainan Sao, Okinawa, Bali, Kinmen, Lakshadweep Islands, Fiji, Maui (Hawai'i), Galápagos, Tasmania, Spitzbergen, Crete, Majorca, Mauritius, Madagascar, Prince Edward Island, the Isle of Man, Sakhalin, Bahrain and Åland. Cities include Hiroshima, Hanoi, Christchurch (New Zealand), San José (Costa Rica), Stockholm, Cape Town and Boston (Massachusetts). One of the expected outcomes is a Peace Island Initiative Resolution (I-20 Resolution) addressing the challenges an opportunities for island societies.

Beyond these activities, Jeju is looking into sustaining the Peace Islands Initiative through an island-based World Environmental University and associated entrepreneurial programs such as a "Peace Island Cruise Tour" through participating islands and cities (Jeju, Kinmen, Hainan, Hanoi, Kerala, Bali, Tasmania, Fiji, Maui, Okinawa, Hiroshima, etc.) (Ko, 2010, personal communication).

Hawai'i

Hawai'i is a well-known archipelago in the Central Pacific, currently administered as a U.S. State but that remained independent as a monarchy until the overthrow of Queen Lili'uokulani in 1893 (Silva, 2004). Even though the Islands suffered an increased militarization since the turn of the 19th century— especially visible since World War II and the establishment of the U.S. Pacific Command in O'ahu—Hawai'i's nickname is the "Aloha State," referring to the so-called spirit of *Aloha*, that can be translated as "peace" or "love" (Ulukau, 2004). Even though Polynesian peaceful traditions have possibly been over-romanticized somewhat ignoring the strong feudal and warrior culture that existed in the islands before their westernization (for another view see Dukas, 2004), the idea of Hawai'i as the "Geneva of the Pacific" (Ikuma, 2004: 17), a place for meeting, has a wide acceptance and has been supported by the State government and promoted by organizations such as the Center for Global Nonkilling and the Matsunaga Institute for Peace.

Hawai'i is both a "war island" and a "peace island." It hosts not only a large military contingent throughout land, sea and air force bases and installations but also a very large percentage of veteran population (over 118,000 in 2008; U.S. Census Bureau, 2010), partially responsible for the State's high suicide rates (approximately 9 per 100,000; id.). This makes Hawai'i, in many aspects, a retirement gift similar to what Roman legionaries were granted with on the completion of their term of service, also serving as place for healing for those wounded in battle. The military accounts for a substantial portion of the Islands income and this close tie is symbolically enshrined by the many war monuments, memorials and museums (Pearl Harbor, Battleship Missouri, Punchbowl National Cemetery, Army Museum, etc.).[6]

On the other hand, Hawai'i's peace traditions are an important part of the Islands' heritage. Queen Lili'uokalani's opposition to armed resistance during the overthrow of the Hawaiian Kingdom and her peaceful struggle during the following decades seeded the basis for the Hawaiian nonviolent sovereignty movement that reemerged during the sixties. The movement's vision of a restored Hawaiian society incorporates many of the Island's traditional values as *laulima* (cooperative work for the common good); *pono* (righteous justice); *lokahi* (harmony in unity); *ho'okipa* (hospitality); *lokomaika'i* (generosity and goodwill); *kokua* (mutual help); *'ohana* (extended family); *aloha 'aina* (love for the land); *malama* (care for each other) and *aloha* (love and peace) (Guanson, 1991: 9). Interestingly, the monopoly over violence imposed by the United States meant that most aggressive aspects of traditional culture where erased—as they would harm the interests of the State—while the peaceful facets of the same culture where allowed

---

[6] Note that some "Peace monuments," even though fairly unknown, are also present. Among them: Hawai'i Peace Memorial (1986), Kennedy Theatre, Mānoa Campus, University of Hawai'i, Honolulu, O'ahu; Mohandas Gandhi's statue (1990) in Kapiolani Park, Waikīkī, O'ahu, given to the city by the Gandhi Memorial International Foundation; the Leahi Millennium Peace Garden (2000), Diamond Head, Honolulu, O'ahu, "[c]reated by teens from around the globe to promote peace and cultural understanding and now stands as a symbol of solidarity and hope" or the "Plant Peace" Mural (2006), Leahi Millennium Peace Garden, Diamond Head, Honolulu, O'ahu. The "Peace Bells" scattered through the islands are also worth noticing, including those of the Byodo-In Temple, Valley of the Temples, O'ahu; Nani Mau Gardens, Hilo, Hawai'i; Hiroshima Peace Bell, Izumo Taisha Mission, North Kukui Street, Honolulu, O'ahu and Nagasaki Peace Bell, Honolulu Hale (City Hall), Honolulu, O'ahu.

to continue[7], even if in a heavily merchandized form, that sovereignty and cultural movements are attempting to surpass.

Hawaiian traditions as that of the *pu 'uhonua*, places of refuge[8] "within no blood can be shed nor unkind word spoken" (Guanson, 1991: 11), provided basis for rethinking the islands as a zone of peace, "a place of refuge for all to go for renewal and protection" (id.). *DMZ Hawai'i / Aloha 'Aina*, a network[9] of organizations and individuals working to counter the military's negative social, cultural and environmental impacts in the islands, is one example of the combination of environmental, indigenous and peace struggles in Hawai'i, confronting military expansion and "promoting the development of environmentally sustainable, socially just and culturally appropriate economic alternatives" for the islands.[10]

The Center for Global Nonkilling's "Nonkilling Hawai'i" project is also akin to these efforts, envisioning the Islands as a working model for modern killing-free societies. Its comprehensive approach includes the promotion of leadership development, research/discovery, education/training, and policy/action initiatives. Among these, the First Global Nonkilling Leadership Academy held in October 2009, the 2009 and 2010 Interdisciplinary Nonkilling Research Seminars convened at the University of Hawai'i at Mānoa, or the Nonkilling Hawai'i Advisory Council (that includes representatives from a wide array of public and private organizations), are some recent examples. (For more on nonkilling, see Paige, 2009; Evans Pim, ed., 2009.)

Lanzarote

Lanzarote is the easternmost of the Canary Islands, a Spanish autonomous archipelago in the Atlantic Ocean. The whole island is a UNESCO Biosphere Reserve and has a long history of settlements from diverse cultural backgrounds, following its strategic location between the Canary Islands and the African continent (just 100 Km away from the coast). Re-

---

[7] For this observation I am grateful to Professor Stephen M. Younger.

[8] Preserved historical *pu'uhonua* include the *pu'uhonua o Hōnaunau*, Hawai'i National Historical Park. (See <http://www.nps.gov/puho/planyourvisit/the-puuhonua.htm>.)

[9] Groups that have been active in the network include: the American Friends Service Committee Hawai'i Area Program, 'Ohana Koa / NFIP, Malu 'Aina, Ka Pakaukau, KAHEA, Life of the Land, Malama Makua, Hui Malama o Makua, 'Ilio'ulaokalani, Hui Ho'okipa, Save UH / Stop UARC Coalition, Kipuka, Na Imi Pono, Kaua'i Alliance for Peace and Social Justice, and World Can't Wait.

[10] See <http://www.dmzhawaii.org/?page_id=2>.

cently, a strong proposal for establishing an "International Zone for Human Rights and a Culture of Peace" (*Zona Internacional para la Cultura de Paz y los Derechos Humanos*) has been brought forward by local and national authorities, to be maintained by a Foundation under the same name. (See <http://zonainternacionaldepaz.org>.)

The proposal is intended to transform the island into a meeting-point for peoples and States seeking understanding and conflict prevention through the use of dialogue and negotiation. The project is based on three central axes, that are to be developed combining local and global actions in the areas of human rights, sustainable development and corporate social responsibility. The initiative builds upon previous experiences as the "*Navegantes por la Paz*" ("Sailors for Peace") UNESCO Associated Schools Programme or the Spanish Network for the Global Compact (<http://www.pactomundial.org>) on corporate responsibility.

The new Foundation is intended to merge research, action and sensitization under the principles of peace, democracy, equality toward global disarmament, conflict prevention and resolution and human security. Beyond promoting cultures of peace in the islands the project seeks to establish an international role for Lanzarote as an active agent of peace. Former UNESCO Secretary-General Federico Mayor Zarogoza recently committed to take the proposal for the establishment of an "International Zone for Human Rights and a Culture of Peace" to the UN General Assembly, and in July 21, 2010 the Spanish Senate unanimously approved a motion in support of the project.[11]

Final Remarks

In his keynote address to the 6th Peace Island Forum: "Security and Peace in Island Societies" (Jeju, July 6-7, 2006), Professor Glenn D. Paige posed the question "Is a nonkilling island society possible?" Paige offers a series of public policy, economic, educational and security recommendations for island development following historical, scientific, social, cultural, spiritual, etc. grounds for confidence on the realization of nonkilling insular societies. Taking into account the second section of this article and considering Kenneth E. Boulding's "First Law" ("Anything that exists is possible", in *Stable Peace*, 1972), the obvious answer to Paige's question is "Yes!".

---

[11] See *El Mundo* (21/07/2010), "El Gobierno impulsará a Lanzarote como Zona Internacional de Paz y Derechos"; *ABC* (22/07/2010); "El Senado apuesta por crear en las Islas una Zona para la Paz".

The other two sections in this article provide further evidence that this possibility has been permanently recollected in human consciousness through the ages, forging a deep-rooted individual and collective archetype of islands as places for peaceful and sustainable development of human existence. This vision and quest—possibly originated in the reminiscences of the biocultural history of our species—not only emerges in utopian literary fictions (some of which have been mentioned) but have constantly been pushed forward as a feasible reality, evident in late medieval and modern oceanic explorations, contemporary seasteading experiments and actual island-based cultures of peace realizations as those presented in the final section.[12] Navigating the future seas to islands where there is no more killing will be fascinating.

Acknowledgments

For comments on a draft of this paper I am indebted to Glenn D. Paige, Glenda H. Paige, Stephen M. Younger, Leslie E. Sponsel, Thomas A. Fee, Balwant Bhaneja, Katherine Li and Robley George. The many shortcomings still present remain my own responsibility. I am also grateful to Alberto Vieira for allowing the presentation and discussion of the initial draft of this work at the International Conference on Islands: "The Islands of the World and the World of Islands", CEHA, Madeira (Portugal), July 26-30, 2010.

References

Avalle Arce, Juan Bautista (1988). "La Ínsula Barataria: la forma de su relato," *Anales de Literatura Española*, 6: 33-44.
Bacon, Francis (1901 [1626]). *New Atlantis*. New York: P.F. Collier & Son. Available at: <http://oregonstate.edu/instruct/phl302/texts/bacon/atlantis.html>.
Bailes, Alyson JK; Bring, Ove; Robins, Graham; Sundback, Barbro (2007). *Åland – fredens öar? Rapport från seminarium den 19.10.2006 på Armémuseum i Stockholm*. Mariehamn: Åland Islands Peace Institute.
Bano, Sara (2007). "Solution of Kashmir Dispute and Possibilities for Peace," *Asteriskos*, 3/4: 85-101.

---

[12] As Ko (2010, personal communication) explains, peace islands are a "healthy working model," and also a metaphor that can be exported to non-insular communities. I extremely appreciate Les Sponsel's idea of (re)thinking of peace islands beyond geographical constructions, as certainly many peaceful communities and areas (such as the Amish experiences or several international peace parks as those of Costa Rica with its neighbours) can be considered enclaves or "continental peace islands".

Bonta, Bruce D. (n/d). "Tahitians," in *Encyclopedia of Selected Peaceful Societies*. Available online at: <http://www.peacefulsocieties.org/Society/Tahitians.html>.

Bonta, Bruce D. (n/d). "Tristan Islanders," in *Encyclopedia of Selected Peaceful Societies*. Available online at: <http://www.peacefulsocieties.org/Society/Tristan.html>.

Camões, Luís Vaz de (1572). *Os Lusíadas*. Lisboa: Antonio Gonçalves Impressor. Available at: <http://purl.pt/1/1/>.

Campanella, Tommaso (1901 [1602]). *The City of the Sun*. New York: P.F. Collier & Son. Available at <http://ebooks.adelaide.edu.au/c/campanella/tommaso/c18c/>.

Donnard, Ana (2009). "O outro mundo dos celtas atlânticos e a mítica Brasil, ilha dos afortunados: primeiras abordagens," *Nuntius Antiquus*, 3: 14-28

Dukas, Neil Bernard (2004). *A Military History of Sovereign Hawai'i*. Honolulu: Hawaiian Historical Society.

Eliade, Mircea (1991). *Images and symbols: studies in religious symbolism*. Princeton: Princeton University Press.

Eriksson, Susanne; Johansson, Lars Ingmar; Sundback, Barbro (2006). *Islands of Peace. Åland's autonomy, demilitarisation and neutralisation*. Mariehamn: Åland Islands Peace Institute.

Evans Pim, Joám, Ed. (2009). *Toward a Nonkilling Paradigm*. Honolulu: Center for Global Nonkilling. Available at: <http://www.nonkilling.org/node/18>.

Ferguson, R. Brian; Whitehead, Neil L. (1992). *War in the tribal zone: expanding states and indigenous warfare*. Santa Fe: School of American Research Press.

Ferreira, Maria Isabel Rodrigues (1999). *Mitos e utopias na descoberta e construção do mundo atlântico*. Funchal: Centro de Estudos de História do Atlântico.

Friedman, Patri; Gramlich, Wayne (2009). *Seasteading: A Practical Guide to Homesteading the High Seas*. Palo Alto: The Seasteading Institute. Available at: <http://seasteading.org/seastead.org/book_beta/index.html>.

George, Robley E. (2010). "Socioeconomic Democracy: A Nonkilling, Life-Affirming and Enhancing Psycho-Politico-Socio-Economic System," *Global Nonkilling Working Papers*, 4. Available at: <http://www.nonkilling.org/>.

Granlund, John (2010). "Det internationella kortet. Altruism och egennytta som skäl till att föra fram Ålandsexemplet," *Rapport från Ålands fredsinstitut / Report from the Åland Islands Peace Institute*, 2/2010.

Guanson, Lou Ann Ha'aheo (1991). "Hawaiian," in Paige, Glenn D.; Gilliatt, Sarah, eds., *Nonviolence in Hawai'i's Spiritual Traditions*. Honolulu: Center for Global Nonviolence Planning Project, Spark M. Matsunaga Institute for Peace, University of Hawai'i at Manoa, p. 1-12. Available at: <http://www.nonkilling.org/node/18>.

Hart, Donna; Sussman, Robert W. (2009). *Man the Hunted: Primates, Predators, and Human Evolution*. Boulder: Westview Press.

Ikuma, Edmond K. (2004). "The question of an office of international affairs," *Legislative Reference Bureau Report*, 1 (2004).

Jeju Development Institute (2006). *Building a Northeast Asian Community: Toward peace and prosperity*. Yonsei: Yonsei University Press.

Kainen, Lauri Hanni; Horn, Frank, eds. (1997). *Autonomy and demilitarization in International Law: The Aland Islands in a Changing Europe.* Den Haag: Martinus Nijhoff.

Ko Sŏng-jun, et al. (2004). *Tong Asia wa p'yŏnghwa ŭi sŏm Chej [Peace in East Asia, Peace Island Jeju].* Cheju-si: Cheju Taehakkyo Ch'ulp'anbu.

Levy, Robert I. (1969). "On Getting Angry in the Society Islands," in Caudill William; Tsung-Yi Lin, Eds. *Mental Health Research in Asia and the Pacific.* Honolulu: East-West Center Press, pp. 358-380.

Levy, Robert I. (1973). *Tahitians: Mind and Experience in the Society Islands.* Chicago: University of Chicago Press.

Levy, Robert I. (1978). "Tahitian Gentleness and Redundant Controls," in Montagu, Ashley, Ed. *Learning Non-Aggression: The Experience of Non-Literate Societies.* New York: Oxford University Press, pp. 222-235.

Lockwood, Victoria S. (1993). *Tahitian Transformation: Gender and Capitalist Development in a Rural Society.* Boulder: Lynne Rienner.

Loudon, J. B. (1970). "Teasing and Socialization on Tristan da Cunha," in Mayer, Philip, Ed., *Socialization: The Approach from Social Anthropology.* London: Tavistock, pp. 193-332.

Lutz, Catherine (1988). *Unnatural Emotions: Everyday Sentiments on a Micronesian Atoll and Their Challenge to Western Theory.* Chicago: University of Chicago Press.

Lutz, Catherine (1990). "Morality, Domination and Understandings of 'Justifiable Anger' among the Ifaluk," in Semin, Gün R.; Gergen, Kenneth J., Eds., *Everyday Understanding: Social and Scientific Implications.* London: Sage, pp. 204-226.

Mallon, Ronald; Stich, Stephen (2000). "The Odd Couple: The Compatibility of Social Construction and Evolutionary Psychology," *Philosophy Of Science*, 67(1): 133-154.

Marshall, Mac (1994). "Social Isolation, Cultural Competence, and Disability in the Carolines," *Micronesian Counselor*, 13. Available online at: <http://www.micsem.org/pubs/counselor/frames/socisofr.htm>.

Mieiro, Elisabete Maria Costa (2001). *A atlantização mítica do Éden. Novos Mundos, Novos Paraísos.* Funchal: Centro de Estudos de História do Atlântico.

Mohawk, John (2005). *Iroquois creation story: John Arthur Gibson and J.N.B. Hewitt's Myth of the Earth Grasper.* Buffalo: Mohawk Publications.

More, Thomas (1996 [1516]). *Utopia.* London: Phoenix.

Munch, Peter A. (1964). "Culture and Superculture in a Displaced Community: Tristan da Cunha," *Ethnology*, 3: 369-376.

Munch, Peter A. (1970). "Economic Development and Conflicting Values: A Social Experiment in Tristan da Cunha," *American Anthropologist*, 72: 1300-1318.

Munch, Peter A. (1971). *Crisis in Utopia: The Ordeal of Tristan da Cunha.* New York: Crowell.

Munch, Peter A.; Marske, Charles E. (1981). "Atomism and Social Integration," *Journal of Anthropological Research*, 37: 158-171.

Paige, Glenn D. (2009 [2002]). *Nonkilling Global Political Science.* Honolulu: Center for Global Nonkilling. Available at: <http://www.nonkilling.org/node/18>.

Kirch, Patrick Vinton (1996 [1984]). *The Evolution of the Polynesian Chiefdoms*. Cambridge: Cambridge University Press.

Republic of Serbia (2007). *Comparative Overview of the Cases of Hong Kong, Åland Islands, and the Serbian Status Proposal for Kosovo and Metohija*. Belgrade: State negotiating team for Kosovo-Metohija.

Silva, Noenoe K. (2004). *Aloha Betrayed: Native Hawaiian Resistance to American Colonialism*. Durham: Duke University Press.

Sponsel, Leslie E. (2009). "Reflections on the Possibilities of a Nonkilling Society and a Nonkilling Anthropology," in Evans Pim, Joám, Ed. *Toward a Nonkilling Paradigm*. Honolulu: Center for Global Nonkilling, pp. 35-70.

U.S. Census Bureau (2010). "Veterans by Sex, Period of Service, and State: 2008," in *The 2010 Statistical Abstract*. Washington: U.S. Census Bureau. Available at: <http://www.census.gov/compendia/statab/2010/tables/10s0508.pdf>.

Ulukau (2004). *Ulukau Hawaiian dictionary*. Honolulu: University of Hawai'i Press. Available online at: <http://wehewehe.org/>.

Vesa, Unto (2009). "The Åland Islands as a conflict resolution model," in *Territorial issues in Europe and East Asia: colonialism, war occupation, and conflict resolution*, Bae, Chinsoo; Vesa, Unto, Eds. Seoul: Northeast Asian History Foundation, pp. 34-59.

Westropp, T. J. (1912). "Brazil and the Legendary Islands of the North Atlantic. Their History and Fable," *Proceedings of the Royal Irish Academy*, (30)8: 223-260.

Wrangham, Richard W.; Peterson, Dale (1997). *Demonic Males: Apes and the Origins of Human Violence*. New York: Houghton Mifflin Harcourt.

Younger, Stephen (2010). "Leadership in Small Societies," *Journal of Artificial Societies and Social Simulation* 13 (3)5. Available at: <http://jasss.soc.surrey.ac.uk/13/3/5.html>.

Younger, Stephen (2009). "Violence and warfare in the pre-contact Caroline Islands," *Journal of the Polynesian Society* 118: 135-164.

Younger, Stephen (2008). "Conditions and Mechanisms for Peace in Precontact Polynesia," *Current Anthropology* 49(5): 927-934.

Ziyadov, Taleh (2007). "The Aland Islands model for Nagorno Karabakh: Searching for optimal solutions to the Armenia-Azerbaijan conflict," *Regnum*, 4/2/2007. Available at: <http://www.regnum.ru/english/805841.html>.

Chapter Twelve

Nonkilling and the Body
Toward a Deep Sociology of Embodiment and Involuntary Death

John Clammer
United Nations University

Introduction

The sociology of the body has emerged strongly in the last two decades as an important sub-field of sociology. Drawing belated attention to the fact that embodiment and somatic experience pervades essentially every form of social interaction and cultural performance, it has to some extent addressed the issue of *dying* as the dissolution of the body as the ultimate outcome of aging and illness, but it has rarely concerned itself with *killing*—with the involuntary termination of life by the agency of others (for examples drawn from a now very extensive literature on the sociology of the body, see for example Turner, 1988; Featherstone, Hepworth and Turner, 1991; Shilling, 1993). The closest that classical sociology has come to the question of killing has been the studies of suicide originating with the work of Emile Durkheim and extending up to the present. This essay will explore the relationship between the sociology of the body and the issue of nonkilling (in contrast to the much more sociologically and ethically neutral issue of dying by natural causes). It will attempt to do so from at least three perspectives: from the perspective of social theory, by contextualizing nonkilling in its wider social, political and cultural context, and from a comparative perspective—by locating nonkilling in terms of the ways in which a number of different societies have understood the notion and its consequences for their moral, political and social orders. These combined approaches will hopefully lead to the clarification of a deeper and more sociologically rooted concept of nonkilling as an aspect of what I have elsewhere (Clammer, 2009a) termed "Deep Sociology"—one that does not confine itself to the surface levels of human social relations and modes of social organization, but that attempts to penetrate to the deeper existential ones on which societies, cultures and religions are ultimately based.

Such an approach requires the exploration of the notion of nonkilling not only as a social/ethical category, but also in its relationship to cultural concepts and practices of embodiment, suffering and religious belief on the one hand, and to very empirical and concrete dimensions of society on the other—including medical practice, especially in the case of terminal or incurable illness; penal practice and particularly the highly controversial issue of the death penalty; war and specifically the concept of the "just war" and acceptable military of individual behavior during wartime; genocide; and even the extension of the idea of nonkilling as an ethical category to non-human nature—to the rights of animals in particular understood as sentient beings and possibly even to the rest of the apparently nonsentient biosphere including trees, plants, minerals, insects and other life forms (on the rights of animals for example see Benton, 1994). Attitudes to killing/nonkilling are clearly embedded in culture and indeed reflect its core values. Many of us however live in very ambiguous and paradoxical cultures—ones in which killing is officially and societally disapproved of, but yet which are permeated with violence in the form of crime certainly, but even more significantly in the content of the media. Film and television in particular constantly carry the message that violence, including extreme violence ending in killing, is "normal," an attitude expressed not so much by the overt message as by the covert ones encoded in the imagery.

The connection of these questions to a sociology of the body should be apparent: a society's understanding of the sanctity, uniqueness and unwillingness to violate or destroy the bodies of its members or those of other societies as much as its understanding of more conventional somatic issues such as sexuality, ageing, gender and illness reveal much about its fundamental core. There is consequently involved what might be called a form of prescriptive or applied sociology at work here as well as a purely normative or descriptive one. At one level the attitudes and practices of a society with regard to killing can be simply described, but at another it may be felt that social science and policy intervention in assisting that society toward a more humane practice may be implied. Cultures cannot be regarded as simply ethically neutral. Even those of us who do not practice it might on good ethical grounds be critical of cannibalism or the ritual killing of captives taken in wars or raids whether or not the perpetrators of these practices consider it to be an integral part of their "culture." We will now turn to spelling out in more detail some of the fundamental connections between a comprehensive sociology of the body and the issue of killing/nonkilling.

The Body and Nonkilling: Toward a Sociological Analysis

Bryan Turner, the sociologist most often credited with reintroducing the question of the body into contemporary sociology, has argued that the essential issue is one of philosophical anthropology—the question of what makes humans what they are and the conditions under which they can best not only survive, but thrive. As he suggests, "The ontological centrality of human embodiment consequently emerged as a focus of universality. The fact of human embodiment (or more technically the fact that humanity is in evolutionary terms a warm-blooded mammal, a species being) gives rise to certain problems which must be satisfied in order for Man to survive. In particular, it raises the question: what range of social and cultural arrangements are minimally necessary for human survival and reproduction?" (Turner, 1991: 1). Primary amongst these is obviously life itself, and where possible the assurance that such life will not be terminated prematurely by anything other than illness or the accidents that human life is inevitably prey to, including natural disasters. These constitute a very different category of risk to entirely avoidable humanly induced threats to life—warfare, murder, cannibalism, execution or the slow death of the concentration camp. One of the reasons that may have attracted so many sociologists to the study of suicide is precisely its very odd ontological status as a form of voluntary termination of the very basis upon which all personal identity, hope and the possibility of social interaction fundamentally depends—the continuation of life itself. But at least, whatever its complex reasons, suicide is self-engineered; killing is not. Killing is, from the point of view of the victim, the violent termination of existence itself. Whatever views may be held about an afterlife, reincarnation or some other form of personal post-death continuity, the fact remains that killing ends personal survival in this world and all the social ties, potentialities and creativity, desires and hopes and development and contributions of the one killed. Casually as it may be treated in real life or in the violent fantasies of the media, killing is in a sense the ultimate crime from which there is no appeal: the final and irrecoverable termination of another's life and all its unfolding possibilities.

In his review of recent work on the sociology of the body, Arthur Frank divides his discussion into four main categories—of the Disciplined Body (as in sport, diet and fasting), the Mirroring Body (with its emphasis on narcissism and consumption), the Communicative Body (concerned with body awareness and expression, as in dance), and the Dominating Body (Frank, 1991). It is this last category that has the most bearing on the issue of killing/nonkilling. Frank begins by making two important observations: firstly that the comparative anthropological and historical literature strongly suggests that dominating bodies are almost exclusively male ones; and secondly that the desire to dominate comes from a sense of lack (Frank, 1991: 69). As a paradigm case he takes the immense two volume work *Male Fantasies* by the German social psychologist and social historian Klaus Theweleit (Theweleit, 1987; 1989 in English translation). The core of volume two in particular is a detailed examination of the German Freikorps, originally formed in the closing years of the First World War to fight the Bolshevik threat on Germany's eastern borders and continuing on into the early years of the Weimar Republic as a vicious militia devoted to combating the Left in general. Many members of the Freikorps later ended up in the SS and SA when Nazism became established by the 1930s. A large part of Theweleit's argument concerns the male sense of lack expressed initially in fear—of the masses, of women, of disorder or the "alien"—which find their expressive form in violence: the will to dominate which, when it cannot be expressed in more subtle or culturally appropriate forms turns to aggression. While much of his position is based on a latter-day version of psychoanalysis with which we may want to quibble, his social psychological and empirical historical analysis show clearly how for the psychologically and socially unintegrated individual, the "other" becomes not simply different, but subhuman, yet nevertheless necessary as the mirror of the dominating self for without the other that self cannot exist. For Freikorps members this meant having someone to fight, for to fight was to live: "The only real thing was fighting. (You couldn't be a man without fighting, and being a man was the only way of being alive.) When there is no more fighting, no more being a man, life ceases and everything (the man, the world) becomes a pulp" (Theweleit, 1987: 395). A "technology of the self" was thus created in which seeking out and destroying the other became the chief method of identity creation. Life is unpredictable: the dominated, or better still the dead, are not. Hence they are necessary in this gruesome dialectic of self formation and preservation. Embedded in this dialectic is a hatred and fear of the body itself: the bodies of others are unclean; one's own must be kept pure through the destruction of that unclean disorder.

   This of course has widespread sociological ramifications. While the Freikorps and the myriad other examples of militarized entities world wide, the glorification of this in the media often in the guise of the war film and the heroism that such productions almost always proclaim, and cases of civilian-led genocide as in Rwanda all involve a definition of the body that excludes other forms of social relating or empathy. As Theweleit summarizes this issue in his characterization of the dominating body as a warrior body: "The soldier male is forced to turn the periphery of his body into a cage for the beast within. In doing so, he deprives it of its function as a surface for social contact. His contact surface becomes an insulated shield, and he loses the capacity to perceive the social corpus within which his insulated body moves... A man so structured craves war, because only war allows him to achieve identity with his alien, "primitive," "bestial" interior, while at the same time avoiding being devoured by it" (Theweleit, 1989: 22). The result, Theweleit suggests, is that for the "warrior body" the outcome is the need to oppress the bodies of others, to subordinate them through violence extending as far as murder. What is most significant about his account is that he does not attempt to explain this male-initiated violence and other cases like it in terms of classical psychoanalytical theory or its popular variants (the sexual frustration explanation in particular), but in a sociological context—as socially instituted practices tolerated or ignored by much of the wider society (or even glorified by it) that serve in effect to protect the male from life and its contingencies. While the argument here can come dangerously close to essentialism, the supposition is that women are not subject to the generation of this socially-initiated violence (of which war itself is the paramount example) because of their closer intimacy with life, nature and with blood through childbirth and menstruation which leads them to a much higher benign tolerance of the multiplicity and fluidity of life, something which the sociological seeking for "order" through domination cannot manage.

Comparative ethnological evidence would seem in many ways to confirm this general theory. While the abortion debate (abortion being seen by its opponents as the deliberate killing of the unborn child) has occasioned widespread debate as has the associated issue of reproductive technologies (e.g., O'Brian, 1989), there are many other equally controversial questions. One of these is certainly the issue of the death penalty as the ultimate penal punishment, but others might include cannibalism and the question of its frequency and sociological causes (other than simple response to starvation in extreme situations), warfare as a generalized sociological phenomenon, and an issue that used once to be discussed fairly frequently in anthropology —notably that of sacrifice. In all these cases deliberate and planned killing of other humans takes place, always within a sociological context which may involve ethnicity, religious practices, ideas about fertility and agriculture and so on, class (who gets sacrificed and who does the sacrificing in either ritual or warfare situations?), ideas of justice and appropriate punishment and hence of whole legal cultures, and again, gender. All these instances it is apparent are dominated, initiated and practiced primarily by males. There are a number of important issues here for sociological theory to consider. If the body has a kind of sociological and ontological priority, being the very site of sentient life itself, while it is perfectly legitimate to pursue the many interesting empirical questions that body-oriented sociologists have indeed investigated (ageing, sports, illness and "body maintenance" via such practices as exercise, diet and cosmetic use and the possibilities of life extension and bodily reconstruction through nanotechnology or even cryogenics), in a sense more existentially fundamental questions remain. These include the possibility that even as I am aware of the constantly changing states of my own body and often its suffering especially through illness, so I can achieve a shared humanity by recognizing the same suffering in others, without my own self image being threatened. While bodies separate (as they spatially must), so also the shared experience of embodiment can unite. The deliberate deprivation of that embodiment in another (through killing) is thus not only a fundamental violation of the ontological reality of that individual (and indeed the termination of that individuality), but is also the diminution of the wider humanity that all embodied beings share and on which all call constantly for their own preservation (the supply of food, care, services, emotional support, images and shelter which make up the dynamic and interdependent fine structures of all societies). It is for this reason that Arthur Frank, in concluding his survey of recent work in the sociology of the body suggests that a sociology of the body points to an ethics of the body (Frank, 1991: 89-96).

Philip Mellor and Chris Shilling in their study of the relationship between embodiment and the sacred suggest that the proliferation of "body options" —ranging from diet through alternative sexualities to the prolonging of life by technological means—have introduced a fundamental insecurity into modern society about what the body is, including the idea, reflected in a good deal of contemporary literature, of the existential isolation of the embodied individual, which issues in many culturally interesting ways, including macabre imagery expressed in popular culture, the horror movie and other contexts in which the body can be represented in grotesque ways (Mellor; Shilling, 1997: 54). Part of the reason for this they posit is what they term the "sequestration of death"—most people (at least in the affluent West which is clearly their frame of reference) never encountering an actual death or corpse. This loss contributes in their view to a "banalization" of contemporary culture in which death, formerly an opportunity for self-reflection, contact with the scared and moral contemplation, becomes instead a media image (Mellor and Shilling, 1993). It may indeed be, as Hannah Arendt suggested in her famous and controversial notion, in relation to the trial in Jerusalem of Adolf Eichmann, that "the banality of evil" is now the characteristic of our times, a modernity that has not led, as the proponents of the "Enlightenment Project" hoped, to universal peace, social justice and heightened aesthetic and ethical awareness, but rather as Zygmunt Bauman has so cogently argued, to the Holocaust—to the bureaucratization and technologizing along "rational" managerial principles, of mass killing (Bauman, 1999). Many cultural theorists have come to assume, incorrectly, that this banality, a product of narcissism and the affluent modernity of the West, is universal and that we as a species have somehow evolved from the medieval pleasure in torture, combat and death to a more humane society. And indeed the past was violent: Garland (1991) is his study of the history of punishment, documents not only the brutality of the Middle Ages but the continuation of such practices as public executions well into the Nineteenth Century, and Hanawalt from his study of medieval coroners' reports shows how disputes were routinely settled by extreme violence and homicide and how few perpetrators of such murders were ever actually convicted (Hanawalt, 1976). Indeed such practices as public torture and executions in the later Baroque period were regarded as a salutary means through which "the authorities sought to structure violent passions through spectacles of blood, pain and death. The *consciousness* of violence, and a fascination with its potentialities, reached the point of inspiring what could be called an "aesthetics of cruelty" which, though utilized as a means of repression and subjugation, could also be experienced as pleasurable, entertaining and morally enlightening" (Mellor and Shilling, 1997: 140). Such practices while perhaps now less common in the "modern" West still sadly prevail in a number of recent and contemporary societies, particularly those that are politically dictatorships.

Underlying all of this is a deep and largely unquestioned sociological assumption: that social order is fragile and somehow needs to be constantly maintained, if necessary by violence. It is not clear however what the empirical evidence for this idea actually is: what is clear is that this notion is actually most often an ideology, the interests of a particular group concerned to maintain their privileges in the face of threats from others who may indeed have good claim on their resources. Durkheim's belief that society is based on a fundamental solidarity that somehow absorbs conflict and turns it to functionally desirable ends is consequently very suspect. More "modern" forms of sacrifice may indeed substitute animals for human victims (except in wars), but in either case it is not very clear how from the viewpoint of those victims, all possessing the essential quality of life, their deaths contribute to the true benefit of the wider and largely abstract "society" from which they are being so violently torn. But there is also another, and doubly paradoxical dimension to this. If as Zygmunt Bauman argues (Bauman, 1992) increasing degrees of control over bodies, largely through the means of improving medical technologies, has encouraged amongst modern people a subjective avoidance of death through body maintenance, medicine, exercise, diets and so forth, this individual effort in managing and maintaining their own bodies leads to the end result that in the face of their deaths, such bodily-fixated individuals face a crisis. Having invested all their efforts and a great deal of money and huge amounts of time in maintaining the thing, suddenly it lets you down, not just temporarily, but terminally. The other paradox is a more sociologically macro one: in the very society that invests huge amounts of its resources in body maintenance (the market in cosmetics worldwide for example running annually into many billions of dollars), killing is still widely condoned in warfare, in penal contexts and in the worlds of the imagination as reflected and reinforced by movies, computer and video games, comics, popular literature, sports such as hunting, extensive meat-eating and in crime suppression. Yet even here there are contradictions: much of the opposition to the first and second Gulf wars and the continuing involvement of U.S. and other troops in Afghanistan and Iraq is the death rate amongst those Allied troops (relatively modest by both warfare standards and in comparison with civilian casualties in those "theatres" of war). A "war on terror" itself pursued through counter-terror or even the overthrow of a corrupt and violent regime no longer carries much weight in the modern or postmodern world when measured against the deaths of a small number of combatants, most of whom are in fact volunteers (although often of ethnic minorities, working class or educationally deprived individuals).

Killing terminates the physical, social, emotional and spiritual potentialities of the individual/body which is the vehicle of the life-force. While death in a natural sense is an inescapable fact of the human condition (although obviously there are many competing theories about the post-physical survival of the individual, the soul, the spirit or some other entity widely distributed amongst the world's religions), killing is not. From an ethical viewpoint it can be seen as an extreme aberration, yet since it continues to be a sociological reality, we have to ask ourselves why? To answer this question takes us into another dimension of the sociology of the body: the relationship between self-identity and death and the expansion of the sociologically quite extensively discussed notion of death from simply dying into killing and being killed, into involuntary death as opposed to the outcome of natural processes such as ageing and illness. As Shilling rightly points out (Shilling, 1993: 175) the sociology of the body has been mostly concerned with the living body rather than with the death of that body, and such studies that have largely dealt with aging and "natural" death rather than killing. He reviews the work of a number of prominent sociologists who have dealt with dying in their work—specifically the American Peter Berger, the British sociologist Anthony Giddens, the French sociologist Pierre Bourdieu and the work of the social historian Norbert Elias, especially Elias' *The Loneliness of the Dying* (1985). The outcome of this survey for Shilling is that he sees the current "problem" with death in the context of modernity: "Consequently, I view death as having become a particular existential problem for people as a result of modern forms of embodiment, rather than being a universal problem for human beings which assumes the same form irrespective of time or place" (Shilling, 1993: 177). Essentially the argument is that of Bauman's—that if self-identity is vested primarily in the possession of an attractive, healthy and functioning body, the dissolution of that body is far more painful than in a traditional or religious culture in which bodily death is seen simply as the transition to a higher state of being, a religious consolation no longer available to many modern people (although to far more than one might at first suspect). For Giddens, for example, self-identity and the body are reflexively organized projects which are created through lifestyle choices rather than through (as in pre-modern societies), given roles or shared religious meaning systems (Giddens, 1991). It might be assumed that in the presence of such shared codes, killing would be largely outlawed, but as we have seen from examples from the Middle Ages and later, this is not true. Killing, torture and extensive violence can not only coexist with a body of religious teachings that appears to ban or restrict them, but those same religious teachings may be used to actually promote those very atrocities. Culture, as we have tragically seen from Nazi Germany, does not necessarily prevent barbarism.

Modern control over the body—in both the sense of better medical intervention in bodily dysfunctions and in the sense that Foucault so pertinently pointed out of the development of penal systems and systems of surveillance—then has paradoxical results. On the one hand it allows, for those who have access to such resources, much greater "management" and maintenance of the body and its shaping and presentation in desired ways; on the other it makes the body into something of an object. Objects of course can be manipulated, moved, disposed of at will. Contemporary globalization makes this only too clear: it allows the free movement of international capital, while greatly restricting the free movement of bodies—in the form for example of migrant labor. Similarly "flexible" personnel management systems allow for the hiring of staff on short term or temporary contracts, such that whenever the organization, usually for purely economic reasons, wishes to restructure itself, it is easy and perfectly legal to simply "downsize" what are now regarded as surplus and superfluous individuals, regardless of their social and financial needs. As modernity has spread the possibility of effective management of the body, so too it has pushed us collectively into the so-called "risk society" with its surplus powerlessness increasingly spread over more and more social strata with increasing perception of a generalized vulnerability as complex human systems appear as they indeed are—built on shifting foundations of sand and deeply dependent on the very environment that we are so rapidly and knowingly destroying. Even as modernity has made it easier to manipulate the body in ways designed to enhance the self-identity and image of the "user," so it has made more efficient the means of destroying bodies (especially through weapons), and has simultaneously made us aware of the uncontrolled dangers of epidemics such as HIV/AIDS, SARS, Avian or Swine flu, many of which are either created in human built environments and cultural practices ("Mad Cow" disease, now known to be transmittable to humans for example, or the potential dangers of GM crops or even the introduction of invasive non-native species of plants and animals) or spread by human means (air transport, shipping, long range transport of foodstuffs and industrial pollution), all of which threaten in new and alarming ways the "body projects" upon which affluent consumer societies are based.

Explanations and Models

Of course if one looks at much of the writing in the sociology of the body from a comparative perspective two things clearly emerge. The first is that it is to a great extent the product of a very modernist and Western point of view and largely implies societies of affluence, leisure and consumption. Other studies from the South rather than from the North suggest that these often narcissistic issues are by no means universal. As Nancy Scheper-Hughes (1993) has vividly shown, death can be an event in everyday life and as the direct result of violence, not of natural causes. Nevertheless the sociology of the body points to some essential issues that have a very direct bearing on killing and nonkilling. The first of these is the recognition of the social constitution of the body. Bodies are not just biological entities, they are equally social and cultural: the ways in which they are presented, decorated, clothed, tattooed, fed, exercised, subjected to various medical and dietery regimes, ideas of sleep (how much, when and where?), and how they are represented in art all testify to the cultural construction of the body. If the body itself is situated in a social context, then so is killing. This can be seen in situations of hunting for game or for sport: as comparative ethnography clearly shows, hunting is itself socially structured, with rules, often with rituals to address the spirits of the hunted animals and conventions about the sharing of the game amongst members of the social group. Sport hunting is often even more bound by rules and even laws—what may be hunted, when and in what seasons; for example, hunters often have to be licensed and only certain forms of weapons or traps are considered permissible. Many human societies have also developed sets of rules or conventions surrounding killing—in the context of judicial executions, warfare and the treatment of prisoners, and in hospital settings (the termination of a life support system, for example), but yet these rules are curiously weak and often violated, much more so indeed than the rules for the hunting of game. The atrocities of the Khmer Rouge in Cambodia and the brutal inter-tribal massacres in Rwanda represent two very recent examples of this principle.

But why is this so? To a great extent cultural discussions of death except in the limited and specific areas of penology and medical ethics have taken place in the realm of religion. In a way this is not surprising as death represents both the ultimate limiting factor of human life and an existential crisis not only for those to whom it inevitably occurs, but for the survivors as well or even more so. Some scholars even suggest that the mystery of death is at the root of all religions (Bowker, 1993), and certainly a specific interpretation of death is a preoccupation of all major religions, and to a great extent religions are defined precisely by their theories of death (resurrection and an afterlife in Christianity, reincarnation in the case of Hinduism, and so forth). This is understandable, but a purely religious discussion (and we must face the fact that religions empirically have done little to curb the actual incidence of killing in either historical or contemporary societies) draws attention away from other and more sociological factors. These include the ethical structures of a society and its associated value system, notions of power and legal culture, including ideas of who has an official monopoly on killing (the state in many cases), gender and the relative political and social position of women and men, and something rarely discussed, notably the ecology of a society and access to resources by various social or ethnic

groups within it. Killing is not just a free floating idea then: it too is embedded in an extensive set of social and ethical conventions. Even as the body
itself is both biological and cultural, so too is killing. The achievement of a
nonviolent society in which killing is seen as an extreme aberration cannot
come about simply through propaganda or formal religious exhortations
("Thou Shal Not Kill") important as these may be in at least setting some
kind of objective standard (as with the Universal Declaration of Human Rights
which, often violated as it is even by its signatory governments, does provide
an essential tool of accountability and a standard against which to measure actual political behavior). It can only be achieved by creating a constellation of
these sociological, political and ecological factors that put nonkilling at the very
centre of the core values of a culture, reinforced by social practices (socialization, art, the content of the media, education, etc.) that reflect that principle
at all levels of the culture. Only a holistic model—having at its core the respect for life, and the recognition of the body as having the ontological
status of the right to existence, and the prohibition of violation of that
right—can see a nonviolent society actually come into existence.

Some of these contributory factors have as yet hardly entered the discussion on killing/nonkilling; for example, the role of ecology and resource competition. In his celebrated study of how societies collapse as a result of irresponsible environmental practices, Jared Diamond (2005) convincingly shows
how the horrific inter-tribal genocide in Rwanda cannot be explained simply
as ethnic hatred, but rather as the outcome of a complex of factors including
very high population, scarce and diminishing resources, accelerating ecological
degradation, land disputes and the falling international prices of Rwandan export crops and particularly coffee (Diamond, 2005: 311-328); and how similar
conditions are emerging in Haiti and elsewhere in the developing world.
Some pessimistic writers such as the Italian futurologist Roberto Vacca see a
very gloomy and violence ridden future for the world precisely as a result of
resource depletion, conflicts over access to such diminishing resources, pollution and toxicity in the environment, and the breakdown of complex engi-
neered systems such as power grids and communications (Vacca, 1974).
While the ecological factor is significant in explaining intra- and inter-societal
violence, so are a number of others, and here I will mention what I feel to be
amongst the main ones. The first of these is the representation of the body in
the media and in art. When the media routinely depict the human body as
subject to shooting, stabbing, mutilation, torture, rape, car and airplane
crashes, explosions and entombment, and when the depiction of the body in
realistic terms has largely disappeared from nonfigurative art—and when it

does appear is often in a distorted or mutilated form—and when such images are the routine stuff of everyday image-consumption in films, television, comics, magazines, video games and the news, it is hardly surprising that such representations enter deeply into the social psyche of a society. While the exact relationship between violence in the media and violence in the streets is still debated, that there is some very real connection can hardly be doubted. When a society's media are obsessed with guns, crime and violence, it is not surprising if this spills over into everyday reality: random shootings and drive-by shootings, school room massacres, street crime, and the need for ever higher levels of personal security in the home and when travelling. Terrorism is hardly a surprising outcome when society itself is fixated in its images on the very actions that terrorism simply performs in practice.

This is not to say of course that the media is to be separated from the other factors mentioned above: it too, like all social institutions, is embedded. Indeed a second and related factor is technology—the technology that makes the media possible also has widespread social implications. These include, as we have seen clearly with the first Gulf War in particular, the technologizing of killing: the televised war, the missile strike launched from ships far from the spots that the missiles will hit, the pilotless drone directed to specific distant targets unseen by their operators, the "daisy cutters" (massive bombs dropped on suspected targets by high altitude bombers), and the euphemisms that surround such warfare: "clean war," the "surgical strike." Much modern warfare is carried out from a distance—the carpet bombing of Dresden and Hamburg, the dropping of the atomic bombs on Hiroshima and Nagasaki, the defoliation of Vietnam—such that its perpetrators do not see the results of their activities on the ground, something that easily leads to the "normalization" and even routinization of warfare. The deaths are not seen, they are merely the outcome of the application of a form of industrial technology. And when one recalls that the world's biggest arms traders are the five permanent members of the UN Security Council one begins to grasp the deep immorality of a global system driven primarily by profit, economic expansionism and the "imperatives" of technology.

No doubt also related to this hegemony of technology is the shift from a sacred to a profane conception of the body, partly as a result of secularization and the relative decline of religion, and partly as a result of medicalization and the technologizing of bodily interventions. Even as medicine has become more and more technological, so too have many of its ancillary activities: sport, exercise (machines, constant measurement of aerobic capacities), body maintenance (artificial tanning in a machine, hair-care and cosmetic interventions), travel, leisure and entertainment. When the body is treated as in effect just another machine to be maintained, "tuned," polished and washed, its ontological status shifts and paradoxically while an obsession with the self and self-image can be the result, so too can the denigration of the bodies of others, especially those who are less (by local cultural standards) beautiful, healthy, well presented, polite, or who are simply ethnically different or are the "wrong" color. And denigration is simply the first step on the road to despising those others and ultimately to the wish to destroy them.

Naturally we must be aware that there are many individuals and not a few communities committed to overcoming these negative values. One thinks of course of Gandhi and his central concept of *Ahimsa*. For Gandhi *ahimsa*—the non-negotiable principle of nonviolence—is intimately linked to his theory of truth. As I have suggested elsewhere (Clammer, 2009b: 566), while *ahimsa* in its negative sense means nonharm to living beings, in its larger and positive sense it implies self-sacrifice, love (including of one's enemies) and charity, and as such is a constructive force not merely a prohibition, since it reframes human relationships and human-nature relationships in terms of compassion, and as such represents an existential condition, a whole way of living life. A similar idea is found in Buddhism where compassion (*karuna*) and *metta* (loving kindness) are seen as the foundation of ethics and hence of society, and also as the answer to exploitative power. And this is not simply a "religious" teaching, detached from actual socio-political realities. The basis of a great deal of social and political violence lies not in the individual (deeply influenced as each one is through socialization and the media), but from generative structures in the society and economic system as a whole. As David Edwards phrases it: "Thus with the reversal of truth common to all systems of concentrated power, it is the parties of 'law and order' which are actually the greatest causes of crime and disorder in society. It is they who generate desperation, crime and chaos for the sake of short-term profits for the wealthy, by reducing equality, increasing poverty, stripping down the social security system, increasing unemployment, and above all, perhaps, by keeping people from an understanding of the importance of critical thinking and kindness" (Edwards, 2001: 154). This is not only true of or within individual societies, but is also an outcome of globalization with its huge ecological damage, displacement of peoples, closing of "inefficient" industries in places where employment is desperately needed, amoral currency transactions, stock market manipulations, debt generation in developing countries and many other well documented effects. The body of the individual is situated at the nexus of all these forces. The "value" of the individual person can easily be diminished when they become a statistic in a globalized system of trade, warfare and resource flows in a world where only those few with access to power, funds and prestige "count." The fundamental paradox of modernity is that its humanism and exaltation of the individual has in fact historically led to the devaluation of the human person in many of the economic and political systems that now infest the globe.

Nonkilling and an Ethics of the Body

As we have seen, Arthur Frank rightly suggests that there is a close relationship between the sociology of the body and an ethics of the body: the first indeed implies the latter. This key idea as we have suggested needs in turn to be located in a wider ecological, economic and political context. This is partly because killing/nonkilling is a moving target: the routine nature of judicial execution in 16-18th century Europe or the revolutionary "justice" of the French Revolution, with the possible exceptions of Hitler's Germany or Stalin's Russia, seem to be nightmarish from the perspective of the 20th and early 21st Centuries. We still kill, certainly, but in war, not in the public squares of our major cities. And even then casualty figures have steadily fallen and we pride ourselves that "modern" wars are not as deadly in terms of lives as their predecessors. But a closer look suggests a rather different picture: contemporary violence may not be the result of war, but of "development," not any longer of colonialism, but of globalization and the modernized forms of poverty that it creates.

The Buddha was noteworthy for pointing out that suffering is an inevitable part of the human condition: it is part of the "signature" or species being of human existence. But that suffering, which can be redemptive in the context of Buddhism as much as it can in Christianity or Judaism, requires life as its essential environment, for without life there can be no experience. In a fascinating edited collection, the editors, Arthur Kleinman, Veena Das and Margaret Lock extend this idea of suffering into what they term "social suffering" (Kleinman; Das; Lock, 1997), which they define as the "assemblage of human problems that have their origins and consequences in the devastating injuries that social forces can inflict on human experience" (1997: ix), and which they in turn relate to "a language of dismay, disappointment, bereavement, and alarm that sounds not at all like the usual terminology of policies and programs [that] may offer a more valid means for describing what is at stake in human experiences of political catastrophe and social structural violence, for professionals as much as for victims/perpetrators, and may also make better sense of how the clash among globalizing discourses and localized social realities so often ends up prolonging personal and collective tragedy" (Kleinman,

Das and Lock, 1997: xi). For killing is not only the termination of the experiential possibilities of the victim, it is also an act that both inflicts trauma on the survivors (spouses, children, friends, colleagues) but irrevocably breaks the social order as a space is created (a father perhaps, the skills of an irreplaceable colleague) that can never again be filled. For the dead there is no substitute. A killing is thus not simply an event: it is the initiation of a process—of memory, mourning, adaptation, irrevocable loss—that has deep and permanent effects on those left behind at the individual level. And often too at a social level, as evidenced by the tendency to memorialization of martyrs, of the war dead, of the victims of major tragedies—a social tendency that can easily become political as we see in the Balkans, Northern Ireland and elsewhere when old deaths become the excuse for new ones, for revenge and for fueling ancient communal or tribal animosities. A killing involves loss, displacement and the cutting of emotional bonds (or rather perhaps the creation of new virtual ones to the dead individual), and deeply effects the subjectivities of those who survive. Any death disrupts the ontological economy of the world and its initial effects will be both emotional and sociological, and later perhaps political. A new methodology is required in the social sciences here: one that includes the subjectivities of the victims and of the survivors and their existential interpretation of the circumstances in which tragedy has befallen them.

Such an approach has many very practical applications: therapy with trauma victims generated by war, natural disasters, ethnic and tribal conflict and catastrophic illnesses. In fact three dimensions are revealed here: at one level the suffering of the victims and their survivors; at a second the implication of forces of structural violence in the production of involuntary death; and at a third the memorialization and politicization of such deaths in the ceremonies, historical narratives and myths of the victimized culture. Interestingly this takes place from both sides—the victims and the perpetrators as the former try to come to terms with what has happened to them, and the latter to assimilate the spectacle of their own violence—as one sees today in the Balkans and in the preservation of the Nazi death camps in Germany and Poland—sites of memory of very different kinds for both parties. Very different ideological approaches to these memories can also be taken—denial (e.g., Holocaust deniers), down-playing (as with Japanese school history textbooks that mention only in passing or as a mere aside Japan's colonial and military interventions in China in the 1930s), used as an excuse for continuing conflict (Kosovo, Northern Ireland, Sri Lanka), for attempting to overcome the massive hurts both inflicted and received (the South African Truth and Reconciliation Commissions) or as an exercise in competitive victimology—the survi-

vors of the Hiroshima atomic bombings for example, who refuse to acknowledge that Japan was engaged in a vicious war in Asia and against the USA and
that Hiroshima was itself a major military base and the home base of the
Japanese armies operating in China, as opposed to the American view that the
bombings both brought the war to a speedy end and in fact saved the tens of
thousands of lives that would have been lost had the land battles extended
from Okinawa where they were already in progress onto the mountainous
Japanese main islands (Paris, 2000; Yoneyama, 1999). Post-conflict societies in
particular where psychic and emotional healing is as much a necessity as physical reconstruction greatly benefit not just from interventions by outside aid
agencies and the likes, but by simply having the stories of the victims and the
perpetrators listened to and their narratives of suffering taken seriously (for a
good example from the Sudan see Marlowe, Bain and Shapiro, 2006).

By now this essay may seem to have strayed a little far from the sociology of the body. But not really: violence is quite literally inscribed on the
body, through torture, punishment, malnutrition, execution and fighting.
There has been unfortunately at least in Western social theory a lineage of
ideas from Georges Sorel, through Franz Fanon to Jean-Paul Sartre and
Jacques Derrida and many others arguing for the regenerative effects of violence and its "purifying" qualities including, alas, even artists, the Italian fu-
turists and their leader Filippo Marinetti, for instance, glorifying war (until it
actually happened) as "the only hygiene" that could clear away the dead
wood of a corrupt and materialistic society. Such thinking rarely survives
the actual experience of violence, but the very fact that it exists as a mode
of thinking is frightening. Hannah Arendt in her classic study *On Violence*
(Arendt, 1970) argued that public life was being progressively colonized by
both violent practices and violent ideologies and much of the evidence supports this thesis—the casual recourse to war that we have witnessed in the
opening years of the 21st Century and, despite so much talk of "civil society," the inability of a weakened public sphere to actually influence the outcome or nature of political decisions (Dallmayr, 2004). But violence, even
when directed at the other, is ensnaring: it can all too easily engulf the perpetrators themselves as they turn the violence inward as we see so often in
the history of revolutions, and in the internecine violence of groups such as
the Tamil Tigers in the recent prolonged conflict in Sri Lanka, where
"death...became a polysemic emblem, signifying not only the recovery of
dignity, honour, self-respect, nationhood and freedom, but also an instrument for the recovery of the Tamil ontic self in its 'hiddenness'—i.e. the
sense of authentic being destroyed by trauma" (Sivakumar, 2001: 336-7), if

necessary turned onto those within the movement itself not deemed pure or enough, sufficiently committed or ideologically suspect for some reason. Killing then is never a "solution"—it does not address the underlying problems (e.g., judicial execution in relation to crime), it breeds further problems for the perpetrators and the survivors, and it violently disturbs the peace and harmony of society, and, if one takes a more metaphysical approach, of the wider universe beyond society. Its epidemic quality in the past and in contemporary societies seems to stem from two kinds of sources: on the one hand structural qualities of societies that generate cycles of violence whether these be war, "development," or globalization. And on the other a lack of appreciation, both ethical and aesthetic, of the uniqueness and beauty of the human body and its ontological status as the vehicle of life and all that implies: experience, love, creativity, potentialities and the contribution that only that person can make to the life of the universe. The mechanization of the body through medicalization, its fragmentation through its representation in art, its easily destructible nature as depicted in the media, its purely functional qualities as presented in pornography, easily lead to the diminution of its significance and hence of its disposability. Sociologists on the whole have concentrated on the external dimensions of social life, including the many counter-movements that exist to institutionalized violence (for example, Zunes, Kurtz and Asher, 1999), but here my intention has been to draw attention to the existential aspects of embodiment and social life and the fundamental violation of these through involuntary death—toward a "deep" sociology rather than a shallow one. The body, as the "material" carrier of life, far from being peripheral to such a sociology, is implicit in its very nature: embodiment is the mode of our Earthly being and is the very thing that unites us with the rest of nature. Indeed I would hazard that it is our current alienation from nature that so many are now struggling to overcome, that lies at the source of so much of our social violence and alienation, a view now strongly supported by the emerging field of eco-psychology. The overcoming of killing as a "solution" to any number of issues, deeply embedded as it is in human societies and cultures, requires a holistic mode of thinking: one that recognizes and affirms not our separation but our co-dependence. And this is not only true psychically: it is through our bodies that we communicate (which is why the sharing of food is a universal sign of friendship and good will), we actually breath the same air and it is through our bodies that we love and reproduce. The root problem as is so often the case in human cultures is one of imagination. The peace scholar and activist John Paul Lederach in a luminous book on the peace process raises the fundamental question: "How do we transcend the cycles of violence that bewitch our human community while still living in them?" (Lederach, 2005: 5), and he answers his own question as follows: "Transcending violence is forged by the capacity to generate, mobilize, and build the moral imagination. The kind of imagination to which I refer is mobilized when four disciplines and capacities are held together and practiced by those who find their way to rise above violence. Stated simply, the moral imagination requires the capacity to imagine ourselves in a web of relationships that includes our enemies; the ability to sustain a paradoxical curiosity that embraces complexity without reliance on dualistic polarity; the fundamental belief in and pursuit of the creative act; and the inherent risk of stepping into the mystery of the unknown that lies beyond the far too familiar landscape of violence" (Lederach, 2005: 5). This "moral imagination" is for Lederach the one thing uniquely gifted to our species.

He is, I think, correct. Seen from this perspective the role of the social sciences becomes a revolutionary one: not simply to describe existing societies or to make policy recommendations based on the generation of empirical data, but a far greater task: to build the moral imagination through a dialectical recognition of the weaknesses and strengths of actually existing or past human societies on the one hand—the data—and the building of the humane, creative and ecologically responsible kind of society that we all ultimately desire to dwell in and where the flourishing of human species being is, in as far as we can make it, assured—the moral task of sociology.

References

Arendt, Hannah (1970). *On Violence*. New York: Harcourt, Brace, Jovanovich.

Bauman, Zygmunt (1992). *Mortality, Immortality and Other Life Strategies*. Cambridge: Polity Press.

Bauman, Zygmunt (1999). *Modernity and the Holocaust*. Cambridge: Polity Press.

Benton, Ted (1994). *Natural Relations: Ecology, Animal Rights and Social Justice*. London: Verso.

Bowker, John (1993). *The Meanings of Death*. Cambridge: Cambridge University Press.

Clammer, John (2009a). "Sociology and Beyond: Towards a Deep Sociology," *Asian Journal of Social Science*, 37(3):332-346.

Clammer, John (2009b). "Beyond Power: Alternative Conceptions of Being and the Reconstitution of Social Theory," in Giri, Ananta Kumar, Ed., *The Modern Prince and the Modern Sage: Transforming Power and Freedom*. New Delhi: Sage, pp. 559-575.

Dallmayr, Fred (2004). *Peace Talks - Who Listens?* Notre Dame: Notre Dame University Press.

Diamond, Jared (2005). *Collapse: How Societies Choose to Fail or Succeed*. New York: Penguin Books.

Edwards, David (2001). *The Compassionate Revolution: Radical Politics and Buddhism*. New Delhi: The Viveka Foundation.

Elias, Norbert (1985). *The Loneliness of the Dying.* Oxford: Basil Blackwell.

Featherstone, Mike; Hepworth, Mike; Turner, Bryan S., Eds. (1991) *The Body: Social Process and Cultural Theory.* London: Sage Publications.

Frank, Arthur W. (1991). "For a Sociology of the Body: An Analytical Review," in Featherstone, Mike; Hepworth, Mike; Turner, Bryan S., Eds. *The Body: Social Process and Cultural Theory.* London: Sage Publications, pp.36-102.

Garland, D. (1991). *Punishment and Modern Society.* Oxford: Clarendon Press.

Giddens, Anthony (1991). *Modernity and Self-Identity.* Cambridge: Polity Press.

Hanawalt, B. (1976). "Violent Death in Fourteenth and Early Fifteenth Century England," *Comparative Studies in Society and History,* 18(3): 297-320.

Kleinman, Arthur; Das, Veena; Lock, Margaret, Eds. (1997). *Social Suffering.* Berkeley: University of California Press.

Lederach, John Paul (2005). *The Moral Imagination: The Art and Soul of Building Peace.* Oxford: Oxford University Press.

Marlowe, Jen; Bain, Aisha; Shapiro, Adam (2006). *Darfur Diaries: Stories of Survival.* New York: Nation Books.

Mellor, Philip A.; Shilling, Chris (1993) "Modernity, Self-Identity and the Sequestration of Death," *Sociology,* 27(3): 411-431.

Mellor, Philip A.; Shilling, Chris (1997). *Re-forming the Body: Religion, Community and Modernity.* London: Sage Publications.

O'Brian, Mary (1989). *Reproducing the World.* Boulder: Westview Press.

Paris, Erna (2000). *Long Shadows: Truth, Lies and History.* Toronto: Vintage Canada.

Scheper-Hughes, Nancy (1993). *Death Without Weeping: The Violence of Everyday Life in Brazil.* Berkeley: University of California Press.

Shilling, Chris (1993). *The Body and Social Theory.* London: Sage Publications.

Sivakumar, Chitra (2001). "Transformation in the Sri Lankan Tamil Militant Discourse: Loss of the Tamil Self, Violence and the Hermeneutics of Recovery," in Giri, Ananta Kumar, Ed., *Rethinking Social Transformation.* Jaipur; New Delhi: Rawat Publications, pp. 304-353.

Theweleit, Klaus (1987). *Male Fantasies, Volume 1: Women, Floods, Bodies, History.* Minneapolis: University of Minnesota Press.

Theweleit, Klaus (1989). *Male Fantasies, Volume 2: Male Bodies: Psychoanalyzing the White Terror.* Minneapolis: University of Minnesota Press.

Turner, Bryan S. (1988). *The Body and Society: Explorations in Social Theory.* Oxford: Basil Blackwell.

Turner, Bryan S. (1991). "Recent Developments in the Theory of the Body," in Featherstone, Mike; Hepworth, Mike; Turner, Bryan S., Eds. *The Body: Social Process and Cultural Theory.* London: Sage Publications, pp.1-35.

Vacca, Roberto (1974). *The Coming Dark Age.* London: Panther Books.

Yoneyama, Lisa (1999). *Hiroshima Traces: Time, Space and the Dialectics of Memory.* Berkeley and London: University of California Press.

Zunes, Stephen; Kurtz, Lester R.; Asher, Sarah Beth, Eds. (1999). *Nonviolent Social Movements.* Malden: Blackwell.

Chapter Thirteen

Toward a Nonkilling Society

A Case Study of Individual and Institutional Changes in Social Affinity within a Religious Context

Matthew T. Lee
University of Akron

And ye shall know the truth, and the truth shall make you free. (John 8:32)
If it's your truth, you can't not do it. (Palmer, 2009: np)

In the parable of the Good Samaritan, one of the most well-known and powerful stories of the New Testament, Jesus responds to the question, "But who is my neighbor?" The question was posed by an expert in Jewish law who was seeking to justify his narrow definition of the word "neighbor" and thus limit his responsibilities to others. Jesus provides a surprising answer in the form of a story. This parable sought to undermine a social hierarchy that drew sharp distinctions between classes of people and change the consciousness of those who held hypocritical views about the Biblical command to "love your neighbor as yourself." In the parable, a man was robbed and beaten on his way to Jericho and left for dead. Two high-status religious figures, a priest and a temple functionary (a Levite), pass by the beaten man and offer no help. Why? Perhaps they were obeying religious rules about not coming into contact with the "unclean," in this case a dying man. Or maybe their thoughts were preoccupied with religious matters and they failed to notice the victim (Darley and Batson, 1973). But a despised, "half-breed foreigner" (Cox, 2004: 155) and "religious outcast" (Darley and Batson, 1973: 101)—a Samaritan—stops to help the robbery victim. This low-status character binds the victim's wounds and transports him to an inn, where he pays for the victim's room and board until he recovers. The moral of this story is that everyone is our neighbor, regardless of how they have been labeled by society. No exceptions. Equally important, according to Jesus, it is the low-status Samaritan who has done God's will, not the two representatives of organized religion who are both distracted from what it means to truly follow God by their blind adherence to religious rules prohibiting contact with the dead or dying, or simple inattention to reality in the present moment.

According to Jesus, when religious rules interfere with a compassionate act these rules must be abandoned. When dogmas distract us from living the spirit of God's law ("do unto others"), Jesus would argue that we have a duty to improve ourselves and transcend our social and religious conditioning. But why do we sometimes behave like the priest or the Levite, rather than the Samaritan? Why does religion seem to encourage love of neighbors (and even love of enemies) for some people, but aggression and even violence for others? These questions are important for individuals, as well as social groups like religious denominations. For example, some Christian denominations (e.g., the Episcopal Church and the United Church of Christ) took an official position opposing the current war in Iraq, while others, such as the Southern Baptist Convention, supported the war (Beliefnet, 2006). Individual members of these groups did not necessarily agree with the public pronouncements, so it is important to remember that individuals do not blindly follow the leaders of the groups to which they belong. But religious institutions do exert a strong influence on people, including the behavioral forms that "love of neighbor" and "love of enemy" may take. For some, a "just" war is sometimes necessary to secure the peace, and participation in killing can be understood as a loving action. Religion has important implications for the creation of a nonkilling society and the impact of religion on this issue is not monolithic.

This chapter considers the role of religion (beliefs, practices, and communities that deal with the sacred) and religious experience in fostering killing or nonkilling attitudes and behaviors. It does so by drawing on a sociological concept (social affinity) to analyze the oral history of a Pentecostal theologian and minister (Paul Alexander) whose orientation shifted from supporting killing to opposing it. I also consider the context of Paul's denomination (the Assemblies of God), which supported nonkilling at the time of its founding in the early 20th century, but now has become one of the more pro-war denominations in the United States. At present, "the majority of Assemblies of God people in the United States support Christian combatant participation in warfare" (Alexander, 2009: 22). But Paul is working to change that by shifting his denomination's hermeneutical center back to its original "Christocentric" (p. 334) orientation. A hermeneutic is a framework of interpretation, and Paul's research makes a convincing argument that the "non-Christocentric hermeneutic" (p. 334) that is dominant in the Assemblies of God today contradicts the Jesus-centered (Christocentric) interpretive lens of the denominational founders. More important than simply returning to the denomination's roots, Paul argues that the nonkilling way of life modeled by Jesus is theologically defensible and that the current orientation of his denomination is grounded in a faulty theology and a poorly reasoned set of ethics. Paul's personal narrative is sociologically important for understanding the process by which an individual can overcome past pro-killing socialization—often at great personal and professional cost, including the loss of a full-time academic job (Alexander, 2009)—and also for demonstrating how this changed person might begin to confront the cultural supports that make killing possible. Individual and institutional change is required for the creation of a nonkilling society. Paul's story incorporates both of these levels of analysis and serves as a beacon of hope that significant change in a nonkilling direction is within reach for individuals and the institutions in which they are embedded.

Social Affinity, Social Distance, and Nonkilling

Like the Good Samaritan story, Paul Alexander's biography raises the issue of *social affinity*, which concerns our perceived similarity to others, comprised of "empathy and identification between individuals and groups" and "the sentiments underlying the social bonds" that hold societies together (Vela-McConnell, 1999: 8, 10). The degree of empathy and shared identity fostered by social bonds within and across societies is of critical importance for the creation of a nonkilling world, while dehumanization and a sense of social distance are important ingredients of killing (Kelman and Hamilton, 1989). Most of us do form strong bonds with others, when our social circumstances foster such connections (Vela-McConnell, 1999; Boulding, 1988). And although we may tend to describe our behavior in individualistic, self-interested terms, many of us also exhibit a "strong sense of communal membership," which suggests a disparity between our "individualistic rhetoric" and our "instinctively communal behavior" (Palmer, 1998: 68). In other words, our words imply selfishness, but our behavior does not. But is our behavior equally beneficial to all people?

The concept of social affinity directs our attention to an important fact: we are less likely to "love" neighbors and enemies from whom we feel separate or distant. This distance can be geographical, temporal, or social. We tend be less concerned about people on the other side of the planet than we are about those who live in our own backyard. Temporal distance also weakens our altruistic impulses. For example, many white Americans do not want the U.S. government to make financial restitution to Native Americans or African Americans who were exploited, killed, or enslaved in the past and who continue to suffer from their disadvantaged position in society (Winbush, 2003).

The idea of reparations for acts that are centuries old seems unthinkable to many who do not perceive the connection between their own place in the current social hierarchy and historical patterns of conquest and subjugation.

As with the other types, increases in social distance reduce the likelihood of benevolence toward others. The issue here is not geography or time, but the distinction between *us* and *them*. We may feel an obligation to help members of our in-group (family, country, race), even to the point of risking our lives, but we may not perceive a similar duty for those we define as *other*. In fact, we might even feel justified in exploiting or even killing members of the out-group. Social distance is based on the degree to which we feel similar or different to a group of people, where similarity is based on ascribed or achieved characteristics (Vela-McConnell, 1999). Ascribed traits are those you are born into or otherwise cannot change, such as biological race, sex, or age. Achieved characteristics include such factors as educational attainment, wealth, or occupation. For example, wealthy people may see themselves as more similar to each other than to other social classes and justify their privilege on the grounds that they possess superior traits or a stronger work ethic. Similarly, Israelis and Arabs may conceive of each other as out-groups. One Israeli father who lived in a mixed community of Jews and Arabs noted that, "Between my children and my neighbor's children is a wall of glass.... They do not exist as people in the same psychological world" (Hunt, 1990: 91). Separated by such walls, killing can become justifiable.

Of course great diversity exists within such groups, so we must be careful not to over-generalize. But the point is that once we start making distinctions between ourselves and others who are different in some way, there is a tendency to create a hierarchical order in which some are less deserving of our help and possibly even a threat to our way of life. As Pitirim Sorokin (2002[1954]: 459) argued:

> ...in-group altruism tends to generate an out-group antagonism. And the more intense and exclusive the in-group solidarity of its members, the more unavoidable are the clashes between the group and the rest of humanity. Herein lies the tragedy of tribal altruism not extended over the whole of mankind....

As an example, much has been written about the sense of superiority the Nazis felt toward the Jews during World War II. Many considered Jews to be a "lower species of life, a kind of vermin which upon contact infected the German people with deadly diseases" (Hunt, 1990: 92). This kind of dehumanization is a universal requirement for massacres and genocide (Kelman and Hamilton, 1989). The perpetrators believe that they must kill others to save their in-group, but before this can occur the victims must be stripped of their humanity and independent identities in the minds of the killers. The problem of out-group antagonism also confronts us with the fact that we are faced with contradictory social norms: our duty to help a stranger in need conflicts with our duty to take care of our own, to put the needs of our in-group first (Hunt, 1990: 80).

In light of these issues, it is clear that in order to increase love of neighbor/enemy and reduce killing in the world, we must eliminate the social distance that we perceive between ourselves and others. In this act, we are able to transcend our past socialization through which we originally learned the disastrous falsehood of the us/them dichotomy. Only when our concerns "extend beyond family and beyond nation to mankind" can we claim to have "become fully human" (Leon Eisenberg, quoted in Vela-McConnell, 1999: 219). French novelist Albert Camus (1972[1946]: 53) makes a similar point when he states: "We are asked to love or hate such and such a country and such and such a people. But some of us feel too strongly our common humanity to make such a choice." But how can we increase social affinity in our society in order to move from "tribal egoism to universal altruism" (Sorokin, 1954[2002]: 459)? Similarly, how can we make the transition from a killing to a nonkilling society (Paige, 2009 [2002])? These questions will guide the rest of this chapter. Before we turn to our case study, we must first unpack the different types of social affinity.

A Typology of Social Affinity

James Vela-McConnell's (1999) thoughtful research on social affinity has identified four types that fall along a continuum from low to high affinity. Note that a person may exhibit a low degree of affinity on one topic, but high affinity on another. For example, an individual may be quite concerned about preventing deaths caused by a preventable disease, but unconcerned about deaths caused by war or other forms of violence. Similarly, a low level of affinity may exist for one group, while a high affinity may exist for another group, even though the same issue is involved (e.g., a person may be quite concerned about hunger among Americans but unconcerned with hunger among other nationalities). The person with the lowest affinity is described as *nonreferenced* with regard to a particular issue and expresses the attitude that "it's not my problem" (Vela-McConnell, 1999: 49). They often have little or no awareness of the dimensions of the harm involved and are not particularly concerned for the well-being of the group affected. The *self-referenced type* displays a higher affinity with victims, but their concern is primarily motivated by self-interest. For example, many hetero-sexuals were unconcerned about AIDS as a social problem when they be-lieved that it only affected homosexuals (i.e., they were nonreferenced). But when the disease began to spread among members of their own group, they became much more interested in treatment and prevention as a means to protect themselves. A person who is self-referenced will donate money or time to causes that actually or potentially affect them personally. Vela-McConnell (1999: 61) writes that nonreferenced and self-referenced peo-ple have "compartmentalized their selves.... The broad ties of social affinity are cut off at the root.... In the tradition of sociologist C. Wright Mills, they have not translated their personal troubles into public issues."

The *relationally referenced type* has been able to look beyond personal self interest to consider a problem that has afflicted someone in their in-group. The closer the relationship, the more likely the person will help. For example, family members with strong ties look out for each other. Count-less examples come to mind of celebrities who have brought a formerly un-known cause to the attention of the public because their child has contracted a particular disease or their close friend has experienced the ravages of sub-stance abuse or some other malady. Their beneficence is laudable, but there is still some element of indirect self-interest involved. But their self-interest does extend to others, which is a more expansive kind of affinity than the previous types. The "deepest level" of social affinity is the *socially referenced type* (Vela-McConnell, 1999: 70). This group is concerned about issues that affect strangers. For some people, the very idea of a "stranger" is not a viable con-cept—we are all one interconnected, indivisible whole. Some—but clearly not all—religious traditions deny the validity of the self/other distinction. Although these four types do not necessarily unfold as a series of sequential steps, they can be displayed as a continuum of social affinity (see Figure 1):

Figure 1. Continuum of Social Affinity

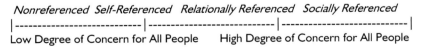

Nonreferenced Self-Referenced Relationally Referenced Socially Referenced

|---------------------------|---------------------------|---------------------------|

Low Degree of Concern for All People   High Degree of Concern for All People

One potential pathway to a nonkilling society is for people to build a cul-ture that fosters a strong social affinity with all people in a way that helps them to see past the geographical, temporal, or social distances that blind others. Religion can play a constructive or destructive role here, depending on the extent to which love of neighbor/enemy extends to all people and whether or not violence is legitimated.

Toward a Nonkilling Society:
The Importance of Religion and Religious Experience

> But what is meant by a "nonkilling society"? It is a human community, smallest to largest, local to global, characterized by no killing of humans and no threats to kill; no weapons designed to kill humans and no justifications for using them; and no conditions of society dependent upon threat or use of killing force for maintenance or change.... Religions do not sanctify lethality; there are no commandments to kill. (Paige, 2009 [2002]: 21)

The Center for Global Nonkilling (<http://www.nonkilling.org>) has made important contributions to the interdisciplinary analysis of killing and nonkilling. In this body of scholarship, a nonkilling society is "characterized by no killing of humans and no threats to kill" and includes "no conditions of society dependent upon threat or use of killing force" (Paige, 2009 [2002]: 21). A nonkilling culture would not contain ideological justifications for killing or institutions that support killing. Paige's (p. 73) foundational work argues for a "four-part logic of nonkilling political analysis" involving the "causes of killing; the causes of nonkilling; the causes of transition between killing and nonkilling; and the characteristics of completely killing-free societies." The current chapter follows the shift from a killing to a nonkilling orientation within Paul Alexander's oral history as well as—paradoxically—a shift from nonkilling to killing within Paul's religious denomination. This case study supports Paige's (p. 74) orientation that nonkilling analysis "does not assume irreversible linear progression" and seeks to shed light on the question of why "individually and collectively... ideas, individuals, leaders, organizations, institutions, and policies [have] shifted to nonkilling" or to killing. Paige (p. 78) also identified the need for a "seven interdependent sub-revolutions" that are required for the creation of a nonkilling society and this chapter speaks to two of them: "a *normative* revolution from acceptance of killing to rejection" and "an *institutional* revolution to transform and create organizations to facilitate nonkilling change." Paul Alexander's life is devoted to fostering these two revolutions through scholarship and activism, particularly within his religious tradition (see <http://www.pcpj.org>), and illustrates the struggles inherent in working for normative and institutional change.

His work has attracted growing support, and although the Assemblies of God is not currently a nonkilling denomination, documenting and analyzing the early stages of what will hopefully become a major institutional shift toward nonkilling should be of great value to scholars interested in this issue. Much of the research in this area is conducted retroactively, but Paul's life story involves both historical components and ongoing work, making it a strategic case for analysis. It is also important because many Americans both self-identify as "Christian" and are also supportive of specific forms of killing (e.g., preemptive war, capital punishment). Paul's theological analysis and ongoing empirical research seeks to demonstrate the incompatibility of killing and Christianity. Leo Tolstoy's classic work of Christian nonviolence, *The Kingdom of God is Within You*, has had an enormous influence on people and cultures since its publication in 1894, including on Gandhi and Martin Luther King, Jr. Indeed, Walter Kaufmann (2007 [1961]: 7) is not entirely off the mark in arguing, "It would be a gross understatement to say that Gandhi owed more to Tolstoy than he did to Hinduism." Whether Paul's work will have a similar impact remains to be seen. What seems clear is that religious support for killing in the U.S. is a strategic site for normative and institutional nonkilling revolutions.

As Paul—like Tolstoy before him—persuasively argues, it is difficult to reconcile the life and teachings of Jesus with participation in killing. In fact, denominations like the Assemblies of God do not attempt a systematic reconciliation, instead preferring to interpret Jesus through the lens of the Hebrew Scriptures and a few proof-texts from St. Paul (in other words, through a non-Christocentric hermeneutic). In this way, "the Hebrew Scriptures controlled what Jesus and the Sermon on the Mount could mean" (Alexander, 2009: 334). According to Paul Alexander (p. 334), this is exactly the opposite of what people who call themselves Christians should do because they have received a "more complete revelation" of God's will in the life of Jesus than the authors of the Hebrew Scriptures had during their lifetime. In other words, for CHRISTians, Jesus should be the lens through which other Scriptures are interpreted, not the other way around. A Christocentric hermeneutic is more legitimate than a non-Christocentric one.

This argument could provide the necessary logical and theological leverage needed to transform American Christianity into a nonkilling religion. Whether this will happen is far from certain, since other cultural and institutional forces strongly oppose such a revolution. As Robinson (2009 [2002]: 13) points out, such a shift would need to:

subvert certain globally prevailing values and the institutions that shape those values. Among such values, goals, preferences, demanded outcomes, events, and acts, as well as corresponding institutions, are those relating to the acquisition and use of power. "Power" designates the processes by which people participate in making decisions for themselves and others that bind them to comply, by coercion if necessary (Lasswell and Kaplan, 1950: 75). Institutions associated with values of power include more than governments and their decision makers who wage war and apply severe sanctions including death to those who do not conform to public order. Interacting with power institutions are economies of organized entrepreneurs some of whom produce wealth from the inventions, manufactures, sales, and threats to use "arms"; universities among whose faculties some creative members conduct research and devise strategies of force and "coercive diplomacy"; associations of skilled athletes and artists that include those who specialize in violent games and entertainments; hospitals and clinics of venerated medical and health personnel who abort lives and assist in euthanasia... and certain religious organizations with faithful adherents who countenance killing deviants from approved doctrines, formulae, and miranda.

So the situation is complicated and much interdisciplinary scholarship is needed to fully understand the interrelationships among these various forces. But I suggest that sociological and theological attention to religion and religious experience might provide one avenue for progress toward a nonkilling society. Looking at the issue from the perspectives of both sociology and theology, the question we would like to answer concerns how Paul shifted from being non-referenced to socially referenced with regard to killing and how his denomination moved in the opposite direction. The answer, as I have suggested, turns on the hermeneutic center, which for Paul has shifted from non-Christocentric to Christocentric and for the Assemblies of God has become reversed.

Another level of complexity is added to this story when we consider the impact of Paul's experiences, both religious and nonreligious, and the contingencies that shaped these experiences, on his current nonkilling perspective. Paul's transformation involves more than a simple religious awakening—he had many Pentecostal Christian experiences both before and after his conversion to a nonkilling paradigm. Sponsel's (2009: 35, 41) "reflections on the possibilities of a nonkilling society" include a brief discussion of pacifist churches like the Quakers who have "courageously persisted in their pacifist commitment in the face of terrible violence" and posed a question about the possibility of "a similar Christian response" in the aftermath of the attacks on 9/11. It is important to raise these questions, but the "peace churches" represent a minority position in American Christianity because

394 Nonkilling Societies

most American Christians supported the military response to the attacks. More information is needed on how the majority of denominations might be transformed in nonkilling directions, and Paul's work within the Assemblies of God represents one plausible pathway that others might follow. To this point, the nonkilling research agenda has emphasized other social institutions instead of religion (e.g., none of the chapters in Evans Pim's 2009 edited volume focus on religion) and the current chapter provides an initial step toward addressing this gap. Religion involves more than the holding of certain beliefs; religious experiences are in a reciprocal relationship with beliefs and this relationship should be more fully explored.

Drawing on the social constructionist perspective within sociology, Kathryn Feltey (2009: 374) helpfully points out that "a society organized on the basis of militaristic principles, defining war and killing as inevitable, will produce and support what is necessary for people to kill one another, including weapons and ideology." In order to move beyond this social organization, Feltey argues that we must develop social frameworks that provide the capacity to envision an alternative future—one free of killing—and support work that attempts to realize this future. Drawing on the work of sociologist Elise Boulding, Feltey notes that people do seem to have these frameworks and capacities, while sociologist Wendell Bell's scholarship has identified a global set of shared values that can provide a foundation for this effort. Feltey also mentions social affinity as a helpful concept in this larger dialogue. So the foundation appears to be there, but what impedes progress in building on this base and working toward a nonkilling society? And what are the potential solutions? We can build on Feltey's general observations and begin to answer these questions on a more concrete level by examining the emergence of Paul Alexander's social affinity for the issue of nonkilling as applied to all people, rather than simply an "in-group."

The Flame of Love Research Project:
Exploring the Relationship between Religion and Altruism

Paul has told parts of his story in public talks that sometimes involve an audience of thousands[1] and in written form (e.g., Alexander, 2009). This chapter draws on his published work as well as an interview that was collected for the Flame of Love Research Project. This project is a multi-year interdisciplinary effort organized around the concept of *Godly Love*, which

---

[1] <http://ia341007.us.archive.org/0/items/PaulAlexanderPaulAlexander-MCUSASanJoseJuly4_2007/PaulAlexanderMCUSAJuly42007.mov>.

is defined as *the dynamic interaction between divine and human love that enlivens and expands benevolence* (see <http://www.godlyloveproject.org>; Lee and Poloma, 2009). Godly Love is not a synonym for God's love. It is rather an attempt to capture a process of interactions between an individual's perceived "vertical" relationship with God and "horizontal" relationships with other people in which benevolent service becomes an emergent property. Social science must remain agnostic about whether God exists, but perceived interactions with God do have real consequences on behavior (Lee and Poloma, 2009). The project is an ongoing venture of The University of Akron and the Institute for Research on Unlimited Love (see <http://www.unlimitedloveinstitute.org>), with funding from the John Templeton Foundation and the active involvement of a team of scholars in a variety of social sciences and theological traditions.

Some background on the Flame of Love Project is helpful for understanding the context in which the interview with Paul was conducted. The project began its investigation of Godly Love within the broadly-defined Pentecostal tradition. This tradition includes historic Pentecostal denominations, neo-Pentecostalisms found in mainline and independent congregations, as well as others who adhere to a Pentecostal worldview in which the Holy Spirit is deemed an active force in daily life. The Flame of Love Project was designed to unfold in a series of stages. The first phase involved interviews and surveys with the exemplars of Godly Love and their collaborators. The interview guide, the list of questions for the written survey, names of interviewees, and a detailed discussion of the sample and research methods have been described elsewhere (see Lee and Poloma, 2009). The second phase involved funding five sub-projects at $150,000 each to study Godly Love within specific Pentecostal communities. The third phase fielded a telephone survey of benevolent service among a nationally representative sample of American adults regardless of religious orientation or other personal characteristics, which was conducted in the second half of 2009 and the beginning of 2010.

The 116 people we have interviewed as exemplars (or collaborators) of Godly Love are seen as benevolent *within their own communities* and frequently within the larger culture. Their status as exemplars was ascertained by reviewing local and national news sources for feature stories, public recognition for benevolent service, and through the Flame of Love Project Institute Core Research Group's (ICRG) extensive connections with the Pentecostal community. The ICRG is comprised of an interdisciplinary group of twenty-two scholars who have established national reputations in the study of Pentecostalism, benevolence, or both (see <http://www.godlyloveproject.org> for the list of members). This group debated the selection of specific exemplars and developed criteria with regard to benevolence and the extent to which an individual was "Pentecostal" (Lee and Poloma, 2009). Interviewees reside in the following states: Alabama, California, Colorado, Florida, Kentucky, Missouri, North Carolina, New York, New Jersey, Ohio, Pennsylvania, Tennessee, as well as Canada, Puerto Rico, and Mozambique.

Exemplars in our sample have attained some degree of public notoriety for their benevolent work. Many have received awards and honors in both secular and religious contexts. Most are highly involved in the supernatural, with over 80% having the following experiences according to our written survey: experiencing divine healing, being used as an instrument of divine healing for another, or having an ineffable experience of God (i.e., one that words cannot express). Paul's survey indicated that he has participated in these experiences and also has a strong social affinity for strangers which was on par with the level of affinity that he felt for loved ones. He also donates to charitable and religious causes at a rate that is almost five times the national average. Margaret Poloma and I conducted his face-to-face interview on January 29, 2009. The interview lasted two hours and ten minutes and generated just over 45 single-spaced pages of text (page numbers for interview quotes refer to this printed copy). Paul signed an Informed Consent form waiving his right to confidentiality and his form is on file at the Flame of Love Project Office at the University of Akron. This form has been approved by the University's Institutional Research Board.

The Story of Paul's Nonkilling Transformation

> Well, you don't just choose an issue. It chooses you.... It's more like what seizes you. (Jason, an activist quoted in Vela-McConnell, 1999: 156)

Margaret Poloma and I were quite familiar with Paul's story prior to our interview with him. As a result, the interview focused on exploring the reasons behind his thoughts and behaviors, according to his perceptions, rather than on the biographical details of his life. Paul was unique among our interviewees, in that he was selected both as an exemplar of Godly Love for his benevolent work in the area of peace and justice (see www.pcpj.org for more on the organization, Pentecostals and Charismatics for Peace and Justice, that he co-founded), and his research project on high-risk social action ministries (with psychologist Robert Welsh) received funding in the amount of $150,000 from the Flame of Love Project's competitive Request for Proposals. His collaborative research is ongoing and has taken him to the site of dangerous conflicts throughout the world. His work as a theologian, minister, author, speaker, and activist demonstrates a high level of integrity around the core issues of peace and justice in a Pentecostal context. These issues have "seized" Paul, to borrow the words of the activist quoted at the beginning of this section. Paul has—to refer to the quotes from Jesus and Parker Palmer that opened this chapter—come to know a "truth" that differs from that of his upbringing, to the point that he "can't not do it." He has made significant personal sacrifices for his benevolent work on behalf of others.

He started on a very different path. As Paul recalls in his book *Peace to War: Shifting Allegiances in the Assemblies of God*, as a student in a Pentecostal college in 1991 he was a "tongues-talking, pro-war, hardcore patriotic, Assemblies of God follower of Jesus" (Alexander, 2009: 19). He "cheered as Operation Desert Storm began and the missiles rained down" and he "thought the song, 'Bomb, bomb, bomb... bomb, bomb Iraq' (to the tune of 'Ba Ba Ba... Ba Barbara Ann' by the Beach Boys) was hilarious" (Alexander, 2009, 19). As he mentioned in our interview, he was "raised in a Pentecostal home in Kansas [as a] 4th generation Pentecostal" (p. 1) with a limited consciousness of social justice, stating, "Well, it would have been anti-social justice. It would have been pro-social injustice" (p. 6). In terms of Vela-McConnell's typology, he would have been nonreferenced with regard to social justice and killing at this time in his life, which he calls the "pre-critical time" (p. 5) that lasted through part of his graduate school experience (he received a Ph.D. in Religion and Theological Ethics from Baylor University in 2000). He noted that he was a "good kid" growing up who did "everything right," but he did not perceive "the greed and the racism and the sexism" in his society (p. 12). He did engage in hunting practices that resembled shooting fish in a barrel:

> You know, killing 18 or 20 snowbirds in the snow... I'd throw out the feed and I'd hide in the garage and snipe them. That is, violence toward animals, it did go along with very much of a willingness to kill people in war (p. 6).

The social norms in his religious community and in his small Kansas town focused on issues of personal sin, such as smoking or premarital sex, but not structural "sins" like poverty or institutionalized violence.

His parents "were very compassionate and very giving" (p. 7) and his church was quite involved in foreign missions. He later learned that the pastor in his church "was very mean," particularly to his father. But his father shielded Paul from this conflict: "He bore the stuff that just about destroyed him. It's led him into serious depression as he's tried to work through this now, since then. But I come out with this great childhood.... I was just having a great time growing up, going to school, going to church, [with] loving parents" (p. 10). Paul's parents and grandparents prayed for him constantly when he was a child and his father prayed him to sleep nearly every night, which gave him a sense of "constant affirmation" and "encouragement" (p. 8). During the interview, he became quite emotional when he reflected on the fact that his "grandparents are praying for me every day" (p. 11).

Despite the high degree of care-love he received from his parents as a child, Paul's religious and nationalist socialization left him "quite judgmental" (p. 13), with a "hard-core belief in war and profit" and "American exceptionalism" (p. 7). He recalled his early outlook which emphasized "profit over people, rather than people over profit" (p. 7) and listening to conservative commentator Rush Limbaugh, which was his favorite "three hours a day" (p. 18). Graduate studies and interactions with his wife (also a Pentecostal) would later soften his judgmental perspective. As Paul tells it, "this ongoing relationship with Deborah... that sort of expanded my understanding of [God's] grace" (p. 13). Although a confirmed Christian since age 5, Paul explains getting in touch with God's grace and love through the compassion of his wife as being "saved":

> I just got saved. I have never actually been saved until now. This is what salvation is. I'm saved. It was that big of a deal that I use that language. You just saved me, Deborah. I was filled with the Holy Spirit, spoke in tongues from 12 on up and I'd been "saved" since 5, but... talking to Deborah and having this change, I *felt* saved. I felt really [sighs deeply] delivered.

Salvation thus took on a new meaning for Paul around age 21 or 22, which shifted his conception of a judgmental God as he "gave up the God of wrath" (p. 12) and the legalism that ruled his youth in favor of an image of God that included greater grace and compassion.

Paul eventually experienced a crisis of faith, which he referred to as a "dark night of the soul" (p. 5), during graduate school at Baylor University. He "started realizing just how absolutely ridiculous my faith was" (p. 19). He goes on to say:

> I can't give Baylor all the credit... that was a piece of it. The other piece of it is my wife's deep compassion and her empathy and identity with the suffering of the world. So I married a woman who is very compassionate and very aware and very thoughtful.... One of her closest friends was molested repeatedly from the age of about 6 until she finally got to leave home at 17.... Deborah's question is simply, "If God is love, and has the power to do anything, why would God let that happen?" (p. 19).

When asked whether he grappled with these issues in his prayer life at that time and whether he received any answers from God, Paul stated that during that period, "there is no God to pray to or talk to. So I didn't believe in that God or a God. And then I started realizing there are a lot of different Gods. That's helpful in the reformulation of faith in me. That God died" (p. 19).

In other words, the image of God that Paul had learned as a child had to "die" and be replaced with a new understanding of God in order for him to reconcile the difficult issues his compassionate wife was raising. It is difficult to know for certain which contingencies in a person's background are central in shaping the direction their life might take, but it is certainly possible that Paul's life might have gone a different way if not for the influence of his wife. Paul certainly believes that his wife has been "integral" (p. 31) in his emergence as a Christian exemplar of Godly Love devoted to issues of peace and justice. He remarked that "her love surpasses, far exceeds mine. I mean, she, yeah, it's a way in for me" (p. 31). This is an important sociological insight for those who wish to foster a nonkilling world: the significant others who populate our social networks exert a profound effect on our worldviews and behaviors. For the exemplars of Godly Love interviewed by the Flame of Love Project, such as Paul, God is certainly a "significant other" (Lee; Poloma, 2009: 8). But relationships with people are important too; they sometimes serve as a "way in," to use Paul's words—a pathway to a new identity that includes nonkilling. This idea is captured nicely by the African phrase "ubuntu," which loosely translated means that a "person [becomes] a person through other persons" (Barasch, 2005: 188).

Psychologists might want to argue that dispositional factors would have led Paul in this direction anyway. Or, according to some theologians, God may have been working through the events in Paul's life to reach this pre-ordained outcome. Interviews like Paul's make it difficult to draw firm conclusions about independent causal factors because so many intertwined processes are working at the same time and some of these processes may not be perceived by the person giving the account. In Paul's case, his identity change was at least partially shaped by the social network in which he was embedded, which included his wife and his professors in graduate school (as well as the written works he was reading at the time). He recalls:

> So I'd come back to faith, to following Jesus and believing Jesus and God. I don't really know how that happened experientially other than I think reading and talking about it and working through it and kind of, maybe, feeling drawn. But I, belief was kind of gradual. But what I do remember is

that it seemed too hard.... [At the time] I wasn't speaking in tongues. I wasn't having any kind of relationship with God in the way that I did earlier in my life. Those hadn't come together yet, even then (p. 25).

At the early stage of the identity rebuilding process, after losing his faith completely, Paul decided, "OK, I'll be an atheist, but I'll follow Jesus, so Christian atheism was part of this." He had moved away from a belief in substitutionary atonement, a pro-killing perspective which Paul learned as a child meaning that "God wants Jesus to die so He can forgive us" (p. 15), to a "nonviolent atonement" in which Jesus is "murdered and vindicated by resurrection" (p. 15). A nonviolent atonement is premised on the idea that God does not use violence to achieve goals. Paul came to this understanding after he finished his Ph.D. and it served as another social and theological influence on his emerging nonkilling perspective.

During Paul's crisis of faith while in graduate school, he discovered pacifism in the early history of his denomination, the Assemblies of God. One of his professors knew Paul's denominational background and suggested that he read a recent dissertation on "ethical issues in the Assemblies of God" (p. 22). Through this work he discovered other scholarship on pacifism among the founders of the Pentecostal movement in America at the turn of the 20th century. His reaction was not positive: "That was pretty significant for me because it was stupid. I thought it was the dumbest thing I'd ever heard. I mean, for real. I had to start looking into it" (p. 20). He ended up writing his dissertation on the topic (Alexander, 2009). It is not an overstatement to say that Paul discovered nonkilling unexpectedly. Between the compassion of his wife, and the early history of his denomination and broader Pentecostal tradition, he began to see the life of Jesus in a different light:

So that opened me up to thinking about issues of justice or issues of peacemaking and conflict transformation, or economics in a different way. I can't say that, at that particular time right then, there was a correlation between, "I love God, God loves me, I am a follower, I am a Christian, therefore I'm concerned about justice." It wasn't like that. In fact, it was pretty strongly disconnected, except that I was reading all of these early Pentecostals who were tongue-talking, "Jesus is coming back," "everyone is getting healed," "save the world quick," and "don't dare fight for America!" [They preached] "Look at this stuff with the Native Americans, all this injustice. Our wrong to the black people is evil." I thought, "Whoa!" So that was really crazy.... They were non-violent and they loved their enemies... I hadn't heard [that] before (p. 21).

As with his interactions with his wife, Paul's ultimate concern with peace and justice was an emergent outcome of a social network. This network included acquaintances both corporeal and virtual, as it quickly expanded to include the writings of people like Martin Luther King, Jr.

It was through this network that he re-discovered Jesus and came back to faith, but this new faith was premised on nonviolent love:

> I see myself as part of the story. Sort of an ancient story that's continued that will go on for I don't know how long. So that I am now participating in this story. I learned about it from others. And I've seen it lived by others. I'm just one part of it. So catching the vision, I guess, is a way of seeing Jesus and what He did and what His followers did. Then how Dr. King did it, or others, and the way that it gets lived out. This is not my idea, [laughter], the idea of forgiveness, or of love to the point of death, or social action. Yeah, I didn't invent any of it. I'm just trying to live it and share it with others. I have a friend who called me. He said, "You know, if you think about this, you're kind of like a peace evangelist. It's changed you, you like it and are passionate about it and you want others to experience this transformation" (pp. 37-38).

In Paul's words, "what makes it all fit together is that I am crucified with Christ. Nevertheless, I live. I said 'walking dead' before. I can't distance [myself] from that. That is really what rocked my world" (p. 36). This is why Paul appreciates the term "crucifism" as much as "pacifism," a word he picked up from well-known Christian activist Shane Claiborne in 2006 (Alexander, 2009: 33). He argues, "Discipleship in this context always included a rejection of the sword and a willingness to follow Jesus to the death" (Alexander, 2009: 33). But Paul originally came to a more general understanding that Jesus—as the living God, not just as moral exemplar—was the heart of this perspective, through the work of Mennonite theologian John Howard Yoder:

> [W]hat happened to me with Yoder is that [nonviolence] only makes sense, it only makes sense if Jesus is the way. If Jesus is the son of God. If Jesus is the revelation, He's the way, the truth, and life. If there is a God and that God is incarnated in Jesus and we are to follow Him. Because my approach to this is theological. If that doesn't work.... It is Christian. It is so deeply Christian that if Jesus is not the Messiah then forget it. It doesn't work. It does not hang together (p. 23).

Earlier in the interview he noted that "when you follow Jesus, you're a walking dead man/woman, you've given yourself over to God. That becomes deeply, that's belief again... that's [sighs deeply]" (p. 23).

By trailing off with a sigh, this last quote is one example of a common occurrence throughout his interview: Paul's beliefs are tied to strong emotions (e.g., "great emotional release," p. 3). In contrast to the overly cognitive emphasis on belief alone that often characterizes Protestant Christianity—but not Pentecostalism—as well as social scientific analysis of religion (Yamane, 2007), Paul's beliefs co-occurred with emotions such as anger, confusion, catharsis, and peace. Is belief driving emotion, or the other way around? It is sometimes pointless to ask. Similarly, what proportion of Paul's peace work is motivated and sustained by God and what proportion is driven by other forces? He is not distracted by such questions:

> So you could find out about [nonkilling or social justice] practices in many different places, that might not be connected with the love of God or the experience of God. But then to practice the practices or to engage in loving actions or practices in the world, then how you do it, the sustaining of that is maybe where the love of God works in. I mean, so you don't have to, I don't know that I learned about it from, well, you never know though. [Laughter]. I won't analyze it (p. 30).

Such questions are ultimately unanswerable for Paul. What is clear to him is that a "Christocentric," or perhaps better "Christomorphic" (p. 35)—referring to a process of spiritual formation in the shape of Christ—approach to theology is an improvement over the partially Christomorphic socialization he experienced in his early life. Unlike the Paul Alexander of his "precritical" (p. 5) phase, he now believes that you cannot do "peacemaking through violence and call it peacemaking. I disagree with that. I would make a theological argument against that" (p. 35). What exactly is his theological argument? Basically, "that is not how Jesus lived and showed us how to live…. You take violence off the table…. Why am I doing this and not other people? I have caught a vision of God, of the God who is love revealed clearly in Jesus with concrete implications for the way I live my life" (p. 35). He now reads "the Old Testament, hopefully through Jesus' eyes, the way Jesus read it…. I try to stay pretty close to Jesus" (p. 39). Staying close to Jesus is the method of becoming a nonkilling Christian peacemaker. Paul's journey from pro-killing to nonkilling and becoming socially referenced (Vela-McConnell, 1999) with regard to peace and justice for all people was complicated, gradual, and filled with contingencies, but in the end it is centered on staying close to Jesus. This is the method he would have other Christians follow in order to have a nonkilling and pro-social justice presence in the world.

From Peace to War: The Sad Story of the Assemblies of God

Paul's journey has been toward peace, but the story of his denomination has been just the opposite. The Assemblies of God started out socially referenced with regard to nonkilling but is now relationally referenced at best (Vela-McConnell, 1999). Paul is working to change this situation by raising historical and theological issues that he hopes will convince his denomination to adopt a nonkilling and pro-social justice orientation (see Alexander, 2009; note that the rest of the quotes in this chapter are from this book). Paul's Preface explains that he discovered that "most early Pentecostal denominations had been 'pacifist'" (p. 19) quite unexpectedly. Through the study of this issue:

> My understanding of Christianity died, my understanding of God died, my faith died, I died. I was murdered, crucified with Christ... and yet I am still alive. I am a walking dead man—fully alive but having died to my old gods, allegiances, and ways of life. It is no longer I that live, it is Christ who lives in me (p. 19).

That final sentence is a reference to Galatians 2:20 and contains the crux of Paul's argument for Christians: a "Christocentric hermeneutic" (p. 334) requires a commitment to the nonviolent love of neighbor and enemy. He laments that his denomination has allowed its ethical norm to shift:

> from appeals to Jesus to a norm in line with politically conservative or fundamentalist teachings that support a nationalistic American agenda. Whereas in the early period they discussed killing and war with reference to Jesus, they now deal with war by quoting the first part of Romans 13 and by appealing to conscience based on Romans 14 (p. 336).

He notes the contradiction inherent in the official position of the Assemblies of God with regard to killing, pointing out that, "On other issues dear to the American Evangelical politically conservative agenda—abortion, drinking alcohol, lotteries, gambling, and tobacco—the stand of the church is clear, and the authority of conscience is never mentioned" (p. 336).

Elsewhere Paul indicates that the theological argument he is making (stay close to Jesus) is more important than the historical fact that the Assemblies of God started out as a pacifist denomination: "my theological arguments are much more important because they call us to a faithful way of living regardless of what our ancestors did" (p. 329). Yet for nonkilling sociologists, the institutional shift in the official position of this denomination is also important. In a nutshell, the Assemblies of God shifted from a nonkilling to a pro-killing stance largely through a gradual process of cultural accommodation. This story is a common one in the sociology of religion: a radical sect abandons its counter-cultural tendencies as it seeks mainstream acceptability and integration into the wider society. In the case of the Assemblies of God, the issue was gaining "acceptability from the American culture and government as well as from the fundamentalist religious establishment" (p. 330). In the end, the denomination "held to radical orthodoxy (right worship—speaking in tongues) but not radical orthopraxy (right living—nonviolence)" (p. 330). They transformed themselves from "kingdom outsiders" to "political insiders" (p. 331). Paul concludes that there was no conspiracy in making this change. In fact, it was bound up with normal organizational processes inherent in the transition from separatism to social legitimacy.

The historical contrast is striking. In 1917, the official position of the denomination was "absolute pacifism," which was explained in a resolution sent to President Woodrow Wilson outlining the reasons why members could not participate in World War I:

> Therefore, we, as a body of Christians, while purposing to fulfill all the obligations of loyal citizenship, are nevertheless constrained to declare we cannot conscientiously participate in war and armed resistance which involves the actual destruction of human life, since this is contrary to our view of the clear teachings of the inspired Word of God, which is the sole basis of our faith (p. 154).

This resolution, drafted by the Assemblies of God, claimed to represent all Pentecostals and referred to timeless teachings: "these and other Scriptures have always been accepted and interpreted by our churches as prohibiting Christians from shedding blood or taking human life" (p. 154). The Scriptures in question refer to such foundational verses as "Thou shalt not kill" (Exodus 20:13) and "Love your enemies" (Matthew 5:44). Pentecostals in this era and later, including—Paul was surprised to learn, his own grandfather in WWII—became conscientious objectors. Many were imprisoned and abused by the authorities and some were killed. For example, in 1918 "Dave Allen, a twenty-six year old Pentecostal in Alabama, was beaten and shot to death by two police officers in his home, in front of his wife, because he would not fight in World War I" (p. 136).

Paul notes that the gradual move away from a policy of nonkilling was the product of "choices we as a denomination made," which suggests that "perhaps the shift can be reversed by different choices in the future" (p. 342). His historical, empirical, and theological work is oriented precisely to affect this change within his denomination, while his activism is not waiting for this cultural shift to occur. (See <http://www.pcpj.org>.) Yet there are significant barriers within the Assemblies of God to this change. Paul quotes John Howard Yoder who identified a broader problem within American Pentecostalism, which fostered both pacifism and racial integration at the turn of the 20th century when such things were not in vogue:

> But this originality (both the pacifism and the racial integration) was not deeply rooted. They don't believe in being deeply rooted. If you think history doesn't matter, and theology doesn't matter, church structures don't matter, there need be no sense of history in society which could make sense of a radically ethical position in the world. There was no critique of Americanism as such.... They had no alternative view of the meaning of power, the meaning of nationalism (p. 302).

Put differently, they had no *sociological imagination* (for more on this issue, see Feltey, 2009). Contemporary Pentecostals have taken history, theology, and even sociology much more seriously than their founders, but the Assemblies of God—"the largest of the Pentecostal denominations with close to forty-eight million adherents globally, a little less than three million of whom are in the United States" (p. 29)—remains firmly integrated in a politically conservative, pro-military culture that minimizes structural issues such as social justice (Lee and Poloma, 2009). And according to Poloma and Green's (2010) recent survey of Assemblies of God congregants, 65% believe that the U.S. government has the right to take preemptive military action and another 21% have no opinion on the matter. In other words, only 14% oppose this unilateral, prokilling prerogative. Without a sociological "critique of Americanism as such" to challenge this American exceptionalism and to compliment Paul's theological arguments, the sad story of the Assemblies of God's turn away from nonkilling is likely to continue. A Christocentric hermeneutic, combined with a sociological imagination that makes sense of violence and inequality in structural rather than individual terms, is needed to affect a nonkilling change within the denomination. Whether these factors will be sufficient to challenge the entrenched conservative culture remains to be seen.

Conclusion

This chapter has explored the implications for a nonkilling society of a case study involving both individual and institutional changes in social affinity within a religious context. While Paul Alexander developed a strong social affinity for nonkilling applied to all people over the course of his lifetime, his religious denomination has gone in the other direction during its history.

Each narrative demonstrates both the complexity and simplicity of developing an affinity for nonkilling or killing. In Paul's case, various contingencies
and experiences (both religious and nonreligious) contributed to the path
his life has taken. This path has been complicated, but it ends in the simplicity of "staying close to Jesus." For the Assemblies of God, the trail has also
been full of complications and contingencies, only a few of which have been
detailed in this chapter (see Alexander, 2009, for more details). But that sad
story boils down to Paul's contention that the denomination has not stayed
close to Jesus on the related issues of peace and justice. Of course many
members of the Assemblies of God would reject the contention that they
have strayed from Jesus in their search for mainstream respectability.

We end at the beginning, where this chapter started, with the words of
Jesus: "And ye shall know the truth, and the truth shall make you free"
(John 8:32). Paul has found his truth and he works tirelessly to convince
other Christians to join him in peace and justice work. If they wish to
become like Jesus, they must take up this cross. Perhaps the disciplines of
theology and sociology can collaborate in convincing Christians that
nonkilling makes good theological and social sense. In many ways, Paul
Alexander's story is an inspiring and hopeful one: his change has been
dramatic and suggests that anyone can choose nonkilling. But his
denomination's story is less encouraging. Can a Christocentric theology
combined with a sociological understanding of violence and social justice
bring about a socially referenced affinity for nonkilling within this group? If
so, the prospects for a nonkilling society would be dramatically increased.

References

Alexander, Paul (2009). *Peace to War: Shifting Allegiances in the Assemblies of God*.
    Scottdale: Cascadia.
Barasch, Marc Ian (2005). *Field Notes on the Compassionate Life: A Search for the
    Soul of Kindness*. Emmaus: Rodale.
Beliefnet (2006). "Your Religion's Stance on Iraq: A Faith-by-Faith Guide to Where
    the Major Religious Denominations Stand on War in Iraq," *Beliefnet*, Available
    at: <http://www.beliefnet.com/story121/story_12190.html>.
Boulding, Elise (1988). *Building a Global Civic Culture: Education for an Interde-
    pendent World*. Syracuse: Syracuse University Press.
Camus, Albert (1972 [1946]). *Neither Victims nor Executioners*. Chicago: World
    Without War Publications.
Cox, Harvey (2004). *When Jesus Came to Harvard: Making Moral Choices Today*.
    Boston: Houghton Mifflin.

Darley, John M.; Batson, C. Daniel (1973). "'From Jerusalem to Jericho': A Study of Situational and Dispositional Variables in Helping Behavior," *Journal of Personality and Social Psychology* 27:100-108.

Feltey, Kathryn (2009). "Nonkilling Sociology," in Evans Pim, Joám, Ed., *Toward a Nonkilling Paradigm*. Honolulu: Center for Global Nonkilling, pp. 371-378.

Hunt, Morton (1990). *The Compassionate Beast: What Science is Discovering about the Humane Side of Humankind*. New York: William Morrow and Company.

Kaufmann, Walter (2007 [1961]). *Religion from Tolstoy to Camus*. New Brunswick: Transaction.

Kelman, Herbert C.; Hamilton, V. Lee (1989). *Crimes of Obedience: Toward a Social Psychology of Responsibility and Authority*. New Haven: Yale University Press.

Lee, Matthew T.; Poloma, Margaret M. (2009). *A Sociological Study of the Great Commandment in Pentecostalism: The Practice of Godly Love as Benevolent Service*. Lewiston: Edwin Mellen Press.

Paige, Glenn D. (2009 [2002]). *Nonkilling Global Political Science*. Honolulu: Center for Global Nonkilling. Available at: <http://www.nonkilling.org>.

Palmer, Parker J. (2006). Quoted on the radio program *Speaking of Faith* in an episode entitled "The Soul in Depression" (Nov. 16). Available at (consulted 7/18/08): <http://speakingoffaith.publicradio.org/programs/depression/transcript.shtml>.

Palmer, Parker J. (1998). *The Courage to Teach: Exploring the Inner Landscape of a Teacher's Life*. San Francisco: Jossey-Bass.

Pim Evans, Joám, Ed. (2009). *Toward a Nonkilling Paradigm*. Honolulu: Center for Global Nonkilling. <http://www.nonkilling.org>.

Poloma, Margaret M. and John C. Green (2010). *The Assemblies of God. Godly Love and the Revitalization of American Pentecostalism*. New York: New York University Press.

Robinson, James A. (2009 [2002]). "Introduction: The Policy Sciences of Nonkilling," in Paige, Glenn D., *Nonkilling Global Political Science*. Honolulu: Center for Global Nonkilling, pp. 13-19

Sorokin, Pitirim A. (2002 [1954]). *The Ways and Power of Love: Types, Factors, and Techniques of Moral Transformation*. Philadelphia: Templeton Foundation Press.

Sponsel, Leslie E (2009). "Reflections on the Possibilities of a Nonkilling Society and a Nonkilling Anthropology," in Evans Pim, Joám, Ed., *Toward a Nonkilling Paradigm*. Honolulu: Center for Global Nonkilling, pp. 35-70.

Vela-McConnell, James (1999). *Who is My Neighbor? Social Affinity in a Modern World*. New York: State University of New York Press.

Winbush, Raymond, Ed. (2003). *Should America Pay? Slavery and the Raging Debate on Reparations*. New York: HarperCollins.

Yamane, David (2007). "Beyond Beliefs: Religion and the Sociology of Religion in America," *Social Compass*, 54:33-48.